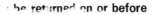
be returned on or before

D0333638

Keeping
a Horse
Outdoors

KEEPING A HORSE OUTDOORS

New edition

Susan McBane

David & Charles

To my parents and family
for the good things in my life

British Library Cataloguing in Publication Data

McBane, Susan
    Keeping a horse outdoors
    1. Horses
    I. Title
    636,1'083

ISBN 0-7153-9992-6

Line illustrations by Ray Hutchins

First published 1984
Second impression 1985
Revised edition 1992

Typeset by XL Publishing Services, Nairn, Scotland
and printed in Great Britain
by Billing & Sons Ltd, Worcester
for David & Charles plc
Brunel House Newton Abbot Devon

Contents

1 First Things First

To a horse-lover, surely one of the most relaxing and pleasing sights anywhere is that of horses grazing peacefully in lush, green pastures with shady trees and crystal clear water gurgling nearby. Imagine a soft, balmy day in late spring, the sunshine warm on our backs as we lean over a gate taking in the restful scene. The flies have not yet become bothersome, and the only sounds we hear above the usual summer music of birds chirping and bees buzzing are those of the horses rhythmically cropping and chomping the grass, and the whirr of a distant tractor bringing with it on the light breeze the heady scent of new mown hay.

The grass is at its best, the horses are well fed, sleek and comfortable; everything is right with their world. These are undeniably the perfect conditions for an outdoor life. Worries such as mud fever, sodden ground, bitter winds and incessant rain, or, in summer, inflamed eyes from the flies, hard ground, jarred legs and broken feet, all seem far away.

But for how long do these ideal conditions last? A month, maybe? Two at the most, and then all the old, familiar problems start creeping back as spring turns to high summer and the year wears on. There is some respite in autumn, but winter takes over all too soon.

Advantages and disadvantages

People keep horses at grass for various reasons, the most common being lack of facilities and/or time to care properly for a stabled horse. Other reasons include the need to give a horse a period of rest and relaxation after a season's hard work, or to economise on food and bedding which can both be replaced by grass during the warmer times of year. Breeding stock and youngsters spend most of their time at grass not only for ease of management but because a great deal of natural exercise and fresh air is vital to the correct mental and physical development of a young animal, and the health and development of a broodmare and her unborn foal.

From the human point of view, the good points about this system of horse keeping are that it is less tying, the horse will feed, water and exercise himself as he wishes and money can be saved if the pasture is adequate. There is no thorough, energetic grooming required, no desperate need to exercise the horse if one has no time, and not such a strict timetable to adhere to as regards feeds and general routine.

But although keeping a horse entirely at grass does not take up so much time and money as keeping one stabled, it is not a cheap trouble-free way of horse maintenance if one is to keep the animal in a healthy, happy state.

The first problem may be finding a suitable convenient field. A cramped, exposed, marshy, starved patch of land is worse than useless for a horse out all the time, as is a rich, lush cattle pasture. There is no stable to muck out, but droppings will have to be picked up daily from the shelter shed (which is essential for a horse out for long periods), and if the pasture is restricted or over-stocked the droppings will need picking up from the grass regularly, too, in the interests of good grassland management.

The horse will still need grooming lightly and examining as regards condition, wounds, injuries and signs of ill-health or other disorders. A grass-kept animal can never be as clean and fit as one kept largely stabled; he could be very wet and dirty when caught up to be worked - if he allows himself to be caught at all and tending and handling a horse outdoors can be difficult and unpleasant in bad weather.

Most owners will probably have a twice daily journey to and from the (possibly rented) field in all weathers, and if the field is some distance from one's home there is the regular bother of transporting hay, concentrates, tack and other necessities, unless secure storage is available nearby.

The horse might need extra food at least once a day, and his water supply checking along with fencing and gates, and an eye will have to be kept on other sources of danger such as litter thrown or blown into the field and poisonous plants developing. Tack, headcollars and New Zealand rugs will still have to be cleaned, rent found, worming medicines bought and the feed merchant, veterinary surgeon and farrier paid for normal maintenance work, as well as emergencies.

A major disadvantage which has arisen over the past few years is the risk of your horse being stolen for the meat trade. Rustling is now rife in Britain and it causes great distress not only to the owners but to the horses, too, who are subjected often to long and repeated journeys in rough waggons crammed with other unfortunates who trample on, kick and bite one another in their panic. Horses, ponies, donkeys, broodmares with foals and also stallions are herded indiscriminately together and hawked from sale to sale until sold, often injured and seriously run down, to the knackerman. Once a horse is sold through a public auction, his owner cannot get him back other than by buying him from the person who bought him there. Some horses, however, are not stolen for meat but simply for joy riding. Some have been ridden to death and others killed by traffic after being released on to a road.

Other considerations from the horse's point of view are just as varied. On the credit side is his obvious freedom to move about as he wishes and to eat to his heart's content. He has full and natural physical and social contact with his friends and the odd skirmish or two simply add interest to life, provided they are not serious. Horses are often happier and healthier when living a properly arranged outdoor life.

Unfortunately, for most of the year there are as many disadvantages as advantages, particularly if the horse is left too much to his own devices. In summer, the worst problem is flies and I believe most people do not realise (or, in some cases, turn a blind eye to) the immense misery these pests often cause. From late summer on, the food value of the grass starts to decrease until, by late autumn, it is worth practically nothing, resulting in an increasingly thin and hungry horse. Then the cold, wet weather comes, accompanied very often by winds of varying severity, not to mention frost, sleet and slushy mud; if the horse has inadequate shelter and food, he is going to start suffering considerably. Notwithstanding shelter, wet conditions are the contributing cause of the painful and common condition known as mud fever, and its allied complaint, rain rash or rain scald.

The right horse for the job

Correct, humane management can greatly diminish many of the problems but, even so, not every horse is a suitable candidate for living out. Although the worst prospects are the thin-skinned, hot-blooded, sensitive Thoroughbred, Anglo-Arab and Arab types and the best any of the hardy, heavy types such as native pony, cob and heavy horse and their crosses (others falling somewhere in between), even within these different types there are individuals showing varying constitutions and preferences. Thus, we may have a half-bred horse who curls up at the first sign of wind or rain or, conversely, an Arab who grazes happily in all but a blizzard, or a Shire who gets mud fever as easily as a white-legged, chestnut Thoroughbred. Much depends on the individual, who must be closely assessed by the person responsible for his care.

The breeding of the horse can be taken only as a broad guide. Some individuals do not have the physical resistance essential for a life of more or less exposure. Intimate observation and knowledge of the particular horse, culminating in an honest opinion as to the horse's suitability for outdoor living, is the only way to decide whether he can thrive and be happy on this system of management.

Basic necessities for the outdoor life

The first essential is obviously a field. This must be well drained or for at least six months of the year it will be out of use because of squelching mud or waterlogging. Wet land cannot support a healthy and abundant growth of the right kinds of grasses for feeding horses and, as mentioned, favours the development of mud fever and also foot rot. If poor drainage is combined with a heavy, sticky soil or clay, the problems will be even worse. Also unsuitable is land

An ideal field, with thick hedges and spreading trees which provide shelter. Company is also important, and even if the horses cannot share the same field, they can communicate over the fence if discretion is exercised over suitable neighbours. The post and rail fencing has had an extra bar run along the 'wrong' side to protect horses who may knock against the square posts. Two-rail fencing is adequate for adult horses, and cheaper than three-or four-rail fencing

which bakes hard or cracks in hot, dry spells, such as, again, clay. This can cause not only poor grass growth but jarring to the legs and feet, plus broken hooves in some cases, especially when flies are bad and horses gallop frequently to escape them.

There must be a healthy growth of nutritious but not over-rich grass to provide food, with no poisonous plants or trees within reach of the horses. The fencing must be safe, strong and high enough, as must the gates. There must be a generous, clean water supply, either natural or provided by the owner, and truly effective shelter at all times of year. General safety must be considered, such as whether there are any pits, dykes or unsafe ponds within reach, any farm implements or litter left in the field or dangerous hazards like concealed tree stumps and rabbit holes. It is worth considering, too, the field's proximity to any residential area which might be the source of vandalism, such as the joy riding already mentioned, razor-slashing, releasing on to the roads or other harassment.

Another important point, dealt with more fully later in the next chapter, and one frequently overlooked by owners, is that the horse must have a companion if he is to be truly content, otherwise he will probably not thrive or will constantly hurt himself trying to get out of the field in search of a friend.

Finally, there is the nature of the human attention available to the horse. Knowledgeable, sensible, reliable human attendance is necessary twice daily, to check on accidents and illness if nothing else. If the owner is not free to attend, arrangements must be made with some other suitable person to take turns.

Back to Nature – with reservations

So often we hear people talking about horses at grass as being 'in natural conditions' and of horses who have been sick, injured or just in need of a break, being turned out for a 'nature cure'. True, a horse at grass is out in the open air, eating grass and wandering about more or less as he wishes, as he would be in nature, but that is where the similarity ends between nature and mere outdoor domesticity.

The fact that a horse is, by evolution, a creature of the plains and wide open spaces often leads people to think that, as he survived in the open in his wild state without human attention, so he can survive in an open field in domesticity. But this is not so, and for several reasons. Life in a truly natural, wild state is very different from life in a confined space, even if this confined space consists of several acres. One would need many acres of reasonable quality, sheltered and watered pastures before one could begin to emulate nature.

To appreciate the difference, consider what the terms 'nature' and 'natural conditions' mean. Perhaps the simplest and most direct definition is that the horse is living in conditions created by nature and to which nature adapted him by evolution. These conditions comprise hundreds of square miles of land with ground of varying texture and consistency, which wears down the horse's constantly growing hooves, and with water holes, lakes, streams and rivers to drink from, and a great variety of vegetation to provide the wide range of nutrients needed for robust health. There is also shelter in the form of caves, cliffs, rocks, thick clumps of trees or bushes, sheltered valleys, hills or just hollows in the ground, which feral and wild horses use to protect themselves from bitterly cold or wet, windy weather, and from the sun and flies.

The 'natural conditions' which most owners are able to provide do not nearly match up to the real ones. Turned out on relatively soft agricultural-type land, the horse's hooves soon become overgrown causing him inconvenience, even pain, and adversely affecting his ability to move about and exercise himself, so man-applied foot-trimming is needed. The grasses in the field may be too rich, restricted in range or unpalatable, or the land may be overstocked and become what is known as 'horse sick', where all the best grasses are over-grazed until they virtually cease to exist, leaving inedible herbage like docks, rank grass, growing nettles (horses relish them when cut and dead) and other weeds, not to mention poisonous plants, which all take over the land.

The water supply we believe to be adequate may, in reality, be insufficient, dirty or stagnant and polluted. And the shelter facilities in most horses' fields are practically non-existent. Wind and rain pass straight through man-made fences and thin, straggly hedges, and there may be no overhead shelter at all.

Overcrowding, which rarely occurs in the wild, results in a build-up on the pasture of the microscopic larvae of internal parasites, which the horses ingest with the grass. In nature, many different species of animal commonly graze together. This not only means that each kind picks out its own favourite grasses (what one leaves another will eat) but the different species eat with the grass the larvae of the other species' parasites, which usually die in an unnatural host.

There are advantages to both ways of life, wild/feral and domesticated. Domesticated horses are normally protected by their owners from carnivorous hunting animals which may exist in their part of the world. The horse is not denied leadership as he has a substitute for the stallion (or, more likely, the matriarchal mare) in a human who makes major decisions and should provide all the horse needs in the way of food, water, shelter and general care. However, the horse does usually have to work, sometimes quite hard. He cannot please himself when he comes and goes but has to wait for his master or mistress to take or let him out or to provide fresh pasture. He also has to put up with various fussings which he may dislike, and is completely dependent on humans for all he needs to keep him well and happy.

The big advantage of being wild is the horse's freedom to do as he likes within the constrictions of his herd's social rules. He has many square miles of country to call home, which amply satisfy his natural, evolved instinct to roam. He is not restricted to bare, unpalatable pastures when he has been in one place too long (unless in competition with domesticated animals like cattle and sheep turned on to his range) but can move on to fresh grazing. He is also not obliged to huddle miserably behind a thin, holey hedge vainly seeking shelter on a cold, wet night, but can roam on to a more sheltered area to rest.

But this wonderful freedom so beloved of all creatures, including Man, has to be paid for. The wild horse in many parts of the world means 'food' to carnivorous animals, and a wild or feral horse has no one to care for him or lessen his suffering when ill or hurt; he must fend for himself. His alternative is death, from disease, starvation, thirst or predation.

The object of domesticating an animal is to use him to make life easier or more enjoyable for ourselves. As we are going to ask more of him in domestication in terms of physical output than would be asked in nature, we must improve his lot to ensure he acquires and maintains the increased state of health and fitness needed for him to work or breed to our satisfaction. If the 'natural' conditions we offer in domesticity are not good enough, we must make up for them artificially. In any case, those of us who care about our horses will want to make life comfortable and happy for them, and not want to see them eking out a mere existence in inadequate conditions.

It is not clever to make animals rough it by subjecting them to harsh lifestyles. This sort of treatment does not harden them up but results in misery and physical deterioration, even in death. Harsh conditions are particularly dangerous for old animals, which have lost the resistance and strength of their youth, yet are the category of animal most often subjected to neglect of this sort, and for youngsters, both before and after birth, resulting in stunted growth and development and impaired constitution for the rest of that creature's probably shortened life.

2 Handling

Apart from knowledge of how to feed and generally care for a horse, of his basic physiology and of the horse as an individual, there is another important aspect of management which can make or mar the relationship between horse and owner, and that is handling. Horse handling and management is very much a 'contact' activity and the handling part, in particular, is one which is often learned the hard way. Just as there is an old saying 'You're not a horseman until you've fallen off' (and very often not then either) you might also say you don't know how to handle horses until you have been kicked, bitten, trodden on, pinned in a corner by a pair of threatening hooves or just a black look, or chased out of a field by a horse you were trying to catch. Even if these experiences do not teach you the right way to do things, they at least teach you the wrong way – plus how strong, heavy and formidable horses are if you get on the wrong side of them. Most of the time, successful horse handling amounts to knowing the correct way to do something, knowing the individual horse's quirks and having the mental presence to put mind over matter and act with calmness and confidence.

Because horses evolved as prey animals they developed an alert, nervous nature, always on the lookout for predators and ready to fly off the instant danger threatened. This behaviour and instinct is still very strong in domesticated horses, simmering just beneath the surface of their acquired *savoir-faire*; even the best trained and worldly-wise horse can be startled by an unaccustomed sight or sound, a thoughtless movement at the wrong time or even a figment of his imagination.

Turning a horse out

Unless a horse associates his field with unpleasantness, he

will be eager to get back to it and keen to greet his friends over the gate. They, in turn, may be milling around generally making life a bit difficult for you. It is tempting to half open the gate and bundle your horse through, somehow slipping off his headcollar in the process, to avoid entering the field and possibly getting hassled by its occupants; but a half-open gate can leave little room for your horse to pass through and he might knock himself on it or the gatepost.

The safe way to lead a horse through a gate is to hold the horse in the hand nearest the gatepost and open the gate with your free hand, allowing enough room for you and the horse to pass through without injury and *keeping hold of the gate all the time.* As the horse executes a perfect turn on the forehand round to face the gate, you begin closing the gate at once with your free hand and fasten it securely again. You and your horse are now facing the gate and you have performed a neat, nifty movement giving you both safe access to the field without allowing other horses to escape. Now lead the horse a few paces into the field and turn him round again to face the gate, release him and step back. If he whirls round on his hind legs and gallops off with a buck and a kick, you will now be well out of the way of his heels. If you release him while he is still facing into the field he might accidentally knock you down or kick you in passing in his haste to get to the middle of the field. (He is unlikely to want to gallop off towards the gate he has just come through!)

Taking him out through the gate is similarly easily achieved once the horse gets the hang of the sequence of movements involved. Again, hold the horse in the hand nearest the gatepost and open the gate with your other, free hand wide enough for you both to pass through safely; another turn on the forehand from the horse while you pull the gate closed behind you and fasten it, having kept hold of the gate all the time, as before, to prevent it swinging or being pushed open further by other horses, and you have safely extricated yourself and your horse without letting others get out.

A well hung gate which will open and close easily with one hand is a big help, as is a catching pen (detailed in Chapter 3).

Catching

Catching horses can be a process fraught with frustration, anger, blood, sweat and tears as there is nothing more infuriating than a horse that will not be caught. One learns quite early on that it is pointless running after a horse, who can keep well out of a human's way by simply trotting, never mind proceeding at a Derby winner's speed, so again it is mind over matter.

It is always said you should approach a horse from the shoulder, but the reason has never satisfactorily been explained to me. Whichever direction you use, except directly behind, he will see you and take evasive action if he wants. If you do approach from behind and he does not spot you until you are nearly upon him, you run the risk of being inadvertently or purposely kicked.

To catch a horse who is co-operative, you simply walk calmly and confidently up to him, slip on a headcollar (or bridle if you are going to lead him on a road where more control is needed), and you've got him. Horses who are slightly difficult to catch are often quite amenable if you can get them to come to you for something desirable, like oats or sugar lumps. A friend of mine had a horse who was impossible to catch if she went after him, so she would sit in the field eating sweets out of a very rustly, large white bag. The horse eventually gave in to curiosity and temptation, approached for his share and she would catch hold of the short rope hanging from his headcollar. He was not allowed a sweet until he had permitted her to grasp the rope, and would then come quietly.

I have spent many hair-raising hours trying to help other people catch their horses by various means, such as herding them into a corner, sometimes with a long rope, buckets of food and a positive army of helpers, and occasionally have succeeded, but who wants to go through that performance every time the horse is needed? A much better way is to try to effect a permanent cure and I have found the following very effective.

Buy yourself a brightly coloured bucket for water, something distinctive from an ordinary feed bucket, and give the horse regular drinks from it or at least show him it full of water, so he gets to know it contains water. Then turn him out in a field with no water supply or block off the existing one somehow. Turn out with him a horse who is easy to catch.

Go to the field and take the full water bucket to offer to the horse. If he approaches, make sure you do not let him drink until he has let you catch hold of the short rope hanging from his headcollar (I am presuming he is so equipped if he is difficult to catch). If he refuses to let you catch him, take the water out of the field without letting him drink. The 'good' horse should be allowed to drink its fill, so you will probably need a helper with an identical bucket.

Return a few hours later, let the good horse drink again, but do the same with the bad one – no catch, no drink. Repeat this procedure every few hours until the horse *will* let you catch him. If the horse has gone half a day or more without drinking, limit him to half a bucketful on the first and second occasions and thereafter let him have a full bucketful. I have used this method on two particularly bad-to-catch animals. The first was permanently cured, the second relapsed after a few weeks and was put through the treatment again. The last I heard of him he had remained good to catch.

Once the horse seems cured, return him to his original field or restore his water supply, when he will almost certainly remain good, having established the habit within himself of allowing you to catch him, although you may always need food of some kind as an attraction. Do, however, always remember to insist on being able to catch hold of him *before* he gets his reward.

The above method works better in mid-summer to autumn, when the grass is drier and the weather warm. It works even better in large, grassless yards or dirt corrals, although these are rare in Britain, as the horse can get no water from the grass. I would not use the method, however, in circumstances where horses are receiving only hay and concentrates, which are comparatively dry foods, as digestive troubles could occur through lack of moisture. The treatment does not work so well using food instead of water, particularly when the grass is good.

There will always be the animal who remains almost impossible to catch all its life and I feel such horses, who relapse no matter what cure you try, can only be abandoned to an indoor life.

If you are unfortunate enough to have to turn out your horse with another which is bad tempered with humans, life can become fraught with anxiety and foreboding every time you have to go to the field (which will be at least twice a day). Provided the animal is not actually dangerous (in which case it should be removed from the field for the sake of all concerned) attack is often the best form of defence. Such horses are often bullies and if they come at you with teeth bared, ears back and an unmistakable 'get-out-of-my-field' look, try going towards them smartly, making yourself look aggressive, waving arms, headcollar or a big stick, and bellowing at them. A smart rap on the advancing nose with said big stick has worked well for me several times in the past, and I was never harassed by those particular animals (often ponies) again. A horse which subsequently turns on you with determined-looking heels should, in my view, be swiftly removed from the field as walloping it on the rump will not usually work. Disturbing the peace warrants solitary confinement.

A lot depends on your personality. If you appear strong, confident and knowledgeable to a bully horse, it will often back down, but if it thinks you are weak it will take advantage. A bit of acting ability on your part can be a big help!

Tying up

If you have to care for your horse entirely in the field, having no stable, you will need a secure tying-up point, preferably a proper ring bolted through the wall of the shed, if it is strong enough, or to one of the support posts. Here you will be under cover and, if you temporarily block off the entrance to the shelter with sliprails, you can tend to your horse in peace.

Leave the sliprails on the ground outside close up to the wall of the shelter where they are less likely to be trodden on by the horses.

If, for some reason, you cannot tie up your horse in the shelter, try to find a convenient tree branch or, if all else fails, use one of the fence *support* posts, never one of the rails which will probably break quite easily if the horse takes a determined pull backwards. A horse can exert a pull of roughly one and a half times his own weight, so you can see that whatever you intend to tie him to must be virtually an immovable object. Of course, his leadrope and headcollar would probably break first if he were exerting a really determined pull on a strong anchoring point, and many people maintain that horses should be tied up to a loop of string so that they will break free rather than risk breaking the structure or their headcollars, or risk injuring themselves.

My own feeling is that horses should be taught when young to tie up – and to learn that they cannot break free – not by force but by means of a long rope to their headcollar dee, through a ring on the wall and back to their handler's hand. Then, by give and take, the handler can give some rope when the youngster pulls back, and gently bring him back again. The horse does not then get the feeling of restriction imposed by the 'old school' who maintain they should be left securely tied up and left to 'fight it out with themselves'. The method may well work, but I feel the horse's spirit and personality lose something in the process.

With a mature horse who has learned that he can break free (a truly accursed vice), improvement can be effected by a friend standing behind and to one side of the horse with a stiff-bristled yard broom while you groom him. Then, when the horse makes to pull back, a couple of sharp scrubs under the tail will warn him to think better of it. Another method is to fasten a lungeing rein to the headcollar D, back under the horse's tail and through the dee again to the tie-ring (it can be secured from dropping down by a driving pad or by running it through run-up stirrups on a saddle). Then when the horse pulls back he will feel the rein behind his thighs and few horses will resist against that.

Whatever method is used, it is essential that a horse which has to be tended outdoors must be able to be tied up reliably and safely. Always use a conventional slip knot which you can pull undone with one jerk (a half bow) in case of emergency.

Friends and enemies

Horses are gregarious animals craving the company of their own kind. Although this may be inconvenient to us at times, it is understandable, as they evolved as herd animals always surrounded by at least a few others of their species. For millions of years they lived in this way and for good reason – there is safety, in the wild, in numbers. A solitary animal is easy prey to a carnivore in search of a meal, but if there is a herd of you, there is a good chance it will pick someone else!

This, and many other aspects of behaviour, has become instinctive in the horse, and instinctive behaviour is not wiped out by a mere few thousand years of breeding in domestication. The need for the company of others, even if only one, of its own kind is firmly ingrained in most horses. There are a few animals who do not seem to care for other equine company but they are rare.

Most horses, then, should be provided with company to ensure their happiness and contentment, and although animals such as goats and donkeys are often used as substitutes, there is really nothing quite like another horse, or a pony, as a companion. Anything else must seem rather like giving a human a chimpanzee to talk to.

Horses, like all animals, have their own code of social etiquette, and it is quite easy for an observer to discern which are the Boss Horses in given situations and which the underlings. The usual bones of contention among a herd of horses in a field are choice patches of grazing, water, shelter, chosen companions and, believe it or not, humans. When the human brings with it hay and other foods, there is another bone to fight over.

Sometimes there is an overall herd leader. In the wild this is usually an old, experienced, assertive mare rather than the stallion. She even bosses him about and tells him when he can mate her (as, indeed, do the other mares). In domesticated conditions, sometimes a mare and sometimes a gelding is boss. In many herds, however, you will find one particular animal has first choice where, say, food is concerned, another where access to the water trough is concerned, and so on. If an underling is sheltering under a particular tree and the Shelter Boss saunters over, all the latter may need to do to get the other horse to move is simply put its ears back, and sometimes not even that, so secure is its position. If a horse not so high up the Shelter Hierarchy comes along, however, it may need to do a bit more, not only ears back but maybe a quick nip or even a good bite, too. When two horses of similar rank have it out over a jointly desired property, the results can be serious indeed, particularly if the horses are shod. Severe kicking (resulting in, at worst, fractured bones) and biting take place, with ears back, tails thrashing and generally threatening looks.

It may be of some reassurance to know, however, that in a herd with an established membership and hierarchy, each animal knows its place and true fights are very rare. If two animals really form a seemingly permanent antagonistic relationship, their human owners must simply resolve never to turn them out within reach of each other, otherwise constant injuries will be the result.

Apart from physical injuries, a horse which is always being bullied by one or more others will be unhappy and under considerable stress. Stress seems to be a much-used word these days, and with good reason, for it is now known and accepted that mental stress, or rather too much of it, does lead to physical disorders of various sorts. A miserable horse will never thrive physically to its full potential and will be unable, therefore, to work as well for its owner as it would if happy and prospering. In any case, most owners will want their horses to be happy and so will do their best to create happy surroundings and lives for them.

Introducing a new horse

One situation, in connection with herd relationships, which

can cause a good deal of trouble is when one tries to introduce a new horse into an established herd. This will
inevitably completely upset the apple cart until the horses
sort out for themselves (and only they can do it) where the
newcomer is going to fit in. Even so, there is a good deal
humans can do to try to smooth out the wrinkles and avoid
as far as possible the serious fights which could ensue if the
introductions are wrongly carried out.

The worst way to introduce a new horse into a herd is
simply to open the field gate and bundle him through into
the mêlée of curious bodies on the other side, and just leave
them to get on with it. This method will almost certainly
result in a badly hurt newcomer and permanently soured
relationships between him and the others.

The correct way is to allow the new horse to make friends
with at least one of the herd first, preferably one fairly low
down in the general hierarchy (who might be glad of a new
friend) or one noted for its congenial attitude towards other
horses. These two should be led around in hand (wearing
bridles for extra control) and perhaps taken for a ride
together. If stables are available, they could perhaps be
stabled next to each other for a night, or just an hour or two,
and finally turned out together in a preferably small paddock
(where they cannot get up too much speed but can get out of
each other's way, if necessary), ideally with plenty of grass, to
take their minds off each other. There will be some nose and
tail smelling, a few squeals and a bit of stamping and
prancing around but, if care has been taken to match them
temperamentally and status-wise, there is almost certain to
be no real trouble.

The next stage should be to put these two *alone* into the
main field which is to be their home and gradually bring back
the other herd members, low-ranking ones first, one by one,
letting each new arrival have up to half an hour to fully assess
the newcomer, until the herd is complete. Again, there will
be some introductory sparring and maybe a couple of 'try-
outs', but there should be no serious problems.

This might all sound like too much of a palaver, but it is an
ideal way, and may not be possible in all circumstances.

Another method would be to put the newcomer *and his friend,* to prevent the sole horse trying to jump in to the others, into a safely fenced adjoining field so that the rest of the herd can weigh them up over the fence. It is better for the horses not to be able to touch each other over the fence if at all possible, but this may be difficult to arrange. After half a day in this situation, preferably more, the two chums can usually be put in with the others with little trouble, although two people should stay around for up to half an hour in case of trouble should the horses need separating again.

The new horse will settle in surprisingly quickly, if properly introduced into the herd and, likewise, the others will accept him. On the other hand, if the introduction is carried out wrongly, the animals could well be permanent enemies and the newcomer constantly unhappy – a pointless and miserable situation for all concerned.

Numbers
The personalities and temperaments of the horses turned out together will ultimately decide the success of their relationships. Numbers do not normally matter and, in any case, horses will be coming and going into and out of the field as their owners arrive to work them or return them after exercise, so, especially in communally used fields, it will be impossible to always have a set number of animals turned out together.

It follows that there will be times when an animal may well be left alone for a certain period of time, which it will probably not like. If it cannot be safely shut in at such times, the only way to teach it to put up with such a situation is to leave it to get used to the idea. It is true that animals which object to this can work themselves up into a sweat and start charging the fences and gates trying to get out, so the fencing will have to be truly deterring, high and strong. Only experience will tell whether such an animal is going to learn to tolerate occasional solitude, and most do; if it does not, its owner will simply have to accept that it can only be turned out if there is at least one other animal in the field.

If only two horses are turned out together as a regular

procedure, another problem arises in that they can become impossibly attached to each other. Not only does the one left behind behave as described above, but the one taken out for work will be an absolute pest, whinnying to its soul-mate, not working well and, in bad cases, jibbing and napping and becoming not merely a nuisance (and therefore not enjoyable) to own but dangerous as well.

A horse *must*, almost above all else, learn to go where and how its rider or driver tells it, alone or in company, and this takes very firm, determined and knowledgeable handling – and you must win the 'fight' as soon as trouble starts to develop. If you are at all unsure of your capabilities to do this, I strongly urge you to engage professional help, otherwise you may well find that you end up not being able to use your horse at all.

3 Accommodation and Facilities

To a horse kept at grass, obviously his whole world is his field. He will probably spend at least twenty-two hours out of twenty-four in it, and it needs to be a place which offers him health, happiness, comfort, safety and, as far as is possible in an open field, security.

Much depends on what the horse's owner expects of the field. Does he or she want it to provide most of the horse's food, or is it to be merely somewhere to put the horse because there is no stable?

This book is mainly for people who are keeping horses at grass twenty-four hours a day at any particular time of year. Therefore, even if they are happy to provide their horse's food in the form of concentrates and hay, for their horse's sake and their own convenience and peace of mind, they will need to consider the general suitability of the field.

Many owners know little about land and grass, and it is easy to think that any plot with practically anything growing on it will make a good enough home for a horse. But this is by no means the case. Most owners do not have their own land and are not in a position to be too choosy, but the fact remains that an unsuitable environment can make life difficult and worrying for the owner and most unpleasant, even dangerous, for the horse.

Type of field

The best horse paddocks are on light, well drained land which does not easily waterlog in wet weather or bake hard in dry. (The quality or 'richness' – or otherwise – of the land and, hence, its productive abilities, can be to some extent changed by treatments and fertilisers, about which more in Chapter 4.) Fine grained soils like clay quickly go from one extreme to the other while peaty soils are only really good in the driest weather, soon becoming sticky or flooded at other times. Sandy soils can be good and are often naturally well drained, although they will not grow the lushest grass. For horses, however, this is not important, as protein-rich herbage causes digestive troubles in them. The ideal soil is what every farmer wants, a rich brown loam. The rock over which the soil lies can determine soil quality, eg limestone areas are traditionally desirable for breeding bloodstock because of the calcium (for bone and teeth development) they impart to the soil. But nutrients can be added to the diet easily enough in deficient areas.

Drainage
Drainage is vital especially for a field which is to be used heavily in wet seasons. A couple of horses living on a wet and, particularly, a small field will soon poach it into a morass of liquid mud quite unfit for habitation.

Wet land is cold land. Not only does it make the growth of ample good grass difficult by starving the roots of air and warmth, it creates favourable conditions for mud fever. If the land is your own or you have it on lease for some years, it could be worth putting in a drainage system to make it usable, healthy and productive, otherwise you will be able to use it only in dry seasons. If the land is also used for agricultural purposes (say, fattening bullocks, which is excellent for horse pastures incidentally) you could also get a grant towards the work.

Even in dry weather, it is often possible to tell if a field is too wet by the type of herbage growing on it. If there are rushes or marsh grasses with round, spiky blades, forget it. You will need a reclamation programme rather than a drainage system to make it acceptable.

Fields with natural drainage in the form of a gentle slope to some outlet such as a ditch, stream or road with drains are good, as are those drained by the old method of ridge and furrow, where the land has wide, gently domed ridges, the water running away in the furrows. Fields of both these types are good for horses as they help keep them muscled and balanced in their paces. Flat fields do not have this advantage and often need expensive drainage systems installed as the water has no route of running away. They become water-logged, even flooded, very easily, particularly in lowland areas. Such fields need deep ditches on all sides cleared out regularly, to take the water, and even then may not be a success. They also tend to seethe with flies in summer.

Other considerations
Steep hillside fields, too, have disadvantages. Apart from the fact that it can be impossible to get machinery on them for agricultural jobs, they can be uncomfortable and wearing for the horses, who are constantly bracing themselves against the gradient and can neither lie nor stand in comfort. There must be at least one flat, sheltered area where they can relax without having to combat the slope. Such fields are unsafe for in-foal mares, and youngsters who gallop about a lot, as they cause falls and stumbles which can bring about abortions and other injuries.

Although unpleasant, hard ground is less of a problem than mud as the horses can at least be put on it. Jarred limbs from excessive galloping occur most often when horses are overfed, underworked or forced to charge away from flies through lack of shelter.

Another point to consider is whether the field is sheltered or exposed. A fairly sheltered field is best even if your horse is quite commonly bred. He will then not be battling against the full brunt of the weather and will not need so much food to keep flesh on him in winter. Some people argue that an exposed field is best in summer as the constant breeze keeps flies away, but in my experience the difference is minute.

New leys (fields which have been seeded less than a year) are not really suitable for horses. Unless the seed mix contained herbs and a wide variety of grasses, the herbage will most likely be too limited. This is usually the case with mixtures sown for cattle. It is not until the second year that indigenous herbs and weeds appear, providing interest and variety (of taste and nutrition) for the horses, plus essential nutrients often lacking in cultivated grasses. Also, in young fields the turf has been destroyed by ploughing. After years, sometimes centuries, of undisturbed growth, the roots of grasses and other plants form an underground network, a 'cushion', which makes the perfect surface for horses' legs and hooves. Old turf is heavenly to walk on. It feels springy underfoot and absorbs the jar when the foot hits the ground. It is also more resistant to the destructive action of hooves. With new leys, the ground is still loose, there is no protective network of roots and the grass is easily pushed in or torn out and wasted.

Orchards and woods

These do not make good homes for horses. The grass under trees, although it may look luscious, is often poor and sour as it lacks sunlight and is not cared for like genuine pasture. It often contains much useless stuff like old matted grass, moss or rotten fruit, not to mention poisonous plants, conkers and acorns. Chemical residues from preparations sprayed on fruit trees may linger and poison the horses, who also often make themselves ill by eating windfalls or pulling fruit off trees. The ground in woods and spinneys is often very rough, and I once saw a pony with the most sickening injury to his leg, caused by an old, forgotten trap hidden by grass and brambles.

Generally, I should prefer to fence off such areas even though they might seem to offer good shelter, unless one can be quite sure none of the above dangers exist.

Size of field

Generally speaking, if the land is in good condition and producing varied, medium quality grass ideal for horses, 2 acres (.8ha) properly managed should just support one horse in light work all year round (plus supplementary feeding in winter) or two horses during spring and summer. As a horse should always have a companion, this means that for two horses getting much of their food from the grass, at least 4 acres (1.6ha) will be needed on a year-round basis. The poorer the land or grass, the more you will need. In fact, horses keep happier and healthier with a large area of medium to poor grazing than a small one of rich grass; they have more space to roam and have to walk and exercise more in search of their food.

As will be shown in the next chapter, the land must be divided if it is to be well-managed and productive. It is best to try and keep one's driest land mainly for winter use, resting it as much as possible during summer, and laying off the wetter land in winter. If renting land, try to acquire one field for spring and summer, changing for a drier and more sheltered one in winter.

Hedges and trees

These are a definite advantage to a paddock. Apart from providing interesting titbits, as horses often nibble them, they give some protection from the weather. One of the best windbreaks possible is a belt of trees and/or a high, thick hedge on the windward side of a field. The horses will gather there during wind and rain and be grateful for the protection. Trees, if thick enough, also give overhead shelter and hedges, if well kept, make excellent fencing.

To be effective as either windbreaks or fencing, hedges must be periodically trimmed, although left high and thick and, ideally, laid. A farm worker or agricultural contractor can do this and the finished job has an aesthetic as well as a practical value. If a hedge is left to grow wild it becomes thin and straggly with large gaps which not only invite horses to escape but allow wind and rain right through. Laying (which involves reinforcing the hedge with its own branches laid diagonally across it) strengthens the hedge and helps fill in gaps. A well done job, although expensive because it is a skilled craft, should last many years. A hedge can be left at 5ft (1.5m) or higher, and left fairly thick by the trimmer, when it will appear neat, discourage the horses from jumping out and provide an effective windbreak.

Man-made fencing

Fencing can be an expensive item, particularly if much new

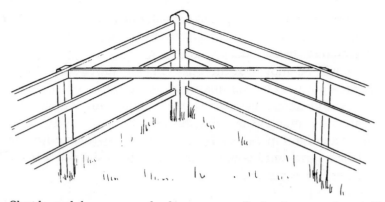

Sharply angled corners can be dangerous to galloping horses, and to timid animals who can be cornered and bullied. This bar, fixed at a safe height, will steer a fast-moving horse round the corner, and will prevent one horse being hemmed in by others

material is needed, but few things detract more from the appearance and safety of a field than dilapidated, unsuitable or badly erected fences.

Effective fencing can save a great deal of inconvenience and expense to the owner, whose liability it is if his horses stray from their proper place. Any damage they cause to neighbouring property, not to mention road accidents, is the responsibility of their owner. In addition is the pain and suffering caused to humans involved in an accident, and to the horses themselves if they are injured or eat a surfeit of growing corn in the next field. So apart from an insurance policy with a trustworthy company to guard against damages, the provision of effective fencing really is a must. Some insurance companies may not pay out in a claim action if a horse has been enabled to stray through neglect of the owner to provide proper fencing.

If your land lacks suitable natural hedges, even those rein-forced by man-made fencing in the gaps, you will have to provide an alternative. No fencing should be lower than the height of the horse's back, with the lowest strand or rail no lower than 12 in (30cm) from the ground to reduce the like-lihood of a horse getting a leg over it and damaging both himself and the fence trying to pull it back.

Rounding off the corners of the field helps prevent

galloping horses colliding with the corner by steering them round it. This can be done by erecting the fencing in curves rather than corners or, with existing fencing, by fixing a 6ft (1.8m) rail diagonally across the corner at horse's shoulder height.

Wooden support posts should be sunk into the ground for one-third of their length so that when the horses rub against them they will not become easily loosened. Needless to say, wooden structures should be treated with a reliable wood preserver, especially if going underground. Many suppliers now have their own excellent systems of preservation for their products and creosote is now largely being superseded.

Wooden posts and rails (preferably hardwood for wear) are still considered the most traditional and safest fencing by many horsemen, and are still the most expensive. Some economy can be made, though, by buying only two-rail fencing which is quite adequate for mature horses. The bottom rail, in this case, can be about 2ft (60cm) from the ground. Breeding stock and ponies should have four- or three-rail fencing respectively to prevent foals and small ponies getting through the gaps. With foals, there is a danger they will roll or lie down near the fence and, in getting up, end up on the other side of it with panic stations resulting, so the bottom rail for them should be low enough to prevent them doing this, about a foot (30cm) high.

The tops of the posts should be flush with the top rail, never above it, to minimise the dreadful injuries which the protrusions can inflict on horses trying to jump out, and to prevent their catching in a loose headcollar. The rails themselves should be fixed on the inside of the posts, making a smooth barrier for a horse rubbing along them. Horses can injure themselves on fence posts inside the rails. If it is impossible to arrange the rails correctly, or where a single fence separates two fields, run a single rail at horse's shoulder height on the offending side.

Plain wire fencing on wooden posts is a fair and cheaper alternative to wooden rails provided it is kept properly strained and taut. It does have the disadvantage of the whole of one strand collapsing all along its length in the case of

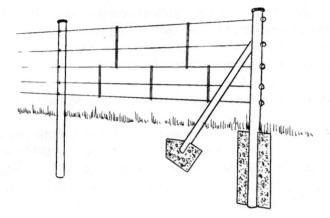

Plain wire dropper fencing (which can be electrified). The vertical dropper rods enable the posts to be spaced more widely apart (for economy) and will prevent full strands of wire collapsing if broken

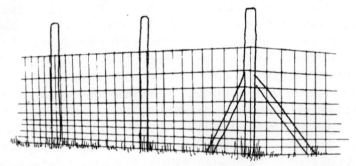

Resilient wire mesh fencing with the lower meshes sufficiently small to prevent a horse's hoof passing through; suitable where horses are grazed with sheep. The joints between strands should be securely fixed to prevent movement. If galloping horses collide with this type of fencing, it tends to 'bounce' them off unhurt

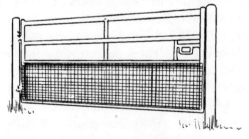

A strong, safe, tubular metal gate, the bottom part filled in with strong mesh to prevent horses' legs getting caught through the bars. The catch is safe and unobtrusive, and easily padlocked to the gatepost with a chain

damage, instead of just one section breaking, but this is avoided with *dropper fencing* which has strainer rods vertically supported on the wires between posts, so restricting sagging to just that one area. Because the strainers support the wire and help keep it taut, the posts can be fewer and further between than with other types of fence, so it is economical.

Resilient fencing in the form of *wire mesh*, heavy gauge, is becoming more popular, particularly on establishments catering for more than one type of grazing animal. The type recommended for horses has lower meshes small enough to prevent a horse's hoof passing through them. With conventional sheep fencing, horses frequently get their legs through the squares with disastrous results.

There is always a possibility, with most wire fencing, of the wire mysteriously finding its way between the horse's hoof and his shoe in accidents or skirmishes near the fence, when the shoe might be ripped off as the horse struggles to free himself, causing a badly torn foot.

Resilient fencing works on the principle that horses colliding with the fence (a quite common occurrence) are bounced off it harmlessly instead of breaking through it or hurting themselves on a rigid structure such as a stone wall or iron railings. Post and rail fencing is often purposely designed with rails weak enough to break if the horse hits them hard enough (rather than the horse breaking his leg) but then you have the problem of an inviting gap being left in the fence.

Flexible fencing has the advantages of being resilient and easily seen by the horses, being usually white, while being in rail, rather than wire, form. It consists of flexible synthetic material which comes usually in a roll and which is simply nailed to conventional support posts. It is excellent for improving existing fencing, instead of wire, and it has been found that often a single 'rail' fixed round the top of a fence is sufficient to warn the horses of its presence and cause them to respect the fence. It is also rotproof and chew resistant, unlike wooden fencing. For those who have to move fields often, it can be a boon as it can simply be removed, rolled up, and reinstated in a new field much more easily than other materials.

Another form of take-away fencing which, I feel, is not made sufficient use of for horses is *electric fencing*. Provided horses are taught properly about it this can be a really effective way of keeping them away from taboo areas such as dangerous dykes, ponds, bogs and faulty fencing. Various makes and systems are advertised in equestrian journals, both mains and battery operated (the latter being especially useful for rented grazing). Not only can it be used to divide a field and so help with correct pasture management, it can easily be removed when you leave and can be used to transform a paddock with unsafe fencing into an acceptable home for your horse. The newest type is in the form of an easily-seen twinkling electrified metal tape.

Electric fencing can be used as the top strand of a wire fence, can be run inside the posts of a conventional wooden fence to keep horses away from it, or used alone on its own insulated rods. Although many people would regard the latter arrangement as temporary, it is a fact that some horses live for long periods surrounded by this type of electric fencing and, because they have a healthy respect for it, will not even go near it, let alone try to jump it.

To introduce a horse to electric fencing, moisten his nose (for added 'impact') and lead him up to the fence, pressing his nose gently but firmly against it. He will receive a sufficient shock to make him jump back, so be ready for him, but will not be hurt. Take him further along the fence and do the same. On the second occasion he will usually decline your invitation. Make sure you lead him all round the field wherever the fencing is and show it to him.

Barriers to avoid include stone walls (very good for breaking horses' legs), wire gardening mesh and chestnut palings (too weak), iron railings with sharp metal joints and spikes (death traps) and the all-too-commonly-seen barbed wire.

Unfortunately, most horse owners enquiring about rented grazing will be confronted with barbed wire, and although it is true that horses can graze happily for years surrounded by this murderous stuff without coming to any harm, to me the situation likens itself to the Sword of Damocles. One day the sword will fall and your horse will come into contact with the fence. You could be lucky and have him escape with a few minor scratches. On the other hand, he could be scarred for life, or even rip his legs and/or body so badly that he is permanently crippled, which, in our economy, usually means he has to be destroyed.

What better case could there be for investing in your own set of electric fencing? Of course, it will cost money, but could mean the difference between accepting an otherwise suitable field (and they are hard enough to find as it is) or continuing your anxious search further afield – or between a safe horse and a fatally injured one. It is worth considering.

Gates

Horses often congregate round the gateway, perhaps at feeding time, when they want to he brought in or are lonely, so it is obvious that gates must be strong and safe. Whether of wood or metal, they should be hung so that their top rail is, again, at horse's back height or slightly higher. If this means adding another rail on the bottom for foals, so be it. The top rails can be horizontal, but if the lower ones also are they should be filled in from the inside with strong metal mesh. Some horse requisite suppliers stock good tubular metal gates with the lower halves of vertical tubing, which are filled in with mesh to prevent legs getting through in impatience or excitement.

It helps to have a gate hung so it swings closed when you let go, rather than open! A gate which has to be lifted bodily (often with two already full hands) before it can be moved is not only annoying when one is trying to manoeuvre horses in or out of the field, but dangerous when the horses are milling around trying to get into your buckets of food. You need as few hindrances as possible so it pays to get the gate properly hung.

It can be a tricky operation, trying to get one horse into or out of a field with several others in it, but the job can be

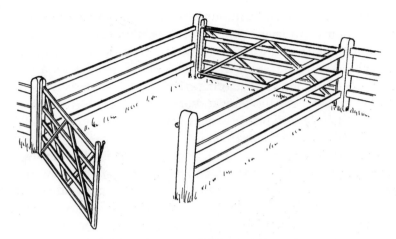

This catching pen enables horses to be taken through or brought out of a field without danger of other occupants escaping during the process

made much easier with a 'catching pen'. Here, the gate from the road, yard or wherever leads into a pen at least 12ft (3.65m) square, with another gate at the other end leading into the field. You open wide the outside gate, lead the horse in, turn yourselves round comfortably to close the gate and finally open the gate into the field and take him in. In this way, if the other horses wangle their way through the field gate, they will not be able to escape because you will have shut the gate leading to the road. Similarly, if your own horse breaks away from you he cannot go anywhere he shouldn't.

A safe width for a gate is about 5ft (1.5m) as this allows enough room for horse and handler to pass through in comfort. However, the width is less important (provided it is not ridiculously narrow) than the correct, calm way of passing through it, as described in Chapter 2.

Nuts and bolts used for securing hinges should be the smooth-headed type if on the inside, otherwise sharp edges should be filed off. The hinges should be the fixed type and not those with open tops which can be lifted off by the horse getting his neck under the top bar. If this type has been used the gate should be chained round the hinges to keep it on. There are several types of fastener for gates. Ordinary bolts and hunt catches (with a long vertical spring handle so that

'Lanes' between fields enable normally incompatible neighbours to live in adjoining fields without being able to contact each other. On studs, this means that stock can be led freely around without passing through occupied paddocks. The slipgate is a refinement of the plain sliprail system. It is simple to construct, cheaper than a proper gate and light enough to be lifted with one hand when leading a horse. It is more secure than ordinary, separate sliprails and easier to operate

they can be opened from horseback) are soon fathomed out by horses, as are hook-type fasteners. A quick, secure way of fastening a gate is to have a length of wide-linked chain passing round the end of the gate and the post, being clipped together through its links with a strong spring clip, such as from the end of a worn-out headcollar rope. Stapling the chain to the gate and clipping the free end to a staple in the gatepost is good provided the staples are well in and firm. Tying the gate with rope or twine has often resulted in horses eventually undoing the knots or biting through the fabric.

Sliprails, slipgates and cattle grids
Cheaper than gates, *sliprails* should be strong, smooth poles (two or three depending on the height of the fence and the

size of the animals in the field) which slot into holders on each gatepost. Holders with open tops are useless unless the rails are fastened in at both ends, as horses soon learn to lift them out. A secure fastening is to have a heavy-duty nut and bolt (kept lightly oiled) passing through aligned holes drilled through the holder and pole. Even with enclosed holders, some horses can learn to jiggle the poles sideways, so it is always safer to secure one end of each pole. For safety's sake, the poles should be let down completely when the horse is passing through.

Slipgates are simply a framework looking like a gate, but slotting on to holders, as shown in the illustration. Again, their advantage over a gate is simply economy and, like sliprails, they are not so convenient for the handler, although effective in use.

Cattle grids are lethal to horses who are not usually in the least deterred by them. They wander unconcernedly across and fall with their legs trapped between the metal slats. I have seen more than one horse suffer the most horrible injuries this way, sometimes resulting in permanent hideous scars on the limbs. One pony I knew, having once been injured in a grid, was later returned to the field by his owner who thought he would have 'learned his lesson'. Certainly he did not walk across the grid again, but took to jumping it quite happily.

The need for shelter

Shelter seems to be the most neglected aspect of the management of horses at grass, even more neglected than feeding. The horse's natural coat and grease do not give anything like the protection often imagined. Nature intended these only as partial protection and without additional shelter horses suffer much more than people realise, or wish to admit.

A common remark seems to be: 'There's no point giving a horse a shelter, he wouldn't use it anyway.' This statement is often just an excuse for not having a shed, and unfounded, too, for I have only ever met three animals in my life who refused to enter a suitable shelter and in each case it was because it was frightened to do so.

(Reasons for this fear could be: (1) a bully horse inside the shed keeping out a more timid one; (2) the shed appearing dark so the horse cannot see that it is safe inside; (3) the entrance being badly poached, which will put off a sensitive individual; (4) the entrance being too low and/or narrow so that the horse might feel unable to enter without injury; and (5) the horse associating the shed with some unpleasant incident such as being cornered in it and kicked by another horse or knocking himself on the way in or out.)

In winter, leafless hedges and trees offer very little protection from driving sleet, relentless, biting winds and penetrating rain, but horses still vainly gather round them and the ground there becomes poached into a mass of oozing mud. I have seen common-bred horses and Thoroughbreds alike with rotted feet, painfully swollen legs and raw backs from constantly standing in mud, soaked to the skin and frozen. Miserable and shivering, they huddle together seeking moral support from one another to enable them to bear the unbearable.

Horses like dry, still, cold weather and often play and roll in fresh snow. It is when the snow turns to slush, when the sleet and rain pour down for days or when the frost freezes the mud round their legs and the wet on their backs that they suffer. Bitter winds in addition double the effects of the cold and wet, and many horses each year die inwardly (and, indeed, actually) from being forced to endure these atrocious conditions.

In summer, life without a shed can be no less agonising for different reasons. Undoubtedly, the worst part of summer is the flies and midges which mercilessly torment horses from dawn to dusk. Even at night some insects are active, but the worst times of day are from mid-morning to early evening. Flies happily follow horses into the shade of trees, but only a small hard core seem to go into a man-made shelter.

Some flies feed off the secretions from a horse's eyes, sheath and dock, others bite him to suck his blood – but all of them are capable of inflicting severe torment. Because we tend to overestimate the protective qualities of the horse's natural defence mechanisms, it is necessary to stress the chain of events which occurs during attacks by flies, something I have witnessed many times in horses inadequately protected (by their owners) from fly-strike. Some individuals, as always, are more susceptible than others, but they *all* suffer.

Nature has bestowed some defences on the horse, such as a mane, forelock and long neck and head which, combined, enable him to reach almost any part of his forehand, and also a tail which, when long enough, can deal with the quarters. There is also a large, flat sheet of muscle just under the skin on the sides and shoulders which twitches off insects effectively.

There is one big drawback to these built-in mechanisms. To keep the flies at bay the horse has to keep up a ceaseless campaign of head-shaking, muscle-twitching, leg-stamping and tail-swishing which soon wears him down. He can make himself sore, even raw, by biting himself or rubbing on any convenient object to relieve the itching and eventually, driven half out of his mind from the torment, he starts to run – the horse's natural defence against anything with which he cannot cope. Flies cannot keep up with a galloping horse, so he gallops, and gallops, and gallops, until he can go no more. He stops from exhaustion, probably in a heaving sweat which attracts the flies even more – and once again they attack to crawl upon and irritate the most sensitive parts of his body and particularly any raw areas caused by rubbing or other wounds.

In the end, all the horse can do is stand defeatedly nodding his head up and down like clockwork in a futile attempt to free himself from his tormentors, his eyes half closed from the soreness and swelling they cause. The galloping on hard ground does damage, too. His legs and feet can become jarred to the point of lameness and his lungs and heart overstressed from the constant overwork. The eyes can ulcerate eventually and wounds become infected, which simply compounds the problem as the flies greedily feed on the discharges produced.

A good residual insect repellant (dealt with in Chapter 5) is an excellent preventative of fly-strike, but to get away from flies completely an effective shelter shed really is essential.

A shed should be regarded as a basic necessity for any horse out for more than a few hours a day at any time of year other than late spring, and even then freak conditions can occur. Any horse will use one once he has become used to it and, protected not only from flies and winter weather but from heat and sun, too, his condition will noticeably improve. Horses come to regard their shelter as their anchor, their home base, a welcoming haven to which they can thankfully and confidently retreat when things get rough, knowing they will find peace, shelter, probably hay except when grass is plentiful, and a soft, dry bed on which to lie and rest.

Shelter sheds
I hesitate to give too many requirements for a shelter as almost anything is better than nothing, but there are certain standards to aim for and below which a shed will become dangerous and possibly discouraging to the horse.

This barn provides safe shelter for several horses at once; note the high, wide entrance, deep-litter flooring and hayracks around the walls. The animals can be kept in spacious indoor accommodation at night or in bad weather or, with the gate chained back against the outside wall, can come and go as they wish

A practical shed large enough for two horses can be purchased new or constructed from second-hand materials. This shed has an economical single-pitched roof at a safe height, a strong, secure hayrack and deep-litter bedding to encourage the horses to lie down and rest. The open front has no projecting beams or support posts

Ideally, a shed should give as much space per horse as a stable. For two horses who are friendly towards each other, a smaller structure could be adequate, but where several horses are out together and/or there is any squabbling more room is needed to allow the underdog to manoeuvre himself out of the way. Although it might sound impracticably lavish, if there are any real problems of hierarchy, two sheds should be provided so that there is a better chance of at least one of them always being available to a victim of bullying. I have seen it happen so many times that the more timid horses are constantly kept out of the only shelter available, with a consequent deterioration in their physical condition and happiness.

Prefabricated shelters are sold by many firms advertising in horse journals. Cheaper ones can be provided by buying a used building, say from a farm sale or smallholder selling up, or there might already be a building in your field which, with some modification, can be made suitable for horses. For several horses, a disused barn, or part of one, can give shelter for all, with a high lofty ceiling providing headroom and preventing any sense of being closed in, which puts off some horses from using a shed. Satisfactory sheds can also be constructed out of straw bales and supporting wooden framework with a rigid waterproof material such as wood covered by roofing felt, or even corrugated asbestos or polythene for the roof.

The main points about shelters are that (1) they should be sited on the highest, driest part of the field to prevent the inside becoming wet, (2) they should have their backs to the prevailing wind (or where there is none, to the north or east so that the entrance faces south, preferably, or west), (3) they should have high, wide entrances to encourage the horses in and allow room for manoeuvre when several are trying to get in at once, (4) they should not be set against a fence but have room all round to avoid crushing, and (5) they should be free of all projections, rusty nails, splintered wood and so on which could harm the horses; windows should be barred up and buildings with low rafters shunned.

Most shelters are rectangular and have the whole of one long side left out as an entrance. These work well, but provide no shelter from the front should the wind change direction. Do not, however, remove only one half of a long side leaving the other intact as this forms a 'cul-de-sac' inside where a horse can be cornered and injured. If the shed is big enough, have two 10ft (3m) wide entrances on each end of the front, otherwise it is safer to remove the whole side. A single pitch roof, sloping to the back of the shed obviously, is quite adequate and should, at its lowest point, provide at least 2ft (60cm) headroom, preferably much more. Semi-circular shelters (rarely seen) are ideal, as there are no corners into which a victim can be hemmed. He can simply run round the wall and out.

Make the structure as strong as possible to withstand kicks and rubbing, and make provision for providing hay inside the shed, either by means of tie-rings bolted through for haynets or by fixing a cattle-type hayrack down the back wall with the top just above horse's head height. Keep the shelter well strawed down and the droppings picked up, and I am sure you will find your horses treat it as a real home and will show their gratitude in their condition.

Bedding

A concrete base is not necessary for a shelter as the horses do not often stale (urinate) inside. They do droppings, though, and these must be removed daily if you want to avoid an indoor muck-heap. Keep the bedding clean and as thick as for a stable. Used bedding can be scattered (minus droppings) on badly poached areas, such as the shelter entrance, gateways, round watering points and other areas where horses congregate, to help reduce this problem. These areas will not grow much grass anyway, so the practice will do nothing but good. Other substances which can be used to reduce poaching include sand, fine cinders and fine shale. Never, though, tip a load of rubble down as the stones and bricks can cut and bruise the hooves and lower legs. It also presents very rough, unreliable footing to the horses, who may become reluctant to step on it until forced by intense thirst or need of rest and shelter.

If, when you erect your shed, there is grass growing on the floor inside, remember your horses will eat it, until it withers and dies, and will take in any bedding on top. Therefore, use only straw bedding in the meantime as the inadvertent eating of other materials can cause colic.

In Chapter 4, on grassland management, the need for a rota in the use of fields is discussed. By using a little ingenuity, and ground conditions permitting, one shed can be made to serve several fields by siting it where they meet and removing the fencing there. Then, using gates or sliprails and fencing, a pen can be built around and at least 12ft (3.65m) from the shed, and any fields which may be resting or under treatment can be closed off.

Water sources

A healthy horse can need anything up to 12 gallons (55 litres) of water a day. Shortage of suitable water has a bad and most noticeable effect on the health and condition of any animal, so the supply must be ample, clean and from a source which the horse is not afraid to use freely. If he is frightened to approach because of rough or slippery ground,

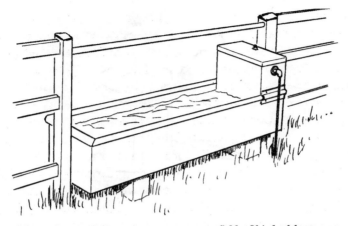

A trough positioned within a fence to serve two fields. If it had been set at an angle to the fence, it would have formed a dangerous projection into the field. The rail above will prevent horses from trying to jump over the trough, and this rail and the top fence rail should be level with the tops of the posts for safety. The pipe should ideally be lagged (below ground as well) and guarded with strong mesh or wooden boxing

low branches or sinking mud, or an unstable container, he will go without until forced, then snatch a quick sip to appease his immediate thirst.

A clear running stream with a stony or gravel bottom is good. A sand or earth bed, it is generally believed, can be sucked up with the water and eventually cause colic. A pond is unlikely to be clean enough, most being stagnant and with unsafe and unwelcoming approaches. In winter, there is the added danger of the horse's venturing on to the ice and falling in, so all ponds should be fenced off. If a horse prefers drinking muddy water to fresh, it is a sign he could be short of minerals in his diet. Ponds and streams should be checked regularly for pollution (consult the National Rivers Authority on analysis services).

If there is piped water to the field, an automatically-filling trough is good provided the mechanism is shielded from the horse and is not taken for granted but regularly checked to ensure it is filling up but not overflowing. These are available from agricultural merchants and stable fittings suppliers, in many cases. Plumbing should be well lagged to prevent burst pipes in winter. If the horses chew lagging above ground,

This post and rail fencing is safely constructed, with the rails on the inside, the bottom one a good distance from the ground, and the top rail level with the tops of the posts. The plastic dustbin, rammed into an old tyre, is a cheap, effective water container. It can be filled by hosepipe and is excellent in fields with no water supply laid on

pour old-fashioned bitter aloes over it – but not into the water! In winter, troughs and all water containers should have the ice broken at least twice a day as horses often seem unable to do this for themselves. If piped water ends in a tap over a water container, there should be some kind of smooth guard over and round the tap which enables humans to use it but keeps horses off, to prevent damage to both them and it.

If there is no piped water, a hosepipe will have to be run from a convenient tap to the field. Any water container, whether filled automatically, by tap or by hosepipe, should be smooth to prevent injuries. Sharp cornered troughs or tanks are dangerous, as can be the rims of old baths. Some metal containers, whether galvanised or not, contaminate the water with rust and rubber ones can make it taste horrible.

Plastic dustbins are good (the lids can be used as dung skeps). Choose the flexible type which will not crack should the horses bite them. Tie each bin to a support post in the fence (not where it will get leaves falling into it) with binder twine or rope round the top and middle and wedge the bottom into a close-fitting large rubber tyre for stability. Many tyre fitters are glad to sell these very cheaply. The advantages of water bins like these are that they are safe, easy to handle for scrubbing out, more than one watering point can easily be provided and they can be moved on a little way down the fence each day, preventing poached ground.

Safety

In rented fields one often comes across dangerous farm implements hidden in the grass which must be taken right out of the field, not just pushed to one side. Horses cannot be trusted to see and avoid even something as large as an old plough, and a chain harrow is easy for even us to overlook if the grass is more than a few inches long. Horses can canter right on to such things with serious consequences. Litter must be regularly checked for and removed, as should fertiliser sacks left lying about or blowing in from elsewhere.

Danger areas such as ponds should be fenced off. Even shallow ditches can be dangerous. Horses rolling near them can end up cast on their backs or sides in the ditch. They can die of exhaustion and shock just by struggling to get out, but if the dyke is deep and/or contains water, it is possible for a horse to drown.

Safety is largely a case of cultivating the habit of observation and imagination as regards the horses' field. Make a point of filling in holes with stones and earth, removing large rocks, loose or protruding tree roots (the tree has plenty more!), fallen boughs and dead (and therefore possibly dangerous) trees. Also make a habit of checking for and spotting damage to fencing, gates or shed every time you visit the field. Rest assured that if there is anything within reach of the horses which could cause them trouble, they will find it.

Security

Anyone keeping a horse out round the clock has to face the fact that one morning when they go to check on him he may not be there, and not because he might have escaped but because someone has stolen him. It is distressing but true that it is very easy to steal a horse from an open field in the dead of night. They are even stolen in broad daylight. But how do you make a field thief-proof? The answer is – you don't. All you can do is make life as difficult and discouraging as possible for the thief.

The first thing to be done is to get your horse freeze-marked. In Britain at present, there are a few companies offering this service, which is approved by the British Horse Society and police forces. The horse has a personalised number freeze-branded on his back. The super-chilled irons kill the pigment in the hair root and it grows back white, showing the number. With white or grey animals the hair follicle is killed completely by leaving the iron on a little longer, so the number is shown in bare skin. The horse is registered at the freeze-marking company's offices, and any freeze-marked horse stolen, or found away from home, is reported to the police, who check with the company for the name and address of the owner. Horses can be marked under the mane, if desired, although the number will not then be immediately visible at, for example, a sale. The marking companies normally offer rewards well above meat price for the recovery of the horse which act as incentives to sales operators and others to report such horses, and not slaughter or sell them. This system is much more effective than lip tattooing. Most companies provide stick-on or sew-on warnings for rugs and metal plates, to fix up in your yard, to the effect that the horses are marked.

The British army burns a code number on to its horses' hooves, and there is a company in Britain offering this service to civilian owners, using their post code. Not so visible as a freeze-mark on the back, it avoids the disfigurement by the latter (although it is under the saddle) and is preferred by many.

As for the field, it is highly impractical to make the fencing thief-proof or even thief-resistant. The best deterrent here is high, thick prickly fencing, which can take years to develop. Saws and wire-clippers will cope with most man-made fencing, unfortunately, but at least you can padlock your gates round the top and bottom hinges at each side so that they cannot easily be undone or lifted off the hinges.

It is a good idea to cultivate the favours of people living in the area and ask them to keep an eye out for strangers lurking around. Give them your telephone number (work and home) and ask that they contact you or some other designated person if anything suspicious is going on.

Breeding stock

Although this book is not specifically meant for breeders, some mention should be made of turning out breeding stock with other horses.

Much depends on the temperaments and personal relationships of the horses involved. If a broodmare's only companion is a friendly gelding, they will probably both be very miserable if separated just because 'the books' say the two do not mix. If a broodmare is turned out with an animal or animals which persistently chivvy her, and which might set on the foal if born when no human is about, it is obviously dangerous to leave her with them. Stallions are normally turned out alone, although, one hopes, within sight of other animals (when they are happy and balanced in their outlook). However, I have known of two stallions who each spent half of each day out in turn with an aged pony mare who kept them both firmly in their places and taught them manners. She would stand for no nonsense and would not let either of them even attempt to mount her and they both appeared extremely fond of her. They were both very well mannered towards their 'wives', too.

If animals which do not mix are to be turned out in adjoining fields, it is best to create a lane of double fencing between the fields. This could simply be done with electric fencing about 12ft (3.65m) away from one side of the fence, provided the horses are taught to respect it as described earlier.

Tethering

Tethering is a very poor way of keeping a horse at grass unless the horse fully understands what the tether is all about and will tie up peacefully, and is left tethered for only short periods to give a change of grazing. The horse must be tethered within easy reach of shelter and water, wear a well-fitting, supple headcollar or neckstrap round the throat and have a swivel on the end of the tether which ensures he cannot wrap his rope round and round the stake and end up with only a little ground. The stake must be firmly and deeply hammered into the ground, and the horse must not be tethered in dangerous surroundings or within reach of any enemies, from whom he will obviously be unable to escape.

The combined system

Although many horses live constantly at grass, there are undoubtedly times when it would be much better to be able to bring them in temporarily for convenience, say to facilitate preparation for some occasion; and it might become essential in times of illness or injury, so every effort should be made to obtain at least temporary use of a stable, perhaps by paying someone a small retainer rent to ensure availability when necessary. At a pinch, the field shed, if large enough, could have part of it safely sectioned off for the horse, although possibly the other animals might try to interfere with the occupant. Also, the 'prisoner' might try to get out to them.

The combined system of horse keeping means that a horse spends some of his time stabled and some outdoors and is really the best system of keeping any horse as it gives him and his owner the best of both worlds: the freedom of the outdoors and the comfort of a stable. When the land becomes unfit to use, usually when badly poached in winter, it may become essential to get the horses off it for at least part of the time and stable them, say, at night, or on summer days to get them away from sun and flies.

Another system of keeping them when the land is out of use, if the facilities can be arranged, is to bed down a large enough building, say a barn, large garage or implement shed, and construct a run or corral outside so they can wander freely in and out and stretch their legs while still having shelter. The surface of the run will have to be non-slip and not hard, or falls and injuries could occur. A covering of peat, sand or used bedding, even though it will get rained on, can make many surfaces acceptable if laid thickly enough. (This is yet another use for used bedding from stables or shed. If the practice is made of mucking out the droppings into one muck heap and the used bedding into another, the droppings will make highly saleable manure and the bedding can be used as described to good advantage.) A corral system such as this is far better for horses than either being cooped up in a stable with no exercise or relief from boredom when their field is out of use, or standing rooted in the mud of their paddock.

4 Grassland Management

It was not until I read an article on conservation some years ago that I realised just how important is grass, not only to horse owners but to the human race as a whole. Perhaps we do not grow grass to eat as we do cereal crops, but we grow it to feed animals on which we depend for food, whether they eat it in its natural growing form, as silage, hay or as processed cobs, cubes or meal. The article made the point that grass is our most neglected crop and the most underrated. Every year, millions of pounds worth of food potential is unrealised through neglect or mismanagement.

To the horse owner, particularly the owner whose horse spends most or all of his time in the field, good grass is a cheap, naturally balanced diet suited to the delicate equine digestive system. Even when meticulously managed, it is cheaper to provide than bought foods and definitely saves money in the long run. Those owners who have more than enough good grazing for their requirements need pay less attention to it than those who have barely sufficient. It is small acreages per horse which need most planning and care, because the smaller the area the more wear it gets. Pounding hooves and cropping teeth inevitably cover the same ground more often and the same amount of manure is dropped as on a larger field, so covering and contaminating with its smell (and probably worm eggs) a greater percentage of the available area.

Together, these three factors – hooves, teeth and droppings – combine to hamper seriously the growth of desirable grass on overstocked or neglected 'small' paddocks. I have placed the word 'small' in inverted commas because the size of the paddock matters less than the number of horses on it, eg while a 5 acre (2ha) paddock might be enough for two horses on a year-round basis, it would be cramped for three and definitely insufficient for four.

Many owners from a non-farming background have no idea what constitutes good or useless vegetation for grazing. To them, grass is just grass and they presume the horses will eat it willy nilly. Also, many of us have no real idea of how to care for what we have. To make matters more difficult, there is a difference between the sort of grass which is good for horses and that which is better for cattle.

Horses these days are normally required for athletic purposes – galloping, jumping, endurance work, trekking or hacking, or for breeding other horses able to do these things. They are expected to have a long, sound, useful life, unlike farm animals which are either used for the production of food (involving a fast growth and weight gain and a short life) or for producing other food animals; and their nutritional requirements and digestive processes and abilities are rather different.

Growth pattern and food content

Grass has 'waves' of growth, being more abundant and containing different levels of various nutrients at different times of the year. It contains most food value and protein in May and early June, which is nature's time when young animals are born and need food, and when lactating mothers need plenty of food to provide milk for this year's young and to nourish next year's offspring which is probably developing inside them. Stallions also need good food during the mating season to make fertile, healthy sperm.

From June onwards, the food value of grass gradually decreases. In early autumn, there is a flush of growth which, however, is not so rich in protein as spring grass, containing more carbohydrate, and by late autumn, there is often practically no nourishment left in the grass. It is almost all fibre. In very mild winters, grass may continue to grow slowly throughout the season and may contain more nutrients than usual, but this is still not enough to support an animal properly.

It has traditionally been believed that horses prefer short, young grass, but in fact they do graze any length of grass provided they find it palatable, and this is the crux of the matter. No matter how perfect, in theory, a grass is for horses, if they do not like it they will not eat it, and it will do them no good at all unless it finds its way inside them!

Because grass is such a variable food, its high food-value level in spring being possibly dangerous (particularly for animals which have a good deal of common or pony blood and which just cannot take much nourishment – this includes donkeys) and its nutritional value in winter virtually nil, we must learn when to restrict grass intake and when to supplement it with other food of a suitable type. Otherwise, the result could be a horse who is not only unfit to use through being unsuitably fed but possibly dangerously obese and suffering from laminitis, or conversely starved to emaciation or death through ignorance. Supplementary feeding and the recognition of condition (understanding when a horse is too fat or thin) are dealt with in Chapter 6.

It is nature's plan to provide plenty of food in the breeding season, tailing off the supply during the year. In winter, horses still eat grass from instinct but they will really be living off the reserves of fat they have built up in their bodies from good summer feeding (supposing they have been allowed to grow fat from ample food and a work-free summer). By spring, they will be noticeably lean and, indeed, the weaker animals will have starved to death before the spring grass appears. This illustrates the survival of the fittest, and shows nature ensuring that the weaklings are not around when breeding commences, to reproduce their weaknesses within the species. In domestication, of course, this sort of treatment is not only regarded as the height of cruelty (although it happens each winter) but as stupid from an economic point of view, as it surely costs more to build up a thin horse or replace a dead one than it does to keep an existing one properly fed.

Suitable grasses and herbs

It is not only the nutritional content of a grass which decides its value but also its physical characteristics, such as whether it has a long or short growing season (some grasses grow for only a few weeks, then die), whether it is palatable to the animals and whether it is strong enough to grow and tiller (spread) vigorously despite competition from other grasses and plants nearby. It should also be of a type which recovers quickly after grazing and which will persist in the pasture for several years without the necessity to keep reseeding the paddock.

It is advisable to include some grasses which appear early in the year and some which go on growing well into autumn, thus ensuring the field will be productive for a long season as when the early grasses have had their day the later ones will still have weeks of young, active growth left. It is important to top (mow) early grasses not grazed or they will smother the later ones.

For horses, whose hooves and teeth are particularly destructive to turf and grass, it is also advisable to have some hard-wearing turf-forming grasses (such as *Agrostis)* included in the mix to help form a resilient turf to protect the horses' feet and legs and the land itself. It is worth hand-sowing areas of these grasses in much-used areas which tend to become hard and bare in summer or badly poached in winter, eg along fences, in gateways and round troughs and shelters.

The climate and soil in your district will also determine what will and will not flourish under local conditions. Some grasses grow best in warm areas and others in cold; some prefer dry land and others damp. Formulating a seed mix is a job for an expert, and new species of grass are constantly being developed, and seed mixes formulated as research in this field continues.

It is well worth consulting, in the UK, the Equine Services Department of the Agricultural Development Advisory Service (part of your local Ministry of Agriculture, whose telephone number is available from your 'phone book or local reference library) or an independent consultant such as the Equine Management Consultancy Service, based at 20 Victoria Road, Bulwark, Chepstow, Gwent NP6 5QN, Wales.

The nutritionist at the firm whose seed mixes you are

considering should also be able to advise on a suitable mix for athletic horses, and if one doesn't exist ask if a mix can be made for you. Some firms will not want to bother, and may not have the knowledge. If you feel this is the case, or they try to sell you an alternative or substitute which is not tailor-made for horses, go elsewhere. These days there is no need to accept the sort of seed mix guaranteed to increase milk yields in cattle, for example, which will be almost sure to give your horse laminitis anyway. You want a mix which is for working horses, not the slightly 'richer' pasture with its different nutrient balance which is suitable for equine breeding stock – unless you are a breeder, of course. You have to be extremely careful over your seed mix if you keep native ponies and cobs. These animals were evolved to do well on the very sparse, low-energy, low-protein keep of unimproved land before the advent of agriculture, and must have a mixture made up accordingly if you do not have natural ranges for them. The type of land grazed by sheep is plenty rich enough for them.

The benefit of clover is often misunderstood, possibly because the term 'living in clover' is taken to mean contentment and luxury. Clover is valuable as it adds essential nitrogen to the soil whereas grass removes it, but too much clover will stifle the grass and, as it is rich in protein, could cause digestive and other troubles in horses. Another valuable property of clover is calcium, which is vital for all horses, not just breeding and youngstock. Limestone or chalky soils (high calcium) are traditionally best for rearing horses, but a deficiency in other soils can be corrected artificially by the application of lime and/or chalk, which also helps keep the land sweet. The calcium/phosphorous ratio should ideally be 1.5:1, giving more calcium than phosphorous, and the advice of a consultant should be sought before indiscriminately applying calcium, or indeed any other supplements, to your land for fear of doing more harm than good.

(Some years ago, I visited a famous stud near Lewes, at the foot of the Sussex Downs. The owner of the stud told me that the calcium from the Downs was constantly washed down on to the lower land in the area making it far too high in calcium so that he had to take retaliatory action by means of his horses' other feed. Apparently, the calcium also got into the drinking water, causing arthritis in human and animal occupants of the area, but because he closely controlled his horses' diets they did not suffer from arthritis – and some of them were very old – although he did!)

Apart from nitrogen and calcium in clover, there are also many important minerals not found in grass, so it can be seen that a balanced proportion of clover in horse pastures is a most important factor.

Herbs

Herbs, too, contain protein, plus calcium and minerals not available from grass alone, and should be included in all pasture seed mixes for horses, or sown separately if the pasture is otherwise in good order. The following herbs are suitable for horses: ribgrass, burnet, yarrow, sheep's parsley, dandelion and chicory, which is especially palatable. It is generally considered that clover and herbs together should comprise not more than one tenth of the whole pasture.

Horses' grazing habits

Horses designate sometimes quite large parts of their field as lavatories where they go to deposit droppings and urine. They do not contaminate the chosen dining areas as the smell of their own manure is repugnant to them, consequently the grass in the lavatory areas is ignored and wasted and that in the dining parts can become overgrazed and weakened. In practice, this means that parts of the paddock are constantly cropped down tight, even bare if the horses are left on long enough, while others are never touched. This in turn obviously implies that although you may have, say, a 4 acre (1.6ha) paddock, the actual grazing area may only be 3 acres (1.2ha). After a few weeks, a horse paddock begins to look uneven, showing short areas interspersed with areas of what looks, to the uninitiated, like plenty of lush grass remaining but what is really, in the horses' eyes, rank, contaminated grass, inedible even to hungry animals. Because these areas are receiving 'fertiliser' in the form of dung and urine, they become rich in plant nutrients excreted by the horses while the overgrazed parts become deficient in them, constantly giving and never receiving. This can eventually result in retardation of grass growth in the grazed areas and a practically unproductive paddock from a food viewpoint. A paddock in this state is called 'horse sick'. It is now that the owner's troubles can really start, because the horses become increasingly hungry. They chew the fencing, strip the trees and make themselves ill by trying out poisonous plants within their reach which they would probably normally ignore, or they can injure themselves trying to jump out to greener pastures in search of food.

The subject of the contamination of land by the smell of droppings was studied at the Equine Research Station (Animal Health Trust), Newmarket, England in the 1970s. It was found that even after using land over which ponies had established a grazing pattern for two or three arable crops, and then returning equines to it, the same areas were grazed as previously plus some not grazed before. By and large, the lavatory areas remained the same, however, so it would seem that the smell of the droppings persisted after all that time.

It was discovered, however, that liberally spreading the entire field with well-rotted farmyard (cattle) manure had the effect of disguising the smell, and when ponies were eventually returned a completely even grazing/dunging pattern resulted which persisted for many months afterwards. It appears that farmyard manure is valuable for horse paddocks not only because of the nutrients it provides but because it seems to mask the smell in the areas contaminated by equine droppings. The horses no longer find these areas offensive and so will graze there, thus putting to use land which was previously wasted.

Unfortunately, 'good old-fashioned' farmyard manure mixed with straw is becoming harder and harder to get as modern farming practices embrace the increasingly common (and to my mind appalling) policy of not giving the animals bedding, so all that is produced is slurry. When spread at normal rates this is regarded as far too potent for horse pastures. If you can somehow spread it thinly, or get hold of the 'real McCoy', I feel it would be worth while.

Many owners not unnaturally would like to use their own horses' manure on land, and it does seem that provided this is well rotted and over a year old the problem of contamination with smell does not occur. However, as so many owners now use shavings, it should be pointed out that shavings deplete the land of nitrogen so this would probably need carefully supplementing, under expert advice.

Parasites

The subject of internal parasites will be dealt with mainly in the next chapter, but some mention of them must be made here. Almost every horse and pony has worms to some extent, whose eggs and larvae are passed out in the droppings and so on to the pasture. The eggs hatch and the larvae crawl on to the grass, often quite some way from the droppings, to be eaten with the grass by grazing horses. Once inside the horses they mature, migrating through organs and arteries and causing sometimes fatal damage, finally establishing themselves in the intestines to suck the horses' blood, breed and begin the cycle over again.

It is known that consistent, frequent dosing (every four to six weeks) results in large numbers of parasites being killed and their breeding activities curtailed for this time, during which very few eggs and larvae are excreted. Therefore, with adequately-wormed horses, parasite infestation is not much of a problem.

It can be seen, however, how in horses *not* so wormed parasites can soon build up to dangerous levels, and good husbandry from this point of view alone would then demand that droppings were picked up regularly – as often as every day in warm, moist weather, the worms' optimal breeding conditions. The formerly recommended practice of spreading droppings in the lavatory areas to expose them to sun and air to desiccate and decompose them more quickly

is not now recommended as it is felt that this will spread the
larvae around before the sun kills them off. Every effort
should be make to pick up droppings as often as possible
(certainly where youngstock are grazing, and other breeding
stock). However, hot sun and a dry atmosphere does kill
many worm eggs and larvae, as does a sharp frost.

Cattle

Although it is possible to counteract the results of horses'
grazing habits by mowing down the long grass and adding
artificial fertilisers to the deprived areas, the results are not
so good as another workfree and completely natural method
– the use of cattle on the land.

Horses graze by cropping the herbage with their front
teeth. They can and do take it right down to soil level, which
is bad for pasture as it then takes weeks or even months to
recover. They are also, as already mentioned, very selective
in their diet and will leave much good grass if they do not
happen to find it palatable, even when hungry. Cattle,
however, obtain their grass by wrapping their tongues round
it and tearing it off some way above the ground. They are
physically unable to take it down to ground level and so are
not able to feed off the areas overgrazed by the horses.
Instead they eat the long parts the horses have left, being
unoffended by the horses' droppings and also not so fussy
over what they eat. They use for their lavatory areas, largely,
the horses' grazing areas, thereby depositing much-needed
nutrients there. When the horses return, after the short grass
has grown again, they keep to their same pattern and graze
in their previously selected areas, being similarly unoffended
by cattle manure.

Cattle also play a valuable part in parasite control. As
they graze in the areas containing the highest numbers of
equine parasites, they will inevitably ingest them with the
grass. Parasites cannot live in an unnatural host, and will be
killed off. Likewise, any parasites of cattle eaten by the
horses are also killed off, so each species again complements
the other.

If nothing else were ever done to the land, the use of cattle alone would go a long way towards correcting the 'damage' done by horses. In most districts where there are horses, there are usually cattle nearby whose owners will normally be pleased to use your free grazing (I have never yet known a farmer who had enough land) at no cost to you.

Renovating and maintaining your land

If the land is your own or you have the use of it for some years, it is worth implementing a programme of drainage and reseeding (if necessary) and of subsequent fertilisation, treatment and use in order to get the best from it, whether the area is large or small. If you are unable to do the work yourself, a few enquiries among local farmers or a glance through your district's farming journals will produce either a farmworker or agricultural contractor who will do it for you.

The first step is to put right the drainage (for which you may be able to get a grant, especially if you are grazing cattle, too), if this has been advised. This is vital, as no methods of husbandry will work to good effect on badly drained land. It is best done in late summer or autumn as the grass is then past its best but the land should not be too wet for the work to be carried out.

To drain a field, tubular field-drains must be laid below the surface to collect the water and run it off into some suitable outlet, such as a ditch. Clay drains have been used for many years and last well, but a few years ago they began to be replaced by long plastic tubes which were felt to be easier and quicker to lay. However, in practice it has been found that these can crack too easily from the weight of soil above them, and whilst there is some return to clay drains, other materials are now being tried. Your field would be considerably disrupted by the work, as trenches have to be dug at intervals across the land, the drains inserted and the topsoil replaced, so it could be out of use for several weeks.

The second step is to rid the land of any unwanted herbage as far as possible. Spraying with herbicides should only be a last resort if the land is really bad, and then the clover and herbs will have to be replaced. It is much better in the long run to gradually get rid of what you do not want by persistent mowing down and uprooting, which in time will effectively kill off the unwanted growths. In this way, there is no risk of killing off valuable herbage or of having chemicals washed down into the land, with possibly deleterious side-effects on the soil or animals.

The third stage is heavy harrowing, a marvellous treatment for the land. A pitchpole harrow should be drawn across the field by Land-Rover or tractor twice both ways. This aerates the soil by loosening it and tearing out old roots, moss and dead, matted vegetation without going too far and destroying the precious protective turf, as does ploughing. (Once the land is back in use, it will do nothing but good if it is chain harrowed once each way each month throughout the growing season.)

Fourthly, whatever fertilisers have proved necessary should now be applied at the recommended rates. There are specific fertilisers such as lime, potash, calcium, phosphate and nitrogen, and general ones such as fishmeal or seaweed meal. It is important to follow the advice you have received on this subject, as a great deal of harm can be done to your land and horses by haphazard applications of just any product which sounds impressive in the advertisements. Some fertilisers can and should be applied frequently throughout the year while others are required only every few years. Any product which claims to produce a quick flush of protein-rich grass (eg straight nitrogen, pig or poultry manure) must be used with great care and a hay crop taken first before the horses are grazed, or serious digestive troubles can result.

Fifth, and finally, comes the sowing of your seed mix which, if possible, should be followed by rolling to consolidate the soil again. The only thing to do then is wait. After an April sowing, the land should be ready for you to begin using lightly in August or September, and after a July sowing, say, the following April or May.

Obviously, while the renovation programme is proceeding the horses must be kept off the land, mainly for their own safety but partly to avoid ruining the good work; it will, therefore, be necessary to section off the land, preferably into at least four parts (especially if reseeding with the subsequent waiting time involved) and renovate it piece by piece.

It is usually recommended that after the application of most fertilisers and weedkillers pasture should be left ungrazed for at least three weeks, unless there is a very heavy fall of rain, to ensure that the toxic properties have either become inactive or been washed away. Some products, though, are safe as soon as they are dry, but this point must be carefully checked with your adviser or veterinary surgeon.

Your land should be left until the grass has reached 4-5in (10-12cm) before being subjected to grazing, and at first should be grazed lightly. The following season, normal grazing in accordance with a sound management rota can be practised. Newly seeded paddocks should not be used for hay otherwise all the herbs, clover and fine-leaved grasses will be smothered and killed off. As mentioned earlier, the grass should be kept 'topped' to 3-4in (8-10cm) to allow these slow growers to establish.

A suggested management rota

A carefully thought-out rota is essential if the land is not to revert quickly to its former condition. The following routine is only a rough sample of what might be suggested for, say, an owner with two horses and 5 acres (2ha) of land. Precise details must depend on individual circumstances but the following might provide some guidelines at least.

If not already done, the land should be divided into three paddocks of roughly the same size (ensuring each has access to water and shelter facilities, which can be centralised as shown in the illustration on page 66. If one field is noticeably drier than the others it could be kept mainly for winter use and be sown with a good proportion of *Agrostis* or similar grasses to stand up to winter conditions. This field could also be used for exercising the horses (ridden or lunged) if required, so as not to spoil the others. The two 'summer'

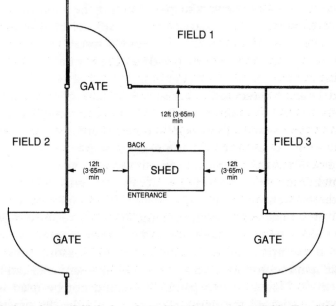

This shows how a field shed can be positioned to serve three fields. Two fields can be shut off for treatment and resting while the third is in use, and the horses can still get to the shelter

fields could have some early-growing grasses for early spring use, by which time the 'winter' field will be ready for its rest.

For convenience, let us call the winter paddock Field 1 and the others 2 and 3, and imagine that the rota has begun in spring, with the horses in Field 2.

When the grass in Field 2 begins to look uneven, with some short patches and some noticeably longer ones (in roughly three to four weeks) move the horses into Field 3. Ideally, now, Field 2 should be grazed by cattle for a week or so. Once they have gone, a few hours should be spent scything or mowing down any remaining long grass (preferably spreading it on to the over-grazed areas to rot down) and weeds. A light chain harrowing should now be given; then the field should be closed off to rest and grow.

When Field 3 begins to look patchy, move the horses back to Field 2. Field 3 now needs the cattle, mowing, harrowing and resting treatment, and by the time Field 2 is looking a bit ragged again, Field 3 will have recovered and be ready for use once more – and so the rota goes on.

From about mid-July on, Field 1 could be reintroduced into the rota, but should subsequently receive the 'treatment' and be allowed to grow during September before being put into sole use for the winter. At this time, Fields 2 and 3 should be grazed by cattle, mown, harrowed and given a good general fertiliser, before being shut up all winter. When the land is dry enough in spring, harrow these fields, and once the grass is making a good showing again they can be brought back into use as before. Field 1 should now be mown, harrowed thoroughly and fertilised, and shut up until midsummer.

It will be noticed that this rota allows a good deal of rest for each paddock, something most horse paddocks used for non-breeding stock rarely get. However, in order to keep land in good condition, at least three months' continuous rest is vital. With the type of system described, your land will repay you not only by looking pleasant but in the amount and quality of the grass it grows for your horses. The grass will be right for horses as opposed to dairy cattle so you should not have the problems of obesity and digestive troubles, including laminitis, so often associated with the latter, and in spite of the money you will have spent on it, and will continue to spend, it will still be a cheaper source of food by far than bought-in fodder and concentrates. Sick, neglected, overworked land is depressing to look at, bad for the horses' health and contentment and hard on your pocket in terms of reduced production and enforced supplementary feeding.

Compromises

It is quite possible to operate a successful rota with two fields. Even if you do not have enough land to enable the horses to receive considerable dietary support from the grass, do divide whatever you have into two and operate a rota as best you can, making up for the lack of grass by giving supplementary feeds. In such a case, try to rent some other suitable grazing for, say, six weeks during May and June and the same in September and October, as during these times the grass is growing and will have no chance to develop on your own land if it is eaten off or trampled down as soon as it appears. If your land never gets a reasonable rest it will become useless for anything but exercise and you will have to buy almost all your horses' food. Such paddocks could each be given alternate winters off to ensure that they get their three months' continuous rest once in a while. Those who are able to obtain grazing only on a casual, fairly short-term renting arrangement, usually from farmers, are obviously extremely limited as to how they can manage the land, if at all. It is probably best to rent one field for spring and summer and one for autumn and winter, or, better still, one for each season, if possible, depending on the space available per horse.

Mixed grazing with cattle is perfectly acceptable and the two rarely bother with one another. The main points to check are, first, that the cattle should not be dairy cattle as they will almost certainly be on grazing too rich for horses, secondly, that they are free from ringworm which is contagious and can be difficult to cure and, finally, that they are hornless, otherwise a nasty accident could occur.

Making hay

It is always a temptation for horse owners to save money by taking a hay crop from their land, and this possibility can certainly be discussed with whoever you consult about your land. Mostly it is a waste of time and money unless the land can comfortably be spared and the crop is certain to be well made and of high quality. Specialist knowledge is needed to know when a crop is ready for cutting (most are left much too late until past their best) and to judge the weather if the crop is to be field dried. Expensive machinery is also needed unless you are going to scythe and truss it by hand – to the benefit of the crop, I might add! Even if you engage a contractor to do the work, it is unlikely he will be free to come at a few hours' notice when you judge your crop to be in its prime for cutting or baling, and a few hours can make a big difference to a crop, let alone a few days.

Unless you can overcome all these problems, I feel it more

satisfactory and economical to feed your grass growing and buy the best hay you can find.

Poisonous growths

A good deal is written about poisonous plants and trees, but in fact genuine cases of plant poisoning are rare. The trouble mainly arises in hungry animals because poisonous things are usually bitter tasting and normally only eaten when horses become desperate enough to experiment with almost anything. The moral here is obvious – if you do not have enough grass to keep your horses content, give them supplementary food (probably hay or hayage – see Chapter 6) so that they are not forced to satisfy their hunger on lethal vegetation.

It is not always easy to know what is poisonous and what is not as some poisonous plants look like others which are harmless or actually beneficial. Short of a practical lesson from an expert, the best most of us can do is learn from books and compare the descriptions with any unfamiliar growths in our own fields. It is no good renting a field only to find out too late that it is full of ragwort.

Two common poisonous trees to watch for are laburnum and yew. Yew, apparently, is not bitter tasting but quite deadly. Short of chopping down the trees, the best solution is to put fencing round them several yards further away than might seem necessary, so that there is no chance of the horses' reaching them. Many garden plants are poisonous, also shrubs, two common ones being laurel and rhododendron. Other common plants which are poisonous to a greater or lesser degree, some when alive, some when dead and some both, are: acorns, conkers, plants of the nightshade family, thorn apple, some privets, hemlocks, horse and marestails, buttercups, aconite, foxgloves, dodder, bryonies, some types of bracken, old man's beard, mature charlock and potato plants.

Garden cuttings can also be dangerous to horses, and lawn clippings can cause fatal colic by fermenting in the intestines and rupturing them. If the intestines do not actually rupture, the excess gas from the fermentation will cause considerable pain and the poisons will cause illness. Horses should be kept well away from compost heaps, therefore.

Poisonous plants thrive on neglected, sour land, by ditches and ponds and under hedgerows. There are specific sprays and treatments available, with new ones coming out all the time, and your local branch of the Ministry of Agriculture can give up-to-date advice on this, as can your veterinary surgeon or pasturage consultant.

As with other unwanted vegetation, it is better to spray only as a last resort if the land is really bad, it being preferable constantly to mow down, uproot and remove the plants, which are often equally poisonous when dead and also more appealing, as they then often lose their bitter taste. Dead plants should, therefore, be cleared out of the field and burnt. All animals must be removed while these processes are going on, and not put back until all chemicals are inactive, the exact safety margin depending on the product used.

A full dissertation on the subject of poisonous plants would be too long for this book, but an excellent publication is available from local offices of Her Majesty's Stationery Office or through the Ministry of Agriculture, Fisheries and Food. This is Bulletin No 161 *British Poisonous Plants*.

Ragwort
Special mention should be made of this plant as it is very common, very poisonous and very difficult to eradicate permanently. Furthermore, the Ministry of Agriculture is empowered under the Weeds Act of 1959 to enforce owners of infested land to clear it, although this rarely seems to happen judging by the spread of the plant in recent years. Ragwort (and there are various types) grows to a height of 2-3ft (60-90cm), with a straight, ribbed stem and dark, ragged-looking leaves. The flowers resemble large, bright yellow daisies growing in umbrella-like clusters. Ragwort thrives on land which is horse sick or neglected. It is stifled on well-managed land with a close-knit, ample sward.

Its alkaloid poisons act mainly on the liver. They accumulate (not being excreted) and in trying to render them harmless some of the liver cells die, being replaced by fibrous (cirrhotic) tissue. The liver does not work to full capacity anyway, and a few cells at first are not missed. But as the poison builds up from repeated grazing, or if a lot of poison is suddenly ingested at once, the liver becomes progressively destroyed by which time treatment is often pointless and mostly aimed at relieving discomfort. The healing process of the liver may take days, weeks or even months, depending on the amount of ragwort eaten. Just a few plants may cause great illness. The symptoms are varied as the liver is a vital organ performing many different functions, and it is advisable to consult your veterinary surgeon on this point. He is the person to tell you what signs to watch for.

There are now weedkillers to treat ragwort but it is necessary to spray yearly for several years as the plant is a perennial. Spraying, if decided upon, should be carried out in the 'rosette' stage, ie when the leaves are flat on the ground, and just before the flowering head begins to come up. The leaves then wither quickly and the paddock is fit to use quite soon. Plants *can* be sprayed up to the early bud stage but large plants need removing as they take too long to really rot away.

In practice, ragwort is not generally eaten when growing as it is most unpalatable, but *is* eaten when wilted or dry as its bitter taste then disappears. It should be stressed again that ragwort plants in a dead or dying condition – sprayed, cut down or uprooted – *must* be scrupulously picked up and taken right out of the field well out of reach of horses, not just dumped on the other side of the fence. They should preferably be burnt to avoid accidental access. If such plants are left within reach of horses they are almost bound to be eaten.

In addition to spraying, hand pulling is recommended, when the flower head is long enough to get a good grip, and uprooting with the aid of a garden fork, as a constant practice throughout the growing season. Get into the habit of taking a sack and a fork with you whenever you go into a paddock supporting ragwort. Although the plant has an extensive rootstock and will shoot from a tiny fragment left in the ground, constant uprooting is really the only way to get on top of it, and will eventually eliminate it altogether.

Readers are advised to obtain a copy of *Pasture Management for Horses and Ponies* by Gillian McCarthy, published by Blackwell Scientific Publications. This detailed, authoritative and very readable book is the standard work on the subject. It is very helpful, informative and practical and an essential source of information on a subject which is of vital concern to owners of outdoor horses.

5 Health and Condition

As the owner of your horse, you are responsible for his health and well-being. He is totally dependent on you for providing him with the necessities of life such as food, water and shelter, and for maintaining him in good health. It is also the owner's responsibility to provide veterinary care when the horse is sick or injured.

A great asset for anyone involved in caring for horses is the possession of a good, up-to-date veterinary book. In recent years, veterinary research has progressed considerably in several fields and although a veterinary surgeon is always the person to consult in matters of health and who will have access to the most recent knowledge and ideas in his field, reading at least one veterinary book on horse health matters will equip you with good basic knowledge of the afflictions to which your horse can succumb and of the type of injuries he can sustain (and these are many in such an athletic animal). Equally important, you will gain knowledge of how your horse's body functions in normal health. If we do not know what is normal, how shall we know what is abnormal?

Finding a suitable veterinary surgeon

Although all veterinary surgeons receive the same lengthy training, some prefer to specialise in certain fields after qualification. There are veterinary practices which deal with all types of animal, some only small animals, some large animals and some specialising in only one type of animal. Although any veterinary surgeon could adequately treat your horse, it is logical that one who has chosen to specialise in horses, or at least in large animals, will naturally have more interest in them and so probably be more up-to-date in their treatment than one wishing to work with only dogs for example. You can learn from other horse owners which practices deal with horses and which specialise in them, and choose from one reasonably near where you keep your horse. If you suddenly find your horse with a broken leg in the field, you will need help from a vet based two or three miles away, not from one working five or ten miles away. It is important that you have a veterinary surgeon you can talk to. Vets always seem to be extremely busy, but it is a disadvantage to have one who, because of lack of time, does not explain exactly what is wrong with your horse or what treatment he is having.

Veterinary surgeons' charges are usually reasonable when set against their long training, the hazardous nature of their work and their level of knowledge and skill. The main charges will be for drugs, treatments and travelling expenses. It is my experience that veterinary surgeons liberally give out advice free, especially to their regular clients, and your vet's advice will be one of your greatest assets in maintaining your horse's health.

A yearly care-plan

Have a talk with your vet and explain what you are going to do with your horse. Any horse in work should have a yearly medical check to make sure he is still likely to be able to perform the work you require of him. Heart, lungs, eyes, action and many other things will be taken into account. Blood tests can be carried out to check various aspects of the horse's metabolism, plus urine tests and anything else which your vet feels will be of use.

An annual routine should be worked out for vaccinations (mainly against influenza and tetanus) and for the administration of anthelmintics (worming medicines). Teeth also need periodical checks, every six months in youngsters, possibly once a year in older horses. Organise a routine and get several jobs (and maybe several horses) done at the same time, which will save on visit/travelling expenses. A suitable time for vaccinations should be carefully planned. Although it is normally better to vaccinate horses against influenza shortly before a busy season is about to begin, when they will be frequently exposed to the disease due to travelling, many owners find that their animals go slightly off colour after vaccination, so time must be allowed for any recovery necessary. Vaccinations are normally needed every six months in horses frequently exposed to influenza and once a year or even every two or three years for tetanus. These are matters on which your vet can advise.

Signs of health and disease

Anyone closely connected and working with a horse on a regular basis will get to know that animal very well unless he or she is insensitive. When a person also cares greatly about an animal, the chances of reaching a deep relationship and understanding with it are considerably increased, and so are the chances of noticing, or even just feeling intuitively, when something is amiss. Maybe it is just a look in the horse's eye, or perhaps it is something more noticeable. Whatever it is, no one will ever get to know your horse like you do, and it is you who will probably be the first to notice something wrong. It is also to you that your vet will look for information about your horse when normal. Many a time I have been asked by a vet: 'Are his glands swollen?' (when the vet has been standing right next to the horse), 'Does he always stand like that?' or 'Does he usually stay lying down when you go to him?' This is because the owner is more likely to know the answer to such questions than the vet. Each horse's make, shape and action is slightly different, and its behaviour can be very individual indeed. So we must study and really get to know our horses in order to help our veterinary surgeons as much as possible.

Some physical signs

A horse in good health will have a general appearance of 'bloom' about him, even when filthy with wet mud. His coat should have a certain sheen to it and, even in winter, lie close to the skin. If it is dull and 'staring' (ie the hair is standing stiffly away from the skin) the horse is probably either very cold or in poor health. He should have an alert, interested expression, unless sleepy, and should take note of his surroundings. Any horse which takes little notice of humans or other horses or who isolates himself, standing apart in the field, could well be sick. Even if he is the herd outcast, he will linger about on the fringes of the herd seeking company by instinct when well.

Horses rarely lie down flat out for more than half an hour; if they do, suspect trouble. Lying down excessively, in any position, should be noted, particularly if the horse also seems dull and withdrawn. When horses lie down to roll they very often do one side first, get up and then do the other side. After this they should have a good shake. Rolling without shaking afterwards can be a sign of internal disorder, particularly if done often.

The horse's eating and drinking habits should also be watched although this may not be easy in an outdoor horse. Take the time to stay and observe him for several minutes. If the horse appears to be eating and swallowing normally this is often a general sign of good health, but note whether he takes in and chews food, then drops it out of his mouth again in lumps, or whether food is coming back down his nostrils with saliva. The latter could be a sign that his gullet is blocked (known as 'choke') either from chewing wood (fencing or shelter) and swallowing pieces or from being given dry food. Dropping food out of the mouth ('quidding') is a sign of worn and sharp teeth causing pain and preventing the horse from chewing his food properly.

If you can manage it by being close to your horse for long enough, note whether he seems to be drinking very often or hardly at all, as both are signs of possible disorder. It is difficult to check this in a grass-kept horse, however. When several horses are kept together, it is also difficult to know if the water level in a non-automatic container is going down because some are drinking too much and others not enough, or whether they are all normal, so try to watch them all and get to know their habits. Self-fill containers, obviously, although saving a lot of work, are no help at all in enabling owners to check consumption. Check also that no horse is being kept off water, food or shelter by more dominant companions. If so, the best answer is usually to remove the

The spot under the jaw where the pulse can be taken

bully to another field, but it may be necessary to find somewhere else for the harrassed horse.

Getting to know your horse's normal temperature, pulse
and respiration rates can also be a big help. The horse's
normal temperature will be around 100.4°F (38°C), and his
at-rest pulse rate between 32 and 40 per minute with
breathing about 12 per minute. As your grass-kept horse will
be almost constantly on the move, these rates will be varying
all the time, but if you try to get initial readings at the same
time, under the same conditions every day for a week, you
will at least have some idea of what is normal for him. If you
are in the habit of standing your horse in a stable regularly,
say to prepare him for work or some other care procedure, he
will be used to this and could well relax and give you more
accurate readings. If he is not used to it, however, he could
become upset by it, which will send up his pulse and respiration rates.

To take a horse's temperature, buy a stubby-ended ther-
mometer from your vet and ask him to show you how to
shake down the mercury to below 90°F (32°C) before use.
Moisten or grease the end and, holding it by the top, insert it

into the horse's rectum (holding his tail to one side towards you) with a gentle side-to-side twisting motion. Leave it in place for a minute or half a minute, depending on the time stated on it, and read off the temperature.

To take a horse's pulse always use your fingers (not your thumb which has a pulse of its own) where a main artery passes over a bone. The most common spot is inside the jawbone just under the rounded bone, as shown in the illustration on page 77. Other places are inside the elbow a few inches down, and under or alongside the dock about a hand's breadth from the root of the tail. This latter spot has the advantage that you can take the horse's temperature at the same time. Feel around with your fingers and press so that you are sure you have got the pulse. Count for half a minute (you will obviously need a watch with a second hand), double the count and you have his rate per minute.

To take a horse's respiration, stand just behind and to one side of him where you can see the outline of his opposite flank, ie stand on his left and watch his right flank. Watch for the rise and fall of the flank, sometimes difficult to spot, especially in a fit horse, and count each lift and fall as one breath. Again, count for half a minute and double the count.

When horses are standing and resting, they often rest one hind leg alternately, and occasionally a foreleg, too, changing over from time to time. If a horse persistently rests the same leg, suspect trouble in that leg, even if he is not actually lame.

A horse's droppings, the remnants of his food once it has been digested, will also give a good guide to his state of health. Grass-kept horses' droppings are moister and greener than stabled horses', but they should still form into recognisable balls which break easily on hitting the ground. If they are sloppier or much harder than this, the horse could have some digestive disorder.

The horse's general demeanour will tell you a lot, not only whether he is well but also whether he is unhappy out at grass. If he stands with a forlorn expression, head down, ears back and tucked up (pinched looking in the hip/belly region), he could be ill or generally unhappy. In winter, this, perhaps combined with shivering, is a sure sign that the horse is cold and miserable. Horses can stand below-freezing temperatures quite happily if the weather is still, and dry, especially if it is sunny. Indeed, they seem to find such weather conditions exhilarating, as do many humans and other animals. It is when cold is combined with wind and/or wet that they begin to suffer most and seek shelter. The horse's natural winter coat insulates him quite well normally, holding a layer of body-warmed air within it all round the skin. When the wind disturbs this hair and lets out the warm air, the horse obviously feels cold, and when rain or snow wet the coat it clings together, flattens and cannot hold the layer of warm air. The wet in itself accentuates the effects of wind and cold.

Those animals with naturally thick coats (cold-blooded or heavy-weight types or those with a lot of cob or pony blood) stand such conditions better than the shorter, finer coated warm-blooded and hot-blooded types, which originate in warm climes and do not have the inherent protection against the British climate. It is usually such horses who benefit most from a New Zealand rug (see Chapter 7). Some people maintain that these rugs destroy the warm-air layer by flattening the coat, and this is true, but the rug itself is both windproof and waterproof, and *some* air will remain under the hair. Generally, when well maintained, these rugs have more advantages than disadvantages.

The horse's skin and coat are an excellent guide to his condition, a supple, movable, glossy covering to his body being indicative of good health and also providing a weather-resistant protection for him. Feeding a higher fat diet, most conveniently by adding soya oil or corn oil to each feed in amounts recommended by a vet or nutritionist (probably about a dessertspoonful (10ml) in each feed), does help improve the condition of skin, hair and hooves, as does adequate methionine, biotin, MSM and calcium in the diet, maybe by means of supplementation. Linseed oil can be used but if you opt for this make sure it is the type for animal feeding, not that used by decorators and artists for cleaning brushes, which is poisonous.

Some specific disorders

There are many disorders which can affect horses, of course, and the study of one of the previously-mentioned veterinary books will familiarise you with most of the more common or serious ones, plus usually giving you a good deal of information about the horse's general physiology. In this section, I should like to give some basic information on conditions likely to affect outdoor horses more than stabled ones so that owners can be particularly on the lookout for them.

Laminitis
see under Feet and Shoes, page 88.

Mud fever/rain rash
These two conditions are caused by the same organism, *Dermatophilus congolensis*, which attacks the skin when weakened by constant wetting. Rain rash is as common in warm, humid conditions as in cold weather, but mud fever usually seems to occur most in colder conditions.

Mud fever can be initially noticed by the heat it causes in the skin, so owners should regularly feel their horses' legs (particularly white socks) for warmth. The condition usually starts up the back of the pasterns but can spread knee- or hock-high in fine skinned or susceptible individuals. The organism causes inflammation and great soreness, scabbing and swelling of the affected limbs, with chapped, cracked skin oozing yellow pus. It lives between the scab and the skin, so part of the treatment is to remove the scabs and expose the 'bugs' to the air. If the scabs are very hard and secure and the legs painful, it may be necessary to administer an anaesthetic to do this job, or the scabs can be softened with sulphanil-amide powder creamed in water and mixed with castor oil. Whatever treatment is prescribed by your vet (and it is definitely a job for a vet), he or she will almost certainly tell you to bring the animal in and get its legs thoroughly dry, for obvious reasons, so stabling will have to be arranged. Horses can transfer the infection to their muzzles if they bite their legs, or to their bellies when they lie down.

Rain rash, although rarer and usually less serious, is a similar condition occurring on the shoulders, back, loins and quarters during very rainy weather. The skin becomes sore, the scabs cause the hair to look tufty (a characteristic appearance) and with both rain rash and mud fever, raw (not just bare) skin will result at some point, and maybe re-scabbing in bad cases. Dermatophilus infection can be very unpleasant and painful for the horse, especially on the legs, and can certainly put the horse off work. Treatment of bad cases can be long drawn out so alert vigilance on the part of the owner is essential.

Thrush
see under Feet and Shoes, page 92.

Allergies to chemicals/fertilisers/plants
Skin allergies to products used on the land or blown over from neighbouring land can occur and cause unpleasant skin conditions. Some of these occur on the muzzle and white socks, sensitive areas constantly in contact with the grass and soil, and take the form of blistering, cracked, peeling skin and swelling with soreness. Animals with liver disease can become sensitised to some plants, contact with which causes white areas to become reddened and sore. Allergy to pollen, especially from oilseed rape, causes COPD symptoms in susceptible horses in summer.

Removal of the cause is at the root of any treatment of allergies, so it may be necessary to remove the affected animal to other grazing. Not all animals in a field may be affected, allergies being as individual in horses as in humans. Veterinary treatment should be applied according to the condition prevailing, as these symptoms often do not subside just because the causative factor has been removed.

Parasites
A great deal is spoken of worms and other parasites, and it is true they do cause a great deal of unthriftiness, illness and even death.

The most common internal parasites are ascarids (mostly

affecting young animals) and strongyles (redworm) which cause serious trouble in mature animals. Outdoor horses are particularly susceptible to infection with every bite they take, being permanently exposed to infection, unlike stabled animals which spend a good deal of time away from the source of infection, unless they eat infected bedding.

The life-cycles of parasites vary, but generally they begin with eggs and worm larvae being passed out in the droppings on to the pasture. Eggs and larvae are both microscopic so it is no use poking about in the droppings trying to spot them. Even adult worms are difficult to see.

In warm, moist weather, eggs will hatch within twenty-four hours and the larvae crawl on to the surrounding grass, sometimes for quite long distances, where they can be eaten by some unsuspecting horse and regain access to his intestines. Ascarid larvae migrate through the horse's lungs, often causing coughing and runny noses in young horses; strongyles do more damage by migrating through the blood vessels, often congregating at certain points in vast numbers, causing damage to the arteries (aneurisms or 'ballooning'). Usually, it is arteries serving the intestinal tract which are affected, causing the blood supply to a certain part of the tract to be cut off, with the result that the area dies off causing a very serious problem for all concerned. This is why worms are said to cause colic in horses, as the horse will show typical colic signs (pawing the ground, biting the flanks, rolling and lying on the back) in such cases.

Treatment of ascarids and strongyles, and so prevention of the above horrendous problem, is quite simple and effective. The trouble is that infection starts very early in life, as a foal first begins grazing, and if worm-control methods on the stud were less than exemplary a good deal of damage will already have been done to the horse's body by the time the larvae eventually migrate back to the intestines, hook their teeth into the lining (causing more damage), suck the horse's blood and begin laying eggs to start the process all over again.

Modern thinking indicates that horses should be treated for worms every four to eight weeks, depending on conditions prevailing. Obviously, in small fields or on overstocked land which never sees anything but horses, never has the droppings picked up and is never rested, the infection levels will be much higher than in well managed land (as discussed in Chapter 4). Your veterinary surgeon will advise on suitable treatments and drugs.

Counts of eggs and larvae in droppings can be made to ascertain what species are present and in what levels, but the results are unreliable as the worms' egg-laying and 'passing-out parades' are erratic.

The worms do become resistant to drugs after a time, so it is normally recommended that drugs from different groups are used alternately to help prevent this. There is, however, a school of thought which believes that frequent switching of drugs introduces the worms to them all and that they will, therefore, become resistant to them all. As usual, the vet is the person to discuss this with. At present, no resistance has been reported to the drugs pyrantel and ivermectin (zimecterin in USA). The use of ivermectin has made parasite control even easier and more effective as it will also kill migrating larvae at single dosage rates, vastly reducing the numbers of larvae returning as mature adults to the gut. Livery owners whose horses are out with those of owners who do not worm their horses properly are advised to use ivermectin to keep their individual horses' infection levels down, as otherwise they will significantly reinfect themselves with every bite of their infested pasture.

Dosing a horse at grass is just as easy as dosing a stabled one, as the relevant drug can simply be squirted in paste form from a safe and handy plastic syringe on to the back of his tongue. Some crafty horses wait, holding the paste in their mouths, and spit it out when you are not looking, so try to get the paste back far enough and give your horse some relished titbit afterwards to make sure he has swallowed.

Tapeworm
There has been an increased incidence of tapeworm infestation in horses in recent years so ask your vet to also check for this. A double dosage of the drug pyrantel will take care of tapeworm, normally in early winter.

Lungworm

Unfortunately for donkeys, they have received a bad press in the past as harbourers of lungworm and as the source of passing them on to horses. They are not so badly affected as horses, who often develop coughing and unthriftiness when infected.

Again, the larvae are picked up from pasture and migrate to the lungs to mature. The eggs they lay pass up the horse's throat (whether he is coughing or not), are swallowed down into the intestinal tract and passed out on to the pasture, and so it goes on. Usually, in horses, the larvae do not mature but just remain to cause trouble as immature forms, so if a horse at grass begins coughing, suspect lungworm and call the vet for advice and treatment.

Bots

These are not worms but the larval stage of the bot fly, which lays its eggs on the horse's legs in the summer. The horse licks them off and swallows them, and they hatch out in the stomach, clinging to its lining and causing tissue damage and indigestion. It is for this reason that many vets recommend using a worm medicine effective against bots as well as ascarids and strongyles in the autumn and winter months, to expel the larvae from the stomach.

From the above descriptions of parasites and their misdoings, it can be understood why it is constantly recommended that droppings are picked up from horse pastures very frequently (every day in warm weather) as this is one sure way of keeping down infestation. Unfortunately, this is highly impractical for some owners, particularly those who have to hold down a job as well as care for a horse. Cattle (and, less usefully, sheep) grazing the field do eat some of the larvae, but one quick and sure way of killing adults and larvae inside the horse, or so seriously debilitating them that they cease egg-laying for several weeks, so not infecting the droppings, is to treat horses every four to eight weeks with an effective drug on the advice of a vet. If using ivermectin the time between dosing can usually be increased.

Every horse on the pasture should be done on this basis as just one infected horse can seriously affect the health of the others and nullify their owners' attempts to keep them worm-free.

Flies and other insects

Flies, although not strictly parasites, do cause considerable distress to horses, as described earlier in this book. Inflamed, swollen eye membranes, jarred legs from galloping and constantly harried and exhausted horses are the results of fly-strike in summer. Warble flies, now more or less eradicated, lay eggs on horses' legs, the larvae from which hatch out, burrow under the skin to the back and cause hard, painful lumps there. The culicoides midge is responsible for a very distressing condition known as sweet itch, which is brought on by a horse's allergic reaction to the saliva of this biting midge. The areas most affected are around the withers and tail, the severe itching making the horse rub himself raw and compounding his distress. As the midge is most active for the first two or three hours after dawn and the last two hours or so before sunset, it is often recommended that horses are brought in then, which does help.

It does not help the owner of a grass-kept horse, however, and although there are various methods of relieving the distress, surely the best treatment of sweet itch and other fly-related disorders is to prevent the insects landing to do their damage in the first place. This is comparatively easy to do by using a really effective fly repellant on the horse. There are various types available from saddlers and veterinary surgeons, also agricultural merchants, but the best come into the category of 'residual' repellants, which state clearly that they are effective for a certain number of days (usually a week). Other types are only effective for a few hours, if that, and are not sufficient for a horse out all the time (some insects fly at night, too).

Check with your vet (yet again) on the best type or make to use, and follow instructions faithfully. Usually use of these products must begin in spring before flies get bad, so their effects build up on the horse and provide a really effective invisible 'shield'. If the horse sweats a lot, or the weather is wet, they will have to be applied more often but, even so, they do work. If your horse objects to aerosol sprays (which most do) apply the product on a rag. Most residual products have to be mixed with water and applied with a rag or sponge anyway. The help and comfort these products give to outdoor animals really are considerable and I strongly recommend their use. A fly-fringe on the headcollar gives some help to sensitive eyes, too.

Lice

Apart from worms, almost every horse or pony at grass will be infested by lice to some degree, normally during cooler weather as this most favours their development. They are tiny yellowy-brown insects which bite the skin to suck blood, causing intense itching and rubbing in the horses affected. Lice spread from one horse to another as they rub against each other and the rubbing and biting which occur result in bald, scurfy areas of skin. The louse population on any one horse can build up very quickly but effective shampoos and powders, available from your vet, will clear up the condition.

In bad cases, as the horse will probably have a winter coat at the time infestation is worst, it is necessary to clip off the hair in the affected areas (usually the neck, shoulder and forward part of the back) so the horse may have to be stabled due to the loss of his coat. The clipped hair should be burnt to kill the lice which may otherwise infest other animals, and the affected horse's clothing (including New Zealand rug) must be treated as well.

Ringworm

This is a fungal infection which horses can catch from one another, from cattle and from fields, fences and shelters (and, obviously, clothing and grooming kit) with which infected animals have been in contact. The spores remain active for many months, so proper treatment of the disease is essential. Small crusty bald patches of skin are the giveaway, caused by the hairs breaking off at their bases, and can appear anywhere on the body.

Apart from the antibiotic griseofulvin which can be given in the feed, two new treatments (at the time of writing) can be applied to the areas infected and also to clothing, buildings, grooming kit and anything with which the horse comes in contact. These treatments are Imaverol and Mycophyt. Horses can develop a degree of immunity to ringworm fungi of the same type so if a particular kind is prevalent in an area resistance to it could develop.

Grass sickness

Grass sickness, which affects only grass-fed animals, is a well-known disease now reported all over Britain. Research has been extensive, and some hope is now emerging that we shall soon understand the cause and prevention, although it is still usually incurable and nearly always fatal. Horses can graze fields known to be affected and, presumably because they develop resistance to the causative agent, remain well and healthy, but when a new horse is introduced to that field it becomes ill very quickly.

During the course of the disease, the nerves supplying the digestive system become damaged and the stomach and intestines simply stop working – sometimes the horse is even unable to swallow – and fill with a green liquid to the extent that they burst. The pressure of the full stomach on the diaphragm compresses the blood vessels supplying the heart, and the horse can die in shock. Sometimes animals die within hours or days, sometimes it takes weeks or months, but the horse always suffers greatly.

Symptoms of grass sickness are inability to swallow and general colic symptoms of pawing the ground, repeated rolling or lying down and getting up again, biting the flanks, lying on the back and a general air of great discomfort and pain. Any symptoms resembling the above in grass-kept horses should cause owners immediately to call the vet to diagnose exactly what is wrong.

Before taking on new land for grazing your horse, sound out everybody in the area as to the incidence and localities of the disease and never graze your horse in a field known to have had a grass sickness case on it. It is worth adding that every opportunity should be taken to support research into the cause and treatment of grass sickness.

Feet and shoes

The feet of a grass-kept horse often need considerable attention even if unshod, as the horn is constantly exposed to wet conditions for much of the year, and to hard, and possibly rough, ground at other times. Horses with healthy horn should not cause too much trouble, but those with poor quality horn are often subject to chipping and cracking in summer and to softening and easier wearing away in winter. Sometimes the bulbs of the heels wear badly, too.

Generally, soya or corn oil added to the feeds and adequate amounts of methionine, biotin, MSM and calcium, maybe in a supplement or specialist feed such as alfalfa (lucerne), will greatly help in time, but as it can take about six months for horn to grow from coronet to ground, badly affected feet will need help from an expert farrier to get them over the waiting period. Of course, the farrier's services will be needed approximately every six weeks for trimming, and shoeing if the horse is working, in any case, but you could need him more often if the horse is experiencing foot problems. The farrier can best cope with cracks in the feet, broken (and probably unbalanced) feet and soft horn by judicious shoeing, nail placements, shoe choice and other, surgical procedures.

If the horse is to be without shoes (and this is quite feasible even for a working horse if most of his work is on soft ground) the feet should be trimmed and balanced and well rounded off to help minimise chipping and cracking. Rounding off is only done slightly and cannot be equated with that heinous crime, dumping, in which the toe is shortened to fit the shoe instead of the shoe being made to fit the foot.

If the horse is to be shod for the sake of protecting his feet, lightweight race exercise plates may be quite adequate. If your farrier feels he needs a broader webbed (wider) shoe for added protection, he may fit a conventional lightweight

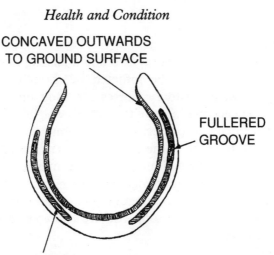

CONCAVED OUTWARDS
TO GROUND SURFACE

FULLERED
GROOVE

NAIL HOLES

A concaved, fullered hunter shoe (without calkin or wedge) suitable for general wear. The concave shape lessens suction in mud and the fullering provides better 'grip' on the ground surface

hunter shoe without the wedge on the outer heel. These shoes are concaved on the inner edge so that they are wider where they touch the foot (the bearing surface) than on the surface which touches the ground. They are also 'fullered out', which means the ground surface is not flat (known as a 'plain web' shoe) but has a recess running around the shoe on the ground surface presenting an upward groove. This means the surface which touches the ground is, in fact, two narrow ridges of metal. This pattern of shoe gives greater grip on the ground surface while reducing suction from mud, which can pull off a shoe and tear the foot in wet conditions. It also lightens the shoe for horses in active work.

It is best to discuss your horse's living conditions, feet and work with your farrier, and decide between you how best to shoe him (if at all) and care generally for his feet. You should, in any case, keep a daily eye on the state of his feet and shoes. The feet should be picked out and checked at least once a day for wedged-in stones, worn or loose shoes, risen clenches and cracking or softening horn, and appropriate action taken.

Kicking

If several horses share a field and a kicking match develops, serious injury can be inflicted by shod hooves. For this reason, many outdoor horses are shod only in front (the forefeet carrying more of the horse's weight and, so, being in greater need of protection). Inveterate kickers are a curse and, for the sake of the other inmates of the field, should be removed and turned out alone. This may cause problems of its own, but the fact remains that 'innocent' horses must not be made to suffer because of one fly in the ointment. Kickers often kick humans, too, who are less able to retaliate than other horses.

Laminitis

Commonly called 'fever in the feet' or 'founder', this foot disorder is extremely painful for the horse and, if allowed to go unchecked it can become serious to the extent that the horse has to be destroyed. It is caused by disorders (usually overfeeding or toxins in the blood for some other reason) which cause an alteration in the blood flow to and within the feet. The outer, horny wall of the foot is joined to the inner, fleshy part covering the bones by vertical leaves of horn interlocking with fleshy, blood-containing leaves. This interlocking system holds the bones of the foot in place inside the wall.

In laminitis, the blood circulation is impaired, which starves the sensitive laminae of oxygen and nutrients, causing them to deteriorate and start separating from the horny laminae, breaking the bond between them. In bad cases the main bone of the foot, the pedal bone, starts to move, sometimes even piercing the horny and fleshy soles beneath it. The horny wall at the toe separates from the bone and the gap may fill with a degenerate, softer type of horn. This can be seen in the white line area at the toe as the line seems to widen and soften, often producing the condition known as seedy toe where cheesy-type horn exudes from the area.

In chronic cases, the foot may take on a concave appearance from the side, with a long toe and high heels. The toe wall may break away and produce a horizontal crack just below the coronet with the strain of walking on detached horn, while the heel horn continues to grow, giving the horse higher heels with upward slanting horn rings in the heel area. Great strides have been made in the diagnosis and treatment of the different sorts of laminitis in recent years, mainly by the Laminitis Clinic at the University of Bristol in the UK. In bad cases, the detached wall at the toe is removed and supportive shoeing applied to prevent further movement of the pedal bone and to realign new horn growth in line with the new position of the pedal bone.

Apart from overfeeding and the circulation of toxins in the blood, or a chemical imbalance in the intestines due to faulty feeding, laminitis can be caused by concussion, but especially by incorrectly dressed (trimmed) feet. The overlong toe/low heels fashion of trimming, currently rather too common, not only in the UK, is a definite causative factor. It places inappropriate stresses on the sensitive tissues and can physically damage them. Feet must be dressed with the toes well back and the heels high enough to support the foot and leg.

Signs of laminitis are a pottering, short-stepped gait and a back-on-the-heels stance as the animal attempts to get his weight off the most painful part of the feet in the toe region. Usually both feet of a fore or hind pair are affected, but one foot, or all four, can be affected. If the animal lies down he often refuses to get up again because of the pain in his feet. If a foot is waved in the air, this indicates great pain.

If you suspect laminitis (and heat in the feet is not always present as the blood supply is reduced, not increased), muzzle your horse if he has to remain at grass, or bring him in on inedible bedding, and call the vet at once. If the animal is very lame, however, forcing him to walk can cause permanent and fatal damage, so leave him as he is. The vet should be called as an emergency and frog supports (maybe simply folded bandages taped to the feet) should be fitted. Corticosteroids should **NOT** be given as these will reduce the blood supply even further and do even more damage. They can even bring on laminitis when used in other diseases such as sweet itch.

Feel carefully with a finger all around the feet, immediately above the coronet. If you feel a 'ditch' or depression here this is a most serious sign as it indicates that the pedal bone is, indeed, moving, maybe at the front or maybe all round. However, provided the horse gets specialist help within 24 hours he may be saved. Many GP-type vets will prefer to refer the horse to a specialist in the treatment of laminitis.

Thrush

This is an infective foot ailment usually caused by dirty stables, ie horses standing on wet, dirty bedding, but I have also seen it in horses kept on wet land. The infection is assisted by the damp conditions and softened horn, and thrives, normally, in the inaccessible areas, such as by underrunning the frog. Horses affected by thrush usually go 'feeling' (cautiously) on the affected foot or feet because of the discomfort, may actually be lame (although as the lameness is often even in both feet, it can be difficult to spot) and 'paddle' (hop from foot to foot) when standing still.

Thrush smells foul and there is usually a dark discharge. If the frog is pressed with the hoofpick the horse will often show pain by flinching. Thrush is definitely a job for your veterinary surgeon as it will not clear up on its own. The horse will have to be brought in and the feet kept dry while the condition is treated.

Rings on the feet

Horn growth is greatly influenced by diet, and horses kept at grass, with its fluctuating growth pattern throughout the year, often develop 'grass rings' running horizontally round the feet. These are small ridges on the wall of the hoof and are quite normal in such cases, and nothing to worry about. In fact, they often appear in any horse, grass-kept or not, who has been subjected to a fairly sudden change of diet, ie one brought in after a season at grass.

Rings caused by laminitis are usually much more pronounced and, if the case has been a bad one, the hoof wall will often have 'sunk' in, giving a concave appearance to the foot when seen from the side. Once a horse has had laminitis it is always prone to another attack and these rings, caused by altered blood circulation to the feet which, in turn, affects the production of horn, should act as a warning to a potential purchaser or anyone put in charge of such a horse. (See also pages 90–2.)

6 Feeding and Watering

Feeding is the single most important subject to be mastered in horse management. A horse, like other animals, is what he eats. To the horse at grass, apart from disease or fatal injury, it is the one aspect of his care which can make the difference between life and death to him. Although, as we saw in the chapter on grassland management, his paddocks can, with care, be made to provide a good deal of his food, in winter or at times when he is working fairly hard, supplementary feeding will be needed. The type of food he can be given is just the same as for a stabled horse, although outdoor horses do not normally need roots and succulents such as carrots, apples, or soaked sugar beet pulp in their feeds as the grass provides the juicy element of their diet.

Digestive disorders seem to be much rarer in outdoor horses than in stabled ones, probably because their digestive systems are functioning more naturally, having a little food passing through them more or less constantly as in the wild. Even in winter, when the grass is practically useless from a nutritional point of view, horses still pick at it from instinct to keep that little something inside them all the time.

Their natural food, vegetation, is a fibrous food which takes up a lot of room in the intestine and which has to be consumed in large amounts to provide the horse with enough nutrients for his needs. This means the horse has to keep eating for about sixteen hours out of twenty-four just to take in his food requirement. Conversely, the food of meat-eating animals is very concentrated, and they can manage easily on one meal a day, or sometimes only one feast every few days. They need to spend little time eating, therefore, and their stomachs are comparatively large to accept the big, sudden intake, whereas the horse's stomach is small for his size because of his eating habits.

Purposes of food

Food is obviously needed to keep your horse alive, but its uses are given priority by his body. Food is used for:

1   Maintenance of body temperature at about 100.4°F (38°C).
2   Formation and replacement of body tissue (skin, muscle etc), bones, teeth, hair and horn.
3   Building up condition or putting on weight (storage of food reserves as fat).
4   Providing energy for life processes and movement. (Even standing still, your horse is using up energy to keep his heart beating, his lungs working and his digestion functioning.)

The first two requirements are the most important and if there is insufficient food and water to sustain them, the horse will die.

If a horse is worked hard and/or subjected to harsh weather on an inadequate ration, what nourishment there is will be used in priority to keep up body temperature (requiring more food or 'fuel' in cold weather), to replace tissue (more quickly used up during work) and to provide energy for these increased demands. On an inadequate ration, there is nothing left for body condition. In fact, the body releases some of its fat reserves to make up the deficit and the horse loses weight. If he exhausts these reserves of fat, he starts using his own body flesh (muscles, skin etc) to provide the fuel to keep up his temperature and just keep going using as little energy as possible, and eventually becomes emaciated. Vital tissues then suffer, body temperature drops – and the horse dies.

If the horse is not working and/or the weather is warm, yet the diet still inadequate, this process will still go on, but will take longer, as the food ration will not be used up so quickly.

Water
The body of the horse is about 70 per cent water and an ample supply is vital to life and health. Water is needed for

the body's fluids, such as blood, digestive juices, lymph and milk. It is also needed for the functioning of the excretory systems as the poisons produced by everyday living are excreted in urine, sweat, in vapour from the lungs and in droppings, which contain moisture. Water is, therefore, essential for the existence and working of the body and without an adequate supply the horse draws on his own body liquids to keep his system going. If he is worked hard in hot weather, he sweats profusely to help keep his temperature down. In either case, he can become dehydrated, so the production of body fluids becomes impossible, as does the maintenance of the body's systems, and death will result in a few days.

Constituents of food

The food constituents and their purposes are:

Carbohydrates (starches and sugar). Used for production of heat and energy. Excesses are stored around the body as fat for use when intake drops.

Proteins. These are the only foods which can make and repair body tissue, but can also supply some heat and energy. Some can be stored as fat, but then lose their tissue-building abilities, therefore a constant supply of protein in the diet is essential.

Fat. This is a good energy and heat producer and small amounts are needed for the absorption of the fat-soluble vitamins. Some researchers claim that up to 20 per cent of the entire diet for hard-working horses can be made up of fats (also called oils, lipids or lipins), as they are excellent concentrated sources of energy and are useful for feeding to high performance horses as a way of supplying extra energy without overloading them with concentrates. Horses with small appetites can also benefit from being fed a higher fat diet for the same reason.

The best way to feed extra oils is to give the horse soya, corn or maize oil in amounts recommended by a vet or nutritionist; possibly, as a guide, a tablespoon (15ml) per feed well mixed in. There is no need to follow the old practice of boiling linseed as the benefits of linseed can be provided more easily by using the products mentioned above. Also, linseed was (and still is in some quarters) used as a weekly or twice-weekly additive or as a linseed mash, going directly against one of the Golden Rules of feeding: to make no sudden changes. If you do want to feed boiled linseed you should feed a little in *every feed*, so that the horse's digestion is not upset by an erratic diet, for reasons given later. As this is impractical for most people, and linseed is unpalatable when kept in a fridge to prevent its going 'off' and fed cold, there is no point bothering with it.

Fibre (roughage). Needed to break up concentrated food (oats, barley, maize) for penetration by the digestive juices. Such food could otherwise impact into a doughy, impenetrable mass causing blockage, fermentation and possible rupturing of the intestine. Fibre also stimulates the movements of the intestine which push the food along and knead it up. Hay is a common and important source of fibre, also coarse grass and hayage products. Hayage is a moist substance which is simply grass conserved to a point midway between hay (a dry product) and silage (a grass product with a high moisture content). It is marketed to the horse world under various brand names. It is basically a roughage feed, but the higher energy grades can be used as a complete feed for horses in quite hard work. Horses should be gradually accustomed to it by introducing small amounts at first mixed with their hay, and gradually (over a period of two or three weeks or more) having the hayage portion of the ration increased and the hay portion decreased proportionately. The makers of hayage products advise that concentrates, if used, should be fed in smaller amounts with hayage than with hay, due to the higher feeding value of hayage.

Vitamins, minerals and trace elements. Needed in small quantities but nevertheless important. Foods possess differing amounts of these vital substances, which, in turn, have individual purposes. Modern farming methods often reduce the quantities of them in horses' food and a good comprehensive supplementary product is often an advantageous addition to the diet, fed in accordance with the directions on the package or upon specialist advice.

The main staple foods for horses (including cubes, or nuts and coarse mixes, which are an amalgam of different foods compounded together) contain different amounts of all these constituents. For example, although oats are mainly a carbohydrate food, they also contain protein (roughly 11 per cent to 14 per cent depending on the quality of the grain) and fibre in the form of the grain's husk, so no food fits solely into one category.

The horse's body can, when faced with a mildly unbalanced diet, convert some substances into others, and make some itself in its own intestines, so absolute precision in the formulation of a diet is not essential, and is, in any case, almost impossible when the horse has free access to grazing with the liberty to pick and choose which grasses he likes. To ensure a reasonably balanced diet, the land and grasses growing on it need assessing, and maybe analysing, by an expert nutritionist and the supplementary feeds formulating on top of that knowledge. If this sounds impractically ideal, it remains the most reliable way of working out a horse's full diet. Many owners, however, simply rely on assessing their horse's condition and providing supplementary feed (or not) in accordance with it. This does work to some extent, but the fact remains that the horse may be suffering from some slight deficiency, or in some cases a serious deficiency, of some essential nutrients. Excesses can also cause problems, so whether your horse is a family pet or a valuable broodmare or youngster, expert analysis and advice occasionally are well worth while.

Types of food

Basically, foods are divided into two main types for practical purposes – bulk, coarse or *roughage* foods such as hay, hayage, straw and chop (hay and/or straw chopped up small), and *concentrated* or energy foods such as grains (oats, barley, maize) and most compound feeds such as coarse mixes and cubes.

As discussed, all foods contain some elements of each

A horse in good, fit working condition, not so lean and 'tuned up' as a racehorse, but certainly not fat. An outdoor horse could carry more flesh in winter, for warmth

constituent (carbohydrate, protein etc), and it is the same with concentrates and roughage foods. Although hay is classed as a roughage or bulk food, containing much fibre, it also contains carbohydrates, proteins, a little fat and also vitamins, minerals and trace elements. Good hay, and particularly some of the hayage products now on the market, can alone provide an adequate balanced diet for light to moderate work.

How much, what and when?
A simple guide to working out how much food to give your horse is to take his height in hands and double it, reading the answer in pounds. For example, if your horse is 15 hands high, 15 x 2 = 30lb (13kg). I stress that this is a *rough guide* to use as a starting point, and represents the total poundage of all foods. For a stabled horse in medium work (two hours active hacking per day, riding-club-type work and so on), this should be split into one-third concentrates and two-thirds roughage.

Of course, a grass-kept horse is eating grass all the time so this confuses the issue except in winter when the grass is usually no good. Then, the above split would probably work well for a working horse living out in winter. The formula is on the slightly generous side, but a grass-kept horse must be fed to keep out the cold as well as provide for work.

A much more accurate way to determine a horse, cob or pony's dietary requirements as regards daily weight of food is to feed him according to his bodyweight, using the tables given here, or by taking him to a weighbridge if there is one within reasonable distance of your yard. Simply use a tape measure (or a piece of string, measured later) and pass it round your animal's girth just behind the wither. The result can be read off from the appropriate table, using the Ponies table for cobs. Of course, you have to know when your animal is too fat or too thin, and allow a little less or more as appropriate. Special measuring tapes are available from some feed firms and saddlers, or from the Equine Management Consultancy Service, 20 Victoria Road, Bulwark, Chepstow, Gwent, NP6 5QN, Wales.

Table 1. Ponies

Girth in inches	40	42.5	45	47.5	50	52.5	55	57.5
Girth in cm	101	108	114	120	127	133	140	146
Bodyweight in lb	100	172	235	296	368	430	502	562
Bodyweight in kg	45	77	104	132	164	192	234	252

Table 2. Horses

Girth in inches	55	57.5	60	62.5	65	67.5
Girth in cm	140	146	152	159	165	171
Bodyweight in lb	538	613	688	776	851	926
Bodyweight in kg	240	274	307	346	380	414

Girth in inches	70	72.5	75	77.5	80	82.5
Girth in cm	178	184	190	199	203	206
Bodyweight in lb	1014	1090	1165	1278	1328	1369
Bodyweight in kg	453	486	520	570	593	611

(Tables based on work of Glushanok, Rochlitz & Skay, 1981)

Once you know the bodyweight you can work out the total daily food requirement as, generally, horses will need 2kg of feed per 100kg of bodyweight (2lb/100lb) split as mentioned earlier. Ponies and cobs usually require less feed per lb or kg bodyweight than horses.

The tables show that just a ½in (1.23cm) change in girth can mean a 14-15lb (5-6kg) alteration in weight, which may not be noticeable to the eye. Also, take the measurement after the animal has just finished breathing out, or you could get a false reading.

Of course, grass-kept horses can be a real problem which is why expert advice on the state of your soil and grass should be taken so you can assess just how much nutrition your animal is getting from the grass and, therefore, what he might need in the way of supplementary feeding.

The old fetish about high-protein levels in feeds for hard-working horses is quite inappropriate: feeds should be assessed by *energy*, not protein, content, as even horses in full work do not need more than about 8 per cent protein in their total diet. Breeding stock (particularly growing youngsters), old horses and convalescents will need more.

For a riding-club-type horse out in winter, look for feeds which contain 10-12MJ (megajoules – a scientific unit of measurement) of digestible energy (DE) per kilogram. If the bag does not give such information contact the makers and ask for it, preferably in writing. For ponies, cobs and animals in light work, plus good doers, 8.5–10MJ of DE per kilogram is enough.

An eagle eye should be kept on the horse's bodyweight and condition at all times. A working horse should be in well covered but lean-ish condition: you should *not* be able to see his ribs, but you *should* be able to feel them fairly easily. With very fit endurance-type animals you could probably just see the last couple of pairs of ribs, which is acceptable provided the horse's top line is well muscled and he is not actually thin.

Assuming that the horse is in medium work most of the year, it can be taken that in winter he will need ad lib hay backed up by sufficient concentrates to maintain condition (bodyweight). In spring, summer and autumn, depending

An emaciated pony; note the angular shape, visible ribs and seemingly large head, exaggerated by the lack of flesh on the body

on the growth of grass, he will probably not need hay but could need concentrates for working energy. In spring, a problem could occur with protein-rich young grass causing overweight and laminitis and other digestive troubles, so supplementary feeding should not be given then. Much depends on the abundance and quality of the grazing available.

A horse which is much too fat, not only for work but for general good health; a prime candidate for laminitis

As a guide, if a grass-kept horse refuses hay, he is getting enough fibre and bulk from his grazing. Given normally good grazing, hay or hayage should be offered from about late September onwards and discontinued when the horses start leaving it in spring. Concentrates (which a grass-kept horse will rarely refuse even when rolling in fat) should be added mainly in winter or if grazing is poor and/or the horse working. Otherwise, good hay and grass are better feeds.

Eating creates heat as it uses energy and from a feeding point of view the best way to keep outdoor horses warm in winter is to make sure they have a constant supply of good hay or hayage which provides them with a natural central heating system. Carbohydrate (concentrate) feeds may provide more of an immediate boost of warmth-giving energy but their effects are relatively short-lived, and a hungry horse or one anxiously seeking out roughage or waiting for another short feed soon becomes cold, maybe dangerously so.

The horse digests his feed by means of enzymes and micro-organisms in the intestinal tract which live off his food and process it for him. Without an adequate healthy population of gut micro-organisms the horse could suffer chronic indigestion or colic and be unthrifty, with other digestive disorders. The micro-organisms are short-lived and need regular supplies of their different foods, different 'bugs' being responsible for digesting different foods. If the supply fails they die off, not only reducing their population and, therefore, the efficiency of the horse's digestive system, but also rotting down and causing a putrid environment in the gut which again can cause mild or serious colics. This is why it is important to give your horse the *same ingredients* in every feed and not to chop and change by giving, say, cubes for breakfast, coarse mix for lunch, barley for tea and so on. Alter the amounts of your ingredients if appropriate, but include at least a little of everything normally fed in each feed.

It is also a bad practice to feed a mash (usually the familiar, old bran mash) once or twice a week. Bran is not a good horse food. It contains too much phosphorous and far too little calcium, and this imbalance can create bone problems, even if barely noticeable, but which could be responsible for such things as the horse easily becoming concussed on hard going, throwing splints or going frequently but inexplicably 'feeling' or actually lame. Bran (or other) mashes constitute a complete and sudden change in feeding which is very bad for the horse's digestive system. Bran mashes are *not* easy to digest; on the contrary, they irritate the horse's digestive tract and this is why they appear to have a laxative effect as that system tries to get rid of the offending material as quickly as possible. This is *not* good feeding policy, obviously, and the practice of mashing horses is not now recommended by nutritionists and many up-to-date vets.

If you want to give your horse a low-energy feed (he should not need an actual laxative if his feeding is correct) because of reduced work, give chop (maybe the molassed kind) with soaked sugar beet pulp and, if you wish, grass meal and/or some other roots such as carrots or apples (plus one handful of his usual concentrate) and make sure these ingredients, even in small amounts, are present in his other feeds. This way you will keep his digestive bugs alive and thriving and your horse comfortable and correctly, *consistently* fed as he would be in nature.

Horses needing most feeding, of any type, are those in hard work, breeding stock and elderly animals. If in doubt as to your horse's diet, do consult a vet or an equine nutritionist or management consultant.

The horse's condition as a guide

Keeping a careful eye on your horse's condition or bodyweight is a good practical way of assessing his food requirements. You must first know your horse well when in normal condition for the work you want him to do. Is he naturally a rounded, chunky type, or the lean, more angular sort? When you are familiar with the 'real him' you will know whether his outdoor life is causing him to become too fat or too thin, and can act accordingly.

Even when resting, a horse should not be allowed to grow

too fat because of the risk of tendon strain and laminitis. Conversely, if he is too thin, he will have a lowered resistance to disease and the ravages of the weather and flies.

Apart from his general appearance, the parts of a horse which most quickly show condition are his top line (upper neck, back, loins and quarters) and his belly. In summer, assessment is easy, but it is more difficult when hampered by a thick and maybe long winter coat. In winter, therefore, get into the habit of really digging your fingers through his coat and feeling how much flesh he has on him over his top line area. You should not be too aware of his ribs and hips but rather have to feel and press for them.

Bearing in mind his individual make and shape, then, generally a thin horse will show a lack of flesh or muscular development along the top of his neck. A giveaway sign is if the neck appears to sink in front of the withers. His withers and spine will be noticeable to both look and feel, his so-called hip bones (in fact, they are the pelvic bones) will be prominent (often known as hat-racks!), and his quarters will show a lack of flesh by appearing to 'fall away' or sink away from his hips and croup, and maybe even showing 'poverty lines' from front to back and down the backs of the thighs when seen from behind. His belly, instead of being rounded and seeming to continue all the way to his stifles (at the tops of his hind legs) will probably show an upward-running line from front to back underneath, and the horse will look pinched in (known as 'tucked up') in the area between belly and hind legs.

A fat horse often takes on a barrel-like appearance and a waddle to go with it. He could develop a big, 'bull' neck, hefty shoulders and huge pads of fat on both sides of his spine. His belly will be gross and low-slung while his quarters will look 'appley' and rounded with fat. He will actually feel soft if you prod him, rather than sleek and hard as a fit horse. Between these two extremes of the slab-sided, starved horse and the walking barrel is the ideal for your horse. Only you can really get to know him and assess his condition and fitness (about which more in Chapter 8) to ensure he is just right.

Practical considerations

The entire object of feeding your horse is to make sure he gets his ration down him one way or another. This he will not do if it is just tipped on to the ground to be trampled in winter mud, blown away or stolen by other horses. It is always more economical to give both hay and concentrates in some sort of container.

A popular way of giving hay is to fill a haynet and tie it up in the shed (there should be at least one more net than there are horses so that the timid ones always have one to go to) or to tie it to a fence post and top rail for firm support. Nets sag lower as they empty and hooves can easily become entangled in them, so they should be tied at horse's head height when possible. They can also be tied to a convenient tree branch against the trunk. If all else fails, hay can be fed in a mobile field rack often seen for cattle, the rack being moved daily to prevent poaching the land. It is always best to feed hay under cover in the shed to prevent its being spoiled by rain. Again, nets can be used, or a long rack can be fixed along the back wall at horse's head height.

Concentrates can be fed in wide shallow cattle buckets or even plastic washing-up bowls if the horses are quiet eaters who will not tip up the container and spill the contents. The containers can be put on the ground at least 16ft (5m) apart, which is outside the horse's natural 'personal distance', and here it is best for at least one person to stay around to see fair play, and that each gets his proper ration. Quiet, friendly horses can have their containers on the floor of the shed. Do not leave buckets or bowls around after the horses have finished as they can be a source of injury.

Horses who waste their feed by throwing it around can be fed from portable travel mangers which hook on to the fence or on to a strong bar on the wall of the shed. These mangers may have two bars running from front to back of them across the top to prevent a horse scooping food out with his nose.

Any animal who is timid and constantly chivvied by the others may not be able to eat his concentrates in peace, so should be brought out of the field for the twenty minutes or so it will take him to eat up.

A word about feeding cubes alone to grass-kept horses. Although rare, it has been known for cases of ruptured stomach to occur when the easily chewed up cubes meet up with the soft soggy grass in the stomach, forming a stiff, gooey mass of food which is hard for the digestive juices to penetrate. It is always safer to mix a double handful of chop (also known as chaff) with the cubes to ensure the presence of sufficient fibrous roughage to break up the food. If the horse winkles out the cubes from the chop, use molassed chaff, which most horses like. Bran is is less good for this than chop, and not advisable in large amounts.

Horses should not be given more than about 4lb (1.8kg) total feed of concentrates at one time. The stomach works best when two-thirds full, and if more food then keeps coming in, food which is not yet adequately digested by the stomach muscles and digestive juices could be released further down into the intestine to make room for the continuing input, and cause colic. This means that if your horse is needing 8lb (3.6kg) concentrates a day he will have to have two feeds, necessitating two visits to the field, say morning and night. If he needs more than this, at least three visits are going to be needed. Two visits a day should be paid anyway but you can possibly cut out the third visit by feeding very good hay with a high feeding value, so you will not need to supplement with so many concentrates. If good hay is unavailable, use one of the hayage products. These are available in different protein and energy levels and can often drastically reduce the amount of other foods needed. Consult your vet about this, if required. However, remembering what has been explained about the workings of the digestive system and the micro-organisms, efforts should be made to give two feeds of concentrates, if very small, as this makes for better digestion and less risk of problems.

Most people stress that horses should be fed at regular times, otherwise they gather around the gates, become impatient and fractious and start scrapping with each other. In practice, I find that an owner need not tie himself or herself to rigid times *provided* the horses are never allowed to get really hungry, which they will not when grass is plentiful or, when it is not, they have enough hay left with them to last them easily until the next feed time. Half an hour to an hour late now and then will not be the end of the world in such circumstances. Do not, however, miss a feed completely, and do not feed on some days and not on others, even if the horses' workloads are erratic. Once you start supplementary feeding, keep it up, but adjust the ration by quantity, if necessary. Routine *is* important to the horse. If animals are to receive only one concentrate feed a day, make it at night, so that they have the benefit of 'central heating' for the colder hours of the night.

Storage can be a problem in the case of isolated fields, unless you have adequate transport to take the full rations needed on each visit, ready packed in haynets and buckets. If you are using a barn as a shelter, perhaps part of it could be securely partitioned off for feed storage, preferably locked, or a building could be rented at a nearby farm. Remember you will also need storage for other equipment, even if you carry your tack or harness each day. It is preferable to be able to store veterinary supplies and grooming kit nearby, and New Zealand rugs, rather than be forced to transport your horse's entire life-support system every time you visit him.

Water sources have already been mentioned in Chapter 3, together with the fact that a horse can need up to 12 gallons (551) of water a day when working hard or in hot weather. Whether the water is from a natural source such as a stream or pond (regularly checked for pollution) or from a trough or plastic dustbins, the supply must be checked at least once a day (bins need filling to the top twice daily, depending on number, as a horse may be reluctant to put his head down to the bottom for a drink), access to the source must be kept secure and inviting (no rough going such as rubble, and with mud lessened by scattering used bedding thickly on badly poached areas, as described earlier) and time should be taken now and then to watch and see if any animal is being persistently chased away from water. If so, he should be watered separately morning and night before being given his feed. He will be quite all right on this method *provided he is allowed to drink his fill at each watering.* He will drink, then probably lift his head and look around, resting. In all likelihood, he will then drop his head for another drink, but it is always better to let him leave the water source himself rather than be led away. Then you can be sure he really has had enough.

Although good modern stable (and field) management indicates that water should always be available (and I agree with this) the fact remains that this is not so in the wild. Herds of animals often make long treks to water holes morning and night, returning to their grazing grounds in between. They do not hang around the water all day, so if a horse in your care needs separate watering do not worry about him. He will be quite all right watered ad lib, night and morning. Do water him first and feed him (if necessary) afterwards. He will doubtless have some grass in his stomach, but concentrates can cause problems if given before a full draught of water. Water intake can be increased by feeding salt to an animal, and many people forget to provide a salt lick for horses at grass. It is advisable to place a salt lick on the wall of the shelter in a plastic (not metal) holder, but do not site it over a water container.

7 Turn-out and Clothing

Structure and function of skin and coat

The only things separating your horse from the rigours of the environment are his skin and coat; and the thickness of the skin varies from only 4mm (⅕in) down to less than 1mm (¹⁄₂₅in) (depending on its location on the body and the breed of horse).

The skin has two main layers, an inner layer called the dermis and an outer layer called the epidermis. It is the dermis which contains the hair follicles, the sebaceous glands which secrete oil (sebum) to lubricate and waterproof skin and hair and which open into the hair follicles, and also the sweat glands which excrete sweat on to the skin to help to get rid of waste products and to cool down the body by carrying some excess heat to the surface for evaporation. It contains nerve endings and blood vessels; it also contains the means of manufacturing vitamin D.

The epidermis is composed of dead, horny cells which protect the dermis. These cells are gradually shed (being replaced by cells from the dermis below) and are seen as the dandruff in an ungroomed horse's coat. The epidermis also contains the colouring pigment, melanin, which strengthens and helps protect the skin. White markings usually have pink skin underneath, which really means the skin (which obtains its pinkness from the blood) is colourless, in fact, and so without the added protection of melanin. This is why white legs and the large white patches on coloured horses (known as piebalds and skewbalds in Britain and pintos or paints in the USA) are often more susceptible to the weakening effects of weather and so more prone to conditions like mud fever and allergies.

Skin protects the body from germs, foreign bodies,

sunlight and poisonous substances, it provides the horse with his sense of touch, enabling him to tell the difference between hot and cold, pain and pleasure, friction, pressure and relief. The hair which grows from the skin assists in some of its functions, giving added protection against weather and temperature. The mane and tail hair also protect the horse against the outside world, and the tail in particular is useful for helping dislodge flies from the back half of the body.

Skin is thicker over the areas most exposed to weather and prone to injury, such as the top part of the neck, shoulders, back, loins and quarters and also the fronts and outer sides of the legs, being thinner in the other, more sheltered areas. Growth of coat hair coincides with this pattern, being thinner on the lower part of the body and inside the legs, and also around sensory areas such as muzzle (the horse's equivalent to fingers) and eyes.

The coat has two main forms, the short summer coat and the longer winter coat. The thickness or thinness of the coat is related to the length of the hairs and not to their number, longer hairs obviously overlapping more and so making the coat appear 'thick', and vice versa. Nature has 'programmed' the horse to shed, in stages, his thick winter coat in spring, when the climate warms up and the days lengthen, and to similarly cast his short summer coat in autumn and replace it with longer hairs for the colder winter months.

Grooming and shampooing

Generally, the rules of good horse management discourage owners from body brushing and shampooing grass-kept horses as these procedures remove natural grease from skin and coat and, therefore, much of the horse's protection. It is possible to produce a clean-looking horse without heavy body brushing or shampooing, although your horse will never be as clean as a stabled animal. Light body brushing will do enough to make the horse presentable without stripping him of too much coat grease, even through a winter coat. Remove dust and dried mud from the coat either with a dandy brush (and possibly a plastic or rubber curry) in the normal way, or with a vacuum groomer used lightly. These are useful especially for a mudcaked, wintercoated teddy bear of a horse. Follow up by a light body brushing and a final wipe over with a damp stable rubber. The mane and tail can be washed as normal, when necessary.

It is best not to shampoo a grass-kept horse, especially in winter, unless he is going somewhere really special, as this will obviously remove nearly all his natural oils, and they will not be replaced in time for his return to the field. You can get away with it occasionally if you have a waterproof rug to put on the horse for a day or two afterwards (even if he does not normally wear one) but generally it should be avoided. If done, the horse must be dried very quickly and thoroughly.

The horse should, on a daily basis, have his eyes, nostrils and lips damp-sponged clean of dried-on discharges (not only for cleanliness but to help avoid chapping in winter and fly-strike in summer), and the whole under-tail area cleaned, too, with a different sponge. The inside of the sheath of geldings and stallions should not be just damp-sponged, which has little effect on the greasy discharge (smegma) in this area, but washed every two weeks or so with warm water and a mildly medicated soap on the 'back end' sponge. Rinse with the sponge very thoroughly (adding a dash of mild antiseptic to the water) and smear inside the sheath with a little liquid paraffin which helps prevent the smegma sticking to the skin. It is also excellent for rubbing into the entire lower leg area of horses susceptible to mud fever as a protection, as is udder cream or E45 barrier cream (available from most good chemists). These will all have to be washed off occasionally with mild, medicated soap and renewed.

Feet should be picked out daily and checked not only for the fit (and presence) of shoes but for softening horn in wet weather or cracks if the ground is hard. Particularly in winter, even if the legs are caked with mud, put your hands on the heel, pastern and fetlock area for several seconds to feel if there is any abnormal heat which could herald the onset of mud fever.

It pays to tease out and gently brush the mane and tail daily, to help prevent a build-up of tangles which are time-consuming to remove and almost certain to cause broken hairs in the process.

If the horse is being prepared for a special day, it makes your task easier to bring him in to a cool, well-ventilated stable the night before. It will be almost impossible to get him respectably clean on the morning of the event if he has been out all night (especially in winter). One night indoors will not soften him up and he should spend the next night out as normal.

Trimming

Even though your horse does live out, there is no need for him to look unkempt with a rough, overlong mane and tail. Mane and forelock can be pulled to thin them out, if necessary for manageable plaits, and shortened to a length of about 5 or 6in (12-15cm) (depending on the size of the horse) by just snapping off the ends of the hairs with the fingertips in a quick, snatching movement. If your horse objects to pulling, a razor comb (from many chain stores) used underneath from the roots has just as good an effect and does not produce a bristly re-growth.

The tail of a grass-kept horse should not be pulled at the top but left full. Racehorses have, in many cases, full tails at the top combined with a neat, level 'bang' at the bottom, and look lovely. To bang a tail, get a friend to stand with an arm under the dock so that the tail falls as it does when the horse is in action. Get hold of all the hairs inside your fist at the bottom of the dock, run your hand down to just below hock level, and cut off the hairs below this evenly with sharp, large scissors.

The tail should not be longer than this in winter or it will get clogged with mud and snow, although in summer it can be left a little longer to help with the fly problem. The top of the tail can be plaited for special occasions if the hair is too thick to look elegant left full. Do not be tempted to pull it; horses stand with their tails to wind and rain in winter and

A full (unpulled) banged tail, sometimes known as a 'racehorse' tail. Grass-kept animals should retain the hair on the dock for protection against bad weather. This type of tail can easily be plaited up for special occasions, and could be banged to a slightly shorter length in winter to avoid clogging with mud and snow

the dock hairs spread out and protect the sensitive areas between the buttocks, so helping prevent heat loss. Standing this way, with the full protection of his natural tail and the thicker skin on back and quarters, the horse presents a small body area to the elements and is able to protect his all-important head and the underparts of his body from the weather. (In summer, horses often stand broadside to the sun, to absorb maximum sunlight and warmth – the opposite to their winter stance.)

Long hairs under the jaw can be trimmed off (with fingers or scissors) without much detriment, although they do act as drainage hairs in wet weather. Opinions vary as regards fetlock hair. Some claim it is best to leave most of it, at least on the point of the fetlock, again for drainage, while others maintain legs are easier to keep clean, and to treat if mud fever develops, if excess hair is removed. I tend to find that if a horse is susceptible to mud fever, he will get it, hair or no hair, and feel it best to compromise by removing the shaggiest growth but leaving enough on the point of the fetlock to help drain away water.

Trimming off the long whiskers from muzzle and eyes is another bone of contention. These whiskers are the horse's feeler hairs and some animals become most disorientated, refusing to eat and banging their heads, if they are clipped off (they should *never* be pulled out). Others do not seem to bother. Personally, I prefer to leave them on.

Clipping

Whether you clip at all or not depends on the work you will be giving your horse and the weight of winter coat he grows. If the horse is a breedy type with a short coat and you are not doing any very active work in winter, such as hunting, you could well manage without clipping, but if you want to work him fairly hard and/or his coat is very woolly, some of it will have to come off if the horse is not to sweat heavily and get chilled and probably lose condition.

A normal trace clip, the most extensive clip which should be given to a grass-kept horse in winter. Trace-clipped animals can be made quite fit enough to hunt respectably, even in galloping country, or to undertake extended hacks or drives. They do need a proper shelter shed, and almost certainly a New Zealand or other waterproof rug

Provided he is hardy enough, a horse living out without a rug or temporarily without a shed can have the hair on his breast and under his neck clipped if in work. The hair should be left everywhere else, to provide some protection from the weather and mud

An 'Irish' clip, where the hair is removed as in a trace clip, but the line is tapered off at the stifle, leaving the hair on the thighs. The belly hair could be left on up to the dotted line, for further protection. This is a good clip for a horse in light to moderate work

Having stressed the necessity for a proper field shed in an earlier chapter, I am assuming that there is one, kept well bedded down, and in such circumstances, with the addition of a waterproof rug, the horse can be given a trace clip with no harm resulting.

A trace clip removes the hair from under the neck, breast, belly and round the tops of the legs, as shown in the illustration. Even so, I think it best to clip once only in early to mid autumn so that a little hair will re-grow, and to leave it at that. Remember, even moving about their field horses kick up a certain amount of mud on to their bellies and without the protection of hair there, chapped skin and mud fever can so easily occur. If the horse is having to manage without a shed (for a short period while arrangements to provide one are in progress), he will lie down (if at all) on wet, muddy ground. If he is even trace clipped, he will have little or nothing to protect his underparts from the mud and, again, could suffer from skin complaints. In such cases, the hair can be removed from the breast and under the neck as shown. I should feel it wrong to clip more extensively than this until a bedded-down shelter were available.

Many people feel a head looks smarter clipped in winter and no doubt it does, but with a grass-kept horse it should not be done. The ears can be tidied up by holding their edges together and carefully cutting off with scissors any hair protruding beyond them, particularly at the base, but that is all. If this is done, and the long under-jaw hairs neatened up, he will not look too bad at all.

Waterproof clothing and headcollars

There are as many differing views on the advantages and disadvantages of waterproof rugs as there are on most other aspects of equestrianism and horse management. Some maintain these rugs are more trouble than they are worth and cause problems of their own (which they can) and others say they are an absolute boon and they could never survive the winter (on behalf of their horse) without one (which may well be true). My view is that *properly fitted and maintained* water-

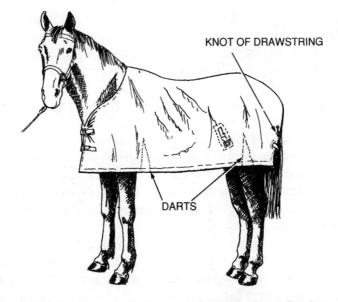

KNOT OF DRAWSTRING

DARTS

A well-fitting New Zealand pattern waterproof rug. It comes well in front of the withers and extends beyond the root of the tail; it is shaped to fit the horse's spine; there are two breast buckles (the top one can be fitted more loosely than the bottom one, to allow the horse to graze in comfort); it has no surcingle (which hinders the circulation of air, and prevents the rug from returning to position after rolling or lying down), and is shaped at the elbows and stifle. It has hindleg straps, and the drawstring inside the hem over the root of the tail can be pulled close to ensure a 'personalised' fit against the weather

proof rugs can definitely be a considerable comfort to a fine-coated or clipped horse living out in winter.

There are three main types available, although many saddlers produce their own designs. The best type, in my experience, is the original pattern from New Zealand which gives waterproof rugs the name by which they are all known in Britain, whether they are the true New Zealand design or not.

This pattern is shaped along the back (spine) seam to conform to the shape of the horse. It has large shaping darts at elbow and stifle to take up the slack fabric (normally canvas or tough sailcloth), breast straps across the front, leg straps at the back, a drawstring fitted inside the turning on the back edge over the root of tail/buttocks area which can be pulled to achieve an individual fit, and, most importantly, it has *no* surcingle. Because of the shaping and the freedom

An Australian pattern waterproof rug, with frontleg straps and a fillet strap round the thighs. This rug is properly shaped and does not need a surcingle

enabled through the lack of surcingle, horses can buck, gallop, play about, lie down and roll, get up and shake and the rug will return to its correct position. Air can circulate freely under the rug (helping to ensure healthy skin) while the horse remains warm and dry.

The second best type of rug (again in my experience) is the Australian pattern. This is also shaped but has frontleg straps, not back (see above), a fillet strap behind the thighs to stop the back end blowing up in the wind, and, again, no surcingle. These rugs are quite good but do not stay in place quite as well as the New Zealand pattern.

The third and most common type is often insufficiently shaped, if at all, has breast and hindleg straps and a surcingle. The surcingle, far from keeping the rug in place, actually prevents the rug's returning to its correct position after the horse has lain down and/or rolled. The rug moves under the surcingle, which then prevents it moving back again. The surcingle not only inhibits the free circulation of air under the rug but also causes pressure on the spine (a heinous crime in horse management) and so a potentially, or actually, sore back – and a horse with a sore back, whether a ride or drive horse, is out of commission. If you already have a waterproof rug which is properly shaped and has a surcingle, provided it is a good fit and you adjust the breast and leg straps properly, you should be able to remove the surcingle and, so, its associated disadvantages, and still find the rug stays in place quite well.

Some rugs are made of heavy sailcloth or canvas and are half lined with wool for warmth, others are of synthetic fabrics with various linings or filling material. Straps are either of leather or strong synthetic material. Whichever type you buy, never consider any rug which is not properly shaped along the back seam, at elbows and stifle and over the tail, and do not buy a rug with a surcingle.

If you already own a poorly shaped rug with a surcingle and cannot afford to replace it, it can be greatly improved by sewing inside it, to the lining and taking care not to pierce the outer covering, four pieces of thick, old-fashioned numnah felt (obtainable from similarly good old-fashioned saddlers) on either side of the back seam where the highest point of the withers goes, and also on either side at the back area directly under the surcingle (see page 121). The felt should be at least an inch (2cm) thick, and will raise the rug off withers and spine and 'wedge' the rug in place, vastly improving the rug's effectiveness and the horse's comfort. (A saddler would probably add elbow and stifle darts for you, in which case you could probably remove the surcingle.)

Fit
Waterproof rugs should be slightly roomier than stable rugs. They must come well in *front* of the withers round the base of the neck, not with the neckline resting on top of the withers or on the shoulders. At the back, they should extend a few inches beyond the root of the tail. Depth-wise, they should come a hand's breadth below the elbow and stifle. The breast straps must be fastened so that they keep the front end where it belongs but allow you to pass the flat of your hand comfortably over the withers under the rug and permit the horse to get his head down to graze without

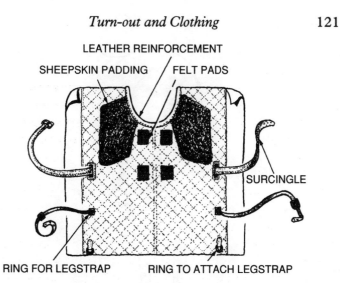

LEATHER REINFORCEMENT

SHEEPSKIN PADDING / FELT PADS

SURCINGLE

RING FOR LEGSTRAP   RING TO ATTACH LEGSTRAP

If your rug has a surcingle, you can improve its comfort and security by sewing thick felt pads to the lining. Those at the withers lift the rug off the horse, and those a little further back prevent the surcingle pressing on to the spine. The pads 'wedge' the rug in position on either side of the spine and help stop it slipping and the sheepskin padding at the shoulders minimises rubbing

significant pressure where his neck joins his breast. He will have his head down most of the time, remember, and tightness here can eventually cause sufficient discomfort to prevent his grazing freely and pull the rug to cause pressure on the withers.

Even in well shaped rugs with no surcingle, improvement can be made and wither pressure eliminated by adding felt pads inside at the withers. Sheepskin padding here simply lessens friction; it cannot remove pressure. Some fine-coated horses also need sheepskin padding at the shoulders to prevent excessive wearing away of hair (the first stages of friction sores). Synthetic fleece is usually too harsh for such horses and does not solve the problem.

There are two leg straps at the back in New Zealand and similar pattern rugs, with a variety of simple fastenings and length adjustments. One end of each strap will fasten about a third of the way forward from the back edge and there will be another fastening, usually a 'D' ring, on or just inside the back edge.

The best way to fasten the leg straps so that they keep the

This method of fastening the hindleg straps (linking one through the other) helps prevent the straps rubbing the thin skin inside the gaskins, as the straps hold each other away from the legs

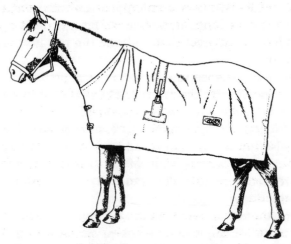

This poor horse is in a great deal of discomfort. The headcollar is much too large, and could easily be rubbed or pulled off; it is sliding down his neck, and pulling on his nose. The rug comes too far up underneath the neck, but is too far back on the withers, where it is pulling, and will eventually cause soreness. It is not properly shaped at the elbows and stifle, and the surcingle exerts pressure on the spine. The leg straps are a little too long for safety, and should only just be visible

rug in place and do not rub the sensitive skin inside the horse's hind legs is as follows: take the left strap at its forward fastening and, making sure it is not twisted, pass it out between the horse's hind legs at the back and clip it to its fastening on the left of the back edge. Now take the right strap and again pass it out between the horse's hind legs, *linking it through the left strap,* then clipping it to its ring on the right of the back edge of the rug. Each strap is now fastened at both ends on its own side of the rug and round the appropriate hind leg, but the straps hold each other away from the inside of the legs and help prevent chafing.

Some rugs hang better if the straps are criss-crossed between the legs, so that the left strap clips to the right back edge and vice versa. Trial and error will decide the best method for your horse and rugs, but try the first method to start with as this is nearly always the most satisfactory.

When the leg straps are fastened, adjust their length so that you can only *just* see them level with the bottom edge of the rug. Adjusted like this, it is extremely unlikely that the horse will tread on them or get both legs 'down one hole'. If they are too short they will annoy him, rub and restrict his movements; if too long, he might tread on them, entangle his legs and have a nasty accident.

Maintenance

Rugs should be removed twice daily, the horse thoroughly inspected for signs of rubbing (rubbed or worn hair, sore or even raw skin) and the rug changed, or replaced if not too wet. You will need two rugs to enable you to remove excess mud and dry off one rug while the other is in use. If the rug is an extra-depth one it will cover the correctly adjusted leg straps, obviously.

Once your horse starts wearing a rug you will have to keep it on until spring as he will become used to it. If you leave the rug off during a mild day and the horse gets wet, he will have to be thoroughly dried before wearing the rug again or dampness under the rug will probably cause skin problems, unless the rug is one of the permeable ones.

Periodically during the winter, if weather permits, and

certainly at the end of each winter, the rugs should be laundered and repaired, and reproofed with a suitable product from a tack or camping shop before being put away for the summer. Synthetic rugs can normally be laundered in a washing machine but canvas and sailcloth ones cannot. Vacuum their linings thoroughly before scrubbing them with warm soapy water and thoroughly hosing out the soap. Hose and scrub off mud from the outside and spread over a fence or hedge to dry completely before reproofing the outside and having any repairs done. Leather parts must be kept cleaned and well oiled throughout the winter and metal parts should be lightly smeared with oil.

Accustoming a horse to a New Zealand rug
Most horses take kindly to their 'macs' but some dislike the feel of leg straps in strange places, so must be gradually accustomed to them.

Put the rug on first in the stable, having let the horse sniff it well. Adjust the straps correctly and lead the horse round his box, in a bridle for extra control. As soon as he is calm in it, lead him round the stable yard, and ultimately lunge him in the rug. Make sure he is quite unworried in it, even if it takes a few days, before turning him loose in the field, as although he is unlikely to suffer harm from the rug itself if correctly fitted, he might gallop in a panic and hurt himself in other ways.

Ancillary clothing
Head and neck hoods are also available for outdoor wear, although not commonly seen. The types made from stretch fabric and fitting closely are uncomfortable for the horse. Neck and head hoods normally attach to each other, with the neck hood remaining open under the gullet, apart from retaining straps, and fastening (overlapping) to the front part of the rug. Obviously the rug must have attachments for the hood and it is usually necessary to buy integrated clothing from one manufacturer. These extra items of clothing can certainly be useful in very cold, wet weather and/or for sensitive horses.

A good type of headcollar; the browband permits a fly-fringe to be fitted in summer, and prevents the headpiece from slipping down the neck and causing an uncomfortable pull on the nose. There is ample room around the ears, and the horse has space to move his jaws when eating. The buckles allow precise adjustment of fit; the noseband does not rub the cheekbones, but cannot be rubbed off

Headcollars

It is best to turn out a horse without a headcollar unless he is hard to catch because there is always the chance of his catching it on any projection, such as a branch in the hedge.

Do use a browband on your headcollar as this makes for greater comfort and security. It prevents the headpiece sliding down the neck and causing an uncomfortable pull on the front of the noseband. The headpiece and browband should fit comfortably around the base of the ears allowing room to pass a finger easily around the area and so that neither strap cuts in. The noseband should fall midway between the sharp face bone and the corner of the mouth and you should be able to fit no more than four fingers inside the noseband. Headcollars with adjusting buckles on the noseband are recommended.

You will not wish to turn out your horse in your best leather headcollar. Chrome tanned leather (as opposed to vegetable tanned), which is often pale green, is a useful compromise for field use. It stretches more before breaking, and New Zealand (and other) rug leg straps are often made of it. Although the headcollar will become regularly muddy, still take the time to clean and oil it often during use to keep it soft. Smear metal parts lightly with oil.

Nylon webbing headcollars, and some other synthetic materials, are extremely strong and so can be dangerous if left on turned-out horses, as they will not snap at all easily if caught up.

8 Working and Resting

Working a horse off grass, even quite hard, is not as impossible as many people think it is. It is true a grass-kept horse cannot be made as supremely fit as, say, a racehorse or three-day-event horse where fast work is performed by an animal carrying no excess fat (a condition difficult to achieve in a horse with constant access to grass), but there are many endurance horses (whose work is slower although very demanding) who perform very successfully while spending a considerable amount of time at grass.

The main 'secret' is that your grass should be of poorish to medium quality compared with normal farming standards. This should not be too difficult to manage if you have taken expert grassland advice as suggested in Chapter 4, or, if unable to sow your own land, have chosen rented grazing carefully (briefly, land supporting sheep will probably be suitable, that carrying dairy cattle will not). Your horse's nutritional requirements can then be made up with 'hard' feed (concentrates) which help promote hard condition for strenuous work. If the grazing is really poor, he will need hay, too, so his diet will approximate even more to that of a stabled horse, and your task will be that much easier.

Poor quality grazing must not, however, be confused with scrub, neglected land bearing many weeds or poisonous plants; it is simply land which has been sown with grasses having a moderate nutritional content. It should still be well cared for and kept clean and in good heart. It could also be land grazed down by beef cattle, or in areas where the soil is not of the best.

In addition, it is an aid to physical fitness if the field is large and undulating as the horse has further to roam and the differing gradients assist in muscular development.

Getting fit

The fittening process for a grass-kept horse is, in principle, exactly the same as for a stabled one – a gradual increase of work and exercise. The main differences are that with the grass-kept animal you do not begin grooming with the body brush, at least not hard, because even in summer some grease and dandruff give added resistance to the skin and coaι. Feeding may cause a quandary because of the grass. In winter, feed as for a stabled horse. In spring, watch the grass and the horse's condition very carefully. If the grass is at all rich and lush and the horse is putting on weight but you cannot bring him in, either move him to a poorer field (easier said than done, maybe) or cut out all his other food and give him long walks on the roads or bridlepaths. If he has been out all winter and/or in regular work anyway, two hours walking a day will do him nothing but good, plus, perhaps, a little slow trotting.

Once the spring flush is over the grass is less rich and lush and you can start fittening work in earnest, judging by your own circumstances whether the horse needs concentrates or not. Make him walk up to his bridle, and trot, too, but steadily. Once a fair degree of fitness has been reached (after, say, a month's walking and trotting) you can, in fact, give the horse more trotting than you would with a stabled horse because he will be walking about the field all day anyway, albeit not marching on in the way he would be asked to do when ridden, so will do much of the slow work for you. However, unless the ground gets hard in summer, his legs will not be hardened without road work to make demands on them, so steady (working pace) trotting on the roads is still part of his programme.

Once the stage of cantering under saddle is reached, the horse may well be as fit as when stabled provided the grass is not too rich or plentiful. You will know your own horse and will be able to compare him in the two states – stabled and grass-kept – but you may well be pleasantly surprised to find that he does not develop a grass belly, that he does not puff and sweat as much as you thought he would and that he really is fitter than you thought you could get him. The three main points to remember are:

1 Avoid rich, lush grass in spring and summer and give plenty of walking and steady trotting at these times to keep him 'tuned up'.
2 It is not necessary for a horse to be body brushed hard to get him fit. The rain will remove excess dandruff anyway and his skin will be perfectly healthy functioning in natural conditions.
3 His lungs will probably be all the better for his outdoor life (indeed, it may have been a respiratory disorder which brought on your decision to keep him out in the first place) and will serve his heart and circulatory system, and so the rest of his body, even better than when stabled – a considerable bonus.

Grass-kept working horses are easier to keep fit than stabled ones as they do not go 'stale' in their work or develop cornsickness (which is mild indigestion due to an unrelieved high concentrate diet). They will stay fit and happy longer provided their normal requirements of food, company and shelter are constantly taken care of. They do not get bored (half the problem with a stabled animal) or develop vices. To keep your horse fit, simply pay close attention to his physical condition, slacken off the work slightly once the desired level of fitness has been achieved and, again, avoid over-rich grazing. As with a stabled animal, vary his work and keep him interested and active, and you should be rewarded with a horse almost constantly fit for your needs. Many horses kept out are likely to be required for work all year round, but remember that the harder they work the more likely they are to need a break (as with a stabled horse). The type of horse kept out like this, though, will probably be doing riding-club or local show or event work during warm times of year and, perhaps, cub-hunting and/or hunting proper at other times, and will probably never need a prolonged break from work.

Care before hard work

As mentioned in the previous chapter, it is much easier to prepare a horse for a special day if he can be brought into a stable the night before. Presuming, then, that you *can* bring him in for a night, choose a stable which is well ventilated without being draughty and leave the top door open. Bed it down well and have a full haynet or rack ready (although the hay can be fed from the ground if the horse is a tidy eater) plus two buckets of water.

If it is winter and the horse normally wears a New Zealand rug outdoors you may be undecided as to whether to rug him up indoors or not. Be guided by the horse. If the base of his ears is cold, he feels cold and should have a single rug on. If you are going to clean him up, the rug will help keep him clean, anyway. If he feels warm, you could either leave him with nothing or just a light summer sheet, for cleanliness.

The horse should not be brought in wet and allowed to dry off on his own if the weather is at all chilly, especially with a winter coat. If you are going to wash him, do so quickly. Rub him down well with straw and/or old towels, and use a hairdryer if necessary. Finish him off by either thatching him with straw under an old rug or putting on an anti-sweat rug under an old top rug. Both these methods allow air to circulate between horse and rug and will keep him warm in cold weather whilst permitting him to dry off. Some horses' coats dry with the marks of the straw or mesh anti-sweat rug on them, but these marks can be removed or considerably lessened by removing the thatch and replacing with an ordinary rug to flatten the coat while the hair is still *very slightly* damp. The permeable rugs now available obviate the necessity for thatching as they allow moisture to rise up through them, and the horse dries off well.

Give the horse his normal corn feed, and check him again last thing to make sure he is not too hot from his unaccustomed accommodation. If he *is* too warm remove any clothing he is wearing but make sure there are no draughts. Next morning, visit him early to check on him, brush off any stable stains and feed and water normally.

Work on the day and aftercare

In winter, as he still has a good deal of his thick coat on, remember he will get hot much more easily than a clipped, stabled horse and cannot do the same amount of work. Do not do any more with him than necessary and do not let him stand about getting chilled. Keep him gently on the move and avoid any more energetic work such as fast cantering or jumping than needed, to minimise sweating as much as possible.

In summer, you will probably find that he performs just as well as a stabled or combined-system horse provided he is not too tubby from spring grass. If he starts to sweat or puff, obviously take things easy, stand him with his head to any breeze there might be and find a shady spot in hot weather.

On the way home, if hacking, your objective in both summer and winter is to arrive home with a cool, dry horse, weather permitting. With a horse wearing much or all of his winter coat, this may not be easy, but if it is pouring down with rain it is better to keep interspersing walk with steady trot to keep him warm, as a warm horse will dry off in his thick coat at home much quicker than a soaking wet, cold one. If boxing a wet horse home, remove the saddle and put on a permeable rug.

In summer, your task, once home, will be relatively easy. Even if it is raining and you feel tempted to let your horse spend another night indoors, don't. The weather is unlikely to be cold enough to cause him any distress and he will probably want to be out.

Whatever time of year it is, deal with the horse as quickly as possible to get him out again. In winter, use your common sense about drying off the horse. If he is wet with rain or sweat, but cool, he can go straight out in the field after a small feed. If he is warm, he must be cooled down by leading round, as to turn out a hot horse into a cold field on a winter night is asking for trouble. If it is raining and you cannot lead him round, put him in a cold stable or somewhere under cover and thatch him (or equivalent) or rub him down with straw until he shows signs of cooling down. Do not let him stand hot and sweating in a draught or in the open in the belief that he will dry off quicker. He will – but he will also probably get a chill. If the horse is to wear a New Zealand rug, he must, for reasons already stated, be dry before it is put on, so get him dry as quickly as possible while he is eating his feed, put the rug on and turn him out.

While your horse is eating his feed or hay, and maybe drying off, check him over for injuries and treat whatever you find. Obviously anything serious, deep cuts or lameness and the like, will need a vet's attention quickly, so the horse will have to stay in until help arrives, and instructions followed from then on. (If a horse has been kept in for several nights and/or days due to illness or injury, he will probably have to be stabled at nights for the rest of the winter as he will have become acclimatised to it, although if you are lucky enough to have a mild spell he would probably adapt once again to nights in the field if you keep a close eye on his reaction.)

Once the horse is out after his day's work, having had an initial feed, try to visit him later that night to check him and give him another feed. It goes without saying that his shelter should have its normal thick bed with hay supply and if he is having an extra feed because of his work, it may be necessary to feed him away from other field companions so that he gets his ration in peace.

The following day, the horse should be caught up and thoroughly checked over from head to hooves for any injuries not spotted the night before, for loose or cast shoes, and undue tiredness, and also trotted up to check for lameness. If he *is* injured or lame, he may have to be brought in to prevent his using the injured part too much in the field, so if you intend turning him out again, as detailed earlier, do not over-cosset him. Try to use a cool, airy stable with, in winter, as few rugs as are needed to keep him reasonably warm, and use your judgement about roughing him off again to return to his outdoor life when recovered.

Working straight from the field

When the horse is just being exercised normally or worked straight from the field without being brought in for a night, remember he will probably have been eating right up to the moment you go to catch him, so at least half an hour must be spent walking to let the grass go down before anything energetic can be undertaken. Normal exercise will take little out of a horse constantly on the move, and there is no need for specially cooked feeds (although outdoor horses, and indoor ones too, come to that, appreciate a warm feed on a cold night, just as we do).

It is often a nuisance to have a rain-wet horse when you want to ride and if the horse has a thick, muddy coat, too, it will not be possible to dry him off sufficiently to be able to get the saddle on if you have only limited time available. For this reason if no other, it is often a better plan to winter the horse out in a New Zealand rug and clip him a bit, than to have a horse who is constantly going to cause you to miss your rides because he is filthy or give you a lot of work cleaning him up. He will need the work anyway if you want him fit for fairly active work, so if the rug enables you to keep to a regular exercise/fitness programme, it is worth using.

In summer, I must admit to having frequently put a cotton fleece numnah on a wet but not muddy back, tacked up and got on with the riding. In this connection I do not see the difference between sweat and rain, and have never had any skin problems because of it. Rubbing mud into the back under the friction and weight of a saddle and rider would obviously be a different matter, and would make the skin sore quite quickly.

After moderate work in warm weather, the horse can have his normal feed (if he is getting concentrates) and be turned out as usual. If he is tired, it may be best to just put him out and let him eat the food which is easiest of all for him to digest – grass – giving him a normal feed later. This will get his digestion going again gently. Giving a tired horse, whether stabled or grass-kept, a full ordinary feed of concentrates is rather taxing to his tired system, and could cause colic as he may not be able to cope with it.

In winter, the grass will not be much use, so give him, say, a half feed perhaps with a carbohydrate booster in it as a quick energy restorative, with another later. After normal exercise, however, just give him his normal feed and put him back in the field as soon as practical.

Letting down whilst remaining at grass

If your horse has had a hard season's work, or you are unable, or do not want, to work him for a while, he can easily be let down for a rest simply by reducing his work over about a week. It is best to do this rather than stop possibly lengthy exercise or work stints all at once. Whether or not you reduce the feed, too, depends on the amount of grass available and on whether or not the weather is getting colder plus, as always, your horse's physical condition. Then, when you want to start work again, begin a fitness programme as normal.

Bringing up from grass

If you decide to bring your horse up from grass completely, try to do it gradually, as sudden changes of diet and way of life can be very upsetting. If the horse is not too fat, start by giving small concentrate feeds while he is still in the field, to begin a gradual changeover in diet if he has been having nothing but grass. If the horse has not been working, either, he can begin by having half an hour a day while still living out, just walking at first, of course. Even just riding him about his field, if he has no shoes on, will start to get his muscles working and his skin hardened up. This process could go on for a month or so, during which time you could call in the vet and the farrier to check over the horse's general condition, have teeth checked, feet seen to and shod, initially with lightweight shoes until the horse becomes accustomed to 'heavy' feet again, and generally get him going.

His grazing should be gradually reduced, not stopped all at once. No matter what anyone says to you, do *not* follow the old advice to 'mash the horse down', ie give sloppy mashes to 'convert' his digestive system from grass to hard feed. This will thoroughly upset his system and seriously unbalance the gut micro-organisms.

From starting work on an unfit, grass-kept horse to arriving at the end product of a fit, corn-fed, mainly stabled one, will take roughly twelve weeks. Over this period, very gradually reduce the grazing and increase the time stabled, until the horse is either being kept on the combined system or completely stabled, according to your requirements. There is never any need to completely cut out grazing for even the fittest horse. In fact, a daily ration of grass, even on the end of a leadrope for ten minutes, helps the digestion and will be relished by the horse.

After the first month or so of a fitness programme, you will start seeing a difference in the horse. During that first month, while you are gradually reducing the grazing and increasing the concentrates, the exercise should also be gently increased, until by the end of the month he could be receiving about an hour and a half a day mostly walking with perhaps a few minutes slow trotting. Concentrate rations depend on the individual horse, but he could now be getting about 2lb or 3lb (0.9–1.3kg) concentrates daily.

During the second month, build up the exercise to two hours a day, walking well up to the bridle rather than slopping along, with two ten-minute stints of steady trotting, using himself properly, and, towards the end of this month, short canter spells. His grazing by now can be cut to the minimum you have decided upon, and his droppings will have lost the green colour associated with those of a grass-kept horse and will be more khaki coloured and slightly firmer. Concentrates could be at about 6lb or 8lb (2.7–3.6kg) a day, always depending on the horse's requirements.

The final month of the fitness programme can be developed further, the horse being on a two-thirds bulk/one-third concentrate diet, or a little less bulk and more concentrates if doing fast work. More than two hours exercise will be unnecessary unless he is going in for endurance work, but grazing can still be given (provided it is not lush and over rich) for an hour or two a day with no harm to the horse.

If the horse is to be brought up from grass but not worked, the grazing should still be reduced gradually, and he will still need exercise of some sort unless sick, for the sake of his health. If he is to be yarded (kept in an area large enough for him to exercise himself but without grass) he should have a permanent supply of good hay or hayage, which alone could be enough to maintain his condition. Concentrates should be used as a top-up ration, in this case, to supplement the bulky diet if the horse appears to be on the thin side.

Should you be unable to reduce the grazing gradually for some reason, say if you suddenly lose the use of your field, graze the horse in hand anywhere convenient as much as you can and give him soaked hay or a hayage product with short feeds of whatever you were feeding in the field. If you were feeding nothing, start introducing small feeds of, say, molassed chop with soaked sugar beet pulp and grass meal. In cases like this where a digestive upset might easily occur, consider using a pro-biotic to help restore a healthy gut micro-organism population, and seek the advice of a nutritionist or vet. At present on the market is an excellent range of alfalfa (lucerne) products from Dengie which provide natural, balanced feeding regimes which could be ideal for your horse.

Turning out to grass

The process of turning a horse out to grass should be treated in the same way as that of getting a horse fit, although this reverse process does not take as long. The main point to watch is the weather; if the horse has wintered in and is being roughed off, and maybe let down, prior to turning out in spring, continuing cold weather can delay the process considerably. Just because the horse is now to be kept out (whether working or resting) it does not mean he can be expected to acclimatise himself within a week from an executive lifestyle, clipped, rugged up, stabled and corned up, to that of a camper, exposed largely to the weather, deprived of most of his rugs before his coat has grown and on a reduced corn/hay diet before the grass is making a respectable showing.

If the weather has warmed up, there is still a danger of adverse effects from a surfeit of rich spring grass, and if a horse is turned out in the autumn the weather could well be getting colder all the time he is being roughed off. It can take anything from ten days to three weeks or more to rough off a horse properly. The points to be borne in mind when working out a programme for it are:

1 The weather. Try to begin during a mild spell, especially if the horse has been clipped.
2 The horse's breeding and personal constitution.
3 How he has been kept (has he been turned out at all or not, is his stable cold and airy or warm and stuffy, how many rugs etc).
4 How much corn and exercise he has been getting. (If the horse is to remain in work these could stay the same.)

Let us assume the horse has wintered in and been 'chaser clipped (basically a trace clip with the head off, too), worked moderately (active hacking/light hunting) and has had short daily spells at grass. He is to become a working, outdoor horse.

The first thing to do is to worm the horse if this has not been done every few weeks throughout the winter, and get his teeth checked by the vet. Then, picking a mild spell, the first step in roughing off could be to start leaving the top leaf of his stable door open at night if it has been closed. Stop body brushing him to let the grease build up in his coat, but tidy him up with the dandy brush and attend to other items of his toilet as normal. As he is to stay in work, continue with feeding and exercising as normal, or cut down slightly. If the horse has been having about an hour a day grazing, double this time now. Continue like this for four days to a week.

The second stage involves leaving off one of his blankets, but only during the day if the weather is cold, and extending his time at grass to half a day, probably wearing a New Zealand rug. Everything else proceeds as before. Continue for about a further four days like this.

Thirdly, leave off a blanket at night and two in the day (if he has had two) so he stands in during the daytime with just his rug. He should now spend most of the day at grass when not working, with his 'mac' on, if chilly or wet. This stage could last four days again. Next, he should wear only a rug at night, nothing during the day when in and be out all day when not working, if possible without his New Zealand rug.

Finally, immediately prior to going out altogether, he should do without his stable rug completely. Pick a warmish night for his first night under the stars even though he has (it is hoped) a shelter and decide by assessing his progress and reaction to your programme whether to put his New Zealand rug on. This stage can be a little tricky as regards the rug. You might want to put it on only at night but find the horse is soaking wet from a day's rain, in which case he will have to be dried off first. Only you can decide if the horse is feeling cold, if he is tucked up and needing more food or if he has taken to the whole thing like a duck to water and is looking forward to his outdoor life, but I hope the above programme will give some idea of how to proceed when roughing off and turning out a horse.

Letting down a stabled horse

If the horse is to be let down from work and is going out for a rest, proceed as above, but also gradually cut down the exercise (by speed and duration) and concentrates. Eventually, if the grass is reasonable, cut down the hay ration too. If early spring, the horse could still need a feed or two a day, and possibly hay, too, if the grass is not properly through. In winter or autumn, although you can cut down the exercise, the weather may demand that his rations remain as when stabled. In summer, of course, it is hoped the grass will be enough to maintain a resting horse.

Acknowledgements

I am grateful for the help given in the preparation of this book by Mrs Marytavy Archer BSc DIC, Ms Janet L. Eley BVSc MRCVS and Mr and Mrs C. G. Taylor.

Index

David & Charles' Equestrian Titles

CLARISSA STRACHAN'S YOUNG EVENT HORSE
Buying, Breaking, Training, Competing
Clarissa Strachan

DRESSAGE
Begin the Right Way
Lockie Richards

GREAT HORSEMEN OF THE WORLD
Guy Wathen

THE GREAT HUNTS
Foxhunting Countries of the World
Alastair Jackson

THE HEAVY HORSE MANUAL
Nick Rayner and Keith Chivers

HORSE BREEDING
New edition
Peter Rossdale

HORSE CARE AND RIDING
A Practical Approach
Susan McBane

THE HORSE'S HEALTH FROM A TO Z
An Equine Veterinary Dictionary
New edition
Peter Rossdale and Susan M. Wreford

THE HORSE OWNER'S HANDBOOK
Monty Mortimer

THE HORSE RIDER'S HANDBOOK
Monty Mortimer

THE ILLUSTRATED GUIDE TO HORSE TACK
Susan McBane

KEEPING A HORSE OUTDOORS
New edition
Susan McBane

LUNGEING
The Horse and the Rider
Sheila Inderwick

A PASSION FOR PONIES
John and Francesca Bullock

PRACTICAL DRESSAGE
Jane Kidd

PRACTICAL EVENTING
Jane Holderness-Roddam

PRACTICAL SHOWING
Nigel Hollings

PRACTICAL SHOWJUMPING
Peter Churchill

THE RIDING INSTRUCTOR'S HANDBOOK
Monty Mortimer

ROBERT SMITH'S YOUNG SHOWJUMPER
Selecting, Training, Competing
Rachel Lambert

THE STABLE VETERINARY HANDBOOK
Colin Vogel

The Lost Letters of William Woolf

Praise for *The Lost Letters of William Woolf*

'A quirky, enjoyable novel about communication, relationships and love' *Woman & Home*

'The Must-Read' *Irish Tatler*

'A strong debut. Cullen's great strength is the way she writes so movingly about how day-to-day life can chip away at a once-solid relationship until it crumbles' *Belfast Telegraph*

'An effortlessly assured debut about how finding a lost letter and a twist of fate can make you question whether the love of your life is really meant for you after all . . .' Rick O'Shea, *RTE Broadcaster*

'What a brilliant book. I couldn't put it down' Larry Gogan, *RTE Broadcaster*

'Once in a while a book comes along that captures your heart, and this one charmed me from the first page . . . An enchanting and bittersweet exploration of what love really means' Maria Dickenson, Managing Director, Dubray Books

'*The Lost Letters of William Woolf* is an entertaining and enriching novel that is capable of inducing in the reader acute apprehensions of the complexities of our inner lives, and of the inner lives of others. Entertaining and enriching' *The National*

'A strong debut . . . Helen Cullen writes movingly about how day-to-day life can chip away at a solid relationship' *The Herald*

'An enchanting, lyrical page-turner and an ode to London, love, Dublin and everything in between' Joy Rhoades, international bestselling author of *The Woolgrower's Companion*

'A spellbinding novel. Compelling, lyrical and deeply moving' Caroline Busher, bestselling author of *The Ghosts of Magnificent Children*

'A wise, imaginative and heart-warming novel about the limits of love, the allure of new romance and the lost art of letter writing' Luiza Sauma, author of *Flesh and Bone and Water*

'A gorgeous love story about the multitude of possibilities and choices in our lives, and how by saying hello to one path, we say goodbye to another. The lost stories in the Dead Letters Depot moved me greatly. A delightfully romantic and original debut' Tor Udall, author of *A Thousand Paper Birds*

'Generous, surprising, full of heart, Cullen's debut leaves you flooded with warmth and gratitude for all the love letters you ever received and pure regret for all the ones you never sent' Ruth Gilligan, author of *A Thousand Folds Make a Paper Swan*

'A rip-roaring, peripatetic tale of love, but also self-discovery set against the backdrop of 1980s London and with hints of *The Shop Around the Corner*. Helen Cullen is an undeniable new talent, whose words stayed with me long after I had read them' Alba Arikha, author of *Major/Minor* and *Where To Find Me*

ABOUT THE AUTHOR

Helen Cullen is an Irish writer living in London. *The Lost Letters of William Woolf* is her debut novel.

The Lost Letters of
William Woolf

HELEN CULLEN

PENGUIN BOOKS

PENGUIN BOOKS

UK | USA | Canada | Ireland | Australia
India | New Zealand | South Africa

'i carry your heart with me (i carry it in)'. Copyright 1952, © 1980, 1991 by the Trustees for the E. E. Cummings Trust, 'you are tired?', copyright © 1973, 1983, 1991 by the Trustees for the E. E. Cummings Trust. Copyright © 1973, 1983 by George James Firmage, from *Complete Poems: 1904–1962* by E. E. Cummings, edited by George J. Firmage. Used by permission of Liveright Publishing Corporation

The moral right of the author has been asserted

Set in 12.5/14.5 pt Bembo Book MT Std
Typeset by Jouve (UK), Milton Keynes
Printed and bound in Great Britain by Clays Ltd, Elcograf S.p.A.

A CIP catalogue record for this book is available from the British Library

ISBN: 978-1-405-93495-4

www.greenpenguin.co.uk

MIX
Paper from
responsible sources
FSC
www.fsc.org   FSC® C018179

Penguin Random House is committed to a sustainable future for our business, our readers and our planet. This book is made from Forest Stewardship Council® certified paper.

Dedicated to Demian Wieland

'More than kisses, letters mingle souls'
                                    – John Donne

I.

Lost letters have only one hope for survival. If they are caught between two worlds, with an unclear destination and no address of sender, the lucky ones are redirected to the Dead Letters Depot in East London for a final chance of redemption. Inside the damp-rising walls of a converted tea factory, letter detectives spend their days solving mysteries. Missing postcodes, illegible handwriting, rain-smudged ink, lost address labels, torn packages, forgotten street names: they are all culprits in the occurrence of missed birthdays, unknown test results, bruised hearts, unaccepted invitations, silenced confessions, unpaid bills and unanswered prayers. Instead of longed-for missives, disappointment floods post boxes from Land's End to Dunnet Head. Hope fades a little more every day, when doorbells don't chime and doormats don't thud.

William Woolf had worked as a letter detective for eleven years. He was one of an army of thirty, having inherited his position from his beloved uncle, Archie. Almost every Friday throughout William's childhood, Archie, clad in a lime-green leather jacket, rode his yellow Honda Dream 305 over for tea, eager to share fish and chips doused in salt and vinegar served with a garlic dip, and tales of the treasures rescued that day. Listening to Archie opened William's mind to the myriad extraordinary stories that were unfolding every day in the lives of ordinary people. In a blue-lined copybook, he wrote his favourites and unwittingly began what would become a lifelong obsession with storytelling, domestic mysteries and the secrets strangers nurse. What surprised William most when he started working there himself was how little Archie had exaggerated. People send the strangest paraphernalia through the post: incomprehensible and indefensible, sentimental and valuable, erotic and bizarre, alive and expired. In fact, it was the dead animals that so frequently found their way to this inner sanctum of the postal system that had inspired the Dead Letters Depot's name. A photo taken in 1937, the year it had opened, showed the original postmaster, Mr Frank Oliphant, holding a pheasant and hare aloft, with three rabbits stretched out on the table before him. By the time William joined in 1979, it was a much more irregular occurrence, of course, but the name still endured. He still felt Archie's presence amid the exposed red-brick walls of the depot, and some of the older detectives sometimes called William by his uncle's name. Their physical similarities were striking: muddy brown curls, chestnut beards flecked with rust, the almond-shaped hazel eyes that flickered between shades of emerald green and cocoa, the bump in the nose of all Woolf men.

In a vault of football-field proportions hidden below Shoreditch High Street, row upon row of the peculiar flotsam and jetsam of life awaited salvation: pre-war toy soldiers, vinyl records, military memorabilia, astrology charts, paintings, pounds and pennies, wigs, musical instruments, fireworks, soap, cough mixture, uniforms, fur coats, boxes of buttons, chocolates, photo albums, porcelain teacups and saucers, teddy bears, medical samples, seedlings, weapons, lingerie, fossils, dentures, feathers, gardening tools, books, books, books. Copious myths and legends passed from one colleague to another; stories of the once lost but now found.

Each detective cultivated their own private collection of the most remarkable discoveries they had made. For William, there was a suit of armour dismantled in a tarnished silver sea-chest, an ebony-and-glass case housing two red admiral butterflies, each wing secured by a tiny pearl pin, and a miniature grandfather clock only three feet tall. 'More of a grandson clock, really,' he always joked.

There were still some deeply unpleasant discoveries to be made. The detectives harboured daily fears of strange stenches, soggy parcels and departed creatures; mostly, white mice, cockroaches and bugs originally destined to feed pet lizards, snakes and rats. At least William hoped that's what they had originally been intended for, before they met another, equally unpleasant end in 'The Furnace', the final destination for contaminated goods, the unrecyclable and unsalvageable. It sat shoulder to shoulder with the gnashing, monster shredder where lost letters became dead letters and all hope was vanquished.

Every day, the detectives opened letter after letter, parcel after parcel, searching for clues. The satisfaction of solving a mystery never faded. The joy of knowing that something so anticipated could find its way after a lengthy diversion remained exquisite. It was the thousands of unsolvable conundrums that wearied bones and wasted skin on paper cuts. Sometimes, there just wasn't enough evidence to trace, no clue to worry over until the blessed eureka moment. Over the years, William had learned not to fret over the truly lost, to let them go and to invest his time instead in those that presented greater hope of a solution. Every week, hundreds of new puzzles arrived, so the mountain of mail in the depot seemed self-replenishing. A pessimist could find much to confirm a bleak worldview in this museum of missed messages. Only a quarter of the post that passed through the depot ever found its way home, but just one very special victory could sustain a detective for weeks in their endeavours.

William had recently reunited a battered Milk Tray chocolate box brimful of wedding photos from 1944 with the bride, Delilah Broccoli. The son of her maid of honour had found them when executing his mother's estate and tried to post the box back to the last known address, but the street, never mind the individual house, no longer existed. When items discovered lost in the post held considerable monetary or sentimental value, or had been missing in action for an exceptionally long time, the letter detectives would courier them to their rightful home rather than send them off into the cavernous postal system once again. A still-breathing tortoise, a crystal chandelier and a silver pendant hanging from a garland of rubies were among some of the undeliverables William had elevated to his personal care. In some very exceptional cases, the letter detectives went one step further and delivered items in person, out of fear that something so precious may become lost once again. On this most recent occasion, William had successfully traced Delilah to the nursing home in East Anglia where she now lived and decided this should be one of those exceptions.

When William entered Delilah's bedroom, she looked confused as she tried to place him. 'We haven't met before, Mrs Broccoli,' he reassured her. 'I work for the post office, and wanted to deliver a parcel to you that went astray.'

He moved a pink plastic cup of water from the table-top tray that lay on her lap and placed the world-weary chocolate box before her. It was the same shade of purple as her dressing gown; velvet with a white lace collar. Delilah's eyes flitted from William's to the box and back again. She tried to speak, but the words caught in a raspy net in her throat. Her silver curls were flattened on the right side of her head from where they were crushed against the pillow. He moved closer and laid his hand gently on her arm.

'It's all right, nothing to be frightened of. Here, let me help you.'

He prised the lid from the chocolate box and placed the crinkled photographs before her one by one. Delilah traced a finger beneath the row of sepia and a look of recognition spread across her face. She picked up one with a trembling hand and held it close to her nose. William watched as a shy smile illuminated her expression and her eyes grew misty.

'I'll leave you in peace now, Mrs Broccoli,' he said.

She reached out and grabbed his sleeve with her

papery grip and held on tight for a second. It was days like those that kept his faith alive.

Lately, William had retreated more and more into the soft silence of the post delivery room, away from the chatter and bustle of the shared office space where the letter detectives worked. He had never been very good at rising above his moods and found it increasingly hard to shake off the melancholia he brought from home in order to join in the collegiate banter. In the solitude of the delivery room, he rummaged deep into postbags, a shirtsleeve rolled up to his pointy elbow, to extract what he hoped would be something special. Each time, he closed his eyes and forced his breath to grow slow and deep. His ribcage expanded like the bellows of old, his lungs paused at their fullest expansion, before he slowly exhaled, with a gentle whoosh. He hunched over the slate-grey canvas bag, with his left hand supporting the small of his back, and wriggled the fingers of his right hand inside. His thirty-seven years didn't command this posture; it was more an affectation that had evolved as part of his hunting regime. With great concentration, he would linger over the folds of the envelopes, squeeze parcels tentatively between forefinger and thumb, until, instinctively, he would clasp one, tugging it gently free and drawing it to the surface. He imagined he was like the mechanical arm of a teddy-bear machine, retrieving a soft toy. These rescue missions were different from the piles of post left indiscriminately on his desk every morning at six by the night-owl team who accepted the midnight deliveries. The letters that he found this way, he believed were destined for him. Over ten years of flirting with coincidence, defying the odds and witnessing serendipity had left him superstitious and more inclined to believe in a divine intervention he would have mocked in his days before the depot. He now was convinced that some letters found him because only he, with his particular personal collection of experiences and insights, could crack their code. Other letters depended upon different detectives, of that he was sure, but some were searching specifically for him.

Last Tuesday, Marjorie, the longest-standing member of his team, had crept up behind him as he indulged in this ritual. He turned and saw her standing there, in her coral-pink mohair polo-neck, multiple gold chains dangling, her hand on her hip. The twinkle of a tease glinted in her eyes. The shock caused him to drop the letter he had retrieved and he felt a blush spread from under his collar and burn through his beard. With no explanation of his furtive activity to offer, he just nudged his black, square-rimmed spectacles further on to the bridge of his nose, mumbled a noise somewhere between a hello, a throat clear and a cough, and brushed past. Her satisfied laugh followed him to the cloakroom, where he rested his forehead against the cool dampness of the mirror and willed his cherry cheeks to fade. His bowel twisted and churned. Why had her seeing his routine bothered him so much? How deeply embarrassed he felt that his secret-self behaviour had been witnessed; actions he performed for himself that had never been intended for an audience. His mortification slowly gave way to irritation. Why had she been creeping about, anyway? No decent person wears shoes that whisper.

William risked a long look in the mirror. His curls looked tangled and his beard needed trimming. Something about his eyes made him nervous. They seemed, well, less brown. Like faded chocolate. It was probably just the fluorescent light bulbs. Eyes don't fade, do they? Was he vanishing? A man diluted? He shrugged his navy-blue pullover into position and braved the sorting office. Stifled giggles followed him as he took his seat at the end of the old boardroom table. He liked to sit with his back to the wall with the window overlooking the street to the right, mysteries lined up in rows to his left. His seat was the furthest away from the furnace trolleys, too. He hated the cremations. Failure in every spoonful of ash.

The faint strains of an old jazz number floated up from the street. It swirled out from one of the heaving hot spots that left William so cold. He could almost place the song, but it danced just beyond his consciousness as he tried to ignore the taunt. Was it 'Old Devil Moon'? He drifted away from the cardboard box of blue fountain pens he had opened, soon to be returned to a warehouse in Leeds as per the enclosed invoice, and tuned into the melody. He closed his eyes and followed his wife, Clare, down the spiral staircase to the jazz club of their first date, the Blue Rooms, on Montgomery Row in Notting Hill. He remembered how his hand had been slippery on the rail, his corduroy blazer too restrictive, his throat dry and knees shaky as he watched her stamp down the stone steps in her white fur boots. Her blonde hair was tied up messily in a yellow silk scarf that looked to be tickling the back of her neck. His fingers itched to do the same. He ached to pull that silky knot loose and watch her hair tumble about her shoulders.

All during the evening, he couldn't quite believe that he was there with Clare in a romantic capacity. Was she just filling in time with him while awaiting a more deserving suitor to woo her? Could she possibly also harbour hopes of something more than friendship?

They had met in very platonic circumstances, when William attempted to organize a book club on their university campus to tackle some of the great literary tomes. Week one: *War and Peace*. No one came. Week two: *The Divine Comedy*. Once again, he was a lonely soul in the Daffodil Room of the library, which he had so enthusiastically reserved; he had even asked the librarian to bring in some extra chairs. *Ulysses* was to be his third and final attempt, and he waited with dwindling hope for some like-minded folk to help him fill that echoing room. When the door creaked open, he was flustered by the vision that floated towards him. Clare, bundled up in a crimson duffel coat and white denim dungarees, looked more modern-day fairy tale than first-year student. Blonde tendrils escaped from an untidy bun held in place on top of her head with green chopsticks. Her left shoulder sagged under the strain of a canary-yellow canvas bag crammed full of books. When she dropped it on the mahogany desk, the contents spilled across the polished surface: *The Female Eunuch*, *Mother Courage and Her Children*, *Persuasion*, sunflower seeds, colouring pencils, a battered and bruised burgundy leather address book and a sepia postcard of James Joyce completely covered in tiny cursive handwriting. For ever after, William would always feel a certain gratitude to Joyce, not just for writing the books he loved so much but for bringing this woman into his life. Her words tumbled out in accompaniment to her belongings as she scanned the empty room.

'Are you William? Am I in the right place? Where is everyone else?'

'Eh, yes, I am, and I've been asking myself that for a few weeks now, but it's just me, I'm afraid. And you – you are?'

'Clare. Clare Carpenter.' She pulled a ratty, striped mitten off her hand and reached out to shake his. 'Do two people make a group?'

'A very exclusive one, perhaps. Or, at the very least, a conversation. That is, if you'd still like to stay?'

Clare slid into the seat opposite him, the legs of her chair screeching violently on the marble floor. His nose twitched at a faint smell of cinnamon.

'Why not?' she answered. 'At least we won't have to compete to get a word in.'

William steeled his nerve to hold her gaze.

'Gosh, your eyes are two different colours. Like David Bowie. How bizarre!' He hesitated for a moment. 'How lovely.'

Clare looked away as she gathered together the contents of her bag. 'It's not as uncommon as you might think. Let's begin, shall we?'

Discussion of *Ulysses* evolved to talk of books in general and favourites in particular. Over the following weeks, Clare introduced William to Iris Murdoch, Edna

O'Brien and Jane Austen; he shared his passion for Albert Camus and Samuel Beckett. Dissecting the worldview of the characters allowed them to delve into subjects that otherwise would have been too emotive for a casual acquaintance.

'Would Virginia Woolf have surrendered her writing for a peaceful mind? I don't know if I would smooth out all my edges at the expense of what she found in those corners.'

'The reason women love Mr Darcy so much is that he changed for the love of a good woman. How many lives have been wasted in the hope of that very outcome to a futile situation?'

'What Jack Kerouac gives me is a licence to be discriminatory about how I spend my time, who I spend it with, not surrendering to small talk and sycophants who need us to reflect and reinforce each other so that we can all feel we're okay. It sounds harsh, but it's true: I'd rather be alone than pretend.'

The sanctuary of the Daffodil Room was soon replaced by cluttered coffee shops and the little alehouse off campus which their professors monopolized. They baked cheese scones and experimented with cooking Indian food, making pizza and mixing mojitos at home. They cheered along the drama society's faltering theatre programme and volunteered at a homeless shelter, dishing out hot soup and self-conscious smiles on the last Thursday of every month. Sometimes, William saw Clare linking arms with other men as they crossed campus between lectures or sat clinking glasses in The Lighthouse pub. He tried to curb his jealousy by reassuring himself that their friendship was different, closer, but he didn't know if that was true. He craved to know her passionate self – whether she dabbed perfume behind her ears or smudged on red lipstick when she heard him at the door – but that part of her eluded him. In the beginning, they left notes in each other's lockers to confirm dates and times to meet, but soon their deposits had expanded to include little jokes, mix-tapes or snippets from newspapers, and William became prone to copying out passages from his favourite poems for her. What he had not yet discovered was how Clare secreted away each one, pressing and smoothing them carefully under the plastic sheaths of an army-green-cloth-covered photo album embroidered with yellow roses. It became a written record of their courtship as it delicately evolved. She gave it to him as his wedding present: the story of them so far, with blank pages left over for them to continue.

William cast his mind back to the afternoon when they had taken their first tentative steps to what would become a shared life. It was autumn. A westerly wind scattered crisping leaves around their feet and stirred a profound change within William. He could not endure one more minute of this constant low-level anxiety about their friendship, nor bear to sustain his neutrality for another second. As he sat on the floor of his bedsit, helping Clare to sand down a rocking chair she had dragged home from a flea market with the intention of painting it duck-egg blue, the urge to speak bubbled up inside him with increasing force. They had been working in silence for twenty minutes when he abruptly stood up and started folding his sandpaper into an awkward square.

'Clare, there's something I have to ask you.'

She looked up from where she sat; her legs stretched on either side of the rocker in a perfect triangle, black-and-white striped socks peeking out from inside the hem of her tartan flares.

'Uh-oh. This sounds ominous. Should I be worried?'

'I hope not.' William's eyes danced across her face, lingering on her own before they darted away at the critical moment. 'I was just wondering, could I, perhaps, take you out on Saturday night?'

Clare coiled her hair into a braid that curled around her throat and watched him fidget in his too-shiny brown leather brogues. Earlier, she had teased him that they looked like they were fashioned out of conkers. She pushed a bruise on her forearm.

'What are you talking about? We go out all the time. We've spent every Saturday night together for the last six weeks.'

William sighed. 'Not on our own we haven't.'

He cursed himself for not considering in advance what to say, but the words had just burst from him like air from an over-inflated balloon. Clare jumped up and punched him playfully on the arm, a huge grin on her face.

'William Woolf, are you asking me out on a date?'

He stood tall, shoulders back, with his hands clasped behind him as if he were appealing to a jury in court.

'Yes, indeed! That's exactly what I am doing and, if you don't want to, well, I guess I'll live down the mortification in about eight to ten years, but I would be grateful if you saved me the pain of having to avoid you for that length of time. I really don't want to have to drop out of uni, or move to Alaska, or start wearing disguises to avoid you. All in all, I think it would be much easier for us both if you just agreed.'

He made a little bow at the end of his speech and a flop of brown curls tumbled across his forehead. She reached forward to brush them back behind his ear and said, 'Well, when you put it like that, it does rather appear so. Hypothetically speaking, if I were to say yes, where would we go?'

'I haven't quite worked that out yet, but does that mean you're coming? Stop smirking – you're torturing me.'

'Well, I'll think about it and –'

'Oh, I see. Well, I appear to have misinterpreted things here,' he interrupted, his face crestfallen. 'I'll carry this home for you so you can be on your way.'

He struggled to pick up the rocking chair in a bear hug and began wrestling it towards the door. Clare's guffaw followed him and intercepted his flustered flee. He turned towards her and she helped him lower the chair to the floor.

'Of course I'll come, you fool. You wait four months to raise the question and then expect an immediate acceptance! You're not very good at this, are you?' She sighed and sat back down on the floor with fresh sandpaper in her hand. 'Maybe that's a good thing,' she said.

And so William had followed a yellow silk scarf down the wrought-iron staircase of a smoky jazz club, wondering if a kiss waited in the air between them. They sat in the smallest booth, tucked away in an alcove. Clare drew circles in the threadbare blue velvet of the banquette with her finger and tucked one bare leg beneath her. William reshaped the melting wax of the candle into odd little figurines and nudged closer to her. Over rum cocktails they could not afford, and bowls of olives they stole from other tables, stories saved for night-time were told. They shared confessions in the shadowy candlelight: tales of childhood, secret dreams of the future, the little worries they carried like pebbles in their pockets.

'I don't need to know where you came from to know you had a happy childhood, William. I have a sixth sense now for children of my ilk; I can see it in their eyes, but yours have no shadows at all.'

'In all honesty, I'm terrified that I'll end up a mediocre man who never had the nerve to turn his dreams into something real. I don't want to become an English teacher bashing teenagers over the head with books they don't care about. I want to write my own, one that will set their brains and hearts on fire!'

'I've never wanted to get married and I hate the thought of a wedding; parading my dysfunctional family in front of my friends while I waddle along in a big white dress. I really can't imagine anything worse. Could you see yourself doing it?'

Not long after midnight, they ascended the stairs from the basement back out into the city night. This time, Clare led William by the hand. It had started to snow. He spun her in a circle, a light, white dust sprinkling down on them. Clare wrenched a red-and-white polka-dot umbrella from her denim rucksack and released it above their heads.

'There are,' she said, 'few things more romantic than a shared umbrella.'

He kissed the top of her head and whispered, 'I can think of one.'

Their first kiss chased away any lingering doubts he had about her feelings for him. When they arrived back at William's, he unpacked a Super-8 camera from a compact charcoal leather suitcase under his single bed. They stood on the front steps of the Georgian house where he rented the basement flat and filmed the snowflakes dancing in the moonlight. Clare lay in the garden in her crimson duffel coat and fanned her legs and arms to make an angel. William captured it all on film; it was a silent movie he often returned to in the years to come as he settled down to sleep. He remembered drying her legs in his only good towel, the orange one with a giraffe in the centre, which had been airing on the radiator. He rubbed life back into them as she hummed along with David Bowie singing 'Wild as the Wind' on the radio. It was much too early to tell Clare how much he loved her, but Bowie sang the words for him. It was easy to believe they were the only two people listening to John Peel that evening and that he had chosen the song just for them.

William sat in the depot and ran that film through his mind once more but, these days, the actors felt like strangers. His wife's hair was brown now, rather than blonde. And much shorter. She had stopped dying it when she started her work experience at the solicitor's. Nobody takes a pretty blonde barrister seriously, apparently, and definitely not one with silk scarves in her hair. It wasn't just their physical selves that had changed, though, that part was easily understood; what confused him was trying to identify when their feelings had altered. Was it a million little incremental changes over a long period of time? Or something obvious he had missed? If their essential selves were still the same, couldn't they find each other again? Or had they travelled too far down separate roads to reconnect in a different but happier place? The music swarmed over him like a misty fog rolling in from the Atlantic Ocean, and he luxuriated in it. The past felt more friend to him, now, than the present.

2.

Marjorie snapped William to attention for the second time that day; she clinked a silver spoon with a peach-coloured plastic handle against the side of his Charlie Chaplin mug. 'Yoo-hoo, William! Time for elevenses! It's your turn to do the honours.' He touched his lips with his fingers. Were these the same ones Clare had kissed? Had he really pulled that sliver of silk free? He rose and carried his mug to the kitchen, where he guiltily stirred two spoonfuls of sugar into a fresh cup. Sugar was banned in his home and William had made a ludicrous promise to stop taking it in tea altogether. Now, the refuge of a milky, sugary mugful was tainted by Clare's cross voice, but he couldn't resist the sweetness. When had he lost the will to argue over sugar? The right to surrender to tooth decay, false highs or type-two diabetes of his own free will had been robbed from him. Why admit defeat on this point when they had slammed doors over so many other things: moving the driver's seat in the car back and forth; whose turn it was to wash up; what the answering-machine message would say; where to spend Christmas; whether to go on holiday and, if so, where; temperature control; volume control; affection control?

So many power struggles, but the sugar ban could not be contested. Each grain was a thread Clare longed to pull. One pinch led to his self-indulgence, another to his alleged Peter Pan syndrome, a third to his lack of ambition. It would leave him open to questions concerning his lack of responsibility and her unhappiness with their lot. William had become acutely aware of the triggers. He walked blindly into so many kitchen catastrophes that their early life together had not prepared him for: finishing the leftovers, not finishing the leftovers, buying a rose for her from a market stall, not posting her mother's birthday present, admitting he was thinking about reforming his old band, the Bleeding Hearts, with Stevie.

The very thought of William cavorting about the country with Stevie and his misfit collective caused a muscle in Clare's temple to throb visibly. At university, she had possessed a greater level of tolerance for their antics and peculiar brand of glam-folk, but her enthusiasm waned when advancing years did nothing to deter Stevie from his flamboyant misadventures in self-destruction. William looked back on their 'Toilet Tour' triumphs with a bittersweet nostalgia that sometimes overwhelmed him. He missed the swagger by association of playing keyboards for Stevie; the confidence and confidants; the potential for calamity and hilarity erupting at any moment. He pined for the nights when Clare had swayed in front of the stage, arms bedecked in dozens of silver bangles that twinkled in the light, purple leg-warmers sliding towards her ankles as she danced. Whenever he looked out at the audience, she always caught his eye, and he felt himself grow taller by her witness.

These days, the only moments of unpredictability in

his life came within the walls of the depot. At home, he felt like a frightened rabbit, constantly sniffing the air for an ill wind. Clare was a queen of entrapment, but some traps the rabbit saw glinting miles away. The sugar was a dare he would not challenge. He wasn't trained for this heart-to-heart combat and was desperate to avoid any more injury. William nursed his contraband and tuned back into the conversation that was circling around him.

'I just think,' said Marjorie, 'that valentines only matter if they arrive by the fourteenth. A couple of weeks could be the difference between 'appily ever after and takin' out a personal ad. There'll be a lot of soggy pillows an' sulky silences if some of this lot don't make it.' Her left hand, stained with orange fake tan, nails painted metallic pink, formed a right angle with her hip.

Mr Ned Flanagan, the Dead Letters Depot director, opened and closed the kitchen cupboards with increasing speed.

'That's all well and good, Miss Clarke, but there are just as many other undeliverables we need to get through that are far more important than Sarah in the sixth form telling some pimply *footie* player that she is *up for it*, or what have you. We cannot simply ignore everything else and prioritize love affairs over all the other, more important, business of the world. There could be –'

Marjorie cut him off as he removed his glasses to polish them in a peach linen handkerchief.

'Well, with all due respect, sir, it's clear you ain't ever been in love. Nothin'll slow down the business of the world like broken 'earts. We 'ave to help Cupid do his job. That's *our* part to play.'

'More like we must help Stupid! I'll have you know, Mrs Flanagan and I have enjoyed a love-filled marriage for over thirty-five years now. If you don't love someone enough to remember their post code, it doesn't look too good, from where I'm standing. Billy, what do you think?'

Mr Flanagan rapped his knuckles on the counter-top to get William's attention. He was the only person who called him Billy.

'William, sir. It's William.'

'Yes, Yes, William, Billy, Willy – it's all the same. Now, what do you think about this idea to move everyone on to valentines duty?'

William scratched his fingers through his beard. 'As much as I share Marjorie's soft spot for a love story,' he said, 'I think everything should be dealt with by normal procedure, and the valentines just have to join the back of the queue. Otherwise, it's not fair on the others.'

In truth, however, William was not sure he was in the right frame of mind to be facilitating love's young dream, not when his own great love story was being stretched so thin. A thought struck him: if he and Clare completely dissolved, did that mean she wasn't his great love, after all? He shook the question away as he watched Ned's back retreat.

'There you are, Miss Clarke,' he called over his shoulder. 'The voice of reason. Good man, Billy. Now, go team!'

Mr Flanagan had recently attended a seminar on Staff

Motivation and Morale, with, at best, mixed results. He thrust a self-conscious fist into the air in lacklustre victory and skipped out of the room, away from Marjorie's look of blatant contempt. William splashed the dregs of his drink into the sink and ran after him, catching him on the stairs.

'Mr Flanagan, I was just wondering if you've had a chance yet to read my presentation on the Supernaturals? If you think it's worth developing, I'd love to get started.'

'Yes, Billy, I gave it a glance. First of all, I don't think God can really be considered a supernatural being.'

William shuffled a little on the step, pausing before he spoke again. 'I see. Well, I just meant it as a collective term for those addressees that don't exist in reality. We could try something else. Maybe "Mythical Creatures" or "The Others"?'

Mr Flanagan raised his eyebrows and leaned in a little closer. 'So you think God is a *mythical* creature, Billy?'

'I don't really think anything at all about him, sir. What we name them isn't really the point. It's more what we do with them.'

Of all the fascinating worlds opened to William by the Dead Letters Depot, the Supernatural Division (as he thought of it) intrigued him the most. On the fourth floor, rows of mail sacks were lined up in metal-framed structures like flip-top bins. At the front of each row, a laminated sign in bold moss-green capitals was taped to the floor to identify each category: GOD, SANTA, SCIENCE FICTION, SAINTS & PROPHETS,

TV/FILM CHARACTERS, LITERARY FIGURES, STARS and OTHER. It was true that much of the mail in the depot was intended for flesh-and-blood people who walked the earth. It was the degree of magic that people must believe in for *the other* types of mail to be delivered, however, that forced the fourth floor to adopt a supernatural element for William. An uncanny number of people all over the country took pen to paper and wrote to idols, icons and ideas: Elvis, the Tooth Fairy, Yoda, St Anthony. These messages in a bottle, trails of bread left in the forest, obsessed William. Who were these true believers and how long did they wait for a reply? Was the writing more important than the response? Did the writers tell anyone that they had written these letters? Were they relieved or saddened that their unanswered prayers had fallen on deaf ears?

For some time, William had wanted to create a volume of these missives for public record. He felt there was a cast of thousands currently speaking into the void but who deserved to be heard. Other letter detectives had their own obsessions: Trevor had sought his job purely to fuel his philately; Morgana had a collection of questionably private photographs that everyone pretended didn't exist; Roger diligently worked on translations from foreign languages; Dolores was determined to reunite manuscripts, books of poetry or short stories with their scribes; and for Marjorie, it was, of course, love letters and, in particular, valentines. The Supernatural Division was William's great obsession and what inspired the stories of his imagination.

There was already a Seasonal Santa Unit, commissioned every December to answer all the children who wrote to Father Christmas and helpfully included their addresses. The staff tried to personalize the letters a little so as not to dispel belief, should the children compare with each other. Fan mail to stars of stage and screen was sent to production companies or agents. Missives to deceased celebrities were despatched to next of kin, their fan club or the manager of the estate. It was the letters to God, to mythics and mystics, to the *other*, that haunted William and formed the basis of his work. He had started collecting his favourites in the filing cabinets that lined the echoing Supernatural Division. He painstakingly typed out those he wanted to include in the volume and took photographs of the original documents. In his mind's eye, he saw the two laid side by side on glossy, ivory pages within hard covers, the book entitled 'A Volume of Lost Letters'.

Mr Flanagan peered over his spectacles at William. 'The truth of it is, Billy, we shouldn't really be opening those letters. You know very well it is illegal to open any mail unless we believe that there is some chance we can forward it on to its ultimate destination. If a letter is addressed to God, what do you think you are going to learn from the contents about the intended address? It seems a bit dubious to me, if I'm truthful.'

'Some of the letters we have here are over fifty years old,' replied William. 'Nobody is going to lodge a complaint, and I think people would get a lot out of being able to read them. They're cultural artefacts, really.' William stopped his left foot tapping on the marble step when he saw Mr Flanagan peering at his mustard polka-dot socks.

'I admire your enthusiasm, Billy, but I just think it's terribly unfair on those people who believe they really *are* writing to God. If they discover in your book a whole edition of other people's letters and understand that the only recipient was one of us, what will that do to their morale?'

'Maybe they'll just be pleased to know that someone is listening?'

'Dear boy, with all due respect, I doubt they were hoping for *you*. I'm afraid we'll never get it past the board. Not at the moment, anyway. I agree that the archiving you are doing is worthwhile – a time capsule, if you will – but making these letters public is just not feasible. Also, it has been noticed that you have been spending too much time on the fourth floor. It's time to get back to the business we hired you to do. God can take care of the others.'

Mr Flanagan gave William's shoulder an awkward squeeze before hastening downstairs to hide in his office until Mrs Flanagan collected him at five o'clock in their turquoise Ford Fiesta.

William gulped back disappointment, ran his fingers through his hair, pulling the frustration from his scalp, through the messy curls. The tugging released some tension and he indulged in a long, deep breath that made his woollen jumper swell and collapse. In an act of self-satisfied defiance, he continued up the stairs to the fourth floor, despite Mr Flanagan's warning. A new trolley of fantastical endeavours awaited him, and he dived straight in. The first letter he pulled out had just one word on the envelope: 'God'. It looked like the handwriting of an old lady: curvy and elegant, letters practised first in chalk, then pencil and, eventually, ink. The 'G' started strong, the nib tearing a tiny scratch in the manila envelope. The 'o' and the 'd' were frailer, as if the writer had grown tired even before finishing the word. William read slowly.

Dear God,

It has been a long time since I went to confession. The last time I went, Fr Fitzpatrick told me a woman with six children could have no sins, so I never went back. It's not right, though, because, as you well know, I am a sinner. Every morning, I wake up and curse the light meeting my eyes. I wish that you had let me go in my sleep – to be with Joe. I know that's a terrible sin. I should be grateful for the new dawn, more time with my children and the grandkiddies. But I'm a burden on them now, and Joe's the one who needs me. I'm sure you're looking after him, but he has his own way of going on, and I'm not sure he'd make a fuss if he was worried. He's never been very good at speaking his mind to strangers. He'll just draw in on himself, like he did during his spell in the hospital. After all those years, I think he'll miss having me to talk to, and the way I helped him into his overcoat, and out of his boots, made sure none of the different types of food touched each other on his plate. Unless you have more work for me here, will you let me go to him? I had a dream last night that I was in Heaven. Joe was sitting beside me on a promenade by the finest-looking sea – bluer and greener than I've ever seen in Blackpool, that's for sure. An orchestra was playing on the bandstand and Joe asked me to dance, and we could. His old hip was like new, his hands steady, back straight, and no touch of arthritis in my legs. We danced like we were sixteen again. And when I woke up, I cried like I was a silly sixteen-year-old, too.

Dear God, forgive me and please let me come to you. Help me find my Joe.

Your faithful servant,

Mrs Vera Flynn, Number 16

William folded the pale-blue page back along the crease and slipped it carefully inside its envelope. He couldn't imagine Clare pining for him like that now, worrying about him after he'd gone, wanting to join him. He mourned for *her*, though, so much already, even though he saw her every day. Each time he heard her laughing on the telephone, or saw her hands waving animatedly at a party, he wished the joke were his, the banter with him. He missed her teasing him about what she called his 'grandad chic', how she had persisted in coaxing him on to dance floors, where his two clumsy feet could be only an embarrassment, missed the way she picked all the raisins out of her scones and made a little pile on his plate for him to finish for her. So many little moments, inconsequential on their own, but the cumulative effect was staggering. He stopped himself unravelling before the pang sank in too deeply, placed Vera's letter in the GOD bin, and returned to his desk, where he scooped up a bundle of new letters from the top of a postbag. He opened them one by one. The first was in an A4 brown envelope with sticky residue where once an address label must have lived.

Mr Papadopoulos,

I hope this letter makes its way to you before your wife gets a chance to intercept it. Why must she always stand between us? It won't be long now until we can be together – I am sure of it. Keep saving, as will I, and our time will come. In the meantime, I will blow you a kiss every day as I wait for my bus across from your shop. If the light is right, I can catch a glimpse of your white coat as you work. How I long to lay my head against that starched cotton once again and breathe in the smell of flour and dough from your skin.

Until then, I remain your impatient love,

J.

A baker named Papadopoulos in London? He was hopeful that the letter could be delivered, if not for the outcome of that delivery. Did the man know that J was watching him? It was not his place to judge; just to mediate, where he could.

The second envelope barely housed its contents, so ragged had it become from having, clearly, been submerged in water. The typed letter inside, though streaked, was just about legible.

Dear Ms Joyce,

Thank you for your recent submission to our *Human Bodies* periodical. Unfortunately, we are unable to include it on this occasion, but we do appreciate the time you evidently spent preparing it. Your accompanying cartoons were particularly illuminating.

Yours in writerly felicity,

Elizabeth Tartt

William was sorry that Elizabeth Tartt hadn't returned the cartoons so he could see them; how bizarre! Perhaps some things were best left unseen.

The third envelope had no address at all; 'Desmond Downe' was all that was written on the front. Had someone forgotten to write the address before they mailed it, or had it been posted in error?

Dear Desmond,

I know that I owe you an explanation, and a better one than this letter can offer. I know, too, that I am a coward to run without speaking to you in person, but I was afraid that, if I tried to, you would talk me round. There is no easy answer as to why I can't marry you. You have only been loving and good. I know that any woman would be blessed to have a man such as you to take care of her, but I think that's the problem – I don't want to be taken care of. I feel so safe with you, but so much so that I end up feeling like I'm smothered in cotton wool. I need to see more of the world, to try some more things that scare me and find out what I'm capable of. I know that you will find that hard to understand, but please know you haven't done anything wrong. And I promise there is no one else, at least no one that I've met yet. I'm just chasing the dream of another sort of life that's full of sights and sounds and smells that are unfamiliar and mysterious, shocking and soothing. Someone else will come along who will take so much pleasure in your lovely life amidst all your fine things in Herne Hill, a life that would have been wasted on me. Until she comes along, take good care of yourself, and please, try not to think too poorly of me.

Yours in friendship,

Melanie

William left Desmond's letter to one side to see if he could track him down in Herne Hill. He would surely know by now that Melanie wasn't returning, but at least if the letter found him he might have a better understanding of why she had left. He couldn't imagine anything worse than arriving home one day and discovering Clare had gone without a word. How long would you wait before accepting that your partner wasn't coming home? Could you forgive them if they did? The fourth envelope had nothing at all written on it.

Mr Piot,

I return these leather gloves to you in addition to the pot of lilies, the oyster truffles and the silk scarf that I have already sent back. Please stop sending me these presents; it is entirely inappropriate and my husband is becoming increasingly furious. The connection you believe we share is entirely fictional and I have given you no encouragement. The next letter I write will be to the police.

Sincerely,

Mrs Assumpta Llewellyn

Marjorie was right: they were overwhelmed by valentines. William took a perfunctory look to see if the parcel containing leather gloves could have come undone in transit, but there was no trace. He wished Mr Piot, Mrs Llewellyn and Ms Joyce well as he dropped them into the shredder receptacle; there was nothing more he could do for them. He decided to launch one more search mission before he returned to his desk. He assumed position and rummaged around in the overflowing trolley. This time, he dug deep. His fingers brushed against an unusual texture, thick and soft with grooves, like old wallpaper. It was just as he imagined paper might have felt in days long ago, when men on horseback carried letters through the night. When he manoeuvred the envelope out into the light, its colour surprised him. He had expected it to be ivory, or brilliant white, a very elegant wedding invitation, perhaps, but it was midnight blue. The colour just before blue becomes navy; the darkest, most mysterious shade on the spectrum. And his favourite.

The handwriting on the front consisted of curls and spirals, dramatic capitals, carefully crafted lower-case letters, all in a dripping silver ink. There were just three words: 'My Great Love'. William held the envelope close to examine the grooves in the darkness of the pages, and smelled the faintest trace of vanilla. Something stirred inside him. He ached to open this envelope. Not here, though. He slipped it inside his shirt pocket and felt it radiate hot light through the cotton and on to his bare skin. He had never taken a letter home before. He longed to read it but wanted to save it for somewhere else, a private moment on his own. He couldn't risk Marjorie seeing it and whisking it away to be part of her lonely-hearts collection; somewhere deep inside him, he knew this one was different.

The afternoon crawled along, a dying man clawing for the border. Eventually, William and his little mystery could wrap themselves in the cherry-red wool scarf knitted by his mother and vanish into the city. He hoped he would be able to exit the building without bumping into Marjorie, who would insist they walk together up the Bethnal Green Road. She was always 'just ready to run', but still managed to delay for a further fifteen minutes, changing her black patent court shoes for old runners, popping to the *little girls' room*, collecting her Wonder Woman lunch box from the fridge and, most maddeningly of all, turning the coffee-shop sign she hung over her desk from OPEN to CLOSED. Infuriating. As if any work happened when she was 'open', or anyone ever came looking for her. Everyone was far too busy pretending to be on the telephone, rushing to a meeting, or hiding under their desks whenever Marjorie did her rounds. With alarming regularity, she patrolled each floor, resting her ample buttocks on any desk where she sniffed out a welcome. Her 'Auntie of the Year' cup often left a tea-stain ring in her wake.

On the pained evenings when William was subjected

to walking with Marjorie, he cursed his misfortune all the way to the bus stop. She always linked her arm in his, and he worried, with a deep sense of shame, that despite their obvious age difference, passers-by might think they were a couple. He always felt compelled to wait with her until the bus came, holding her plastic bag containing the lunch box and a copy of *Woman's Way* for her while she smoked a cigarette, trying not to stare at the line on her jaw where the orange make-up stopped and the pale, blue-veined skin of her neck began. Clare always stuck up for Marjorie, said she was lonely and he shouldn't be so heartless, that Marjorie could be her Ghost of Christmas Future, for all they knew. William thought it was easy to be compassionate about people who exist to you only as an abstract idea, as opposed to the physical beings who leave tea stains on your files and choke you with Poison perfume. He couldn't bear to see Marjorie again today, to bat away her incessant valentines campaigning, so he broke Rule Eleven of the 'DLD Charter for Good Professional Practice' and slipped out through the fire escape.

Clare would be home late that evening; Tuesday nights were reserved for her pole-dancing class, of all things. She was constantly starting courses that she seldom finished and was often away attending conferences. In the last eighteen months, Clare had lost fourteen pounds of fat she couldn't afford training for a marathon she didn't run; half made a summer dress that hung forlornly without sleeves in their wardrobe; joined a photography group and devoted a whole weekend to making a stop-motion film of the pages of a book slowly turning. She studied

Vietnamese cooking without ever preparing them a meal, and learned Italian with no immediate plans to set foot on the Boot. They talked about her classes, but she never invited him to come along to any final-night drinks or sign up for one with her. He worried it was all a ruse to avoid coming home, but he was too afraid to ask. The pole dancing had unnerved him the most. Clare insisted it was just a high-energy fitness class, a more interesting method of calorie burning and muscle toning than working out at a gym. It had nothing to do with erotica, apparently. And yet, when she packed her bag before work, with a pair of white stilettos, black shorts and a slinky silver vest, he felt jealous to be excluded. When he mentioned the class to Trevor in work, the look he received was one of sympathy. 'If it were my wife,' he'd suggested, 'I'd be asking myself some serious questions.' His reaction did little to ease William's discomfort, but he was determined to believe the classes were less about him and more about Clare's relationship with herself.

There was a time when she used to dress up for him; every occasion, a different ensemble, always when he least expected it. Before he met her, he thought antics like that existed only in films but, somehow, he found himself dressing up as Indiana Jones, eating mango as he perched on the stair handrail. His wife, who was always so sophisticated, elegant, refined. To think she had turned their bedroom into a bordello for his birthday weekend and collected him from work wearing nothing but a black silk ribbon under her winter coat. He sighed at the memory, but truly what he missed most was Clare at her most natural; perhaps stretched out on the couch in her awful lilac terrycloth dressing gown as she negotiated swapping a fried-egg sandwich for a hot-water bottle. Now, the stilettos peeking out of her bag, the flush on her cheeks when she came home after class, were cruel reminders of the fun they had once had. He longed to see her dance, tortured himself imagining how she looked as she span in time to the music, watching herself in the mirror. That part of her was slipping further and further out of his reach now, and he didn't know if he could ever have it back. It reminded him of when they had first met, before their first date, when he could only dream of knowing her so intimately – except, this time, he felt anxiety rather than excitement, because he had so much less hope. Less hope, he admitted, but not none. All was not lost.

William slammed the door of the fire escape and hastened up the street. He and Clare had lived in a flat in Tower Hamlets for five years. Clare had transformed it from a dingy two-bedroom disaster over an unpopular curry house into a home. All the furniture had been collected piece by piece from antiques markets, auctions and fairs. The mismatch of colours, history and texture should have clashed, but each element complemented something else, just as her good eye had intended. She had almost studied art at university before committing to law, and William wished she had, although Clare was pragmatic about it now. Only very occasionally would he hear the drag of her old portfolio across the wooden floor of their bedroom. Once, he watched her from the doorway as she held her paintings up to the light, running her fingers gently over the lines, smelling the paint. He had crept back down the hallway before she noticed him.

Although they loved their flat, had built it together, Clare had wanted to move for a long time. As the years wore on, she became more frustrated that they remained in a starter home, while their friends' houses, families and status grew. William refused, insisting they could only live somewhere if they could split the mortgage equally, and he was already at the limit of what he could afford. With every promotion Clare won at work, her dissatisfaction with their nest seemed to intensify. She thought it archaic that he wouldn't countenance them moving somewhere more expensive when she could afford to pay the mortgage on her own. He wouldn't back down, though, and Clare knew, on this point, she would never be able to change his mind.

William's route had defaulted towards home but instinct told him he should not take the letter there to read. Every so often, he ran his fingers over the pocket of his shirt to reassure himself he hadn't lost it. He thought about stopping in the Carpenter's Arms for a glass of red wine but couldn't face talking to Aggie, the landlady. If anyone was going to ask him about the letter, it would be Aggie, her silver locket tickling the top of the bar as she leaned across it to speak to him in her croaking voice, so he navigated towards Broadway Market. William crossed the bridge and walked along the riverbank to a bench beneath a streetlight. The envelope glowed in the yellow haze of the lamp. He tried to reason with himself for a moment. Where had this rush of anticipation come from? What had possessed him to sneak a letter out from the depot? He exhaled a deep breath and turned the envelope over. He broke the seal, running his finger under the fold, and creaked it open. Eased the letter from its home. Three pages, creased evenly in thirds, writing on one side only. He twisted on the bench to tilt the paper towards the light and started to read.

My Great Love,

Maybe this is the year you will find me. I hope so. I have been saving up so many stories to tell you, and I'm worried that if you stay away much longer they will all have slipped from my memory. I've forgotten so much already. Are you hiding somewhere? Are you lost? Do you not feel ready? I wish you would hurry.

I remember, when I first moved to this city, I loved how everyone was a stranger, but I also remember believing that my solitary state was a temporary situation. You are taking much longer to find me than I'd hoped. This morning, while waiting for the bus, I watched a dapper man's suitcase snap open and a pile of papers dance down Old Street. He was laughing, despite the calamity and the wind poking icy fingers between buttons, down collars and up trouser legs. London was grey and howling and his laugh carried in the wind like a tangerine lasso, pulling everyone in. A gaggle of girls in wine-coloured school uniforms rushed to help him. If he felt foolish, he was a happy fool. I wondered if it could be you. I ask myself that all the time as I walk about the city, when a certain sort of someone catches my eye. I find myself waiting for you to look up and notice me noticing you.

It will soon be Valentine's Day – what a perfect time to write to you, when lovers everywhere are wrapping, writing or worrying. I am in good spirits, although my hands are cold as I grip this silver pen. I've just arrived home from New York and the radiators have forsaken me now that the first spot of snow has fallen. I do love long-haul flights: the suspended reality, the anonymity, the disconnection from everything and everyone. Every passenger, an island. It's the most captivating waiting room in the world: sad eyes from leaving-behinds, excited hearts for going-tos, nervous bellies for the unknown, eager longings for the familiar. High up in the skies, we are free from decisions, action, responsibility, identity – reduced to being toddlers pushed in a pram by a stranger. Landing came almost too soon because, every time I fly, I dread the Arrivals lounge. It is so bittersweet to walk out past Security and see all the expectant faces of people waiting impatiently for someone who isn't me. In times gone by, my father would always be there, watching the Arrivals board for any changes, in position too early, just in case he missed me.

I wish you had been waiting for me when I came in this morning, an unread newspaper twisted under your arm, hair still ruffled from sleep. I wouldn't expect you to bring me flowers, but a fresh carton of milk waiting at home in the fridge would be lovely. I know you would take my suitcase and sweep me off my feet in one swift movement – I would well up, even though I hadn't been away for very long at all. But you weren't there. Instead, I dragged my case along by myself and waited in the rain for a taxi back to the city. When I eventually dripped into my flat, it was freezing. The milk in the fridge had turned sour and the bed was still messy, as I had left it. I'm not trying to make you feel guilty, I promise, but I have to tell you all the ways I miss you. The gaps you could fill are widening and I worry they will soon become too big for one person to satisfy. How can anyone be all the things that another needs? Answer all questions?

I wonder now if the choices that brought me to this city were clever ones. Since Christmas, I feel as if I am slipping further and further away from all that is familiar, all those that I love. I furiously write long letters on my lunch break and crackle down phone lines to try to connect with people at home, but it's not enough. My life is synopsized now into anecdotes and reflections after the fact. News is old before it is told, feelings forgotten before they are cried or laughed over, questions answered before they are asked. My old friends have no window into my life now. They can no longer picture me eating breakfast in Donnybrook, in the little flat over the cake shop that they knew so well. There are no faces for new names as we talk on the telephone. I try to paint some wordy pictures, but it gets harder.

I miss my friends and family so much, and that has made me miss you even more. It's true. I hope you miss me, too. Do you? Are you wandering around London, feeling that you've left your umbrella behind? (I do think you're the sort to carry an umbrella.) Do you have dreams of somewhere you've never been but wish you could go? Is your head full of thoughts that no one has quite the right ears for? Do you read about exhibitions, concerts, tours, plays, trips to the seaside, and wish you knew someone who would want to go along with you? Is your hand lonely in your pocket? It's me, I tell you! I'm your forgotten umbrella!

Oh dear, it just dawned on me that you mightn't be in London. Oh, I hope you are. It's hard enough filtering all those millions of people down to one as it is. Or worse still – you could be back in Ireland! No. I won't believe it. If you're not in London, you must come to find me here.

I'm not sure what I will do with this letter now, although I feel better for writing it. Forgive me for counting all the ways that I am lonely; it is not something I can do out loud.

I hope, somehow, that it finds you, and finds you well.

Yours,

Winter

3.

Clare couldn't force herself to look in the mirror, did not want to recognize herself as the creature before her. She resented her pale, pear-shaped body. Like a turkey hanging in the butcher's window at Christmas. With every year that passed, her bottom half widened but her upper body stayed the same and, in her mind, the disproportion had taken on gigantic importance. Having been effortlessly slender in her twenties, it shocked her how quickly her body had changed in the five years since she became thirty. She signed up for pole dancing, thinking it would make her feel better about her now more curvaceous shape, boost her confidence and help her remember how she used to move. In times past, she had felt graceful, conscious of the heat of men's eyes on her as she strode along the marble corridors between court rooms or danced until dawn at the jazz clubs she and William used to frequent. After she graduated, she bought her first pair of stilettos and practised walking up and down the aisles of the supermarket, pushing the trolley for balance and support. It paid off. Before long, she struggled to walk in anything flat; the arches of her feet were now unaccustomed to being horizontal and she loved the added height, even though William was a good two inches shorter than her. It never seemed to bother him either.

Of late, though, she had felt uncomfortably conspicuous, being so tall; an advantage wasted if you couldn't hold your spine straight, your shoulders back, your head high. Her grace felt balled up in her belly. She constantly resisted the urge to bend over and nurse it. The advertisement on the noticeboard at work for pole-dancing classes seduced her with the promise of sculpting her body back to its 'former glory' and 'rejuvenating her va-va-voom' with this new, vaguely taboo, craze. She knew that her self-esteem should not be determined by her physical appearance, but this wasn't about looking good for other people – this was about her own self-control, what made her feel strong and proud. Feeling like she had lost her fitness, her physique, made her worry that she was in a state of decline, but she wasn't ready to surrender just yet. The advertisement failed to mention, however, two elements crucial for the transformation: loving (or at least tolerating) your scantily clad reflection under fluorescent light and at least some natural capacity for gymnastics. Clare struggled through each class with mounting embarrassment. She could hold her position on the pole but, when the time came to slide down, she just couldn't let go. Instead of elegantly gliding to the base with her back arched, Clare descended inch by inch in stops and starts, burning the palms of her hands and leaving friction marks on her thighs. When all her classmates were ready to mount again, she was still clawing her way to the bottom, trying to ignore the looks of pity and the stifled laughter. She was sorely tempted to quit after the first week, to scuttle away with a feather boa between her legs, but she knew the failure would lower her spirits even further and so she persisted. Every week, Clare was optimistic that she would have a breakthrough moment. Each time, the other girls looked more and more accomplished and she remained clinging midway up the pole, praying for an end to come soon.

When Clare arrived home after class, she then had to suffer William's feigned nonchalance as he asked how it had been, if she had enjoyed herself. She couldn't tell him how awful it was, that it was the least erotic experience she had ever had the misfortune to undergo. In the past, they would have been in hysterical fits as she regaled him with her humiliation at the hand of Miss Fortuna. Not any more. His poorly disguised curiosity was probably the only bit of satisfaction she gleaned from going. After the first class, William had asked her if he would ever have the pleasure of a private performance. Clare was taken aback; she couldn't tell if he was genuinely excited at the prospect, saying what he thought he was supposed to, or mocking her. She walked to the bathroom without meeting his eye. 'Seeing as it took you eight months to install the towel rack,' she said, 'I won't hold my breath waiting for a pole.' William didn't reply. Before the door had fully closed, the tears she had been swallowing squeezed out in streams of salty sadness down her hot cheeks. She buried her face in William's dressing gown, the one he said made him feel like a Siberian prince, and inhaled the lingering peppermint smell of his soap. If she opened the door and showed him how upset she was, wouldn't he comfort her? Couldn't he still find ways and words to pull her out of this molasses? She missed him despite being no longer sure that the man she missed still existed.

On the evening of the day that William discovered Winter's letter, Clare was feeling particularly low. There was an option to sign up for an end-of-course performance and she was the only woman in the class who didn't want to do it. No one was surprised. Nor did they try to talk her into it. She sat in the car outside their flat holding her red-raw palms over her eyes, breathing through the bout of anxiety that crawled over her body like an army of ants. She could see the light on in the kitchen and knew William would be sitting there, reading yesterday's paper, unaware that he had grown cold until he stood up and stretched. A cup housing an Earl Grey teabag would sit on the counter, waiting for him to remember he had boiled the kettle. She knew him so well: the light and shade of his moods; when his eyes strained to see; the spot where his muscles always knotted in his left shoulder blade. Clare had always collected stories from her day which she thought would fascinate him, or jokes that would tickle him. She made a note of films, gigs or exhibitions he would be excited about, and stored them in her 'William' vault. She still mined all those observations, conditioned as she was to the practice, but she didn't share them with him any more. They were just filed away and forgotten. Any affectionate words stuck in her throat; she felt that any act of kindness would be taken as a reward for his disappointing behaviour. At times, she felt the fact that she was still with him at all was more than he deserved. She had done everything she could: keeping them financially afloat, humouring him when he spent the first summer after they were married on tour with Stevie, expecting patiently his great novel that never came. All these years, she had waited for him to fulfil the promise he held when they met. How could he be satisfied with working in that godforsaken depot? When people met them for the first time now, she knew what an unlikely pairing they must seem. If they themselves could meet anew as strangers, she thought it questionable they would even be friends – and a romance would be completely inconceivable. And yet, she couldn't turn her back completely on the memory of how much they once were the perfect pair. When her granny met William, she hugged Clare and said, 'When God made ye, he matched ye. For every sock, there's a shoe.' And she had known it was true.

She had started dating much too young: older boys who somehow tricked her into thinking they were the ones who needed impressing; insecure men who had tried to control her in order to feel more powerful. When she met William, she was shocked at how utterly effortless it was to be with him. And not because she didn't care enough, but because they both cared, and in equal amounts. William knew the punchline to her every joke; in his company, she was wittier, more outspoken, fearless in a way that she had never even considered being before. And in her attention, he bloomed. Before she met him, in her romantic entanglements, she had felt like she was trying desperately hard to recreate an idea of love she had drawn from black-and-white films shot on Parisian boulevards. After him, life was vivid; in full Technicolor.

When she walked into the flat, an aroma of soup wafted from the kitchen. Hearty, thick; real vegetables from the ground, stewing hot in a pot. Warming. Loving. Calling. She followed the trail and was amazed to find the kitchen gleaming in godly cleanliness. Normally, William's cooking involved ingredients exploding into every crevice of the kitchen and a mountain of encrusted saucepans balanced precariously in the sink. He turned down their crackling old record player, softening Bob Dylan's crooning of 'Don't Think Twice, It's All Right', and crossed the kitchen floor to peck her on the cheek. He was clearly very pleased with himself but trying to behave as if this little miracle of domesticity was an everyday occurrence. Clare was immediately suspicious; she hoped he didn't want to have a 'talk' or give her an ill-considered surprise. The last time he had made this big an effort was to announce that he had impulsively adopted a puppy. That was not a happy weekend. William had sulked like a child for a week after she made him take the mongrel back to Morgana in the depot. Why could he not have considered the practicalities of housing a growing dog in their already cramped living space without making her be the spoilsport again? She edged her way to the kitchen table, murmured something about the nice smell and waited for the bomb to drop while he ladled some soup into her favourite sea-green ceramic bowl. They had bought a set of four from a local potter on their honeymoon in Sorrento, but this was the only one that still survived. William had often said that he planned to order more for her, but had never quite managed it.

'So, what's all this in aid of, then?' she asked, while rifling through her briefcase. 'Have you broken something? Or invited a homeless person to come and live with us? Oh God, you haven't bought a motorbike, have you?'

William chose not to dwell on the worrying assumptions his wife made when confronted with his good deeds and swallowed the sting. 'No. Nothing in particular,' he answered, stirring the soup. 'I just know you've been working hard and, well, sometimes I feel I could do more here to –'

'I've been working hard for ten years, William. Don't start feeling guilty now. We'll never get all the worms picked up from the floor.'

Clare felt a pang of remorse when she saw his face but couldn't bring herself to take it back. It was as if the only way she could cope with the weight of her worries was to release a little bit of pressure with a series of tiny blows. She couldn't explain how she really felt to him, not until she could accept the idea that the end of the conversation could herald the end of them, too. Instead, she pulled a copy of *Marie Claire* from her bag and smoothed it open on the table. She scanned an interview with an American opera singer, Carletta da Carlo, who had retired to Rome and was growing ever plumper from a heady mix of sunshine, pasta and a new romance. Her eyes wandered over black-and-white photographs of Carletta posing on the

Spanish Steps in an ivory satin evening gown, and her mind travelled back to her own, more painful, excursion to the city, when she had still been in the throes of her last, angsty affair before she met William.

She could see herself now, perched on the rim of a dried-up old fountain, the sleeves of her jumper stretched over her hands, past their give, the stitches strained at the shoulders. She could still feel the scratchy black wool on her face as it soaked up the angry tears and runny mascara that stung the corners of her eyes. She crouched, her back a half-moon, head upon hands upon knees. A hot little cave of rage, sounds of her hiccupy sobs booming in her ribcage. She could feel the eyes of strangers upon her and was relieved when no one offered any help. Eventually, as she felt the grip of panic loosening, Jamie's shadow fell across her, blocking the relentless Roman sun. She refused to look up and just stared at his oxblood military boots with the ridiculous black-and-white chequered laces and buckles flapping open. Although she desperately wanted some kind of resolution, she wouldn't ask for it. He grasped her shoulders and pulled her to her feet. She didn't struggle but kept her head lolled forward like a puppet with its strings cut until he let her go. With her eyes squeezed tightly closed, she held her breath. A moment passed as she listened to his breathing, fast, hot and impatient, but he didn't say anything. She looked up at him through her frizzy fringe. He was pointing a camera straight at her. The shock stopped her crying. The flash blinded her for a second then he instantly turned on his heel and strutted off across the square.

'What are you doing? What's wrong with you?' she shouted after him.

He turned, cold, and with a smirk of satisfaction stretched across his face. 'Just a little memento of our romantic trip to Rome, Clare, in case I ever need reminding why we broke up here.' Her fury rendered her speechless as she watched him cut through the tourists and vanish from sight.

That night, the humid air hung heavy about them as they held hands across a candlelit table in the courtyard of a quiet *osteria*. Little white lights hung from the veranda as the waiter *prego*-ed back and forth, smiling at these strange young lovers who clutched at each other but looked so unhappy. Her stomach was churning, doubling and dancing with the shame of his disrespect and her inability to walk away, but now he was smiling and she was too relieved to jeopardize the fragile peace that had settled between them. She hoped they would make love that evening but dreaded the thought of it. Had not yet learned how much she could expect from love. And so it continued: the Jamie period of her life. Before their relationship had reached its ultimate crisis point, after so many near-misses. Before Clare's little sister, Flora, was called to come and collect her in the middle of the night. Jamie had pushed her out of the door of his flat, tossing her clothes, books, a mini bonzai and her handbag down the stairs in her wake. When she tried to gather her belongings up in her arms, she lost her balance and tumbled down, down, so far down. She cracked a rib on the bottom step and scraped her hands and knees on the gravel. Jamie just closed the front door and left her lying there. Later, he said he knew she was okay when he heard her crying. A passing neighbour helped her to her feet and telephoned Flora while Clare sat in his parlour, drinking sugary tea.

When Clare eventually tried to talk about Jamie to a counsellor, it felt like someone else's story. As she struggled to understand why she had stayed with him for as long as she had, her account was always interrupted by memories from her childhood invading the narrative. The sessions never caught up to recent events. It was meeting William that eventually gave her the peace to leave Jamie and the emotional fallout of their relationship behind her. He helped her to understand that she deserved kindness and how a relationship could strengthen you instead of stealing your power. The difference between intensity and intimacy. It was an epiphany for her: unconditional love that was so far removed from that of her childhood home or the toxic men she was consistently drawn to throughout college and her first year at university. She hadn't understood that you could find creativity, passion and adventure living inside a dependable, trustworthy man. It was an irresistible combination, with which William had completely seduced her; the memory of it sustained her even now, when the light in him had dimmed so. If they did separate, was that the end of love for her, or could she find it again with someone new? Perhaps it was time to stop resenting William for having grown into someone different and just let them both move on? Maybe some other woman would accept him the way he was and not hold old promises against him.

Over the years, William had sometimes suggested she see a counsellor again, usually when he was campaigning for them to have a baby. It was an easier way for her to show willing than to try to explain to him directly the disappointment she felt in their married life, but she had never really felt that it helped her to resolve anything. On the day of her last appointment, a year before, she left sobbing and swore she would never return. In the therapist's office, she remembered her first day at a drama summer school when she was seven.

Clare had worried herself into a tight little knot beforehand about strange faces, lisping out loud or if she would need to be able to do cartwheels (which she couldn't), but it had never crossed her mind that the shame of unwashed feet would be her downfall. It wasn't that her family was dirty or that her mother wouldn't have been appalled if she saw the black between her toes. It was more that her mother just couldn't see it. She was as oblivious to the grubby soles of Clare's feet or Flora's unwashed hair as she was to the runs in her own sagging tights or the egg stains on her blouse. Her mother, Teresa, felt invisible and so believed that she was, and her slovenly condition too. Somewhere over the years, her mother had transformed from a militant housekeeper who scrubbed kitchen tiles, cloth nappies and scruffs of necks with equal vigour, into a half-person who had abandoned herself to apathy. Clare understood now that her mother had been suffering from a severe depression but, as a child, it just confused her and she tried to cover for her as best she could and to protect Flora from the worst of her episodes.

At the summer school, while the rest of her classmates pulled off their shoes and socks with excitement, Clare retreated into the corner and surreptitiously peeled back her left sock to assess the condition of her feet. The sight of her heel was enough to stop her and she yanked the sock straight back up again. How she wished she had filled the red plastic basin with sudsy water the night before and given her feet a scrub. She always loved the feeling of submerging her feet in the soapy water before wrapping them in a towel and drying away the wrinkly sensation. It just wasn't something she made a habit of. Cleanliness had become political in her house, and being too keen to tidy up or be clean yourself seemed almost a direct assault on her mother, who resented the insinuation, however true, that she wasn't capable of doing these things herself. Of course, there was a certain element of laziness, too. She hadn't learned to care for her own sake yet. Not at that point. Clare slipped around the perimeter of the room and sidled over to Miss Mimi's side, where she tugged on her sleeve and whispered, 'I can't take off my socks, Miss, because I have an infection on one of my feet, Miss, and the bandage might come off.' She watched as Miss Mimi looked down at her twisting feet, where no contour of a bandage was visible through the thin cotton socks.

'A bandage on both feet, Clare?' she asked, bending closer to whisper. Clare smelled roses from her skin.

'No, Miss, just the left one, but I think I'd feel strange with one sock on and one sock off. Uneven.'

Miss Mimi gave her a long look, then turned Clare to face the room, her hands on her shoulders.

'Very well, then,' she said. 'Leave them on for now, but try not to slip. Hopefully, you'll be footloose and fancy free next week.'

Clare couldn't meet her eyes but said a little prayer of thanks for the reprieve. Next week, her toes would squeak. She had learned a lesson: to take responsibility for herself. She longed for the day when she would be a grown-up lady. Not like her own mama but like the other children's mothers, with toenails painted red or pink peeping out of white, high-heeled summer sandals. Smelling of soap and roses.

As she sat at her shining kitchen table now, it crossed her mind that she had perhaps taken that lesson too much to heart. Was she so self-sufficient that it rendered William's role in her life redundant? She wanted them to be equals but strived so hard for perfection and control in her life that maybe she'd made the gap too wide. If she let her grip on things loosen just a little, would he tighten his?

William was one of the few people who understood what her childhood experience had been. When she had nightmares, as she sometimes did, he would brush her eyelids closed with the palm of his hands, over and over again, slow and steady, until her breathing calmed and her forehead cooled, just like her father had done when she was a little girl to calm her down after another vicious row between her parents. It had taken a long time for her to feel ready to explain where those dark dreams came from; to share with William the memories of the alcohol-fuelled rows and psychological violence on the part of her mother. Despite the public façade of respectability they all maintained, she and Flora had suffered. It pained her to explain that when, eventually, plates stopped smashing and shouting gave way to sobbing, her father would escape the aftermath in the kitchen and wearily climb the stairs to see if she was sleeping. She always waited for him on the top step, hugging herself, her nightdress pulled down over her knees. She worried about how tired he would be when the alarm called him for work, dreaded the silence she knew would smother the house at tea-time the next day. She sat on the stairs, shivering, but she would not fetch herself a blanket. Little Clare had believed that, if she suffered, maybe her daddy would have to suffer less. She knew the people she described were at odds with the family William met when Clare finally invited him home to meet them. He found it hard to reconcile them with the stories he had heard, but never doubted her, nonetheless.

'What are you thinking about?' William's voice cut through her thoughts and Clare realized she sat holding a spoonful of soup in mid-air. She was too tired to try to explain to him what was running through her mind.

'Nothing. Just a case I'm working on.' She turned the pages of the magazine, scanning the headlines, and allowed herself a moment to take pride in how far that little girl had come.

After Clare left home for university, she worked hard

to recreate herself in the image and likeness of those other mothers, the career women, not her own mama, who had stayed at home with the curtains drawn. The decision to study law and not go for an art degree was made easily in her head. Her heart struggled to follow suit, but she would not allow herself to be emotional when confronted with the choice between struggle and poverty and success and security. Perhaps that was partly what had attracted her to William, as he floated through his creative-writing degree. She could flirt with his life-style, walk with him as he talked about the challenge of this plot twist or that character's arc; it was light relief from laboriously reading tome after tome, writing essay after essay, until she rose to the top of her class. Sometimes, she allowed herself to daydream of an alternative life where she spent hours choosing the exact shade of green to paint a particular leaf or sketching spectators in the Natural History Museum. The day she discovered William's book club, she had arrived exhausted by yet another battle to prove her position among the public-school boys who fell just short of pulling her pigtails in class. They loved to remind her how recently it was that girls had been allowed to attend the university, as if it were a privilege that could be revoked. Clare was searching for a different tone of conversation, something dove grey, where she could feel her way through a conversation, instead of marching to a black-and-white beat she never felt quite in step with.

William looked like he had been caught eating stolen cookies when she walked in; guilty he had no one else to offer her, worried that he was wasting her time. His thumb curled through a hole in the sleeve of his jumper, his spectacles were lopsided on the bridge of his nose. The glossy brown curls erupted from his head at all angles and fell over his eyes in a fringe that tried hard to disguise how handsome he was. This jumble sale of a man thawed something inside her. While they sat together, he flicked through the yellowed pages of a notebook with a cracking, navy-blue leather cover. She put her hand on his to make him pause. 'What are all these notes?' she asked. A flush sneaked from behind his ears. She soon learned that these blushes seemed always to be lying in wait for any opportunity to creep out and expose him.

'Oh, just some silly stories. Sometimes, I'll notice a stranger on the street and make up a little life for them, imagine where they are going, what they care about, who they are.'

It blew her heart wide open. Perhaps he would become a hugely successful novelist one day and she could forget about the law and spend her days painting in a little studio. How wrong she was. She could never have anticipated that William would surrender his dream so easily for what she saw as the drudgery of the depot; that was never his long-term plan. All that time he spent typing out those supernatural letters on that battered Imperial typewriter. Why couldn't he write stories of his own any more? Even if he had focused on his ill-fated band with Stevie, that might have fulfilled him more. Much as she had loathed the influence Stevie exerted on William and the trouble they always managed to get themselves into, perhaps William would have been happier. It would have been very hard for her to endure Stevie's constant presence in their lives; they were fundamentally allergic to each other. He, with his fantastical dress sense and eccentric lifestyle, thought she was far too pedestrian, despite what she considered to be creative styling of her own; she thought he was a self-indulgent poser who had never done a day's work in his life. She remembered him staggering up to William's bedsit one day with a dozen flattened washing-machine boxes; he was going to put their demo tape inside them and deliver each one to the radio stations wrapped up as a giant present. He had considered getting in himself before jumping out and presenting the cassettes in person, until she convinced him his scheme would most likely end in either suffocation or arrest. This, of course, he had interpreted as Clare spoiling their fun, as usual.

In fairness, though, at the time, she had believed that William really was going to have great success with his writing; otherwise, she might not have been so quick to encourage him to leave the band to take up the depot position. It was supposed to be temporary. In the beginning, he worked only three days, leaving two days to write in the British Library but, over time, he admitted that he wasn't really getting as much writing done as he had hoped and that he might as well do some real work until he felt inspired again. She wondered now if it wasn't inspiration he lacked but courage. It was hard to respect that.

The thought pulled her focus back to the kitchen

table, where William sat looking at her with searching eyes. She avoided looking back into them. The William she first met would never have settled. If she had told him then, flushed with the confidence of too much wine, that one day in the future they would sit in awkward silence at their kitchen table, he would never have believed her. She would have struggled to believe it herself. What chased that man away? Was it her? Was she ready to accept that they had lost the war? That William was missing in action? The questions circled in her mind like sharks. To lay the blame at his door neatly and begin again, somewhere else, would at least allow her to move on from living within this stagnant cloud. Was that what she wanted? She wasn't sure, not yet. Instead, she buttered some bread, her shoulders hunched. At least the vegetable soup was warming. At least there was that.

4.

William was keenly aware of the physical proximity of his colleagues. Every sigh, fidget and sneeze rattled his emotional infrastructure. The scrape of chair legs felt like claws down his back. The atmosphere stifled him. The heating was still on its winter cycle, even though white sunlight speared through the dusty venetian blinds. The cleaners who arrived every evening at seven seemed to make little headway in their eternal battle against the dust; the white-washed frames on the floor-to-ceiling windows were no barrier against the dirty air percolating from the traffic below. The Victorian floorboards offered endless chinks and grooves to hide away the daily debris that gathered with the post. Despite it all, however, the depot always felt illuminated by the streams of sunlight flowing in from the south and alive with the coloured patchwork cushions that lay scattered on the chesterfield sofas and the prints on the walls: Klimt's *Apple Tree*, Kandinsky's *Yellow-Red-Blue*, Monet's water lilies, a black-and-white photograph of Johnny Cash and June Carter looking over their shoulders at a fairground, a pen-and-ink drawing of two penguins, wings touching as if they were holding hands, staring out from the perimeter of an iceberg. The depot colleagues had clubbed together to buy them as an office Christmas present two years before, each detective choosing one, and it made all the difference to their working habitat. Each detective's desk was unique, also, infused with their individual characters: William's old mahogany polished to a shine, Trevor's leather and chrome, Marjorie's wicker and pine. The lack of uniformity complemented the higgledy-piggledy nature of their work.

'Marjorie, could you open the window a crack? It's really stuffy in here,' William asked, as he wriggled in his chair.

'The window? When I'm sitting in the direct path of the draught? I don't think so. If you didn't go around dressed like it's Christmas every day, you wouldn't feel so 'ot and bothered. It's a shame to see a young man dressing like he should be drawing his pension. Why don't you get yourself some nice new jeans, eh?'

William regretted the corduroy shirt and cardigan combination chosen in haste that morning. The grey cashmere, normally such a soft comfort, had a newly acquired texture of Brillo pad. It scratched the skin of his neck unmercifully, but the damp patches forming under his arms prevented him shedding the suffocating layer; he would rather endure feverish discomfort than the embarrassment of being exposed as a man not in control of his bodily functions.

At the Dead Letters Depot, time defied the laws of physics, speeding faster than light one day, dripping along like a tired old tap another. That day wound down like a bucket descending slowly into the driest of wells. Every second a minute; every hour a day. Work did not expand to fill the time allowed for it, despite the volume requiring attention; William's fingers were clumsy figs. His trolley of undeliverables overflowed and parcels and letters formed untidy piles at his feet. Envelopes haemorrhaged out of postbags all around his desk. His reputation for clearing his allocation every week had always been considered an example to all. Usually, by Friday lunchtime, every one of his letters and parcels had been attended to. It wasn't entirely selfless; clearing his allocation allowed him time to focus on the Supernatural Division, bought him some hours of peace to click-clack away, typing up letters to add to his collection. Rather than popping out for a tipple to toast the end of the working week, this ritual was his reward. On Mondays, when a new tide of post flooded into his domain, he was generally excited to start the process all over again. And yet, for over a month now, he had barely been meeting his quota. His typewriter lay sulking under its red leather cover, neglected. He avoided Mr Flanagan, skipped staff meetings when he could and ate lunch at his desk, alone. William struggled to find his usual inspiration in the stories from strangers that passed before him or to get excited by his role in their delivery. He was drowning in lethargy. Lethargy and letters. How could he care about the plight of others when he feared his own personal life was accelerating towards a moment of crisis?

He picked up a parcel wrapped in brown paper and tied tightly in string and turned it over in his hands, grimacing to hear it rattle. No address anywhere. He untangled the knot and peeled back the paper to reveal a shoe box that had once held soccer boots, size five. Inside, a large egg shape was cocooned in bubble wrap; it felt heavy in his hands as he laid it to one side and picked up the sheet of dotted paper that accompanied it. The precision of the neat, joined-up handwriting gave the distinct impression of being a newly acquired skill.

Dear Sirs and Madams of the Royal Geological Society,

My name is Penelope Bernardine Foxcroft and I am a keen amateur geologist. I have built an impressive collection of rocks and fossils, as I am lucky to live in Aberlemno in the north-east of Scotland, where I can hunt for them in the mountains and along the shore by the sea. I have enclosed a photo of me with my display, holding the Cairngorm granite I found last spring. The reason I am writing to you is I think I may have found a lump of fossilized whale vomit, or ambergris, to use its proper name. I know that this could be quite valuable and so would appreciate it if you could authenticate it for me.

Yours truly,

Penelope Bernardine Foxcroft

William found the photograph of Penelope in the shoe box. He smiled at her earnest expression as she stood in front of shelves weighed down by Kilner jars and rocks on little mounts. She was wearing a grass-green-coloured T-shirt with GEOLOGY ROCKS emblazoned across the front. He toyed with the idea of unwrapping the offering but wasn't sure he really wanted to get further acquainted with whale vomit. Instead, he called the Royal Geological Society and made an appointment to meet Dr Rosamund

O'Reilly, who was very excited indeed to hear about Penelope and her discovery – it could be worth thousands of pounds, it seemed, and Dr O'Reilly was shocked that someone had just popped it in the post. He called over Sally, their disinterested but charming work-experience student, and showed her what he had discovered.

'That is the most disgusting thing I have ever heard,' she said, and poked the parcel with one pointy scarlet fingernail.

'Well, be that as it may, it's a victory for us!' he replied. 'Would you like to bring it over to the Society with me? Get away from here for an hour or two this afternoon?'

Sally tried to perch nonchalantly on the edge of his desk but couldn't find a comfortable resting position; she tossed her head and swung her ebony ponytail over her shoulder as she slinked up to standing.

'Absolutely. Shall we go out for lunch and carry on from there? I'll swing by your desk again at one, but this time it's definitely on me.'

William felt the judgemental eyes of Morgana and Trevor boring into him. Sally's father was Chairman of the Board at the depot, and they never missed an opportunity to accuse him of designs of advancement by charming her. That was never his intention, however. If anything, he revelled in the newness of her, her lack of cynicism and her spirit.

William felt the familiar sense of satisfaction on completing a successful mission, but it didn't excite him now as much as it would have once. Lately, his interests had evolved from a general fascination with other-world idolatry to a very specific one. He groped about in the mail sacks, imagining little eyes in his fingertips, searching for a familiar groove, hoping for an instinctive path to another letter from Winter. He tried to accept that there would probably not be any others, just that one message in a bottle tossed into the sea by a lonely woman, but still he searched. Instinct powered him forward; his heart needed this, despite the inability of his head to rationalize why. Every time he reached inside a postbag, hope poured from his shoulder blades down his arms, a waterfall flowing over every bone, nerve and sinew to become streams in his fingers, pulsing and pushing.

Winter's letter lay flattened in the L section of the *Oxford English Dictionary* on his desk, between a page that began with 'lady' and one that ended with 'lamb'. For days, he had agonized over whether or not it might be safer to hide it at home after all, but everywhere he considered, he imagined a beacon of light suddenly calling Clare to it: the manila folder of old bills, a hat box filled with their collection of super-8 films, under the tower of her university texts, which never budged. He couldn't risk Clare ever finding it. The thread of trust between them, already so frayed, would surely snap with any further strain. How could he explain why he wanted to keep that letter? Especially when, for so many years, he had refused to bring any letters home, despite her consistent pestering of him to do so. In the beginning, she had been so curious about his working world and wanted to be complicit in his detective work but, over time, as her resentment about his salary and his preoccupation with the job grew, her interest in discussing these mysteries had waned in direct proportion. He couldn't even begin to explain why Winter's letter had stayed with him without unravelling miles of words unspoken between them about where the romance in their own marriage had disappeared to. He didn't know what the simple explanation was for his attraction to Winter's words, or if one even existed. If they walked even two steps down that road of exploration, he worried they would never come back.

The letter had completely unsettled him. Winter's words swam around in his head, exotic fish in an aquarium: *Are you hiding somewhere?*, *Are you lost?*, *your forgotten umbrella*, *wordy pictures*; bobbing around the everyday, goldfish lexicon he shared with his wife: *What's for dinner?*, *The electricity bill came*, *I'll go and put the bins out*. He thought again of the letters that he and Clare used to write to each other, even though they saw each other almost every day, letters full of yearning and dreaming, a way of sharing their inner selves that found expression on paper but which they sometimes struggled with in person. What would he say if he wrote to Clare now? Had those letters been more honest for the element of anonymity paper brings, or less? Had they allowed them to present an idealistic image of themselves they both wanted to believe in or helped them to become even more real to each other? He wasn't sure any more.

He slipped away to his fourth-floor domain and visualized a midnight-blue envelope waiting for him. He ached for it, calling it into being, beseeching the universe, foolish though it felt, that a good wind would blow through and offer him this reprieve. There were two new trolleys awaiting him, and he spilled the contents of the first on to the floor, a tide of white, browns and greys across the mustard tiles. An occasional splash of colour mingled amid the monotony of everyday stationery: an indigo envelope, a polka-dot parcel, a brown-paper package covered in drawings of Christmas trees. And there! There it was! Brazen and bold, buried two letters deep; a midnight-blue envelope with curling silver writing. William pressed his hot forehead to the cold tiles and offered up a prayer of thanks. Why did he care so much that the first letter had not been the only one? How could he dare hope for more? He knelt among the lost letters, his feet tucked beneath him, and opened the envelope.

My Great Love,

How are you? I just saw a very fetching man walking across the courtyard under my window. He was crunching an apple with admirable enthusiasm and a great sense of purpose while a very excited electric-blue scarf struggled to be released into the skies. Maybe it wanted to be sky blue instead. Oh, that it was you arriving home from work with a Tunnocks tea cake hidden in your satchel for me! I will toast the day.

I'm writing to you from the kitchen table as I spy on my neighbours coming and going below. How I envy the couples as they struggle to carry in their shopping and bicker about much of nothing – they are oblivious to the extraordinary beauty of the ordinariness of their lives. If one or the other were suddenly gone, I wonder how much they would mourn these unexceptional days they take for granted? Or would any of them be relieved? Are any of them trapped in a marriage they haven't the heart or nerve to try to escape from? It must be even worse to feel lonely inside a couple than when you're alone. At least my loneliness offers the hope of someone coming along – and I am free to run into their arms if they do.

My window is a glass door that opens out on to a tiny balcony where regular successions of plants arrive, blossom, then die under my neglectful eye. There is a lovely occasional waft of jasmine on the breeze from the vase on the windowsill. I walked down to Columbia Road Flower Market this morning and staggered home under the weight of my finds. My favourite stall is at the very end of the street and run by a man who is blind in one eye; he wears a patch and a pirate hat! As you bob along the avenue, brushing against the human traffic, traders heckle on every side. I listen and look, greedily drinking in the cacophony of colour, but push through to the very end to my pirate. He hates to see any flower left behind at the end of the day so, as time draws closer to Sunday lunch, he paces beside his stall and combines bunches together, bouquets of wild combinations of everything from chrysanthemums to orchids and wisteria to lily of the valley. It's almost impossible to resist reaching out your arms for them to be filled. Ladies line his parade, waving five-pound notes at him, desperate to catch the flowers of the day. He wrapped up twenty white roses with a clutch of yellow tulips and a woman beside me squealed out, 'Ooh la la!' as if she had seen a living miracle. He plucked five pounds from her creamy, perfectly manicured hand and placed the prize in her arms as if it were a baby. She dashed off, jealously guarding her flora, lest someone bump them from her hands or crush them against her chest.

On impulse, I brought him a coffee today, from the cart that also sells helium balloons; I always think it will float away one day, and secretly hope it will. When my turn came to be given my flowers, the bouquet was a triumph. White paper hugged pink roses, white lilies, my jasmine and the sweetest bunch of daffodils. I have such a weakness for those noble stems. If ever we have a garden, will you plant a whole bed of daffodils where I can see them from the kitchen window? My mother grew them in the garden, and they're the first flowers I ever remember picking. Today on the market, a dilapidated yellow Volkswagen Beetle had been converted into a giant flowerpot filled with those very beauties and dozens of daisies and sunflowers. I used half of my camera film taking photographs of it – I hope when I develop them there is something special to send to my mam. You'll meet her one day, I'm sure.

I keep fantasizing about bringing you home to Ireland with me. I sense that my friends and family are anticipating your arrival also. First, we can visit the little village where I grew up and then we'll abscond to the city when it starts to feel too claustrophobic. We might even take the Dart out to Bray and walk along the promenade. I want to take you on a historical tour of the places that mean the most to me in Dublin: the Italian restaurant where I waitressed for years when I was a poor student; the hat shop where I hosted a student radio show in the attic for a few years, until the Gardaí shut us down. Maybe I can finally buy myself a hat there, after so many years gazing at them in the window. We can go dancing in Whelan's, where all the best bands play – I even saw The Cure there once! It was one of the most spiritual experiences of my life. When Robert Smith sang 'Pictures of You', I was shattered into smithereens. When he sings about gazing at pictures of someone for so long he begins to believe that they are real, I understand.

I want to huddle in the window of the Long Hall pub and drink hot whiskies as we watch the Dubliners dash by. I spent every Friday evening there, and sometimes Saturdays, too, before I moved. It's always overflowing with writers and journalists fishing for stories and drowning their writer's block with potions that are either the cause or the cure of their ailments. When you are squashed into that old Victorian magic spot, it could be any decade in Dublin; the characters there feel timeless, too. Shall we meet there? I can think of no better place to find you. I'll be the girl with the long red hair wrapped in a white rabbit-fur coat. Green eyes, Granny-Smith-apple green. Keep a look out for the most Irish-looking girl you can imagine, and that will be me. I always loved to quietly photograph the patrons in their oblivion, and some of those black-and-white portraits hang on the wall there now. I can point out which ones in the gallery are mine when we finally find ourselves there.

Some of my best work was born in those smoke-filled rooms. Those pictures gave me my first tentative inklings that I wanted to make photography my life's work. It's why I ultimately ended up here in this city, chasing that dream. One thing is for certain, however, this city is an endless runway of incredible portraits to capture; I love to walk the streets at night and spy creatures who come out only under the cover of darkness; to walk with protestors and paint their pain on film; to make invisible people visible. Have I photographed you in my travels? Would I know you if I saw you? I have so many happy memories of Dublin, and I hope I'll feel the same about this city one day. My camera allows me to participate in the life of the town, even though I'm alone; I can hide in broad daylight. No one notices you when your face is hiding behind a lens. Could we turn London into a home together? Write a new history here?

I think I can face the day now. I'm going for a walk along the South Bank to fill my wicker basket with paperbacks from the book stall. What are you doing today? Are you reading the Sunday papers? Cooking a roast? Driving in the country? Maybe you have something more adventurous planned. I'm jealous of whoever gets to spend the day with you.

I hope this letter finds you, and finds you well.

The small of my back misses your hand.

Yours,

Winter

William read the letter a second time, savouring now the words he had first raced through. London was his geographical time machine, as Dublin was for Winter; the ghosts of he and Clare lingered throughout the town, their entire adult lives so far played out on those streets. Were they a couple who didn't appreciate the wonder in their ordinary lives, like the couples Winter watched? Or was he one of the men who did not have the backbone to set them free? Maybe courage was what was needed to save them, too. He conjured up an image of Winter in his mind's eye: apple-green eyes, long, red hair vibrant against white rabbit fur. How he would love to walk with her down Columbia Road and choose a flower to tuck behind her ear. He remembered the excitement of those early dates with Clare, when she answered the door with only hope in her eyes. No doubts. To see that look in her eyes again would take a miracle. Had he any left inside him? How the idea of experiencing that feeling again seduced him; an open heart, a hopeful one. A heart like Winter's.

When he came home that evening, he found himself alone once again. Forgoing foraging in the fridge for fortification, he instead walked straight to the record player and placed The Cure's *Disintegration* album on the turntable. He lay on their cream corduroy sofa, the music swimming among his senses for 71 minutes and 47 seconds, and allowed himself to dream until the fatal click and whirr of the vinyl ending. Instead of waiting up for Clare, he went upstairs to bed, but not to sleep. By the light on his bedside locker, he scribbled pages of his chicken-scratching handwriting along lines and lines of an old refill pad that had hitherto lain dormant beneath a stack of patient books. He had been released.

5.

Clare tried her utmost not to think about what had happened, but the knowledge stalked her like a hungry animal; the memory lingered like the smell of spilt milk on carpet. She knew now that moments of great reckoning happen on days that appear to be as ordinary as any other. They don't involve thunderstorms, premonitions or shivers down your spine.

They feel exactly the same as any other day, until the something happens. The sound of the telephone ringing had penetrated Clare's ears, past the defence of her shampoo. She was luxuriating in the feeling of frothy foam bubbling down her arched back, breathing in the aroma of coconut as she tangled and untangled her tresses. It was probably her mother, or a sales call – no one worth clambering from the shower for with sudsy hair and slippery feet. Blistering-hot water cascaded over her, the strain of a sleepless night swirling down the drain. Last night's annual Dead Letters Depot Fancy Dress Fundraiser had presented a more intense blend of discomfort than usual. Normally, the extent of her suffering was enduring the nonversation of William's colleagues as she feigned interest in their politics, hobbies, careers, and their children, whose names she had forgotten.

'So, when are you and Billy going to grace us with a

little Woolf? I'm sure he'd love a son to kick an encyclo-paedia around with.'

'We didn't see you at the sports day. I suppose it's just for those of us with kiddies, really, but you're still very welcome, you know. We had karaoke for the grown-ups. Would that appeal to you at all?'

'I was reading an article the other day about how the number of youths going through the courts every year keeps rising. What's the answer, Clare? Where did it all go wrong?'

This year's event had presented a further layer of stress. Clare's case had been adjourned to the evening session and so she knew she was going to be late even before the event began. A man was on trial for battery; he had defended his sister when her husband attacked her, and his brother-in-law pressed charges. The sister and brother were depending on Clare to win him his freedom. It was one of only three cases she had ever lost. Afterwards, there wasn't a moment to wipe the prosecutor's clammy handshake from her skin, to drown out the woman's quiet keening as her brother was led away. She couldn't flood her mind with Nina Simone songs or distract her-self with a recording of *Desert Island Discs* as she lay in the tub. Instead of indulging in a little cry before washing her face and painting a new one back on, she was forced to go straight to the party so as not to risk missing it entirely. There certainly wasn't time to don the Georgian-lady ensemble William had collected from the costume-hire emporium for her.

Her heels click-clacked down the marble hall towards

the function room, an echo of her courtroom walk. There, she was respected, powerful, in control. In the Prince Regent ballroom of the Highbury Hotel, she was a misfit among the fairy-tale characters, movie icons and monsters. Mr Flanagan appeared before her in a monk's habit. He looked far too convincing.

'Clare, you made it! Wonderful!' He leaned in with a kiss for her cheek, but it landed awkwardly on her ear instead. 'We called you up during the speeches to acknowledge the most generous donation made by your firm but, alas, you missed it. Your husband was very gracious about it, said you wouldn't want a fuss. Not to worry.'

'I'm sorry I wasn't here, Ned,' she answered, surreptitiously wiping her ear. 'I did hope to arrive earlier, but I was held up in court, unfortunately.'

He gestured her to walk with him and linked her arm in his. 'Don't concern yourself. We all know how busy you career girls are. Shame you couldn't dress up, though. Your Billy looks quite the picture in his tights.'

Clare smarted at being called a 'career girl' and turned away from him to face the dance floor. Mr Flanagan looked confused by her giving him the cold shoulder and, embarrassed by his confusion, scanned the room for William, who could relieve him. Clare's eyes found him first, although it took her a second to register that the bundle of energy spinning a Juliet figure swaddled in lemon chiffon was actually her husband.

'Ah-ha! There he is, with young Sally. Billy has been such a mentor to her over the last six months. I'd say he'll miss her when she's gone.'

So this was the infamous Sally. William had been suffering an extreme case of mentionitis since she had started working there: 'Sally came up with a terrific new catalogue system today – really quite remarkable in its efficiency'; 'Sally brought in home-made brown bread today, you really could taste the difference'; 'Sally told me the funniest joke today about Christopher Columbus'; 'Sally went canoeing at the weekend. Maybe we should try to get out in the world a bit more, try some new things.'

Canoeing! This from a man who wore his pullover to the beach on the hottest weekend in July last year. In fact, the only thing he hadn't mentioned about Sally was how utterly gorgeous she was. Why had she never asked him what Sally looked like? She had pictured a sad creature who got her kicks from birdwatching and making her own soap. The hue of the past few months shifted as she watched Sally shimmying around her husband, bending her back towards him. William was certainly not moping in the corner watching the door, as history had taught her to expect. Clare stood on the periphery of the dance floor, waiting for William to notice her. And on she waited. When he eventually stopped for breath, he was just in time to see Clare's back manoeuvring towards the exit. He shuffled awkwardly across the room, weaving around two vampires kissing, a giant apple and a very sad-looking clown. He caught Clare by her coat-tail as she slipped into the cool hallway, where the party became a strange-sounding, muffled other-world. A dark blush was creeping up from the lace collar of William's costume and his breathing was heavy.

'Clare, hey, wait a minute! Where are you going? Why aren't you wearing your costume? I was worried about you.'

'Not half as worried as you seem to be now. Having fun, were you?'

William's flushed face and burgeoning stammer did little to placate her.

'I was just dancing. Where are you going? How come you're so late?'

Clare readjusted the strap of the charcoal suede satchel that was slipping off her shoulder; the weight of its briefs set her slightly off balance and she cursed herself for not leaving it in the car. She was always so anxious in case it got stolen, details of her cases made public. The fallout from her old habit compounded her irritation.

'Well, I rushed straight here so as not to let you down, but I clearly needn't have bothered. Do you know how long I've been standing, waiting for you to finish your dance of the seven veils? Is that part of the work-experience programme? How to make a fool of your manager? Or his wife, at least?'

Clare noticed Marjorie eyeballing them from the dance floor and nudged William out of her sightline. He tried to take her satchel from her, but she yanked it back and hoisted it once again on to her shoulder. Their words rushed at each other like foot soldiers, focused only on their own purpose: not to listen, just to be heard.

'Clare, what are you talking about? I'm glad you've made it.'

'Don't try to pacify me, I –'

'I've spent most of the evening just sitting on my own, waiting for you. Sally –'

'So, it's my fault? Because I have responsibilities?'

'Sally dragged me –'

'Stop saying her name. I don't want to hear –'

'She just felt sorry for me.'

'What? The neglected husband? It's me she should have sympathy for.'

'I'm sorry I didn't see you, but it's packed in there. You should've come over.'

Clare let her satchel slam on to the floor. The thud on the marble tiles echoed around the lofty walls, and more faces turned to look. She took a breath, smoothing down the lapels of her suit jacket, and her voice became an angry whisper.

'What? And spoil the fun? Besides, I wanted to watch you. Witness how you behave when I'm not there. Who you are. You reminded me of someone I used to know.'

The words lashed out of her before she had time to think about what she was saying. Had she gone too far? William fell silent. Afraid of the look in Clare's eyes. Fearful of the bag of snakes squirming in his belly, afraid that one might circle his heart, rise up his throat and speak.

'Woolfie, Woolfie! There you are! Where's my champagne?'

Sally was aglow with excitement as she skipped down

the hall, her shining ebony hair spiralling in electric curls about her shoulders. She turned towards Clare.

'Hello. They seem to have run out of champagne. Could you ask them to send some more through?'

William jumped in before Clare turned a whiter shade of rage.

'Sally, this is Clare. She doesn't work here, actually. She's my wife.'

'Oh! Oh, I see, it's just . . . the suit . . . Well, it's so nice to meet you.'

Sally offered her hand to Clare, a limp invitation, held closer to her own body than Clare's. William slowly exhaled when Clare extended her own strong hand to complete the exchange. She didn't say anything to Sally, though, but turned to face William once more.

'I'm leaving. Come, if you like. Or stay and play. I've certainly had enough.'

'Of course! Yes, let's go. I'll just grab my coat. Wait here?'

Clare sat stiffly down in a brocade velvet armchair and gripped the arm rest. William hurried down the hall, Sally scampering along beside him. Clare watched as Sally took his elbow and stood on tiptoe to whisper in his ear. It horrified her that William jumped away, like a man receiving a blow. He glanced back over his shoulder to see if she was watching. Clare shook her head at him before rising and stalking towards the front door alone.

The drive home was impossibly long. A new, unfamiliar silence to those they were accustomed to settled between them. They became like three uncomfortable strangers forced to share a bed: a husband, a wife and the row that loomed. Clare clenched the steering wheel, turning the windscreen wipers on against the drizzles of rain, forgetting to turn them off again when the rain stopped, despite their dry screeching over the glass. In the past, theirs had been a gentle love, not prone to arguments, accusations, recriminations. Now, this new world, where a battle seemed always to be in the post, had somehow robbed them of their easy talking and familiar affection. Clare nursed her wounds through red lights, roundabouts and stop signs until the sanctuary of their home gave her licence to let go.

There, she bent over the kitchen sink, scrubbing dried-on cornflakes from the breakfast bowls they had abandoned that morning, running late as usual, escaping from the house. He hovered around the kitchen door.

'I don't really understand what's going on here, Clare. I was only dancing with one of the women from work. I really think you're overreacting.'

Clare froze mid-scrub, and her shoulders closed together another inch.

'William, you don't think I'm overreacting or you wouldn't look like a child who has dropped an egg. If there is nothing going on between you and that teenager, why are you acting so guiltily?' She turned to face him and watched the question flicker across his face while he searched for an answer.

'Because I do feel guilty.' His answer was a slap in the face, and she felt a momentary panic grip her. What was he going to confess to? William registered her shock and rushed over to her, placing his hands on her shoulders. 'Not because I've done anything wrong,' he continued, 'just because I've upset you. I wanted tonight to be a chance for us to have some fun. I can't believe it's turned out like this.'

Clare turned away from him and watched his reflection in the kitchen window.

'So you're telling me that this girl who you've been going on about for months means nothing to you? And the fact that you never mentioned she looks like she's walked off the cover of *Teen Vogue* was an accidental oversight?'

He started wrestling the rubbish bag from the bin, frustrated when the jagged contents caught on the rim. 'Why would I comment on what she looked like? And anyway, I hadn't really noticed that she was anything special to look at, not really.'

Clare clattered two spoons on to the draining board.

'Oh, please don't patronize me. At least if you acknowledged that you fancied her –'

'*Fancied her?* Are we back in Year Ten now?'

'At least then I might be able to believe you. *Pretending* you've never noticed just convinces me even more that you've got something to cover up. Admit it. You find her attractive!'

William's eyes ran around the room, looking for inspiration in the washing on the clothes horse, the glasses winking at him on the dresser, the grout between their no longer quite so white floor tiles.

'Fine. So she's an attractive girl. So what? It doesn't mean anything. I'm sure you meet good-looking men at work all the time.'

She turned the hot tap on full and the water blasted the sink.

'Yes, William, I do. But I don't spend every second I can with them, regale you with tales of how fabulous they are or spend the evening in their arms at work dos.'

'I don't spend evenings with her! You're exaggerating!'

'And I certainly would never lie to your face about them. In fact, as far as I know, that's the first time you've lied to me about anything. As far as I know.'

'I wasn't lying to you! I was just trying to protect you from worrying about something that doesn't matter. And anyway, what about Max?'

She bent over and held her hair in fistfuls in her hands.

'Oh, you've got to be kidding me! What has Maxi got to do with anything? Don't try and turn this around on me!'

William walked towards Clare and reached behind her to turn off the tap.

'Ah, yes, of course, it's Max*ee*. As if it wasn't tedious enough, the way he follows you around like a puppy, he has to have a name like a child's pet, too. I'm surprised he hasn't caused an accident in the workplace, with all the drool he leaves behind him.'

'Don't be so childish. We're just friends, as you very well know.'

'Do I? Really, Clare? Is that what he thinks?'

'Is that why you've been carrying on with Sally? To get back at me for having friends of my own at work?'

'Carrying on? Nothing has happened with Sally, okay? Can we just drop this? I just enjoy the company of a beautiful young woman at work. So what?'

The rage Clare had been trying to control erupted, and she smashed the last of their honeymoon bowls on the floor. It was a second before she realized that the shocked howl which accompanied the sound of breaking china had come from her. The noise reverberated inside her head. She gripped the kitchen sink, her arms trembling. Slowly, she floated back down inside herself, empty now.

William took a step closer but hesitated before he reached for her.

'Clare, that sounded bad, I know, but I didn't mean anything by it. Honestly. Why don't you go into the living room and I'll clean up in here? I'll get us a drink. Clare?'

The fragments of china crunched underfoot as she brushed past him and walked stiffly to their bedroom. Upstairs, Clare turned the lock and rested her head against the powder-blue door frame she had so carefully painted without smudging the walls. William had installed the lock for her so she could barricade herself in if burglars ever came during the night. She had never thought she would use it against him. He wasn't the sort of man who would kick the door down to get to her, although a part of her wished he was. Instead, he shuffled quietly up and knocked softly. A barely audible whisper coaxed through the wood. He told her he would wait outside all night until she was ready to talk, but it wasn't long before his shadow disappeared and she could hear him riffling through the airing cupboard for something to sleep under on the couch. Clare's anger slowly turned inward. She despised herself for losing her temper and lashing out like her mother would have done. She had worked too hard to rid herself of those fingerprints and was furious that William had provoked that in her. There was a reason she had settled with a man like him and not one of the Jamies of this world: he was supposed to be stable, solid, trustworthy; not someone who would cause her to smash crockery.

That night, Clare put on one of her father's old shirts which she had salvaged from the charity-shop pile her mother made when he passed away. Her wet cheeks dirtied the sleeves with her smudged make-up as she roughly scrubbed it from her face. As the clenching in her bowel eased, the emptiness of their bed enveloped her. Was she losing her mind? Maybe she *had* over-reacted. Had he really given her any reason to doubt him? Was she just looking for an easy answer to what was already happening between them? Attack as the best form of defence?

She got up and sat on the floor with her back resting against the bed. William's question about Maxi settled on her now. Her husband was no fool, not really. So far, she had held Maxi at arm's length, but it was becoming increasingly difficult to rationalize why she did so, when William offered her fewer and fewer reasons to stay. Maxi seemed to offer everything William couldn't: an equal partnership, ambition, success. He was the most accomplished partner in their firm but still found time to publish papers in the *Law Review*, train for triathlons and take skiing holidays every quarter. Just the sort of man who would have been out of her league once upon a time. It was enticing, but would he make up stories for her about a superhero named Clare and hide them in her briefcase? Or wake up early to get the papers for her every Sunday, and present them to her on a tray (having taken out the supplements she wasn't interested in) with a pot of tea and toast soldiers with the crusts cut off? Would she ever feel confident enough to sing along to the radio in front of him, even though she couldn't carry a tune? Probably not, but maybe there would be other things, though. New intimacies she hadn't discovered yet.

She shook her thoughts away from Maxi. Maybe she should go to William and try to salvage a night's sleep for both of them, but every time she circled closer to the idea of reconciliation, the image of that girl on her tiptoes whispering to him slammed back into the forefront of her mind and paralysed her. William had looked at that girl in a way she thought he reserved only for her. Something about the way his arm reached out to her, the lean of his head, the familiarity, their closeness on the dance floor. She couldn't convince herself that it was all in her mind. In her bones, she knew something wasn't right. She just didn't know if something had already happened or whether it was brewing. Maybe it wasn't too late, but if, all this time, she had been standing by him while he had been having an affair, she thought she would never recover.

★

When dawn broke, the sunlight was a searchlight exposing the madness of her night. She looked in the mirror in despair at her blotchy face, tangled hair and damp shirt. The crumpled sheets were balled at the foot of the bed. She lay still as a stone at the bottom of a black lake, straining for sounds of William, until she heard the front door close softly behind him. She was momentarily surprised that he hadn't come to see her before he left but was relieved not to have to speak to him just yet. The great purge of feeling the night before had cleared her thoughts. Things could not continue as they were; otherwise, in twelve months from now, five years from now, a decade from now, they would still be stuck. She needed to escape. This flat was oppressing them, and they would never face their fears, their feelings and failures, while they were living here together. She needed to do something drastic to force them into action.

That was when she staggered to the shower, where she attempted to wash the terrible row down the drain and ignore the telephone ringing. The first time. And the second. On the third attempt, with her hair rinsed clean, she surrendered. Wrapped in William's dressing gown, she ran to the telephone, determined to rid herself of the persistent pest. Wet tendrils sent shivers down her spine as she impatiently snatched at the receiver. She was drying her legs with the ends of the gown as she prepared for a quick disconnection, but the voice at the other end surprised her. It was Maxi, and he was calling from the telephone box at the end of her street.

6.

On the morning after the fancy-dress fundraiser, productivity at the depot was particularly low. Mr Flanagan cancelled the morning meeting because of poor attendance, and even Marjorie's constant sound effects were reduced to a low, plaintive whine as she nursed her headache on the mustard leather love-seat in the kitchen. The remnants of last night's mascara remained smudged around her bleary eyes. Sally had not shown up for work at all and William was relieved not to see her, as Clare's accusations continued to crash about inside his head. Nothing had happened between them. To say, however, that the charms of Sally in all her flirtatious glory had been completely lost on him was untrue. The ability to pull the thread lay at his fingertips and, sometimes, they twitched to do it. Perhaps he should have told Clare the truth, but he couldn't imagine any version of that story where he could emerge from the conversation unscathed. He knew there were no bonus points for fidelity – surely that was the baseline for reasonable behaviour – and he was prepared to accept last night as a warning. When that bowl smashed, he felt the very foundations of their marriage shake. Where had Clare's rage come from? It frightened him to think how easily she had snapped; how long had that temper been building inside her? In their early days together, he worried about how completely self-controlled she was, so cold when they argued, but now, it was as if the feelings she had suppressed were exploding from within. How much had she been hiding from him? He couldn't risk any further cracks permeating their marriage; it was time to douse out this frisson with Sally before something happened that he couldn't undo.

The day Sally appeared in the dust-filled hallway of the depot, with her shiny youth and infectious optimism, it had felt akin to an alien invasion. It would have been easy to get carried away by the attention she lavished upon him, surprised though he was to receive it, but in reality, he knew he was just enjoying the distraction. He was more relieved now than ever that he had stayed on the right side of that war; he would put more distance between them.

If only it was as easy to close the door on Winter, he thought; images of her quietly invaded his mind each day. As he walked the streets of London, his eyes searched for her, convinced that he would recognize her if she appeared. What would he do if she did? He was looking for a sign that these letters were brought to him specifically by some higher power, an entity greater than his common sense could control, something that would force his hand in the crucial moment.

William sat at his desk and sorted through a new bundle destined for the Supernatural Division: a letter to Godot, one for 'The Fairy Godmother of Lucy Sparrow' and a tired old envelope addressed in blue colouring pencil to

'The Ringmaster of the Circus'. He sliced through the top of this last envelope with the bone-handled letter opener Clare had given him to commemorate his ten-year anniversary at the depot. It was inscribed 'A decade of lost letters, 1979–1989'. It always felt so heavy in his hand that he felt infused with a sense of great purpose and importance when he used it. He prised out a sheet of grey paper that was almost as fine as tissue and began to read.

Dear Ringmaster of the Circus,

My name is Harvey and I am 10 and ¾ years old. You might think I am younger than that because I am a bit small but I really am almost 11. I might already even be that age before you read my letter so maybe I should have just said that's how old I am but I didn't want to tell a fib.

I don't know how long letters take to get to the circus but I hope not too long. We only have four days left in school before we break up for the summer. Everyone in my class is really looking forward to us getting out and they're all showing off about going on aeroplanes and summer camps and having lessons in all sorts of things. My dad doesn't believe in lessons, not those kinds anyway – just what he can teach me himself. Which I'm beginning to think won't be much good for me.

I'm writing to you because I'm hoping you might have a job for me this summer (and I wouldn't mind not going back to school in September if you wanted to keep me on). I've made a list of things you might need to know and tried to think up all the questions you might ask if you were standing here in your top hat and stripy coat.

- I haven't ever been inside the circus but every year I watch you from the bridge bringing all the animals off the trailers and I know every one you've got. The elephant is my favourite but I would treat them all the same. I'm not even frightened of the lion but don't fancy feeding him being my first job if that would be ok with you.
- I'm stronger than other 10, nearly 11, year olds because one of my jobs at home is bringing in the firewood and it's made me tough so I'm good for lifting and carrying.
- I'm not a fussy eater and don't need much feeding. Spuds give me cramps but I'll eat them if that's all there is.
- I have my own tent and sleeping bag that I've hidden in my friend Polly's shed. I won it at the sports day but couldn't bring it home in case my dad needs money for his stuff and sells it. Polly's mam lets me put it up in their garden sometimes when I need to get out of our house.
- I'm not bothered about making much money but if you could give me enough for stamps to send a letter to my nan now and then it would be great cos I know she'll worry about me.
- I'd be happy to do any work that you have but if I could work with the animals I'd really like that

best. I've a way of talking to them that they like
and I trained my nan's spaniel to do all sorts of
tricks. I wouldn't like having to use the whip,
though. I hope I could just coax them along
instead.

I'll keep my bag packed in case you need me so I'm
ready to run if you send a note to my nan's house.
Please don't come to my house because my dad wouldn't
like it. There's no mam to notice me gone though, so
don't worry about that.

Thanks very much, Mr Ringmaster. I promise I'll
do my best if you'll have me.

From,
Harvey Lawless

William rocked back in his chair, balancing it on two
legs. What happens when a little boy whose only hope
lies in running away with the circus doesn't get an
answer? William looked at the postmark; the letter was
two years old. He made a note of the boy's name, age
and the sorting office that first processed it to share with
Social Services. It wasn't a lot of information to go on,
but maybe they could find him. There was a lady he had
dealt with before when worrying letters such as these
came his way; she was relentless in her efforts to track
down a child in trouble. He couldn't know to what
extent the boy was being neglected, but he wasn't prepared to presume the best. If Harvey was still hoping
for an answer, she was the best person he could send his

letter to, and the best chance he had for intervention. He put Harvey's letter to one side and opened his second envelope of the morning.

My darling Nora,

Where are you today as you turn twenty-one and take your first steps into the world as a young woman? I try to imagine how you might look if your hair had stayed as black as it was on the day you were born but grew into the curls I might have given you. I'm sure your eyes are still the cappuccino colour of your father's and your skin the colour of caramel, but I find it hard to picture you all grown up. You were such a tiny baby, just five pounds, so I would guess you are petite now, like me and your grandma before us, but maybe your legs and arms grew tall like your daddy's. It breaks my heart not to know and to think of you wondering which of your parents you took after, or worrying that we didn't want you.

I can't say how your daddy felt, because he never knew, or at least I never told him, but I wanted you more than anything. When my belly grew big and they sent me away to the convent in Wales, I thought it was so I could bring you up there without anyone knowing. I had a story all made up in my head about your father passing away and leaving me a widow, that I'd had to sell my wedding ring to put a deposit on the flat, but that wasn't what they had in mind.

After you were born, they only left you with me for a day before Sr Assumpta in the hospital came to me and said your new parents would be there to collect you in the morning. I tried to explain there was some terrible mistake, but my father had signed the adoption papers. I was only fifteen, you see, and she said it was too late. I stayed up all night holding you in my arms, crying like the rain. I must have eventually dozed off because the next morning Sr Assumpta woke me as she snatched you and turned on her heel out of the ward. I raced after her, tripping up in my bed sheets as I ran, and made it halfway down the corridor before one of the orderlies grabbed me and wrestled me on to the floor. I could hear you crying through the sound of my own howls but, no matter how much I struggled, I couldn't get free. I remember how cold the tiles on the floor felt as I crumpled into a pile at the feet of the orderly and lay my cheek on the ground. From where I fell, I could see his navy trousers were an inch too short for him and exposed his ankles in two odd socks, one dark grey with a black stripe and one just grey. He pulled me up on to my feet and half carried me back to the ward, where one of the nurses was stripping my bed. I stood at the window and watched a couple lifting a Moses basket into the back of a silver saloon car and knew it was you. He wore a dark-navy suit with a royal-blue tie and she had on a white dress with a pink bolero jacket, a white headkerchief holding back blonde curls from the wind. And that was all I knew of them, the people who took you from me, but I hoped they would give you a good life, a better life than you might have had with me.

Not a day has gone by since when I haven't thought

of you, imagined you going on holidays in their silver car, holding hands with that lady as you walked to school, clambering on to those navy suit legs for a story. And I've tracked every milestone – when you would be walking, talking, sitting exams, every birthday, Christmas and New Year, wondering if you have a boyfriend yet and hoping, if you do, that he's nice to you. I'd give anything to know what your plans are for the future, if you've gone to university, or have travelled to faraway places. And most of all, I just want to know that you are happy and that my great sadness resulted in great happiness for you. I wonder if sometimes you missed me, even if you didn't understand the feeling of loss you had. On my good days, I hope you didn't but, in my heart of hearts, I'm terrified that you didn't miss me at all, that you might never ask the questions that could lead you back to me.

I'll be waiting for ever, just in case.

All my heart and my hope,

Mam

William scanned the envelope again, desperately hoping he had missed the presence of a return address, but it was in vain. He would do some research later: try to identify the convent, see if there was still someone there who might be able to help – but he feared the worst. This was the hardest part of his job; when a letter that had the potential to change a life was irrevocably lost. He could only hope they found each other by some other means.

He swallowed the lump that formed in his throat.

Why did Clare not have any of those maternal feelings? Had she so little confidence in him that she believed they wouldn't be able to make it work? If a fifteen-year-old girl had wanted to try to raise a baby herself, like so many others, why couldn't they, together? He absent-mindedly stirred the mail in the postbag while he tried to imagine it, he and Clare as parents, raising a child. What sort of person would be borne of the collision of their gene pools? He hoped their child would look like Clare; the very thought of a miniature version of her made his heart swell. He would speak to her again; maybe their relationship was stagnating because it hadn't evolved and was stuck at this impasse. Perhaps if he finished *A Volume of Lost Letters*, or was able to write something new, she might have more faith in him. It still felt, after all these years, like she was waiting for him to prove himself. If she wasn't monitoring his behaviour constantly, would he try harder without the scrutiny or give up the ghost altogether? The domino effect was impossible to predict; he had been holding everything so still for so long.

He swooshed letters around in the half-empty trolley while questions joyrided through his mind. His fingers recognized the texture of the envelope before his brain fully understood what he had found: another letter from Winter. He edged it to the surface, heart racing, paranoia prickling his skin. He looked left and right to ensure he was alone, holding it lightly between his fingertips, hands trembling. He leaned on the windowsill, smoothed the midnight-blue pages out before him and allowed himself to nurse an idea that his heart always returned to. Maybe these letters really were destined for him. Why else was it he who found them? No. He would not surrender to the power of this letter. He could not allow some idealistic vision of a one, true love to sabotage the real-life love he had at home. He was going to see his wife and put a stop to this madness.

He cringed a little at the crease he inflicted upon the envelope by folding it into the deep pocket of the Aran cardigan he wore. He closed the wooden button with determination and strode on to the fourth-floor landing. Should he go to Clare's office? No, home first, to change into something more respectable, tame his hair; he wouldn't suffer Maxi looking down his nose at him if he turned up looking like a middle-aged arts student. William wrapped a long tweed scarf about him and tucked it inside his cardigan. He scribbled a note about a minor emergency and dropped it on Marjorie's desk before he left, grateful that she wasn't there.

The wind scattered London debris around his feet as he tried to tidy his mind. He clenched and released his hands against the cold February bite. Had he left his gloves at the party? No, he remembered pulling on a rogue strand of wool that dangled from the cuff on the drive home. He had teased it, daring it to unravel, but the knot just tightened and caused the stitches to wrinkle together. He paused on the pavement two doors away from their flat to watch as the postman leaned from his bicycle to deliver their mail; today was not the day for a lengthy tirade on the internal gremlins of Royal Mail. He waited for him to push on to number twelve, and the sight of a gleaming jet-black BMW parked at the end of the street caught his eye. They must be lost, he thought. No one around here drives a car like that. He walked the last few steps to their door at a funereal pace, beginning to question the wisdom of this impulse. His initial determination was replaced by a sinking sense of foreboding. He rested his forehead against their forest-green front door before opening it slowly. He pushed the letters that had just arrived across their welcome mat and stepped inside. Silence. No sound of life at all. No radio playing. No kettle boiling. No footsteps. And then he saw Clare. Sitting sideways, watching him from the top of the stairs, a pen in her hand poised over a pad balanced on her knee. Her hair, still damp, was bunched in a loose knot on the top of her head, although she was wearing her grey mac, as if ready to leave the house. Her eyes were dry but glass-like, on the verge of spilling over. Their questions collided.

'Clare, what are you still doing here?'

'William, why are you back?'

She stood up and tied the belt on her mac tightly around her as she came down the stairs. He saw she was wearing his old *Star Wars* T-shirt underneath and took a strange comfort in it.

'I was just leaving you a note,' she said.

'What on earth for? Where are you going? Clare, what's going on?'

She walked past him at the foot of the stairs without meeting his eye. He reached out his hand to grab her shoulder as she passed, but she shrugged him away. In

97

the living room, she perched on the edge of the sofa. Her eyes didn't rise to meet his when he came and sat beside her.

'I know last night was awful, but please don't do anything drastic. Maybe we just needed to have a blow-out, clear the air, so to speak.'

She turned to look at him, took his hand between both of hers.

'William, listen to me. I'm going to go away for a few days so that we can both have some proper time to think. It doesn't work, this passive-aggressive way we have of living here. We just skirt around our problems but never confront anything. Not properly.'

He pulled his hand away and stood up to protest.

'No, Clare. This is wrong. We should work things out together.'

She stayed perfectly still, her voice level.

'Why are you so afraid of me having some time on my own to think?'

He was lost for a moment in her gaze: one green eye, one blue. Watching her now from across the room, William wondered when he had last really looked at her. He held such a fixed image of her in his mind from when they first met. He often nursed a memory from when they had just moved in together: Clare lying sleeping in their new bay window, wearing just her Blondie T-shirt, white cotton shorts and blue knee socks. Her nap interrupted them painting the living room a shade of moody plum. The paintbrush dangled from the tips of her long, delicate fingers but she had not let it go. The deep purple paint streaked down her arms, blobbed on her feet and slowly dried in her still-blonde hair. In the fading light, she had looked almost translucent. William stroked her hair; she brushed his hand away and her eyelashes batted open. The smile that spread across her startled face and the love in her eyes were photographed by his heart and filed for ever as an image he would often return to in his mind's eye. They were never happier than at that time, when they had only hope for the future and no idea yet of how disconnected they would become.

Now, he realized with a wave of remorse how much their faces had aged since they met aged twenty-one and twenty-two; the work of fourteen years looked like more. Their youth had fallen between the floorboards of their flat while they were looking elsewhere. Now, a few strands of grey were weaving from her temples, tracing a path through her mouse-brown bob, extending the lines that seemed to have appeared around her eyes over-night. The texture of his skin had taken on a strange pallor, a tint of yellow; only the sun could warm the bloom back into his face. The pink of her lips had become so pale; his muscles, softer. Her eyes remained unchanged, though. The face around them might crinkle, but she could never look old to him when he looked into those eyes. They didn't grow older, only colder. As everything around them shifted, it was Clare's eyes that reminded him she was the same girl he had fallen in love with. The eyes he had made sparkle, flash, soften, cry.

'I'm afraid you won't come home,' he replied, his voice catching.

She smiled at him.

'Isn't that all the more reason why we need this?' she asked.

In his heart of hearts, he knew it was true, but the panic mounting in him wouldn't let him stand down.

'No, Clare. This is madness. I swear nothing happened with that girl. You believe me, don't you?'

She stood up and walked towards him.

'This isn't about anyone else, William. We both know that, don't we?'

He nodded, but kept his eyes fixed firmly on her pointy blue shoes.

'How long will you be gone?'

'I don't know. I've told the office not to expect me for a few days, at least.'

'But what about all your cases?'

'After ten years with barely a holiday, they can't really object to me finally taking some time off. And they know where to find me if there's an emergency.'

'And what about me? What if I need to find you?'

'William, ask yourself this. If I didn't leave and everything continued on as before, do you really think, in one year from now, we'd be somehow happy? Would anything have changed? Or would we still be stuck in the same place?'

He looked at her, searched inside himself for an answer that wouldn't come. The hopeful silence hung between them; if he could just find the right words to make her stay, he knew they would survive, but the atmosphere burst and the moment passed.

Clare placed her hand on his arm and leaned forward to kiss him on the cheek. As she turned away, he noticed his volume of e e cummings' poetry sitting open on the coffee table, where he had left it the night before. At the beginning of their relationship, Clare would often rest her head in the little dip between his shoulder and chest while William read his favourite poems softly aloud as he stroked her hair; cummings, Keats, Yeats, Blake, Wordsworth. For his wedding vows, William had threaded different lines of cummings' poetry together to make his promises to Clare. As he worried the ivory wedding band over her freezing cold finger, his voice cracked as he recited, 'i carry your heart with me (i carry it in my heart)'. He picked the book up in his hands; a worry bead to give him strength.

She placed her hands on top of it and whispered, 'I'm exhausted, William. I don't sleep. You don't sleep. We stay up half the night not talking to each other. I'm too tired. "Tired of things that break, and – Just tired."'

William felt a frost settle over his skin, prickling, numbing, crackling at the familiar words. He paused before he spoke, yearning for his gut to show him the way.

'Clare, wait! "But I come with a dream in my" –'

She pushed him away. '*No, William! No!*' she shouted. 'It's too late for that.'

William fell to his knees and buried his face in the pleats of her dove-grey silk skirt. His sobs were wretched and he couldn't hear her crying over his own wet, thick, desperate sounds of protest. Clare stood with the palms of her hands over her eyes, quiet little tears squeezing

through her trembling fingers. She tried to step backwards without touching William. He fell forward but
didn't let go, so she awkwardly wrestled his arms from
around her knees and stepped over him, a semicircle heap
of a man. He watched her pick up a suitcase in the hallway that seemed to have appeared from nowhere. How
could he not have seen it as he came in? She didn't look
back as she rushed out of the front door and closed it gently behind her. William remained immobile on the floor.

7.

After Clare left, William sat staring at the closed front door until his limbs fell into a sleepy ache. Without anything useful to do, he rose to put the kettle on to boil and stood watching it. He listened to its dry squealing for a moment before he realized he hadn't filled it with water. Steam burned his hand as he held it under the tap. The water flowed over, dampening the sleeve of his cardigan so the wool became soggy against his wrist. He slapped his hand against the edge of the sink and cutlery scattered across the draining board. How could he have let her leave? His gaze wandered around the kitchen he had spent so many evenings in with Clare, talking, kissing, cooking, eating, cleaning, decorating, dancing, fighting. He heard a quiet crinkle of paper as he leaned into the sink and remembered Winter's letter in his pocket. He sighed. Would it make him feel better or worse to read it now? Anything was better than the silence of their empty flat. He abandoned the full kettle on the kitchen counter and climbed to the top of the stairs, sat where Clare had been perched writing to him. The discarded notebook lay open; only 'Dear William' written before he had interrupted her. The hallway looked different from there; so far below, like a theatre set waiting for a performance to begin. He groaned, rubbed his tired eyes, removed the letter from its envelope and balanced it on his knee as he read.

My Great Love,

It is such a comfort to me, being able to write to you like this. To talk in a safe place where I can acknowledge you and how much you mean to me. It's difficult to discuss you with anyone else, of course. It's important to me that others don't know how much it bothers me being without you. There can be something so tragic about anyone whose life revolves exclusively around their search for a perfect mate. I often think, if they just spent less time obsessing about their potential other half, they would find themselves a complete whole, nonetheless. So please don't misunderstand me; I have a very full and, oftentimes, lovely life. I don't need a man per se and know I could carve out a life of great adventure entirely on my own – if I had to. I would just rather not. I'm not ready yet to let go of the idea that there is one great love for me out there, that you are still searching for me, too. I can feel it in my bones. I want someone to travel with and share the experience of discovery. Someone to talk to when I come home in the evenings so we can bear witness to each other's lives and understand the importance of a million little things.

I want someone to see me, all the colours of my personality, and love me anyway. But I would rather be alone than pretend to have found the right someone. To sit here and write these letters and wait impatiently for you rather than to talk myself into loving another. I refuse to settle for anything less than a magnificent love. I want the sort of love people have fought wars over, walked thousands of miles for, made sacrifices, forsaken all others for. I'll never ask you to do any terrible things to prove your devotion, but I want to know that you would. I want poetry and passion, a particular love that is specific to you and me. No roses or champagne or candlelit dinners – no generic romantic expressions but rather ones that could be inspired only by the most intimate knowledge of the very heart of me.

I want to have children with someone I believe will inspire them to be the most brilliant of humans, a man that will love them unconditionally and give them the confidence to follow their dreams. My father always encouraged me to believe that I could do anything, be anyone. If not for him, I might never have left home for London with just my camera and the idea that I could be a proper photographer if this city was my studio. Many people question if I made the right decision, leaving what they considered to be the perfect job at home. I spent years working for a small independent record label, coaxing Ireland's DJs to play songs and to promote albums for the next big thing. It was definitely an adventure – concerts, festivals, tours – but I reached a point where I thought I couldn't imagine doing it for ever. It was time for me to stop facilitating the dreams of others and allow myself the chance to follow my own. So I left. I swapped my wishbone for a backbone, as they say, and committed myself to the realization of the dream that brought me here. Any of the men I have known in my life so far, I have struggled to imagine them as a father and a best friend as well as my lover. Someone who will encourage me to follow my heart, while he does the same. Those two things don't have to be mutually exclusive, do they? That's why I'm still waiting for you. I'm not asking for too much, am I? When the moment comes, please don't hesitate. Seize it. Seize this spectacular love for us.

Maybe you'll see me this evening when I catch the Northern Line to Camden Town. I'm meeting my good friend Peter for some Mexican food and mojitos in our favourite restaurant by the station – a hot remedy to spice life up after a grey week spent in Ireland with his parents. He finds it hard to reconcile London Peter with the Peter from the small town he left behind. I can relate. It's far from Mexican food he was reared. Isn't that the magic of this city? You can experiment with a thousand different lives, experience something new, and then continue or cast it aside. Sometimes, I worry the city makes us do that to people, too. There's always someone else to turn your head; potential lovers race by as frequently as the Tube. What if your great love just hadn't revealed their true self before you moved on?

I declare tonight to be my new New Year's Eve. Why wait until 31 December for new resolutions, new beginnings? I wish you were here to kiss me at midnight.

Happy New Year, My Great Love. Can we please start a new year together?

Yours,

Winter

William lay on his back on the carpet of the landing, his eyes focused on the cobwebs in the corners of the ceiling. *I would rather be alone than pretend*. He whispered the words like a mantra; wasn't that the belief Jack Kerouac had instilled in him all those years ago? Back then, it was still easy to believe in a great love; he hadn't yet been disappointed, worn down. Was Winter naïve? Or was she just less jaded than him? A *spectacular love*: the younger William had believed anything less was a travesty. Now, after being in a relationship with Clare for fourteen years, had his essential self changed? Was the real tragedy not allowing their spectacular love to grow into something perhaps less sparkling but more stable? Was real romance just persevering when times were hard, hidden in the daily domestic rituals of a life shared? He didn't think he would ever convince Winter of that. Could he convince himself?

Perhaps Winter was right, and maybe he was one of those who spent too long obsessing about who should complete him instead of thinking of what he could do to complete himself. He needed to make himself whole. The thought of two people independently pursuing their dreams without either making a sacrifice struck him. Had he held Clare back? Was it fair for her to lay that at his door? It made him shiver to think how well Winter seemed to know him. He was so vulnerable to her command to find her. To want more. If Winter were a flesh-and-blood person standing in front of him and presenting her case, would he be able to resist? Oh, how deceitful his heart was to the logic his head struggled to hold! He remembered the quote from Blaise Pascal that his English professor had carved over her door: 'The heart has its reasons which reason knows nothing of.' He knew now that it was true.

He had to escape the flat. Before he had time to consider the wisdom of his actions, he reached for the telephone and dialled Stevie's number. Clare wasn't there to object. He answered on the first ring.

'Well, as I live and breathe, look who's crawling out of the woodwork. If you're going to ask me to reunite the band, well, you'd better have a good —'

Stevie's voice sounded hoarse, as if he had just woken up, which was always highly probable, regardless of what time you called him.

'I'm not, tempting as it is. Although, if I did, it would be far less mad than what's actually been happening recently.'

William caught the panicked tone in his own voice and tried to swallow it away while Stevie asked, 'Oh? What's going on? Oh God! You're not having a baby, are you? Please don't say that.'

'Why do you say that like it's the worst news I could possibly have to tell you? What if I was terminally ill or something?'

He laughed, despite himself, before Stevie shot back, 'I know which problem I'd rather have.'

William creaked the drawers of the dilapidated sideboard on which the telephone rested open and closed. He seemed incapable of sitting still any longer. 'Look, a baby wouldn't have to be a . . . Forget it. Clare's not pregnant, and I'm not dying of anything, not that I know of.'

'So, what's going on then, stranger?'

A silence hung between them on the telephone line.

'Nothing. Not really. I just thought it might be time for us to catch up and maybe have a few drinks, grab some food or something?'

Stevie snorted. 'For no particular reason? I don't buy it, but I'll bite. I've started working in a cool record shop on the Market, Seven Deadly Spins! You could call in to see me tomorrow? Or I have a gig with Blue Lagoon at the Windmill in Brixton next week, if you fancy it?'

'I'd rather eat my own feet than stand watching those clowns. What about this evening? Are you still in that bedsit in Chalk Farm? I could meet you in Camden, maybe?'

'Tonight? Has Clare not got something scheduled already for you? I didn't think you were allowed out on your own.'

William could hear the smirk in Stevie's voice but knew it disguised a very real hurt that he saw so little of him. He shouldn't have left it so long to call.

'Don't be daft,' he replied, in a softer voice now. 'Anyway, Clare's away. At the moment. With work.'

'Oh, I see. So, while the cat's away, eh? Fiiiiiine, I am free tonight, as it happens. This girl I was meant to take to the cinema cancelled on me because she has scarlet fever. Thank Heavens – she wanted to go and see *Ghost*. Patrick Swayze is in it, which is a plus, but apparently it's all about pottery or –'

William cut him off. 'So, will I meet you at Camden Tube at eight? Do you know any Mexican restaurants around there?'

'Mexican?' Stevie sounded indignant. 'What do you want Mexican for? Let's get a curry, like we always do.'

Why did everything have to be a battle? 'I just fancy it, that's all. Maybe we can have a walk around and see if we find one. You're the one who says I need to try new things.'

Stevie emitted a little whine, but acquiesced.

'Oh, aaaaallll right, then. I think there's one on the way to Mornington Crescent. Sombrero Jim's, or something, it's called, but it looks kind of like a disco bar . . .'

William whooped. 'Yes! I bet that's the place. It's a date.'

'What do you mean, that's the place? What place?'

'Wear something normal, okay?'

'I refuse to be bound by your limited understanding of fashion and your lack of individuality.'

'Well, at least cover up, do you hear? Nothing with too much flesh showing!'

William hung up before Stevie could ask any more questions. He was already doubting the wisdom of re-introducing his old sidekick into the current turbulence of his life, but, for the first time in a long time, he was excited to be taking some action.

The 'S' and 'b' of Sombrero Jim's red neon sign had lost their illumination, and the giant sombrero covered in fairy lights filling the window had faded from years of sunbathing, but the aesthetic decline of the exterior did nothing to stop eager eaters filling the chipped red chairs. The waiting staff wore a strange combination of traditional Mexican clothing and the piercings and punk haircuts of Camden uniformity. Stevie and William made an unlikely coupling as they squeezed into a table for two near the bar. The accordion player touring the tables didn't bother serenading them and manoeuvred past. Stevie had shaved his naturally blond hair from the tops of his ears straight across the back of his head and wore his remaining hair in a ponytail on top with candyfloss-pink stripes. He was dressed in a striking ensemble of lady's purple velour smock, white Lycra leggings and petrol-blue biker boots but, in the dim light of the restaurant, he almost blended in.

'Can I ask you a question, Stevie? What do you wear when you go to visit your folks in the Lake District? I can't imagine your father has ever got used to the make-up or the high heels.'

'He hasn't. If the residents' committee cares, he sure as hell does.'

'So? Do you just calm it all down?'

'No. I just don't go home any more.'

'Never? When's the last time you saw your parents?'

Stevie looked up from the plastic menu he was holding tentatively between the black talons of his thumb and forefinger.

'Daddy dear? I don't know. A few years ago. Maybe. Ma sometimes comes to London and takes me to tea. She pretends for a while that she's cool with it – the band, the bedsit and the bankruptcy – but she always cracks and starts bombarding me with college brochures, job adverts or apprenticeship schemes. It usually ends in a row, and she goes home in tears while I go and get another tattoo or blow my dole on blow.'

He was so matter-of-fact. Always had been. William had long since stopped waiting for Stevie to grow out of his habits; he had realized, eventually, that his friend wasn't going through an extended-adolescence phase. This was just who he was, and William always respected him for having the courage of his convictions. He just sometimes wondered if Stevie had been so rigid in the construction of his identity that he had unwittingly painted himself into a corner he couldn't move on from. He wasn't alone in that predicament, if so. He gave his friend's hand a little nudge across the table.

'Do you never get tired of it all, eh? The struggle?'

Stevie swatted him away with the menu then flicked it towards William.

'Tired of what? Not giving up? Holding my nerve? Do *you* not get tired of it all?'

William rested his forehead on the yellow-and-white-checked plastic tablecloth.

'I do. I'm exhausted. I could curl up under this table and sleep for a decade.'

'Not under this table you couldn't. My shoes were sticking to the floor as I walked in. So, what's going on, then?'

'Maybe in about two drinks' time I can start telling you. I fancy one of those pink cocktails – something fruity, toxic and anonymous that'll work strange wonders on me. Do you know what you want to eat?'

William ordered *camarones borrachos* and *frijolas de la olla* with sautéed spinach and rice. Stevie, always a picky eater, grudgingly accepted that they didn't serve burgers or chips and poked at his *taco de pollo*, seeking out the pieces of meat and wiping off the sauce on the rim of his plate.

'You're lucky Clare isn't here,' William said. 'She really can't cope with fussy eaters. You should try her starters approach – always order something you've never had before as your starter so you get to experience new foods without risking your main meal being something you don't like.'

Stevie waved two sarcastic thumbs up across the table.

'Oh, Clare, she's such an inspiration to us all, with her experimental attitude to life. It really doesn't take much to freak her out, does it?'

'Be fair. When you stayed with us, you really pushed her quite far.'

'What? Just because I like to go out and enjoy myself and don't have OCD about housekeeping, the way she does? Just because not all of us want to work for the man?'

'You wet the bed. Twice.'

Stevie's mouth hung open, the forkful of chicken paused on its way to reach it.

'Did I? Well, it happens to everyone. It's not that big a deal. I cleaned it up.'

'Eh, you didn't actually, and, no, it doesn't happen to everyone. Certainly not anyone over the age of eight.

And you borrowed her grandmother's silk dressing gown that she'd left her in her will and lost it at a rave. And you brought home that girl who stole all her tights. And you woke her up playing the saxophone the night before her big –'

Stevie's perfectly manicured hands fluttered over his food, moving the salt and pepper shakers to one side, refilling their water glasses from a plastic lemon-shaped jug.

'Yeah, yeah, okay. So, there were a few minor clashes, but it was good for her. Loosen her up a bit. Where is she, anyway? Exciting yoga retreat up a mountain? Volunteering to save penguins somewhere, is she?'

William played with the food on his plate; his appetite had absconded with Clare.

'She's a lot more fun than you think, Stevie,' he said. 'You've just never seen that side of her, because when you're around she feels like she has to be the grown-up to stop everyone ending up in jail or the house getting burned down or taken over by squatters. She thinks you're a bad influence. Obviously.'

'So did your mum.'

'She was right.'

'How is the old dear? She never lost it, your mum. Still a cracker.'

William sucked the last of his cocktail into the fluorescent tangerine-orange straw.

'She's gone. I don't know where she is.'

'What? Your mum?'

'Huh? No, not my . . . It's Clare. Clare's gone.'

'As in, a missing person? Like, with police looking for her?'

For once, Stevie looked speechless; his mouth forming a perfect 'O' of pink lipstick.

'What is wrong with you? Of course not. Do you really think, if she'd been abducted, I'd be sitting here with you, drinking cocktails?'

William tried not to notice the faint look of disappointment that floated across Stevie's face as the drama subsided.

'I don't know. Maybe you were going to ask me to do a benefit concert or something.'

'Oh, for the love of . . . She's left me, Stevie. Of her own free will. Run away to God knows where for who knows how long!'

'What the? What did you do? Did she meet someone else? Some dapper gent in the law firm? That's it, isn't it? She was seduced by a nice suit with a yacht? She was always too much of a grown-up for you. How the mighty have fallen!'

William clenched his jaw and pushed his plate away from him.

'I'm already regretting telling you anything. No, it was me. It was my fault. Look, it's complicated. It's not really about anyone else.'

'Don't kid yourself, love. It always is.'

Stevie leaned back on his chair legs, rested his shoulders against the grease-stained walls and summoned the waiter with a toss of his ponytail.

'I think we should get a real drink.'

'Agreed. It's time for Mother's Ruin.'

William hadn't told anyone else about the troubles he and Clare were having; pretending everything was normal made them seem less real. As he tried to put into words how fractured their marriage had become, it felt like he was speaking of strangers in a film or a book; this couldn't be his story. Stevie remained surprisingly silent throughout, but his face registered reactions in waves of sympathy, incredulity and a particularly uncomfortable cringing. William couldn't bring himself to mention Winter. He wasn't sure the dream he nursed would survive the scrutiny of Stevie's particular brand of cynicism. He wasn't ready to defend something he struggled to understand or have faith in himself.

'So, what happens now? Are you going to try to find her?'

'I don't know. It's not as simple as that. I think she's probably right that we both need some space, and I can't force her to come home if she's not ready. What good will that do?'

This time, it was Stevie who reached for William's hand.

'That sounds like you're accepting she's not coming home, dear William. Because, if you are still hoping to resurrect your old life in a straitjacket, you'd better do something fast.'

'Is it really all down to me? She's the one who has run away, after all!'

'Well, far be it from me to defend Her Royal Highness,

but it sounds like not everything was perfect before that happened. Maybe she's doing you both a favour by shining a light on where you are, instead of trying to bury it.'

William drained the last of his gin and signalled to the waitress for another.

'I'm finding your moral superiority a little hard to stomach, I must say. It's not as if you've got the best relationship track record yourself.'

'Nope. I haven't, but I've never made promises I couldn't keep or pretended to be something I'm not. What you see is what you get.'

'Perhaps you should consider a career in relationship counselling.'

'Darling, my mother has had me in therapy since I was thirteen, when she caught me trying on all her lingerie. It's about time someone benefited from it.'

'Your poor mother, how she has suffered.'

'Haven't we all?' He rapped his knuckles on the table, as if calling order in court. 'Now, I think we should shake off all this doom and gloom and seek out some sparkle. Let's go dancing. Or, at least, you can hold my coat for me while I go dancing.'

'Tempting as that sounds, I think I'll just catch the last Tube home. Why don't you head off, and I'll get the bill?'

Stevie was already standing as he snaked a black feather boa around his throat and drained the last of his glass.

'Are you sure? If I run now, it's still free admission to Spiders. You sure you don't want to come?'

'No, you go. But Stevie, thanks. Thanks a lot, for listening to me. Let's not leave it as long next time, okay?'

Stevie leaned over and kissed him on the forehead.

'William, my dear, it was you who vanished, not I. Let me know how it goes.'

With a swish of his feathered coat, he sashayed out of the restaurant, casting a new darkness over the table. William called the elderly waiter over for the bill as he became aware that nearly all the tables were now empty. He left a generous tip and the waiter nodded his acknowledgement. As he began to clatter the plates together, William interrupted him.

'I'm sorry, but could I ask you a question?'

'Of course, sir. Is everything okay? You need a taxi?'

'No, no. I was just wondering if you've worked here a long time?'

'Six nights a week for fifteen years. My wife and I always go dancing on Sundays, and then Cracker's in charge. Why do you ask?'

'I just know someone who comes here a lot and I thought you might know them. A lady called Winter?'

'I'm afraid it doesn't ring a bell, sir, but there's always so many new faces around here, it's hard to remember everyone.' He smiled at William and shook his head as he balanced the dirty plates on his arm.

'She has very long red hair and green eyes. An Irish lady. Does that help?'

The waiter turned back to look at William again.

'Don't a lot of Irish girls look like that, sir? I can't

think of anyone in particular. I'm sorry, but perhaps you can come together another time and introduce me.'

'Perhaps. Thanks again. It was all delicious, really.'

William shuffled into his duffel coat and pulled the hood up. Finding Winter, if that was what he intended to do, was not going to be easy. As he stepped out into the crisp, frosty night, he thought about how much Clare would love this strange little restaurant. It occurred to him how much Winter and Clare had in common. It gave him a jolt: did Winter's letters remind him of the old Clare? The constant flipping in his mind from yin to yang was exhausting. He was trying to compare home with a foreign land he had never visited but had only read about in books. And he didn't know if the writers of the tale were telling the truth.

8.

Despite the late hour, and the circumstances which had led Clare to find herself alone in a hotel room in Wales, she felt surprisingly light and hopeful. As she lay in the middle of the bed, legs and arms stretched wide, her mind wandered back to that morning. It felt like days since she'd said goodbye to William, instead of just the mere hours that had passed since the telephone call that had set her on this path. Maxi had been concerned when Clare was absent from work. Things had become confused between them; he was worried that she was avoiding him, said he desperately wanted to see her and had driven to her street in pursuit. Those words from him on the telephone had rattled her; she was already so anxious to escape, even if it was just for a short while. Maxi told her he would take her anywhere she wanted to go. On impulse, she settled on Wales, where she'd spent summers as a child. Somewhere calm and safe, where she could be alone. Her feelings towards Maxi weren't clear in her mind. Had he become more than a friend? Or was she looking for a life raft to help her leave the lonely island of her marriage?

After they arrived at the hotel, he looked crestfallen when she asked him not to come in with her. They had driven there together mostly in silence; she presumed he thought the talking would come later. Instead, she stared out of the window while Kate Bush's *Hounds of Love* played on repeat. As she hugged herself in the car seat, her fingers found a hole in William's *Star Wars* T-shirt, just below her ribcage. She stroked her skin through it like a baby playing with the label on a blanket. Every so often, she discreetly pulled the neck of the T-shirt over her nose to breathe in the lingering smell of him: the gentle aroma of patchouli and cedarwood from the beard oil she loved.

Every so often, she stole a glance at Maxi out of the corner of her eye: his blond hair was cut short enough to kill the curl, his starched white shirt rolled to the elbows of his tanned arms. He drove like a man in control of a mission, staring straight ahead, weaving gracefully between lanes, accelerating rapidly when any stretch of road became clear. She liked him more for his silence; for not pushing her. After their awkward goodbye in the hotel car park, she was relieved to find a room ready for her and immediately called the office to see how her assistant, Nava, was coping in her absence. A little too well for comfort, it seemed, but Clare resigned herself to the knowledge that this time away was essential. Thinking of the pep talk the managing partner had given her when she had stopped at the office en route, she cringed. It was clear she hadn't been herself recently; it seemed she needed a break. So mortifying after all these years with a perfect record; how frustrating the glee he took in patting her on the shoulder and saying, 'You are only human, after all,' as if confirmation had been pending for years.

She unpacked her suitcase as slowly as possible, arranged her toiletries in descending height in the bathroom and perched on one side of the stiffly made bed, cradling the bedside telephone in her lap. She wanted to talk to someone but couldn't think of anyone she could bear to confide in. All her friends had become their friends. None of her relationships with colleagues had graduated past breezy platitudes or repetitive rants about parking, working hours or the sub-par coffee in the staff kitchen. Flora was the only option; the only person exclusively hers. As much as William had immediately adored Flora when she eventually brought him home, Clare had refused to cultivate the relationship between her husband and her little sister. Maybe she didn't want William ever to witness her through Flora's conflicted gaze. No matter how much you evolve as a person, the extent to which you change or improve, your family holds such a fixed notion of who you are; they won't allow you to leave your past behind you or become someone new. Clare had worked hard to grow out of the girl weighed down by their hefty familial baggage and she didn't want Flora dragging her back into that room. She hadn't really considered before why keeping their relationship separate was so important to her, but she was glad of it now. Maybe she would ask Flora to come and stay with her, after she'd had a day or two to think things through. First things first, though. She stood under the powerful hotel shower to cleanse the city of London from her hair and face. She polished her body with a scratchy flannel and appreciated the unfamiliar scent of the hotel's lemongrass soap. With her hair pulled into a messy bun, she dressed in the most comfortable cotton dress in her possession and was surprised to find she felt hungry. Usually, when she was upset her appetite failed her, but she craved something hot and savoury and so made her way to the restaurant in the hotel conservatory.

Over a dish of Welsh rarebit and a glass of Merlot, Clare watched the other hotel guests and indulged in a little eavesdropping. Her ears pricked up when she overheard dangerous words like 'divorce', or 'cancer', or 'pregnant' being whispered. She breathed a little more easily; the little titbits of other people's lives were a salve to the upsets of her own; a reconnection with a world outside the claustrophobic space she had started obsessively inhabiting in her mind.

'When we arrive at your mother's, please don't vanish off with your dad and leave me in the kitchen with her, Mike. Not again. Not after last time.'

'Can you believe Kay still thinks I'm a vegetarian? After all these years! If she ever catches me with a kebab, she'll keel over on the spot.'

'Valerie thinks I should try alternative therapies, but I'm not so sure. It just feels like I would be swimming against the river.'

'I just don't think I can love a man who doesn't appreciate the brilliance of Depeche Mode. It just shows such a fundamental lack of compatibility between us.'

Clare felt nostalgic for the time when the greatest problems she and William navigated involved not loving the same bands. She smiled, remembering the night he refused to go to the pub with her because she was wearing a Frankie Says Relax T-shirt. She left without him, of course, and he followed her half an hour later. Was it inevitable that two people who had met so young would eventually grow apart? If she was no longer with William, who would she become? Their relationship defined her; she was the responsible one, the careerist who gave them security. How had her identity become so wrapped up with her job? A job she honestly wasn't even sure that she loved. When was *her* time to follow her heart?

When she thought of herself as the little girl who loved painting, music and performing, she could never have imagined she would grow up to become this rigid lawyer with no artistic outlet at all. In her younger years, she was afraid of following an insecure path that could keep her stuck in poverty, but she didn't have to worry about that now. Her success to date would give her the freedom to do something different now, if she wanted. William refusing to allow them to take on a bigger mortgage had at least enabled her to save a significant sum. What was stopping her? She couldn't blame William, or their relationship, entirely. It was just so hard to imagine herself doing something else now. What if she no longer had it in her? She had harboured these comforting notions of her own untapped potential but without ever really confronting whether she had any talent at all. It was easier to believe in the theory while it remained untested. Often, adults have to balance a conflict between what they think they are compelled to do as a responsible person and what they desire to do. Why had that never applied to William? The imbalance of power between them was of little concern to him. He never questioned if she was truly happy to keep them afloat with her job while he pursued his flights of fancy, his writing and his endless fascination with the work of the depot. Would it be different if she was with someone like Maxi?

Perhaps if William had tried but failed, instead of just failing through what she considered an absence of effort, it would have been easier to accept things as they were. She remembered so clearly the day when his charade was exposed; the details were burned on her mind like a photograph kept permanently in her wallet. Sheets of rain collapsed from the skies as she drove her Mini home that day. The drops pounded on the tin roof; the windscreen wipers sploshed water back and forth without increasing her range of visibility at all. It made her nervous, driving through a storm so heavy, the sweltering air that fogged the windows from the condensation spreading, the blinking lights of other cars and traffic lights smearing before her eyes. When she finally splashed to a stop outside their house, she rested her head against the steering wheel in relief and released the tension she had been holding across her shoulders as she drove. Clutching a brown-paper bag of pastries, she doubled over against the onslaught as she dashed to the front door in the downpour. Just two houses away, but the rain soaked through her linen blazer, ran in rivulets down her back and clung to her eyelashes in the time it took her to reach home. The bag was disintegrating in her hands and puddles invaded her court shoes as she ran. She shrieked as she slammed the door behind her.

Wriggling out of her soggy jacket, she kicked off her shoes and wiped a blouse sleeve across her damp forehead as she scuttled through the hallway towards the welcoming fire she anticipated would be glowing in the living room. Shaking off the sudden shock of the storm, Clare became aware of a voice floating from the kitchen. Who on earth was visiting at this time of day? She tuned into the sharp tone of a woman's cut-crystal accent; it was familiar, but she couldn't quite place it.

'I suppose there's nothing else to say, but I hope you realize that this embarrassment is not exclusively yours. I have been covering for you for months, and you've made a fool out of me. I can't say this isn't a huge disappointment.'

The door yanked open before Clare could reach it. Olivia Longworth, William's literary agent, froze in surprise to see Clare standing there. She was flushed and agitated, unrecognizable as the elegant lady Clare had met previously, despite the uniform cream wool skirt and cardigan she always seemed to wear. For a moment, it looked as if she was going to speak, but instead she gave a curt nod as she brushed past Clare towards the front door. A curse exploded from her as she stepped out into the torrential rain. In the kitchen, William, pale and sickly-looking under the fluorescent light bulb, sat holding his head at the table.

'William? What's wrong with Olivia? Has something happened with the book? You look terrible. Tell me what's going on!'

Of all the possible explanations she may have expected, the one that he offered floored her.

'There is no book,' he offered quietly, without raising his head to look at her.

'What are you talking about? Dear God, she hasn't lost it, has she? I told you to keep making copies. Oh, no – they aren't pulling out of publishing it, are they? They can't do that – you have a contract . . .'

She dropped the soggy bag of pastries on the kitchen table as he slowly shook his head. Crouching beside him at the table, she asked again. 'William! You're scaring me. Please tell me. What's happened?'

And so the story unravelled. For eighteen months, no words had come to complete the novel he had promised to deliver. The short stories that had secured him the contract remained the only work completed. It wasn't that he hadn't finished the book; he had never even really begun. Before he had secured the publishing success he coveted, with its advances, opportunity and obligations, the blank page had held no fear for him. He had attacked it with vigour and Clare had marvelled at how effortlessly the streams of consciousness flowed from him. 'Like turning on a tap,' she used to say. 'More like rain running down a drainpipe,' he would joke in response. Now, though, the weight of expectation had flattened him, he explained. Squashed his inspiration. It was as if, by consciously trying, he could no longer access his subconscious. He had scared away his voice.

'Nonsense!' Clare shouted. 'You just need some discipline, hard graft, perseverance.'

She didn't understand, he insisted. 'It's not something I can force myself to do, it's not like building bricks or working in a factory. The harder I push, the further away it pulls.'

Clare dashed into the living room, grabbed the file she believed held his manuscript, the great novel she'd sworn not to read until it was ready, and shook its contents out across the kitchen table in impatient disbelief. Reams of white paper scattered; some had one or two lines typed, others haphazard diagrams, scribbles and crossed-out handwriting. Most were blank. He had been methodically filling the file every day with faux progression; it grew fatter with his lie and the mounting pressure.

'I kept hoping I would have a breakthrough, that I could salvage something,' he whispered. 'I couldn't admit to you what was happening, or to myself. I was sure I could claw it back.'

'And now?' she asked.

'The publishers won't wait any longer. I've missed the deadline for a first draft too many times. The editor demanded to see the work in progress. That's why Olivia was here. It's over. And they want their money back.'

Writing a cheque to repay his advance from their savings was the least painful part of the process. She tried to have some empathy for what he must have suffered while nursing his secret but was floored by the daily deceit. How could he lie to her day after day for all that time? She had learned to accept his explanation, but never to understand it. Who would throw away such a chance? And hide their failure from their wife? Why was he so scared to be vulnerable in her eyes? She remembered tossing the pastries the next evening, stale and conjoined now with the brown paper that had wrapped them. She hadn't brought William doughnuts home for afternoon tea since.

Clare drained the dregs of her wine and walked out of the hotel without a clear idea of where she was going. She followed the lane towards the village, enjoying how the drivers of passing cars waved in acknowledgement, regardless of not knowing her. St Gerard's consisted of just one square with a church, a pub and a school commandeering three of its sides. On the fourth, there was a tea room with striped deckchairs in clusters of twos and threes arranged around suitcases set as tables outside, and an antique shop selling furniture and bric-a-brac. Looking through the window at the paraphernalia, fixtures and fittings, it reminded her of the terraced house where she grew up and she felt a chill. Clare's mother had always told her she had an over-active imagination and threatened to ban her from the library if she didn't get her feet back on the ground. She looked at the heavy spiral wallpaper adorning the walls of the shop and remembered how, in her half-sleep, the ivory flock pattern on the rose-red wallpaper of her childhood bedroom had danced. She lay under pink ticklish blankets, fingers stroking the white silk ribbon around the edge, and tried to trick the dancers into staying until she called her papa, but as soon as she blinked, they were gone. The ghosts from the wall had haunted her nighttimes for years, until she turned twelve and paint became more fashionable than wallpaper and the paper with its dancers was stripped away. Her mother painted the walls oatmeal, a flat, dull non-colour that Clare later covered with the artefacts of her adolescence: black-and-white posters of John Lennon, a giant print of Bowie's *Ziggy Stardust* album cover and framed pictures of Greta Garbo, Ginger Rogers and Judy Garland. She missed the dancers sometimes after they were gone, when she no longer had to fear absorbing their strange, shadowy presence into her mind. They had been long forgotten by the time she found herself looking in that dusty window in the village square when they fluttered back into her consciousness.

The hem of her long-suffering sky-blue jumper snagged on a window box and a strand of wool unravelled. Clare released it, cursing another fray, for she could never part with it, no matter how mangled it became. She loved the white stars as big as her hands that her mother had clumsily knitted into the pattern. There weren't many happy memories from her childhood that she clung to, but the day she unwrapped that jumper was one of them and she didn't want to let it go. As she tied a knot in the loose strand, she watched through the window as little glass balloons bobbed from an oak bough perched on a mantelpiece: orange red and powder blue. Something about the light, how they danced in it, stirred an old feeling. She was eleven and her ghosts were dancing.

Clare shuddered, despite the brilliant white sunshine that illuminated the square, casting shadows and dispersing fragments of dust. She hurried next door, to a newsagent's that promised to sell 'all essentials and even some extras'. She decided to hunt for a novel to read in this newly acquired time for herself; the door jangled a dream-catcher constructed of seashells to announce her arrival. The back wall of the shop consisted of rows of paperbacks, and she made her way to it, past the ice-cream fridge, the carousel of postcards, the shelves of sweets in glass jars. As she crouched down to read the titles on the bottom shelf, a pile of clumsily stacked sketch pads in the corner caught her eye. She mooched closer and shuffled through them until she found an A5 version with thick ivory paper inside a soft mulberry leather cover. It surprised her to find something so exquisite in this little rural shop. Before she could change her mind, she grabbed it and marched to the counter, where she picked up a handful of pencils, an eraser and a sharpener. At the last moment, she threw a sherbet Dip-Dab and a Fry's Turkish Delight on top, too. She was on holiday, after all, of a fashion. She felt a rush of excitement as she tucked the striped lemon-and-white paper bag containing her treasure under her arm and clattered the shop door closed behind her.

Back in her hotel room, Clare opened the sketch pad on the first page and laid it carefully on her dressing table underneath a freshly pared pencil. She backed away from it for a moment, wary about discovering if she could still use these tools with any flair. She paced back and forth, poured herself a miniature gin and tonic from the mini-bar, and sat down; rolled the pencil between her fingers, feeling its weight, before making a few tentative, wispy strokes across the paper. Quickly, she tore the page from the spiral spine, scrunched it into a ball and tossed it on the floor. A memory of her art teacher in school came back to her. 'Leave everything on the page,' Miss Forde had said as she strode around in the room in black leather trousers. 'Be bold or be nothing.'

Clare swallowed the alcohol in two mouthfuls, wiped her mouth on a paper serviette and stared at herself in the mirror where she sat. She sketched out the long, oval shape of her face, drew a line from her forehead to where her chin would be, marked lines for the shape of her cheeks, nose and jaw and then began to define her eyes, mouth and ears. Her work was silent and steady until the natural light left the room, forcing her to turn on the lamp beside her.

She continued working as the drawing became more and more detailed, but her eyes grew weary. When she woke up a few hours later, she had fallen asleep at the dressing table, head slumped forward, pencil in hand. She held up her drawing and saw her own face staring back at her. Clare had to admit it was good. She closed the cover of the sketch pad, held it against her chest for a moment then crawled under the blankets of her bed. Reflecting on the day as she savoured the weight of the blankets engulfing her, she was surprised at how it was ending, despite its horrific beginning. It was a blessed relief to have no anticipation of human or alarm to wake her; to fall asleep with thoughts of herself alone and not the torment that had plagued her so. As she slipped away into a slumber, a small smile rested on her face.

9.

In the three days since Clare had left, William heard from her only once, via a message on their answering machine giving the number of her hotel in Wales. In case of emergency only. What was she doing there? Was she alone? William sat in the Dead Letters Depot, listening to Marjorie gossip about him through the partition walls: 'I'm just sayin', 'e looks desperate. I bet she's left 'im, she always thought she was too good for 'im.'

He leaned back in his creaking leather chair and contemplated escaping to the Supernatural Division as he scanned the postal debris strewn across his desk. A long cylinder wrapped in newspaper caught his eye, an irregular shape amid the pile of impatient homeless post awaiting him. He dragged it closer with a wooden ruler, bulldozing over the other parcels in its wake. The newspaper print was tattered and smudged, the name and address smeared into long streams of blue, a dirty mess conjuring up a damp smell of soggy paper that curled up William's nostrils. He gently tore the now tissue-like newspaper away, flinching as it caught under his fingernails. He edged carefully around the smudged address in case any of it could be deciphered. Ten sheets of newspaper peeled away. A final layer of protection – cardboard from a cornflakes cereal box – before a thin oak case with a copper clasp was revealed. William peeled a grey envelope from the cardboard where it had been secured carefully with Sellotape on all four edges. It was addressed to Mr Harry Prummel; the name was written in small, neat capital letters with a fine-tipped blue pen. William opened the case first. Inside lay a gleaming silver medal in the shape of a cross with an image of St George and the dragon at the centre; it hung from a navy-blue ribbon threaded through a silver ring. The inscription 'Francis Sillitoe', the date 26.07.42 and 'For Gallantry' were engraved around the centrepiece. William felt the cool weight in the palm of his hand, fingered the silk ribbon between his fingers. It reminded him of how Clare's skirt had felt against his face the morning she left, and he blushed. He laid the medal back in its case and opened the letter that accompanied it.

Dear Mr Prummel,

I call you Mister, although in my mind's eye you will always be the little chap of seven that I held in my arms. I don't know if you remember my name, or ever knew it at all, in fact, but I have no doubt you remember the day we met; some days are burned in our memories for ever, even those of a seven-year-old.

I was the man who climbed into your window and carried you from the fire on that last godforsaken night of bombings. We had been fighting the flames for fifty-seven days. I was exempt from active military service because I was a civil engineer but hated feeling like I was dodging my duty as my friends and brothers all did theirs. When the bombing began, I volunteered as an ARP and felt as though I was finally doing my bit, although my bit proved more than I ever could have imagined. When the first bombs started dropping, I coordinated a rescue team and, through the nights and days that followed, we did manage to save a great number of lives, including your own. I will always be proud of that. It was for these rescue missions that I was awarded the George Medal you find enclosed here. It was my greatest honour to receive it and I have held it dear all these years.

What you may or may not know is that on that last night of bombings, my own house was struck, and burned down. My wife, Dorothy, and my little boy, Charlie, didn't make it out. He was seven years old, too. I have regretted every day since that I was not there to save them, but I will never regret that I was there to save you.

I'm not long past my ninety-fifth birthday and I won't see another. I hope that I find Dorothy and Charlie in the next life, and that they've forgiven me for what happened. What worldly possessions I have will all go where they should, but my medal, I would like you to have. I will never forget your face when I picked you up; how your little hands gripped the back of my neck as though you would never let me go. I have never let the memory go.

You may be wondering how I have found you after all these years. Well, after the war, your mother and I stayed in touch. She was very distressed about Charlie and always sent me a letter on his birthday and filled me in on how well you were doing. It has been a joy to read of your successes all these years, and it has helped me to place what Charlie might have been doing if he was still with us. I was very saddened to hear of your mother's passing. She was a wonderful woman, as you know. Please accept this medal with my very best wishes for a long life, full of happiness.

If you do say some prayers, say one for me, if you think of me.

Yours sincerely,
Frank Sillitoe

William picked up the medal again and said a little prayer of his own for an old man who had lost his son while saving another. He gently spread the address label flat under the light of his desk lamp and scrutinized the diluted letters. The first two lines were completely illegible but he was sure the next read 'Clovelly' and, unless he was mistaken, there was only one Clovelly in the United Kingdom and this parcel had been destined for Devon. Without a doubt, this delivery qualified for special treatment. He reclined in his chair while an idea percolated; maybe he would take a road trip and deliver it himself. He dreaded his evenings alone in the flat and everywhere he went he was haunted by memories of Clare and apparitions of Winter. Every time a red-headed girl passed him, he wondered whether it could be Winter; convinced that she was close. Was that her walking ahead of him, reading a book on the opposite train platform, or looking out of the window as a bus whizzed past him? The city was shrinking around his shoulders. He needed some relief from the constant battle that raged inside him as he flitted from despair at the loss of Clare to hope at the thought of Winter. Thoughts of the two women pulled him back and forth. He still loved Clare, so why was he not impervious to thoughts of someone else? Even if it was something of a fantasy. Winter's appeal for folk to find strength in their own person lay heavily on his mind. He would travel to Clovelly, track down Harry Prummel and deliver the parcel himself. It would be good to focus on something tangible and real; he needed to accomplish something.

The following morning dawned crisp and clean. The sky looked as if it were painted by a child with only one blue in his paint box and no time for clouds. William donned the official postmaster blazer he was supposed to wear every day but seldom did and loaded up his beloved Ford Corsair. He willed it, first of all, to start, and then, ultimately, to survive the five-hour drive to North Devon. William had inherited this old motor from Uncle Archie and would never be able to let her go, even as 'Corina' grew more and more exhausted and begged for retirement. It was foolish to risk such a long journey in that jalopy, but William needed to feel the power of really driving, to breathe in the history of the leather seats, to surround himself with the safe cocoon of happier times. He was confident that Corina was on his side and would chug through. He packed chocolate peanuts, a bottle of apple juice and a Tupperware box of dried prunes into a Marks and Spencer plastic bag. In his overnight case, he crammed pyjamas, fresh clothing, a pair of binoculars for exploring and *The Woman in White*. *The War of the Worlds* on cassette would keep him company as the miles rolled under his wheels. He considered calling Clare's hotel to tell her where he was going but decided against it and left a note on the kitchen table instead.

Dear Clare,

I hope that you find this note, because that means you are home. I am sorry I was not there to see you walk through the door. Work has taken me to Clovelly. (Can you believe it!!?) I'll be home soon and I hope more than anything that you will be here waiting for me.

Love,
William

William felt the universe had granted him a little reprieve in placing Harry Prummel in Clovelly, of all places. He had wanted to visit ever since he was a little boy but, somehow, had never made it. As a child, he was obsessed with the legend of King Arthur and the great wizard, Merlin. He worked Merlin into every school project he could and, from as young as eight, had acquired quite an exhaustive knowledge of all the myths related to him. When people spoke about the Troubles in Northern Ireland, he loved to tell them that it was all Merlin's fault, really: 'You see, Merlin had advised King Ambrosius to build Stonehenge to honour the dead, but they didn't have enough stone to do it justice and so they invaded Ireland to gather the resources.' It was a theory that usually provoked some strong reactions.

Legend suggested that there was a waterfall in Clovelly where Merlin was born. William had always nursed a dream to hunt Merlin across the country, visiting all the places that he was associated with and retracing his steps. It felt a foolish pursuit for a grown man, however, and remained an inner-voice whimsy that was seldom vocalized when planning the annual fortnight's holiday with Clare. He was tickled to tick one destination off his list, though, and relished the idea of a night away from the loneliest bed in London.

It was almost six hours later that William proudly parked at the visitor centre on the edge of Clovelly. Corina had taken a little longer than he'd hoped but had not let him down; he felt vindicated. He hadn't realized that the fishing village was a private estate, but he imagined that was how such a famous idyll had managed to retain its old-world charm. He was pleased to see they had prevented the tumbling, four-hundred-feet-long cobbled high street from becoming festooned with tourist traps and souvenir shops. William stretched his arms over his head and shook away the driving cramps that had settled in his legs.

An elderly man with a white beard that twisted into a point at his knees sat watching him from a bench; he was methodically stringing multicoloured beads on to purple yarn to make long necklaces akin to the dozens he wore. William started when he caught his eye but the resemblance to Merlin felt like a good sign and he approached him to begin his hunt for Mr Prummel.

'Hello there. I hope I'm not disturbing you.'

'Not so far. I'm wonderin' if the disturbin' bit comes next.'

'Oh, I hope not. I'm just looking for someone. Maybe you know him, a chap by the name of Harry Prummel? Would you know where I might find him?'

'Is he hiding from you?'

'No, no. We've never even met. I just have to deliver something to him.'

'So you have his address, then? You look a bit long in the tooth for a delivery boy.'

'I work for the post office, actually, and his address was missing on a parcel. I just know he lives in Clovelly somewhere, and I wanted to make sure it gets to him safely, you see.'

'No, I don't see. In my experience, people who want to be found usually present themselves in the end.'

'But he doesn't know I'm looking for him in order for him to be able to present himself.'

'Well, you are in a pickle, then.'

'And even if he did, he wouldn't know where to find me.'

'In my experience, people who want to be found —'

'Yes, yes. They present themselves. I guess I'll just go and stand in the middle of the town, shall I? And wait for Harry to guess I'm looking for him?'

'You could. Or you could call into his office. Young Prummel is the only accountant in town. His rooms are at the foot of the hill, over Betty's tea shop.'

'Oh? Well, thank you, but you could have just said that.'

'Now, where's the fun in that? Enjoy your slow-down, Londoner.'

William walked to the turnstile and looked over his shoulder before he climbed through. His Merlin had vanished. He turned towards the village. His knees slowly adjusted to the bendy way of walking that kept him balanced as he began his descent of the steep cobbled hill. The city he had left that morning seemed to belong to another planet. The little whitewashed cottages, with their flower boxes and pretty patterned curtains, were straight from the lid of a biscuit tin. It looked as if only happiness could live there. Of course, he knew the opposite was probably true, as the inhabitants battled the elements and the private demons everyone faces. He was sorely tempted to stop halfway down for a cream tea in the shade. He longed to roll up his sleeves and drape his blazer over the back of a pastel-painted chair in one of the friendly-looking tea houses that lined the route but decided to complete his mission first. He found himself taking a surprising amount of pleasure at the unexpected sight of the donkeys passing by with their loads.

The entrance to Mr Prummel's office sat to the side of Devon Delights, a café William now understood to be owned by someone named Betty. He rang the doorbell but, receiving no reply, gave the red wooden door a little push. It swung wide for him, revealing a narrow, winding staircase. His knee creaked as he climbed up two flights of stairs before emerging abruptly into a tiny reception room.

A bespectacled woman sat behind an expansive mahogany desk that could not dwarf her formidable presence with its might. Her back was straight as a lamp post, her silver hair wound in a tight coil upon her head. A lilac paisley dress wrapped in a neat crease across her kitten-like frame. Her face was lined, but her eyes sparkled green as they darted from her typewriter to meet William's own. He wondered if Winter's eyes were the same shade of apple.

'Good afternoon. Can I help you?'

'Hello! I hope so. I was wondering if I could pop in to see Harry Prummel for a moment?'

'I should think not. People don't "pop" in to see Mr Prummel. He is a very busy man, you know. Did you not think to make an appointment?'

'No, unfortunately I didn't, but it's not for professional reasons I need to see him. I have a personal matter to discuss. Is he not free at all, just for a moment?'

She started busily squirting water from a spritzer on to a family of succulents on her desk.

'If it's a personal matter, I suggest you see him in his personal time. Otherwise, you'll have to make an appointment.'

'Fine. Could I just make one for later today, then, please?'

She continued squirting for a moment longer before flicking briskly through a desk calendar that could serve as a doorstop.

'The next available appointment would be three weeks on Thursday, 8.45 a.m.'

'But I'm only here until tomorrow. Could you not just pop in to him and tell him there is someone here to see him?'

'Are we back to the popping? As I've said, no one –'

'What time does the office close? I'll wait outside, if you don't mind.'

'Please yourself. Mr Prummel usually leaves at five o' clock, but he may leave earlier, maybe later. I'm not his keeper. I couldn't possibly say.'

William decided to treat himself to some fish and chips on the seafront and find a spot where he could sit and watch for Harry leaving the office. He walked along the waterfront, across the pebbly beach, and squirmed to feel grains of gravel invading his shoes. The vinegar soaked through the newspaper on to his hand and the salty smell intoxicated him as he perched on a low stone wall and relished in his indulgence. As Harry's finishing time drew closer, William began to worry that he had somehow missed him. Maybe he wasn't even working that day and his security guard had slipped out while he was buying his fish supper. Of course, it couldn't have turned out as easily as it had promised to; so little in his life ever did these days. He shuffled from one foot to the other, pulling up an unruly sock that slid under his heel. He rearranged the detritus in his pockets so left became items to keep (house keys, Polo mints, handkerchief) and right became things to throw away (stray button, toffee wrappers, pen lid). He tried for a moment to whistle a tune but lacked the puff and resorted instead to conjugating Latin verbs in his head. As the chapel bell chimed five, William became fixated on the red door. It hadn't opened once in all the time he had been waiting. He strained his ears at every suggestion of a creak, until, after ten more torturous minutes, it slowly opened inward. A jolly-looking man with a retreating hairline of fuzzy ginger hair casually strolled out, as if the most impatient man in England weren't feverishly awaiting him. William vaulted forward.

'Harry! Mr Prummel, excuse me! I was hoping to catch you.'

Harry Prummel turned, the tails of his jaunty red blazer spinning behind him.

'Oh, hello. I've actually finished for the day, but you can speak to Mrs Whisker about an appointment.'

William held up his hand in protest and shook his head.

'No, please. I've already met Mrs Whisker and explained that I'm only here for the day and wanted to speak to you about a personal matter. I've been waiting all afternoon. Could I just walk with you wherever you are going? I promise it won't take long.'

'I see. Perhaps we'd better go back upstairs?'

'That would be marvellous. Thank you. I'll explain everything.'

William followed Harry back inside and up the winding staircase, past a surprised and embarrassed Mrs Whisker, who was applying a little rouge when they appeared, and into an office even smaller than the reception area. There were potted plants everywhere and, as William caught his foot on a fern near his seat, Harry explained his partner, Liam, was 'going through a feng shui phase'. 'I'm not sure he totally understands what it's all about, but one unfortunate element he's latched on to is that plants foster prosperity, so now I'm working in a greenhouse. Anyway, how can I help you, Mr . . . ?'

'Woolf. William Woolf. I work as a letter detective in the Dead Letters Depot in London, and I have a parcel for you that was lost in the post before reaching us.'

'A letter detective? Well, that sounds fascinating. Does everyone get such a personal service, Mr Woolf?'

'No, but some things aren't worth risking losing twice, and I felt I should bring this to you myself, for my own peace of mind.'

'Well, this is all very intriguing. Hand it over, then.'

William placed a padded brown envelope on Harry's pristine emerald-green marble desktop and watched Harry survey it before nudging it closer to him.

'Would you rather I left you alone, Mr Prummel?'

Harry looked more confused than ever but shook his head.

'No, I think it's better if you stay until we see what this is all about.'

Harry slid the contents of the envelope out on to the table and touched the surface of the oak case with his fingertips.

'Can you tell me what's inside, Mr Woolf? I must admit, this is all making me a little nervous.'

'I think it's best if you just read the letter, Mr Prummel. Please. There's nothing to be afraid of.'

Harry swivelled his chair to the right to catch the last

fading light from the window. William stared at the brown spirals in the rug beneath his feet to afford him what privacy he could. A shocked, wet gasp burst from Harry, and William looked up to see him holding one hand across his mouth as he read. Tears were gathering in his eyes as he turned back to face William.

'Forgive me, Mr Woolf, for getting so emotional.'

He opened the oak case and laid the medal before him on the desk.

'William, please. I know this must come as something of a shock.'

'I owe you an enormous debt of gratitude, William. This letter releases me from a guilt that has clung to me my whole life.'

William sat up straighter in his chair, and asked, 'So you knew about Frank Sillitoe?'

'Yes, but I had no idea that he and my mother had communicated all these years. She's passed away now. I don't know why she didn't tell me about him. I've always been afraid that he regretted saving me, resented me for surviving when his son had not. To think I have always had his blessing. I feel a great weight has been lifted from me. Maybe I can go and see him and thank him myself.'

William smiled at him. 'I'm sure that he would be relieved to see you after all these years.'

'I don't know how to thank you. The work you do – you must witness so many people's stories, eavesdrop on their private lives, so to speak. It's a big responsibility.'

'Well, sometimes remarkable things happen, like today. Others, we have to let go because we can't find a way to help. That's always hard, but we try to remember that lives continue long after the last words of a letter are written and hope people find some other way. Maybe the letters who need us the most find us.' William blushed. 'I'm sorry, I'm sure that sounds silly to you.'

'Not at all. How could you believe anything else and do your job? I wish I could repay you somehow; you've come all this way. Will you at least join us for supper?'

William considered this for a moment. He was tempted, but wanted to spend some time alone, exploring the village, contemplating his next move. As he stood to leave, William leaned across the desk to shake Harry's hand, but he was instead pulled into a great bear hug.

His feet danced past Mrs Whisker's empty desk, skipped back down the stairs and into Clovelly at dusk. Once again, he was struck by the power of letters to change lives; the medium they offered those who couldn't or wouldn't communicate in person. How much would be left unsaid if people were devoid of the opportunity that pen and paper offered to speak from a safe distance? He would never underestimate it. This was the message he wanted to deliver in the *Volume of Lost Letters* he was compiling. It motivated him to keep working, despite the apathy he felt at home from Clare and in the depot from Ned. Wouldn't Harry's story be the perfect way to open the book? He was filled anew with the excitement of his project. People would want to hear these stories; he was sure of it.

He made his way to the Red Lion Hotel and was pleased to see that his room offered a panoramic view of the peninsula. He thought about how much Clare would love it here and decided to bring her home a postcard, if he could find one that did the little village justice. He had achieved his mission. Filled with renewed optimism, he set out to explore.

With a little map he picked up from the reception desk, William set off to climb the Look-out. The sun was setting in a blaze of blood orange. Dark clouds crept in from the west, charcoal snakes slithering across the sky and smearing it in blackness. He hurried to the waterfall that was hidden halfway up to the Look-out but, as he climbed through to the cave at the back of the crashing waters, the heavens opened. He huddled for cover from the downpour, cursing himself for not returning to the hotel when he first saw the gathering thunderclouds. The rain showed no signs of clearing, so he surrendered to the soaking and started pushing back towards the harbour, head bent against nature. A fork of lightning illuminated the sky; the world's greatest photographer turning on the flash of her camera to capture the dark, dripping village. William's eye was caught by a lone figure, dressed all in white, standing on the brink of the Look-out. A woman stood with her arms outstretched, staring down at the storm over the harbour. Her trailing dress was plastered wet against her body, blowing behind her like a forgotten sheet on a washing line. Her long red hair tangled in the sea spray, the tendrils dancing in the wind like serpents' tails, ribbons of fire against the electric black sky. He was frozen in time, spellbound. She melted back into the shadows and disappeared into the night.

William staggered back to his lodgings and dried his prickling skin with fluffy white towels that smoothed away some of the corners of his jarred state of mind. Hastening to pull the blinds in his bedroom, he kept his eyes lowered as he drew closer to the window frame. A childhood fear had resurfaced and caught him by the heart; he couldn't look directly at the glass or he would see someone looking in, or worse, another face reflected over his shoulder. 'Get a grip, you old fool', he mumbled. 'You're just winding yourself up.'

He decanted a hefty shot of Jameson's from the mini-bar into a crystal tumbler and breathed in the aroma before he drank his first hot sip. He held the whiskey up to the light: pure amber swirls, no particles or imperfections. When things with Clare had started to unravel, he had made a decision never to drink alone in the evenings, although he sometimes found the urge to resist difficult in mornings and afternoons, too. He didn't want to return to the months following his publishing failure, when most important occasions, and many inconsequential ones, were bookended by something to take the edge off in anticipation and something to savour in reflection.

He curled the liquor around in his mouth; a little ball of heat rolling over every tooth, dancing on his tongue. A slow swallow slid down his parched throat, along his spine, to tingle the tips of his toes. He turned on the radio and bristled at the screeching white noise of uncharted radio waves. The dial found him BBC Radio 3, and the comfort of the musical grace of Beethoven's 'Moonlight' piano sonata descended upon him. He rummaged in his satchel for a notebook and pen and sat straight-backed at the little pine desk in his room. The Prummel encounter had struck a nerve; he knew he had stories to tell. Down the drainpipe, rusty water flowed once again. On and on he wrote, and the words rang true. It was effortless. Just before midnight, he stopped. Ended on just the right sentence. This was the second time the words had come in as many weeks. He sat back in the stiff wooden chair and nodded. Maybe the drought was over.

The electric light from the skies crackled around the perimeter of the window blinds. Occasionally, the laughter and squeals of his neighbours next door reminded him he was not alone in this weather-racked hotel by the sea. If Clare had been with him, he was sure they would be sitting up in bed, excitedly watching the storm vent her fury, clutching each other under the covers with each crash. How he longed for Clare that night; missing her fostered tight pangs in his chest, fists beating the bones of his ribs, denting his heart-box. He desperately wanted to tell her about the writing; needed her acknowledgement. He unearthed the number of her hotel from his travelling bag and stretched to drag the telephone down from the locker on to the plush taupe carpet beside him.

After two short rings, a soft Welsh accent whispered into the phone.

'Good evening. Harvest House, how may I help you?'

'Hello, could you put me through to Clare Carpenter's room, please?'

'Are you sure you want to disturb her? It is after midnight.'

'Yes, this is her husband. It's fine.'

William counted the rings while he waited for Clare to answer. One. Two. She'll be stirring. Oh God, I hope she isn't too furious about me calling so late, or for calling at all. Three. It would be worse to hang up now. She's probably blinking into the dark, looking for the phone. Four. Five. Six. Is she wondering who it is? Why isn't she answering? Seven. Eight. Is she afraid to answer in case it's me?

Click.

'Oh, thank God. Clare, it's me. I'm sorry for calling so late. I just really need to talk to you –'

'Excuse me. I'm sorry. Mr Carpenter? You've come back through to reception.'

'Oh.' William paused, curling and releasing his toes in the carpet fibres. 'Can you try her room again, please? And it's Mr Woolf. My wife kept her maiden name.'

'I'm afraid I can see now that your wife's room is unoccupied at the moment. Her key is here in reception. Would you like me to give her a message upon her return?'

'But it's so late. Where could she be? Are you sure you have the right room?'

'I'm quite sure, and I couldn't hazard a guess. Shall I ask her to call you?'

'Yes. No. Please don't, it's fine. Thanks, anyway.'

William fumbled the handset back into position and

struggled to stand up; he could feel the effects of the whiskey in his knees now. The earlier euphoria drained from him. Where could Clare be? She didn't know anyone in Wales. Not that he knew of. Was it better if she did have friends that he had never heard of, or if she had met someone new and struck up an acquaintance? Surely she wouldn't just fall into conversation with a total stranger? That was really not like her, but she could hardly be out somewhere on her own? Maybe she'd had an accident. Oh God. If she were in trouble, no one would know for days that she was missing. Maybe he should call the hotel again and explain how out of character this was, see if the receptionist could check the hotel bar, enquire if anyone knew what time she had gone out, who she had left with. William paced the room, the storm raging once again inside him. The full force of Clare's distance from him hit him hard, a screw twisting in every one of his soft spots. And there was nothing he could do but wait.

The sooty night vanished into itself as a grey half-light swept in. William eventually fell asleep, muffled by the whiskey, a pillow squeezed tight against his naked chest. His dreams were wild visions of a woman with scarlet hair sitting on the distant rocks, calling him out to sea. Clare stood on the shore, growing smaller and smaller. The water around him turned blood red, thick and swampy, so his movements became slower and he struggled to wade waist-high through the tide. He looked over his shoulder at Clare. Her cries were keening in the wind around him, but she was static, a statue full of sounds who could not move. The sun seemed to shine straight through her, a blinding white light too harsh for him to stare at. William felt fingernails running through his damp hair, scratching down his spine, nibbling at his ears and neck, but there was no one there. He woke up at the wrong end of the bed, tangled in his sheets, a towel hot with sweat across his face. His eyes were glued closed by a salty crust and a little drummer boy pounded away in the darkest recesses of his mind. He staggered to the bathroom and sat in the shower, an ice-cold stream washing over him, shocking his body awake. He relished the cold tiles against his skin as he rested his forehead against the glass and waited for the dawn of a new day.

IO.

When Clare and Flora staggered into their hotel room in the early hours of Wednesday morning, several hours and too many drinks had passed since William's telephone call had rung into the silence. The alcohol bullied Clare's repressed feelings into reappearing, and she struggled to stay in control. It was harder than she had thought, asking for help, and it pained her to show Flora how much she was really hurting. Her first instinct was still to be the strong one; to protect her.

On Tuesday morning, Clare had been awoken by Housekeeping knocking on her bedroom door; the sudden disruption disorientated her as she recalibrated once again to the hotel room, her singular status and the mild throbbing in her temples. She staggered to the door, opened it a crack and asked them to come back later. The heavy brocade curtains were drawn tight, creating the illusion of night. When she pulled them wide, she was momentarily blinded by the sunlight that flooded into the room. For each day of her trip, Clare had slept late in the morning, and her body thanked her for it. After she had showered, dressed and coffee-ed, Clare called Flora and asked her to join her. If Flora was surprised to receive a summons from her big sister to come and stay with her in Wales, she hid it with aplomb.

In advance of her coming, Clare carefully packed away the sketch pad and pencils into her suitcase, evidence of the experiment she had continued to embrace in the last few days. They were the seeds of something very delicate; she didn't want to scare what she had discovered and risk it dissolving in the light.

It should have been a three-hour drive from Flora's garden flat in Clerkenwell to the hotel, but she arrived more quickly than Clare had expected. Upon her arrival, the sisters met in reception with an awkward hug that was all elbows and chins. Clare noticed that Flora's hair was longer now, and her own strawberry-blonde colour for once. She looked fresh in a white woollen dress with a butterfly brooch and wine cotton tights. Clare was surprised to see her little sister looking so put-together. They drank peppermint tea in the conservatory and shared little bits of small talk while they adjusted to being in each other's company again.

Flora rapped Clare's knuckles with a silver teaspoon.

'You're not listening to me. Come back.'

'What? Sorry. I'm here. You were talking about the china being like Nana's.'

Flora rolled her eyes. 'Yes, yes, I was. About fifteen minutes ago. Why don't you tell me what's going on, instead of having me sit here talking to myself?'

Clare poured more tea and gave her sister an exasperated sidelong glance.

'Oh, don't look so pained, Flora. You're making me feel worse, just looking at you.'

'I'm sorry, but I'm trying to keep my cool here, and

it's not easy. Can you please tell me what's happened? You're not sick, are you? Is William okay?'

Clare picked up the teaspoon and let it hover over the sugar bowl for a moment before placing it back on her saucer.

'We're both fine, but' – she hesitated – 'our marriage isn't. I haven't left him . . . but I am taking some time away.' She watched Flora's expression remain unchanged. 'You don't look very surprised. I thought you'd be shocked.'

'Well, things sound worse than I thought, but the last time I saw you both things seemed pretty tense. I guess I hoped I'd just caught you at a bad moment.'

Clare paused to sip her tea. 'It would have been hard to catch us at a good one recently,' she replied. 'I'm sorry. I didn't mean to panic you by dragging you down here. I just didn't want to be on my own. I feel a bit silly now. I hope you won't get in trouble at work?'

'No, you did the right thing. I'm glad you called.'

Flora's cheeks were flushed; it reminded Clare of the blush that had bloomed so easily from under the collar of her sister's ivory school blouse when she teased her at school. She had relentlessly tortured her as punishment for the easier life nature had bestowed upon her; the copper curls so often complimented, the solos in the church choir, her easy facility for spelling, maths and exams. It was a long time before Clare realized the impact her casual cruelty had had on Flora's development, the holes it had torn in her confidence. She had focused so much on protecting her from their mother's mood swings and alcoholic episodes that it had never occurred to her that she herself had caused Flora to suffer. The past was a moth endlessly fluttering at a hidden mohair jumper in her closet, undetected until the damage was done. She shrugged the thought away; this was not the time to revisit it. Their mother was confined to a hospice now; it was more difficult than ever to discuss what went before.

The teapot sat cold and abandoned on a tarnished brass tray; dirty tea stains ran in rings around the royal-blue-and white willow-patterned teacups. The crumbs of almond and raspberry slices stuck to a silver fork and clung to Flora's dress like mice on a life raft. It was all Clare could do not to reach across to brush them away. She watched her sister in silence for a few moments as Flora squeezed her bitten, unpainted fingernails between her legs. She resisted the urge to comment on them.

Flora jumped up. 'I think we need something stronger.'

Clare glanced at the porcelain clock hanging on the wall behind her and was surprised to see it was six in the evening already. She nodded her approval and followed her sister's lead as they ambled to their room. Flora paused on the stairs and smoothed her hand along the art deco wallpaper.

'Remember at Nana's, the way the pattern never lined up? She was so awful at putting it up but refused to get someone in. She would have cracked up, trying to match up all these little circles.'

They collected their coats from the bedroom and strolled up to the village inn, where they curled up beside each other on a rose-and-ivory brushed cotton couch in front of the stone fireplace. A large quantity of white wine spritzers operated as a conversational midwife. They spoke of Flora's trip to Thailand, of Thatcher, of Nelson Mandela's imprisonment and how soon they would start knocking down the Berlin Wall. Clare realized it had been a long time since her thoughts hadn't been completely consumed by either the status of a case or the state of her marriage. Sitting with Flora, she felt on holiday from herself, but she knew she couldn't avoid the headline news all evening. After a comfortable silence eventually settled between them, she braced herself to push the bruise.

'I know I haven't been very forthcoming, Flora, but I don't know how to explain. There's no one easy answer for what's happened.'

Flora waited a beat before she asked the question Clare had been expecting all evening.

'Is there' – she paused – 'anyone else involved?'

'No, not really,' Clare answered. 'I don't think so, anyway. He has definitely been flirting with a silly girl in the office, but I don't think anything really happened. That's never been something I worried about with William, I'll give him that.'

'And what about you? Have you –'

'*Of course not!*' Clare leaned further away from Flora and untucked her legs from beneath her. 'How could you even . . . I'm sorry, I shouldn't have snapped, but no, there's no one else . . . but I can't say that, sometimes, I don't fantasize about the idea of someone new, or a different William, at least.'

Flora leaned forward, eager to keep pulling the thread.

'But why would you want anyone else? You guys gave me a template for a relationship I could believe in. You've no idea what that has meant to me, after the disaster of Mum and Dad. You always seemed so happy. I remember when you did that terrible karaoke on New Year's Eve, I sat there wishing *anyone* would look at me the way William looked at you.'

Clare felt an unwelcome sting behind her eyes as she remembered her and William's atonal Sonny and Cher duet. The moment held a crystallized beauty, from a time when their love and life was much less complicated. She glanced around the bar, distracting herself by surveying the two middle-aged women dancing with great abandon to Culture Club in the corner of the room.

'Things were different then,' she answered. 'Before the depot took on a life of its own and William basically gave up any hope of being a writer, of really making anything of himself.'

'He loves it there, though, doesn't he? And if it's enough for him, why can't it be enough for you? Are you ashamed of it or something?'

'Of course not. I just can't understand how it *could* be enough for him. It was only supposed to be temporary. I just feel like he gave up, and I think it's cowardly. It's really hard to respect that, especially when it means that I have to work twice as hard to support us and still can't reap the rewards of a nicer home or what have you. And don't forget, this *was* his dream, too. It's not like I've pushed it on him.'

Flora poured half of her almost full glass into Clare's; the effects of the alcohol were making her sister's features blur a little. She spilled some on the carpet as she rebalanced herself and rubbed it in with the sole of her shoe.

'Wasn't he putting a book together about the depot, though? He told me about it at Christmas and seemed really excited about it.'

'Allegedly,' Clare snorted. 'But we've been down that road before.'

Flora sat up straight. 'Okay, don't shout at me but . . . If you could let go of feeling disappointed and start imagining what a new future together could look like, you might feel better about everything and he might get his confidence back.'

Clare buried her face in the houndstooth throw that lay across the back of the couch.

'That's enough, please, Flora. My head is going to explode.'

Flora pulled the blanket away from her sister's face. 'Okay, I'll drop it,' she said, 'but all I'll say is, it can't be easy living with someone who assumes the worst of you all of the time and has such low expectations. I mean, you organized your own surprise thirtieth-birthday party because you didn't trust him to get it right.'

'Well, that's only because history has taught me what to expect from him.'

Flora started nibbling on her thumbnail but Clare pulled her hand away. 'Stop it! You look like a crazy person doing that.' Flora snapped her hand back and sat on it before speaking again.

'You still love him, don't you?'

Clare muffled a moan into the blanket.

'Of course I do, but as I get older, I realize that love is not enough on its own. It's the day-to-day reality of living with someone that really counts. What's love got to do with it?'

Flora's horrified face triggered Clare's funny bone and she collapsed forward in hysterical laughter. 'I have an amazing idea,' she whispered. 'Let's dance.' She pulled Flora behind her as she weaved her way around the tables to join the two women who were still dancing with gusto, this time to a Madonna medley. When Clare shimmied up towards them, they threw their arms around her like a long-lost friend and she felt emotion well inside her once again. She was all talked out and wanted to throw herself into the rhythm of the music, to climb out of her own head and feel the beat pulsate through her.

The hours slipped away as they danced to each and every song the DJ played. By the time they found themselves tiptoeing across the wooden floors of the hotel lobby, Flora looked exhausted. Clare had thought about booking a second room for her sister before she arrived but, in truth, she wanted the company during the night. They hadn't shared a bedroom, let alone a bed, since they were children, but it felt less strange than it could have. An unfamiliar shape in the bed was better than no shape at all. For the first time, Clare began to understand the appeal of one-night stands. The need for the physicality of someone else. To hear someone breathing and moving in the night. To know that, if someone touched your arm or leg, you wouldn't shatter into a million pieces. In the darkness of the room, Clare could sense that Flora was still awake. She sat up in bed and started furiously plumping the pillows.

'Why do I feel so guilty? I haven't done anything wrong, not really. I'm just trying to make a change, to get us out of this rut. If I thought there was a way back for us, I would take it. You believe me, don't you, Flo?'

Flora put her arms around her and held on tightly as she shook out angry little cries.

'I just feel like I need to do something drastic. To wake myself up. Before it's too late.'

'Let's try to get some sleep. Everything will be clearer in the morning.'

Clare lay back down, and Flora stroked her hair until her breathing steadied. The touch untangled the knotting threads in her mind. More tears were rising up inside her, but she didn't want to cry in front of her sister again. She rolled over and scrunched up her face against the pillow, wiping her nose on the silky rim of the pillow case. Where had all her self-control gone? She needed to button herself back up and make a plan. Tomorrow would be a new day.

II.

William's craving for coffee superseded the urge to collapse back into bed, so he made his way gingerly to the breakfast room of the Red Lion Hotel. His bones ached from walking, weariness and worrying. He sat out on the patio, where a whisper of wind could reach him and dance away shyly with some of the lingering thoughts that haunted him from the night before. He poured one strong brew after another. The weather gods had made peace and blessed Clovelly with a clear turquoise sky. William felt his mind clearing. The matronly waitress placed a full English breakfast in front of him and gave him a quizzical look.

'Are you all right there, mister? You look a little peaky.'

'I'm fine, thanks. Just didn't sleep very well. I think the storm unsettled me. Silly, really.'

'Not at all. There's plenty to be afear'd of in a storm like that one. Many that wasn't have met unfortunate ends around these parts.'

He nodded and nudged the sausage, bacon and eggs around his plate with a fork, his stomach churning at the thoughts of a runny egg mixing with the previous night's intake of alcohol. He forced himself to eat two slices of buttery toast and half a sausage before his delicate insides called a halt. He walked slowly back to his room and braced himself for another call to see if Clare had returned to her room.

'I'll put you through now, sir.'

One ring. Two rings. Three rings.

'Hello?' Her voice was cloudy with sleep and confusion when she answered.

'Clare! It's me. I just wanted to see if you were okay?'

'William? Of course I'm okay. Why wouldn't I be?'

'It's just, I tried to reach you last night, late, and you weren't in your room so . . . I was worried.'

'You want to know where I was, more like it.'

'No, honestly, Clare, I couldn't think . . . why are you whispering?'

He heard shuffling in the background and Clare's voice rose.

'You shouldn't have been calling in the first place. I asked you not to.'

'I'm sorry. It's just I'm down in Devon and there was a storm and I wanted to tell you that –'

'Devon? Why are you there? Look, actually, it doesn't matter. I'm hanging up now.'

'– that I missed you.'

Clare's voice softened.

'I'll be in touch soon, William. Okay?'

Her change in tone gave him confidence, her defences lowered for a moment.

'Clare, just wait a minute, before you go, *would* you tell me where you were last night?'

The phone call disconnected with a slam.

William cursed himself. Why had he pushed? Why couldn't he have just left well enough alone and ended the call nicely? Wherever Clare had been last night, he knew she wouldn't have been doing anything wrong, didn't he? He repacked his satchel and decided it was time to say goodbye to Clovelly and point Corina towards London.

In reception, a dozen American tourists were waiting to check in. He shuffled impatiently at the back of the queue; an elderly couple in matching salmon polo shirts, plaid shorts and white baseball caps were extracting every possible opportunity to bond with the hotel manager through their check-in experience; 'My parents stayed here on their honeymoon many years ago . . . I love how "vintage" the look is, it's so quaint . . . Are your family from Clovelly? Is the food you serve locally sourced produce? A real fountain pen, how lovely.'

William's patience couldn't stand it. He decided to take a final stroll through the village instead of waiting. In the morning sunlight, his jumper felt hot, scratchy and restrictive as he walked; he tied it in a loose knot around his shoulders and relished the fresh air settling on his bare arms. He stopped at the corner shop, bought a Lucozade energy drink, the *Guardian* and a white-paper twist of peppermints. On a low stone wall that hugged the harbour, he stretched out and inhaled the saltiness in the damp air as he gulped back the sticky orange elixir.

With every passing moment, as he flicked through the newspaper, he felt more revived. On page eleven, he was startled to see a familiar face peering out at him. Where did he know that little girl from? He scanned the article quickly for a name and laughed out loud. The Geology Rocks girl! Penelope Bernadine Foxcroft had made the news with her whale vomit.

Dr Rosamund O'Reilly cited Penelope's discovery and recognition of the value of the ambergris as a remarkable feat and commended her sound judgement. The young geologist has been handsomely rewarded for her achievement as the ambergris is valued at £10,000. When asked what she would do with her windfall, Penelope replied, 'I will invest it in my education, of course.'

William folded the newspaper in two and smiled at the photograph of Penelope and Dr O'Reilly holding the specimen somewhat awkwardly between them. He was a little disappointed that the article hadn't mentioned the depot, but it didn't take away from the huge satisfaction he felt at the outcome. What a victorious forty-eight hours in the life of a letter detective. He leaned back on the wall and turned his face towards the sun.

The good news carried him along the cobbled street, away from the harbour and towards the hotel. Should he bring something back for Clare? He paused outside Clovelly Fudge, admiring the towers of delectable treats covered in winking cellophane, like delicious chunks of edible Lego. Perhaps her sweet tooth would appreciate that. Across the street, a clapperboard sign advertised the Clovelly Gallery: ceramics and paintings inspired by the fishing village. Maybe he could find some new bowls to replace those that had been broken. He stepped into the whitewashed gallery and squinted as his eyes adjusted to the loss of sunlight. The room was cool and still, the stone walls hushed with secrets. He softened his tread to kill the echo of his footsteps pounding on the parquet flooring. As his eyes travelled over the walls, they rested for a second on each picture before skipping to the next. He was surprised to find not paintings of Clovelly but a series of photographs of flowers, indeed, a flower market. A strange sensation akin to déjà vu overcame him: had he seen these pictures before?

He picked up a photocopied leaflet that sat in a tidy pile on a tree-trunk table in the middle of the room.

> Our visiting exhibition is a collection of works captured at Columbia Road Flower Market, East London, by the photographer W.W. The photographs will be on display until 1 May, when they will move to Shoreditch Town Hall, London. For sales enquiries, please contact Harry Prummel, Gallery Custodian, on 01237 422314.

Prummel! William found himself at the centre of some mysterious magic that he felt awaited his understanding before it revealed its intentions. Columbia Road Flower Market; he recognized it from the descriptions in Winter's letters. W.W. Those were his initials. And half, at least, of Winter's – assuming, of course, that Winter was her real name. A crawling awakening overcame him as he paced about the room; there was the Volkswagen Beetle filled with daffodils, sunflowers and daisies; the coffee trike with balloons floating high from the basket; the merchant in a pirate hat. He recalled the uneasy feeling that had soaked into him with the stormy rains: the woman on the cliff, the glow of wild scarlet, how the figure had tormented his dreams. Could this photographer truly be Winter? No. This was fanciful. He was letting himself get carried away. And yet, he had no explanation as to how Winter's letters had reached him. Were the same forces at play here? Was this why he had felt compelled to come, now, after procrastinating for so many years?

Once the thought had crystallized in his mind, he became more convinced of the need to trust his instincts, that his heart understood what his head could not. He dithered on the spot, walking two steps forward, pausing to look at a black-and-white print of a woman wearing a full-length leather jacket belted tightly around her waist clutching armfuls of white roses. Circling the room, he felt his life fast-forward to meet its destiny without the need for his permission. There was nothing else for it: he would have to find this photographer and confront them, however irrational and ridiculous that may seem.

William clenched the leaflet in his hand and called out for assistance. A teenager, a coil of dreadlocks wound about her head, slunk from the back room and watched him with sulky suspicion with her kohl-rimmed eyes, a half-eaten banana in one hand.

'Yeah? Do you need something?' she asked. 'I'm on my break.'

William strode towards her but tempered his tone when he saw her start and step back.

'Could I please use your telephone? I'd like to speak to Harry Prummel about this exhibition.' He waited. 'I promise I'll only be a moment.'

She sighed and beckoned for him to follow her with her banana peel through the heavy steel door she'd emerged from. The telephone was perched on an old wooden school desk with the seat still attached; a battered white leather-bound address book sat beside it, a string with a cracked biro taped to the outside. William attempted to wriggle into the seat but gave up in flustered shame when he heard the gallery assistant snort over his shoulder. He tried to ignore her inevitable eavesdropping and turned to face the wall as he listened to the ringing echoing down the line. Please pick up. Please pick up.

'Prummel residence. Harry speaking.'

William gave an involuntary squeal of relief to hear his voice.

'Harry! I'm so glad you're home. This is William Woolf, from yesterday. I hope you don't mind me calling but –'

'William, your ears must have been burning – I was just talking about you! We're still a bit overwhelmed here, but ever so pleased. Is there something I can do for you?'

The question threw him a little: what exactly was he hoping Harry could do for him?

'Well, this might seem a little strange, but I'm in Clovelly Gallery at the moment and I'm just wondering if you might be able to tell me a little bit more about the photographer who's currently exhibiting there?'

A second's silence hung on the line before Harry answered.

'Why, of course, she's a client of mine who I met through some business in London. Long story. Bit hush hush. Would you like to buy something? I'm sure I could help negotiate a great price for you.'

William's fingers traced the carvings in the lid of the desk – *FC heart PD* and a crooked star – while he considered this.

'I actually just think I recognized some of the pictures . . . I wondered if I knew her. Could you tell me her name?'

William gripped the desk as he waited for a reply.

'Alice-Ann Strout – why, do you know her?'

With those three little words, William was utterly deflated.

'Oh, no. I don't think I do, then, after all.'

He was about to close the call when a thought tugged him.

'Sorry, Harry, but why does it say "W.W." on all the photographs? Why not her real initials?'

'Oh, that's a pseudonym of sorts. I don't know what it stands for – her artistic nom de plume, I believe. You can ask her yourself, if you like. She's staying at Crazy Kate's old cottage. Very lovely woman. I'm sure she wouldn't mind you popping over. Tell her I sent you! But good luck getting away without buying something . . .'

William's mind was racing with the sudden onslaught of new information: there was still a chance. He refocused on Harry's chatter. 'Crazy Kate? Is that a real person?' he asked.

'It was once, God rest her. She was a poor woman who lived in what is now the oldest cottage in the village. She was driven demented by her husband drowning at sea and then, one day, she donned her wedding dress and followed him into his watery grave. Terribly sad. There but for the grace of God, as they say. You can't miss her cottage; it's the one overlooking the harbour with the long white balcony. If you call in, do send Alice-Ann my best.'

William retraced his steps back to the harbour; he could picture the cottage Harry had spoken of in his mind's eye. Euphoria about his epiphany soon gave way to the panicky realization of what might happen next. Could it really be *his* Winter? Or had he finally lost his mind? And if it was her, how would he explain who he was? *Hello, I'm your Great Love?* Was he? She had probably never anticipated anyone reading her letters. Yet, she must have hoped someone would. Would she be disappointed that it was him? Should he mention straight away that he was married? Reality slapped him. He stopped on the pathway for a moment. What would Clare say if she knew where he was going? Shouldn't he be chasing after her instead? She was the one who had left him, though; she was the one running away. If she hadn't left for Wales, he wouldn't even be in Clovelly. He tried to validate his behaviour by condemning hers, but it didn't sit right with him to blame her for him being here. He knew that this choice was his alone.

Having reached the cottage, William paused outside; a planet of uncertainty spinning out of orbit. There was no point searching for a voice of reason now. If Winter was this close, he had to go to her. What if this was all meant to be? If he was Winter's destiny and he was the only one who knew it? Maybe Clare leaving was all part of a grand design of which he knew nothing. Besides, it might amount to nothing at all, just an awkward conversation that ended with Winter fleeing back to London to throw her writing paper in the fire. If so, he could accept that, he presumed, but he knew he couldn't live without knowing. William was unravelling like an old wool jumper with every passing second; he needed to tie a knot in this.

He had never anticipated approaching Winter so impulsively; this pleasure trip was fast becoming one of the least relaxing experiences he had ever subjected himself to. William's resolution was fading rapidly as he climbed the wooden stairs to the front door of Crazy Kate's, but he held his nerve as he lifted the brass knocker and let it drop in one loud clang against the lilac wood. From inside, he heard a squeal and claws scampering across floorboards, then footsteps. As the door peeled inwards, a snow-white cat brushed past his legs and scarpered over the veranda. William's eyeline saw white tights first, inside black velvet ballet slippers, the ends of a purple-and-grey silk kimono, before looking up to find his question asked and answered in the same moment. Alice-Ann's long red hair framed a face William thought must have adventured through eighty years or more. Silver streaks snaked from her temples through the tresses he knew must once have been a spectacular fiery mass. In a lilting Scottish accent, she asked him his business.

'Your photos, Ms Strout,' he answered. 'I was hoping to buy the one of the Beetle, with the flowers.'

She gave him a long, hard look.

'Are you sure that's what you came here for?'

He found her gaze unnerving but held firm. 'Yes. Harry Prummel told me you were here.'

She stepped back into the hallway and handed him a pad of stiff cream parchment paper and a well-sharpened pencil.

'Here. Write down where we can contact you. Harry will organize something at the end of the exhibition. I'm not sure why he didn't take your details himself.'

William smiled at her sheepishly. 'I wanted to meet the artist,' he replied.

She tore off the sheet of paper he had scribbled on and glanced at it before folding it in two and slipping it into the loose pocket of her kimono.

'Did I see you last night, perhaps? On the Look-out?' he asked.

'Perhaps,' she answered, with a shy smile of her own that touched the dove-grey pools of her eyes.

He fought the urge to tell her why he had really come; he felt, but rejected, the impulse under the scrutiny of her gaze. As he walked away from Alice-Ann and tried to shake off the strange feeling of loss that settled upon him, she called after him, 'I hope you find what you're looking for, Mr Woolf.'

He turned and gave her a little wave.

'So do I, Ms Strout. So do I.'

William sat on the edge of their marital bed, unmade, as he had left it when he departed for Clovelly. He pulled off his shoes and socks; grit escaped and vanished in the carpet fibres. It was a dispiriting memento of his excursion. He lay back on the crumpled duvet, turning his face to breathe in the familiar lavender smell that faded but never completely left their Egyptian cotton linen. He remembered arguing over buying such expensive sheets when they first married:

'I just don't think we should be spending money on luxuries when we are trying to save for our deposit.'

'A good night's sleep doesn't count as a luxury. Just imagine rolling around naked under this soft cotton every night. If we had sheets this soft, I might never wear pyjamas to bed again.'

It was an argument easily won by Clare. He envied now the problems he once lost sleep over: adopting a puppy; parental visits; spring cleaning; plans for Bank Holiday weekends. He missed the normality of bickering without subtext, sulks trumped by tickling; the everyday debates over which movie, cereal or newspaper to buy. Those were the days before everything became contentious and the flat littered with landmines that they awkwardly danced around. He knew they could not sustain a marriage through memories of better times alone. William groaned and rolled over, squashing his face into a pillow. It was a never-ending cycle. If they were going to stay together, this couldn't be the way they communicated – or failed to communicate – for much longer. Would Clare be throwing what he had done, or failed to do, back at him until he was eventually granted the sweet release of death? What a calamity his life had become. Clare had absconded to Wales and he was wasting time daydreaming about a woman he didn't even know existed. He fell asleep, still fully dressed, with his dusty toes dangling over the side of the bed.

On the walk to the depot the following morning, William tried to imagine a life with someone new. Being with Clare was truly the first proper relationship he had ever experienced. Could he start again and learn how to love someone else? Would it just happen naturally, if it was the right person? He had married his first real girl-friend. Were they wrong to be so hasty? To marry their future selves together when they didn't know who those people were yet? He knew so little when they met; he had acted purely on instinct and the lessons he had gleaned about love from music and books. Back then, there was no doubt in his mind that Clare was the one, and that such a person could exist.

At eighteen, he lost his virginity to one of his mother's friends; she propositioned him after hiring him to paint her house the summer he left school. Gloria gave him a basic education in how to please a woman, but she was not a challenging taskmaster. William sensed that any young body, far removed from her husband Ron's ageing bones and grey chest hair, was probably sufficient. In a moment of particular cruelty, Gloria once told him that sleeping with Ron was like hugging a big bag of yoghurt. Ron wasn't a hard act to follow. He convinced himself at the time that he loved Gloria, but it was more of a childish crush and it faded as soon as he arrived at university. He still thought of her fondly occasionally, of her leopard-print tracksuit, the smell of hairspray on her sticky perm, the lines on her ankles where the fake tan stopped, and wondered what had become of her, although he never dared ask his mother.

It took longer than he had hoped to meet someone new, and in the years before Clare burst into his life there were only two other girls. Oona was an owly creature, with a long brown ponytail that reached the base of her spine. She was studying anthropology and William dated her for nine months without ever sleeping over. They had passionate kisses that steamed up her glasses, but she held his hands firmly by his side and he didn't know how to either accelerate or terminate their relationship. She eventually broke it off with him after winning a scholarship to study in Bolivia.

Her successor, Leonora, was an entirely different species; she had inherited olive skin, jet-black eyes and wild ebony curls from her Greek mother and the long limbs and chiselled cheekbones of her Swedish father. She was the darling of the science department; men hovered around her, hoping for a secret smile or a soft word.

William became obsessed with her and worked very hard to win her attention, accompanying her to evening lectures he did not understand, learning to cook vegetarian meals, allowing her to sketch him while he posed half naked, scorching with embarrassment. She told him she liked how kind he was; how he didn't try to possess her like the other men on campus; how he bothered to listen to her properly when she talked – he wasn't just waiting for her to finish so he could speak again. When she at last led him to her bed, he felt completely unprepared for it. The night of unbridled passion he had fantasized about proved a quiet affair in reality; she politely offered a moan or two while he tried, with an increasing sense of despair, to understand how her exquisite, voluptuous body worked. He was paralysed with fear and moved without much delay from undressing her to finishing.

A lot of vegetables slowly rotted in his cupboard before he could accept that Leonora would not be visiting again. When they bumped into each other on campus, she always offered him a sympathetic smile, which only compounded his humiliation. He had been offered the forbidden fruit but, instead of taking a delicious bite, had dropped the apple in a puddle.

After the Leonora debacle, William's confidence ebbed away. He became a great friend to many interesting and attractive women, but never tried for anything more, until he met Clare; the fear of losing her far outweighed the fear of trying to win her. Clare patiently taught him how to make love to her; helped him understand how she wanted to be made love to. He began to understand that there was a delicate and powerful point where a woman didn't want to be asked for approval to continue but instead wants the man to proceed with confidence because he understands what she wants. What would it be like to sleep with someone else after all these years of knowing only one woman?

When he arrived at his desk, a note from Mr Flanagan awaited him; a summons to see him that morning. William was sure he was in trouble. The haphazard mound of post that now sat a foot high on his desk offered him little opportunity to convince Ned that all was well. He tore the sticky note impatiently from the cover of his diary, tossed it in the wastepaper basket and rubbed away with a resentful finger the faint trace of residue that remained. Had he come to the end of the road at the depot? Forced Ned's hand to let him go? Even if the time was close, he needed to be smart now. The last thing he needed was to have to tell Clare he had lost his job, even if it was a job she had come to loathe as a symbol of his great failure. If he was going to leave, it would have to be on his terms and not before he finished his *Volume of Lost Letters*.

He shuffled through the precarious pile of letters spread across his desk and tried to conjure up the old enthusiasm he once felt for his work. His life was in such a state of flux, restoring equilibrium to someone else's held little appeal, despite how much his recent successes with Harry and Little Miss Geology Rocks had buoyed him. He had no one to go home to and share the anecdotes with; no one to care if he succeeded in a particular mission or solved one of these puzzles. It reminded him of Stevie once saying that he didn't make as much effort at gigs if there wasn't a girl in the audience he was trying to impress. Maybe William's karmic balance was out of kilter and he could earn some redemption by engaging in professional good deeds. Would karma work in your favour if you deliberately chased it, though? Or was that in fact counterproductive? He decided it was best to do his job because it was his duty and not in the hope of heavenly reward.

He shook himself and decided that today he would seize control of the situation; make a serious dent in his backlog and show Ned that he had nothing to worry about. The great success he had achieved with Prummel and Penelope had to count for something, didn't it? He swept the pile of letters and parcels that had accumulated on his desk into an empty mail sack so that he could clear some space and tackle them one by one. Just tidying everything gave him some peace, and he felt confident as he started to work. He couldn't control what Clare was doing, he couldn't control whether any of Winter's letters came, but he could control what he did at his desk, and that is what he would do.

First, he withdrew a black-and-white postcard of a man walking on a tightrope across the Manhattan skyline. On the back, in a blue marker, the address offered only 'London-Irish Maria with the blue poodle perm, Clapham, England'. The note read:

Maria, my mystery woman with the bag of knitting and home-made cheese-and-pickle sandwiches. Why did you leave without saying goodbye? I looked for you everywhere, but you couldn't be found. Who knows if this will find you, but, if it's meant to be, it will! I'm playing the Astoria on 15 May. Come – I'll leave word at the stage door. Jimi. x

William thought of Jimi waiting on the night for a blue poodle perm to peep around the green room door. He felt for him but wondered why Maria had left him so unceremoniously. Maybe this was an unanswered prayer for the best. He pondered at the choice of post-card: what was Jimi trying to say? Have faith? The William of his younger years, when his faith in the idea of *the one* was so unshakeable, would have celebrated Jimi's perseverance. Nowadays, it was harder to hold on to that idealism. What happens when *the one* becomes a heartbreaking amount of work? As we change and grow older, does the one we need have to change also? Or was it possible he hadn't even met the one yet? Was the real one still out there, searching for him? Maybe even writing him letters? He stuck the postcard on the wall beside his desk with a red drawing pin.

The next, pale green, envelope was barely intact; it was water damaged and crumbling at the edges. A grey blur dragged across the page where the address had been and the stamp curled away at three corners. He pressed the stamp flat and smiled with surprise to see it was a half-cent one from New Zealand. Trevor had been hunting one for as long as William could remember; the orange-and-black butterfly against the powder-blue background was so distinctive. He carried the envelope over to Trevor's desk and placed it there for him to find. His denim jacket, the lapels covered in badges from metal bands, was hanging on the back of his chair and emitting a strong stench of smoke. William hoped he would be there to see his face when he noticed it and felt a thrill of excitement for him.

He was still enjoying thoughts of Trevor's discovery when, reaching into the postbag, his fingers felt the familiar groove of heavy parchment. He scanned the room for inquisitive eyes before allowing himself to pull out into the light what he knew would be a letter from Winter. He glanced down to confirm that it was really from her then quickly hid it inside his satchel under the desk. He knew he should be patient and wait until later, but he needed this today. Before Marjorie could ask him where he was going, he hastened for the corridor that led to the fire escape, where he could sit in peace. The steel steps were damp but he sat down regardless and leaned uncomfortably against the railing as he read. Marjorie's *Auntie of the Year* mug lay on its side in a puddle by his feet.

My Great Love,

I only have a few moments before I head out into the night, but I have to tell you something. I might be meeting you soon. In two hours, to be precise. At the Everyman Theatre in Notting Hill. There is a special showing tonight of the forties film *Hellzapoppin'* with a swing-dancing lesson on beforehand – it feels like just the sort of place I might meet you. There are few things

I love more than swing dancing; that music fills me with joy. In some ways, I feel a bit strange telling you that I may meet another man tonight, but you really have nothing to worry about. You see, the thing is, either it's you, in which case, tonight, a tuning fork will be struck upon the roof of the cinema and all the choirs of heaven will sing in tune, or else it won't be you, and the evening will fade into insignificance and whoever he is will slip away into the night with no damage done.

I'm wearing an emerald-green dress with an under-skirt that makes it swish-swish as I walk. It was made for spinning about in. I bought it just before I left Dublin, in my favourite vintage clothes shop, on Dame Street. The owner of the shop told me the frock brings out the green in my eyes. I hope so. What colour are yours? I hope they are brown. Brown eyes are always warm. Blues can be so cold. I felt that the dress symbolized what I wanted my new life to embrace: adventure, colour and opportunities for dancing.

When you walk inside that store, it is like falling down a rabbit-hole to a Wonderland of possibility. You could not fill your wardrobe with such costumes and live a life of mediocrity. So often I have visited there and shyly tried things on but lost my nerve at the crucial moment. Not that time. I was dressing for London. I was dressing for the me I wanted to become. I had no idea then just how far those feathers and bows would take me. Here is a picture of my most extravagant pur-chase; see how they catch the light of the city and shimmer like a silvery moon? I wore them for the first time today. I'm getting braver. But I think I should save them up for a truly special occasion, don't you?

William peered into the envelope and found a Polaroid picture still waiting inside. It curved in his palm; a photograph of her two feet dressed in luminescent white cowboy boots. Were they covered in glitter? What made them sparkle so? Red woollen stockings peeked out from the tops. How bizarre to see even just this part of Winter's physical self. He returned to the letter.

I am slowly breathing in this city and breathing out a new me. I thought about changing my name permanently when I came here, but I'm not sure a girl by another name would feel as true. Sometimes, though, an adopted persona makes it easier to activate a new life plan. It's like buying a new coat that you can return if you change your mind. Whatever you call yourself, though, wherever you go, you take yourself with you. If you could start all over again tomorrow in a new city, what would you do? Would you choose the same life for yourself or try something new? What would you cast aside? I am grateful for this gift of a new beginning, and I won't waste it.

Oh, please, let it be you standing waiting for me tonight. Let the night take us dancing.

If all else fails, maybe I will at least meet some new people of my ilk. Do you find, as you get older, it becomes harder to make new friends? New people are exhausting: the flirtations with friendships and testing of old stories on new ears. One thing I do find very liberating, though, is the opportunity to reposition the past. Former protagonists are important to new people only if I present them that way. Perhaps this is why I like writing to you so much; on paper, I can be the version of myself I've always wanted to be. I am more truthful here, in a way that it takes such a long time to reach in person. I am determined that the me of my letters and the London me should become one and the same, and soon.

I feel quite nervous about maybe seeing you later. It's so much easier to talk to you like this. No pressure. No expectations. You can't let me down.

I must dash – I don't want to leave you waiting. Him waiting. You. Him. The night.

Yours, as always,
Winter

William picked up Marjorie's mug and walked back into the office. In the kitchen, he stood at the window overlooking Shoreditch High Street. He scanned the river of people flowing past on the pavement. Was Winter one of them? Would he start again, if he could? What *did* he most want? In truth, an end to the struggle and to be in the right frame of mind to write again. He wondered how Winter's evening had gone, if she was smitten now with some undeserving buffoon she had met. Surely she wouldn't have spoken to another man of the inner, secret life she wrote to William about, if that inner, secret person even really existed. It could just be a fantasy she spilled across those pages. Was he the one being fooled? He caught himself in that moment of realization; he really had come to believe that the letters were written for him, but why else would they keep appearing in his life, and at times when he was so open to receiving them? He flip-flopped back and forth as the traffic lights before him switched from green, to amber, to red and back again, but he could not convince himself otherwise: these letters were meant for him and he was meant to respond.

As he tidied up his desk before going home that evening, Marjorie sidled up to him, looking very self-satisfied.

'You had a visit from Mr Flanagan just now,' she said. 'He seemed very disappointed not to find you at your desk. Best go see him first thing in the morning, I should think.'

William sighed. He couldn't avoid Ned much longer.

When William returned to the flat, the bulb in the hallway blew as he turned on the light and made him jump. He fumbled his way upstairs in the dark and dragged the stool from Clare's dressing table to the wardrobe. Too tired to be dealing with this, he reluctantly climbed up to rustle about for a replacement bulb. As he tugged at a sleeping bag to wriggle the box they called 'Miscellaneous Madness' free, Clare's old briefcase tumbled down. Papers spilled out all across the floorboards. He cursed his clumsiness and knelt down to gather them together. His eyes traced over Clare's handwriting, so familiar to him, and he wished he could go back in time to whenever she had written this and start again from there. He tried to assemble the pages correctly but couldn't fathom an order.

An A4 envelope had slid under the bed and now peeked out at him. He stretched to reach it and dragged it across the wooden floor towards him. When he turned it over, he froze. His name was written on the front, in Clare's hand. What was this? Hardly a letter, when it was so official looking. Divorce papers? No! Seriously? Dear God. When would she have organized them? Why hadn't she given them to him? Maybe she hadn't decided yet for sure. If that's what was inside, should he open it? Oh, but then he would have to say he saw the papers and it might force things to a conclusion he wasn't ready for. And yet, he couldn't just ignore the envelope now; couldn't unknow that it was there, waiting for him, radiating a heat from inside the cupboard, burning through Clare's old brown leather briefcase, taunting him. The seal was weak and he reckoned he could open it without causing a tear. He understood that he should put it back but he also knew that he could not.

William tidied the rest of the papers into the case and perched upon Clare's little stool. He had watched her sit upon it so many mornings to put her make-up on, and again, every evening, to cleanse it back off. The strangeness of the things he missed hit him again. He closed his eyes as he slipped the pages from the crisp, white envelope; it was her firm's office stationery. When William looked down, he was surprised to see not a legal document but pages of yellow refill pad covered in Clare's handwriting. It was a letter, after all. He paused. No matter what this letter said, he would never be able to ask Clare about it. He could never pretend that he thought she meant for him to find it, not among her work things. He knew that he had to read it, nonetheless. It was too late to stop now.

William,

I couldn't decide whether to write 'dear', 'hello' or something else, so used no salutation at all. That seems to sum up what these last few months have been like. I don't know how to speak to you, how to address you, who you are to me, so I say nothing at all, or something mean.

When I was little, my mother used to say that emotional talks were always regretted; far better to write it all down and get it out of your system then throw it in the fire. I suppose she learned that the hard way. I don't know where this letter is destined – your hand or the flames – but I'm hoping talking to you like this will help me at least understand what I'm trying to say.

The truth is, I'm afraid to talk to you; afraid to tell you how I'm really feeling in case I push us down a road we can't travel back from. I'm afraid to tell you that I understand why you didn't tell me you weren't writing but that I still can't bring myself to give you absolution. I can't admit that I could feel how lonely you were sometimes and that I know I ignored it. I can't tell you that because I want you to take responsibility and seize control of your life. I've always felt, if I told you everything was okay, that would give you licence to just surrender completely, but I'm beginning to understand now that maybe I was partly responsible for your state of arrested development. We have both felt dissatisfied for so long, but I have held out for the answers inside us which I know could be there. I have never looked outside us for someone or something else, but I'm worried that I will.

In some ways, I feel like I have been teaching myself not to love you so that, when we finally break, I will already have moved on. But it has been hard. Harder than I thought. My stubborn heart won't let go of you. Even as I see you fading away, and moving further from me every day.

You were my best friend. Whenever anyone hurt me, you made me better. Whenever I was scared, it was into your arms I ran. Whenever I was lost, you found me. So what do you do when the person you count on most in the world is the person that's hurting you? Where do you go? To whom do you turn?

I know you think I'm angry all the time. Anger is the easiest place to go to. But mostly, I'm so disappointed at what we've become. I know you want to try and fix things; to go back to how things were. I believe you when you say you're sorry, but I don't know if we can find each other again. I just can't bear the idea that we held on for this long and didn't make it out the other side. Where is the return for all that emotional investment? I dread the thoughts of dividing up our stuff, of people feeling sorry for us, our friends choosing sides. But every day, I'm building my strength to do it.

Do I miss you? Every second.

Do I want to go? No.

Do I want you to stop me? Yes.

Do I think you can? I'm not sure any more.

This is an impossible letter to send. These are impossible words to say. Do you need to hear them? Probably. Will I ever have the courage? I don't know.

And I don't know how to sign off now, either.

Love/Yours – neither is a given any more,

Clare

William carefully eased the letter back into its envelope before shoving it inside Clare's briefcase as if it were the case's fault he had read those things. As if, by making the letter disappear, he could shake the words from his head, too. If only she had given this to him instead of running away, maybe everything would be different now, but he couldn't help but feel that her time away would pull them even further apart. He found the light bulb that had brought him to the wardrobe but, even so, he continued ransacking the deep shelves, without knowing what he was looking for. His fingers touched something warm and furry: the head from the wolf costume he wore on Halloween two years before.

He pulled it on and squinted through the eye slits to catch his reflection in the black wooden full-length mirror that stood propped in their landing. Six years on, and he had never attached it to the wall, as he had promised. He twisted his neck back and forth, up and down, straining for an angle, but he couldn't get a clear line through the shaggy brown wool. The headpiece felt tighter than he remembered. Hotter. Itchier. Disorientating. More ticklish. Less liberating. He remembered his grandfather telling him the ancient Native American proverb of the two wolves who lived inside each person, one representing evil and the darkness of the world and the other the light. 'They battle every day to control you, these two wolves, and you know which one will win?' he had asked William, as the boy sat on his knee. William shook his head. 'The one that you feed more,' his grandad answered. He hadn't thought about it in years but, today, he felt acutely aware of the battle raging inside him.

William wrestled the fur head from over his own, struggling like a little boy stuck in his pullover. There was no Clare to wriggle it free and toss it over her shoulder this time. He perched against the white wooden windowsill and smoothed the hairs on the wolf's face. The last time he had worn it, the mask brought out a mischievous streak in him that now lay dormant again. It had kindled a momentary internal fire which domesticity, doubt and drudgery usually squashed. Was it two years ago? Three? Clare had dressed up as Little Red Riding Hood, well, Little Dead Riding Hood, of course. They repeated the same jokes to every guest at the party, jokes that grew incrementally funnier – to them – each time: 'I'm normally a wolf in sheep's clothing, so tonight I'm finally living up to my name' and 'I'm Little Red after the wolf has had his way with her.'

For the party, Clare's red cloak was torn and covered in mud from the garden. Her tights showed long flashes of skin, her skirt was ripped in a diagonal across her thighs. A red corset burst out from under a shredded white blouse, black ribbons undone. Her hair was a tangled mess with twigs poking out at awkward angles. Red lipstick smeared across her bow lips; black make-up smudged around her eyes. Her feet were bare. With dirty hands, she led William through the party. A terrible guide, spinning him round and bumping him into doorways. It was the most fun they had shared in a very long time. When they staggered home to their flat that night, he fell on his knees and howled at the moon before Little Red dragged him to bed. Why had he not spent more nights like that, enjoying Clare, making her laugh?

He shoved the costume back into the wardrobe and resumed his search. What was he looking for? Clare's journals? The thought circled him like a cat of prey. No. That would not help him; there were quite enough of Clare's words swimming in his head from her letter. Now on a mission to clear out their wardrobe after so many years of neglect, he was completely committed to the task; he just hadn't fathomed what the purpose was. A hunt for this old typewriter with no ribbon? These old cassette tapes? That battered old biscuit tin filled with Christmas baubles? He spilled the contents of a padded envelope on to the carpet; a set of sepia photographs from Clare's parents' honeymoon: Teresa sitting on an inflatable beach ball, wearing a straw sun hat, eating an ice-cream cone; the couple posing outside their caravan, Teresa in a floral-print dress that blew sideways in the breeze, Eddie in blue swimming trunks, sun cream across his nose, his arm draped proudly around her shoulders. Such happiness as you might find only in a Saturday matinee movie from the fifties. He reached further into the shelves and his fingertips touched something squishy and soft. From the darkest recess, he eased the photo album Clare had filled for him as his wedding present.

Could his wounds bear another lick of salt from more nostalgia? He slowly turned the pages, and images from the past blasted him:

Clare holding her degree certificate in front of the university gates; she looked small against their might and her smile was shy.

William emerging from the water after a swim in the Lake District. He had taken his glasses off for the photo and squinted at the camera like a mole surfacing from the earth.

Clare dressed as a flapper on her hen night, wearing a little black wig and string after string of pearls.

William and Clare sitting awkwardly in a gondola in Venice, the gondolier hovering over them with a scowl on his face.

Clare and William sitting in deckchairs on Brighton beach, hands held across the space between them, faces sunburnt but happy, Clare's broken arm in a sling.

William closed the album, unable to look at any more pictures, and placed it safely back inside the wardrobe. As he stretched to reach the back of the top shelf, his elbow knocked a sports bag to the floor and a pair of old running shoes tumbled out. William rapped his knuckles on the wooden shelf. Eureka! His beloved white trainers with the navy stripes. He hadn't worn them in years, but now they had appeared just when he needed them. A run would clear his head, vanquish some cobwebs. He stretched each shoe out of the crippled, bent shape they had settled into. Dust scattered from their creases as he forced his feet into their old shells. The interior was hard and stiff. He sat on the floor and pointed each toe upwards in turn, then flexed each foot, rotated each ankle, wriggling his toes inside their rediscovered home. He stood and bounced on the balls of his feet, hopping from left to right, right to left, then ran on the spot as fast as he could. His lungs surrendered before his feet did but he was ready. He pulled on his brown hooded fleece, zipped the house keys into his pocket, jogged downstairs and out of the front door without a second thought. The abandoned contents of the wardrobe lay strewn behind him; bed-linen, a sewing machine, a red canvas bag full of odd socks and pieces of cloth, Volumes A, R and T of the *Encyclopaedia Britannica* and a retired Polaroid camera. How had they managed to squeeze it all in?

William's muscles scanned his body for memories of how to move. There were faint whispers of long runs in the woods during adolescence, occasional bursts about the streets of London, but nothing recent enough to train them for this sudden expedition. He refused to acknowledge the burning sensation on the soles of his feet, the tightness in his chest, or the slowness of his pace. The strain in his calves could not conquer him. His heart pounded in his ears and drowned out the Greek chorus in his mind. Glorious oblivion. He pushed past the rain spitting on his skin, shook his hair into the wind and clenched his fists. The streets stretched out before him like a call to arms; puddles splashed cheers around his ankles, the city watched him run. All along the Bethnal Green Road, he pad-a-thumped, his right leg stronger. When he reached Weavers Fields, he slowed down to do a lap of the lawns, before dropping on to a bench. He arched his spine over the backrest and let the sudden downpour of rain run down his cheeks, drip from his chin, along his throat and under the collar of his hood. Never had discomfort felt so luxuriant. He closed his eyes and called to mind two letter writers: one, his wife; one, a ghost. Whose call would he answer?

Indecision paralysed him. He must push his heart harder than he had his feet. He must take control, take action, take responsibility. It was time to make some decisions. First, though, he must find enough power in his legs to run home.

William sat in the depot, lost in a daydream of letters; on his typewriter, he typed furiously for hours the stories he had been mindfully collecting. Clare had told him she was coming home tomorrow, and the prospect filled him with anxiety. He needed to escape his own thoughts and drown in other people's worries, their words and their worlds. Marjorie's voice cut through his concentration; she sounded even more excitable than usual, if that were possible. Poor Trevor was on the receiving end.

'This is my favourite bit,' she gushed. ' "I miss talking to you late into the night, but I'm saving my stories for you. Hurry up, now, dear man. The nights are drawing in." ' William watched her pause for dramatic effect and put her hand to her heart. "e's 'er Great Love. Oh, I wonder what became of 'er, or if she ever found 'im.'

A sickening dread crawled over his skin as his eyes found the midnight-blue envelope tucked under the arm of Marjorie's fluorescent pink blouse. How had this happened? Those letters were meant for *him*. He tried to feign nonchalance as he strolled towards her.

'That sounds interesting. Can I take a look?' he asked, hoping his inner desperation was not showing on his face. Marjorie wagged her chubby forefinger at him. 'Oh, no, no, no, when I wanted to champion the valentines, you 'ad no interest. Why now, eh?' she asked. 'You've barely said a word to anyone in weeks. This is *my* discovery and I will take care of it, thank you very much.'

She perched on the edge of Trevor's desk, despite his wilful attempt to ignore them both, and read the letter again, mouthing the words to herself and emitting little sighs. William was flabbergasted; this could not be borne. Winter's letters were not a remedy for Marjorie's lonely heart, something to add to her private collection.

All morning, he surreptitiously watched her idling away her time, working as little as possible, and realized he was a victim of his own success. It was no wonder Ned was upset with his diminishing productivity if they were depending on Marjorie to actually carry her own weight. She had Winter's letter in the back pocket of her stonewashed jeans. The indignity of it! He watched and waited for his chance.

Eventually, she took the letter out to read it again at her desk. This was his moment. He slipped into the corridor, sidled along it with his back against the wall, head darting left and right for any colleagues passing by. Then, before he could change his mind, he triggered the fire alarm with gusto. The shrill screeching was shocking as he dashed back into the office, on the pretence of grabbing his blazer.

'Leave everything!' Marjorie commanded, thrilled to finally put her fire-marshal training into action.

William deliberately stalled to evacuate last, and swiped Winter's letter as he slipped past Marjorie's desk, tucking it into his interior breast pocket. Little beads of perspiration gathered at the nape of his neck with the intensity of the moment. His obsession had reached new heights.

After the commotion of the false alarm, the depot settled back into its usual routine, with the exception of Marjorie, who lamented her missing letter for the remainder of the day. Trevor joked about the irony of her losing a letter here, of all places, but she wasn't amused.

'You seemed very interested earlier,' she said to William. 'Are you sure you don't know anything about it?'

He stared her down. Indeed, he impressed himself with his coolness.

'Positively certain. I have far too much of my own work to be getting on with, thank you very much.'

The relief he felt, however, was palpable.

That evening, he was the last to leave. All Winter's letters were laid out across the top of his desk, the earliest ones now thin and a little grubby along the creases from too much folding, excessive holding and reluctant hiding. The one he had salvaged today, however, gleamed fresh and crisp before him, despite Marjorie's interference. Still unnerved by not having found it first, he questioned what this could mean. Had he taken too long to find it so the forces at play intervened and threw it in his path via Marjorie? Was it supposed to propel him into action? If he didn't act, would the opportunity be taken from him? Or was he simply the victim of Marjorie's meddling on the fourth floor, where she knew he didn't want her to interfere? There was no easy answer, but he settled down to read it for the second time.

My Great Love,

I wonder if I'll instantly recognize you when we meet? Even in some subconscious way? Will our great potential love be immediately obvious, or is the greatness something that will emerge over time? What if I mistake someone else for you and don't realize until it's too late? You could be sitting across from me on the Tube from Monday until Friday and never even look up from your newspaper to notice me, or the fact that I was reading your favourite book. You would look up, though, wouldn't you? And notice something in particular: that I have worn down the heel on my left shoe more than the right, that a real handkerchief was stuffed in my pocket, how my left eyelid droops a tiny bit more than the right? Anything? Any question it burned you to know the answer to. You would feel compelled to ask, even though good manners had taught you not to. Please, do ask.

I said a prayer for you today, lit a candle in the chapel in Hoxton Square. I don't believe in the church, not any more, but some traditions tug at my heart strings. Lighting candles is one; sitting in the peace of the pews stills fills me with a sense of calm like no other. I suppose it's just meditation, really, but I grew up learning to call it something else.

William paused. How do you know if someone is the one? You have to trust your instinct, he supposed. He remembered asking his father the same question once, and he'd answered, 'When you know, son, you know!', but he thought he had known about Clare, and look at them now. He turned his attention back to Winter.

Yesterday, I heard a mother drag the strangest promise from her teenage son on the Tube. She made him swear that, if he ever dropped anything on to the tracks, he wouldn't jump down to try and save it. He argued that he wouldn't do that unless he was sure he could reach it in time before the train came. His mother's eyes widened, and she squeezed his arm; 'That's exactly what scares me,' she said, 'You would always believe you could make it. Always. But you wouldn't. Promise me you'll just leave it there.'

It was as if his mother had already succumbed to a self-fulfilling prophecy that she would one day lose her son by his own hand, if not one way, then another. She could try and enforce her nurturing over his nature, in as many instances as she could think of, but one would eventually slip through. I could imagine her warning him about not running into traffic, not talking to strangers, not having unprotected sex, not taking drugs, not drinking too much alcohol, not climbing high walls, not skateboarding on busy streets, not giving cheek, not walking with too much swagger, not standing too close to the ledge, but his mammy's voice would soon get drowned out by more seductive ones; those of girls with long ponytails and short skirts, boys with long Saturdays and short attention spans. How often

split-second decisions define us; how we expose ourselves when we don't have time to decide who we want
to be. My mother always reminded me what Maya
Angelou said: when someone shows you their true
character, believe them the first time.

William looked up from the letter again. Was that
why he procrastinated so much? Was he trying too hard
to decide what was the right thing to do instead of just
trusting his instincts?

There is a jukebox playing fifties songs in the corner of
this bar, and any one of them could be a letter from me
to you; it seems all the singers were just looking for love.
I wish I knew what your favourite songs are. Maybe
you'll make me a mix-tape one day. I love how they
breathe new life into old songs, arming them with
superpowers that allow them to creep in through the
back door of your heart. The lyrics are a language you
can borrow for all that you feel but cannot find the
words to say. And so songs can become ghosts that haunt
us. They are time machines to old flames, lost cities,
melancholy summer days and nights danced away. We
breathe them into our composition like a cold fog. When
the songs surprise us, as they often do, by being played
in the most unlikely of places, years fall off our faces and
we are sixteen again, or twenty-one again, in Paris
again, or holding your face again. Emotional arrest. I
hope we have our own song one day.

I miss talking to you late into the night, but I'm saving my stories for you.

Hurry up, now, dear man. The nights are drawing in.
Yours,
Winter

William shuffled all the letters together with a new sense of purpose; he had stalled for long enough, and it was clear to him that the time had come for action, to take back control of his life. He could not resolve things with Clare one way or the other while the ghost of Winter haunted him. She must be banished. Or summoned. Secreting her away into a dark space inside him, a spot reserved exclusively for her, would not work. He knew her shadow would creep from her cubbyhole into any light he could use to search for Clare. In unguarded moments, it lingered overhead like a black star. What was he to do? He could not endure these two voices competing in his mind for attention. He listed his options on a clean new page.

Shred the letters and try to squash each memory of them as it arises with one of Clare. An act of active forgetting.

Try to find Winter and allow the reality of the woman to confront the fantasy.

He knew that there was no choice. Not really. Find Winter, he must. Or he'd be tortured for ever with the question of what if? Was he completely giving up on Clare if he pulled the thread of Winter? No. It wasn't that simple. He wasn't abandoning his marriage. He was just clearing up a mess he had stumbled into unwittingly.

Winter held so much power only because of her mystery. He would illuminate that room of speculation where his imagination so happily festered and expose the truth. It could just as easily save his relationship with Clare as destroy it, couldn't it?

William stood and stretched his calf muscles, still cramped and sore from yesterday's spontaneous sprint. What a fool he had been to force his body to such unexpected extremes. He kneaded the knot of tension at the back of his legs and remembered the last time they had seized up on him like this. Clare had cajoled him into going for a hike in the Coventry countryside for their anniversary. When they finally arrived at the inn after ten miles of tramping in the rain, they might have been celebrating their fiftieth instead of their fifth year together. They collapsed into bed, soggy and sore, almost too weary to make love. William ordered hot ports and roast-chicken sandwiches up to their room, and Clare ran a bath with lavender. Their shared suffering was a sweet one. Not like this teasing throbbing that taunted William and felt punitive and mean.

He walked twice around the office floor anticlockwise, lifted his leg on to the desk and felt the stretch burn through him, before turning back to survey the evidence before him. All those letters. They must hold dozens of clues. Would they be specific enough to help him find her? Wasn't that his job? Surely, now, he could put all that training and experience into good use for a personal mission. Was this why he had found the letters? Could it be that he was the only one who could use them to find her? He was facing what could be the most important letter mystery of his career.

He started with the postmarks, the first stage of any letter investigation. They reconfirmed what he already knew: all London – but the italic font told him that nearly all had been processed through the Bethnal Green sorting office, as close to his own front door as the grocery shop where he bought a pint of milk nearly every day. He could have passed her in the street so many times. It was no wonder he thought he saw her standing at every Tube stop, buying fruit at the market, waiting at the traffic lights to cross the street. He traced his finger over the pale-blue postmark and noticed that the collection time was the earliest possible on all but one of the envelopes. Was she a night owl prowling in the dark or an early sparrow flitting through the dawn? Did she slip them through the brass slit in the wall of the post office or feed them to the silent mouth of the red post box in the street? Maybe she held her ear close to hear the soft thud of paper landing on a blanket of envelopes. Maybe she kissed the seal before she let the envelope drop. Or did she toss it quickly in before dashing up the pavement, putting footsteps and seconds between real life and her foolishness as quickly as possible? Winter could never have imagined that her messages in a bottle would float to shore so near to her home. If it came to it, he could knock on every door in the borough. Could he? Wasn't that the sort of thing people did out of desperation when they were looking for a missing child? How could he ever explain what he was looking for? The letters pulled his attention back. Tug. Pull. Drag.

With renewed focus, he rearranged Winter's letters in the order he had received them and turned his pad sideways. Using a sharp pencil, he drew almost perfectly straight columns from top to bottom and wrote in capital letters along the top:

NEIGHBOURHOOD
WORK
NAMES MENTIONED
SOCIAL SPOTS
ROUTINE
PORTRAIT
DUBLIN

It was difficult at first to look past the language of the letters and seek out the reality of her life, the concrete world she lived in. It shouldn't have been so complicated for him, whose job it was to solve mysteries such as these, but he had never been so invested in his subject before. One thought haunted him like the brewing ache of a bad tooth: would the reality of Winter destroy the fantasy? When she wrote her letters, she had the power to be so selective about her life, about how she presented herself. Was it possible to get a true impression of someone, judging only by dispatches from their private self? How different would the public version be? What elements had she chosen to leave out? Webbed feet? Bad debts? Substance abuse? Did she lie in baths for hours at the weekend weeping as she listened to Barbra Streisand records until her skin grew wrinkled? Was her name even really Winter? Or did he have a secret portal to her truest self? One it could ordinarily take nights, months, years, of onion-peeling to get to.

In his mind's eye, the scant details of her appearance painted a portrait of a woman who could never have passed him unnoticed in the street: long, flame-coloured, waving hair, apple-green eyes, alabaster skin, a white rabbit-fur coat, those boots! Would she be recognizable from her description? Had he imagined her as being more beautiful than she was? How could a woman with that head and heart not be? Even if it was just something that glowed from inside her. Did it matter? He thought not. His imagination could conjure only so much; it was the words within her that had bewitched him.

He populated the columns with more debris from her life: the Mexican restaurant in Camden that had already proved futile, Columbia Road Flower Market, the Long Hall pub, former work in the music industry, a vintage clothes shop on Dame Street in Dublin, a bar with a jukebox of fifties records, a mention of photographing protestors. Where could he begin? Not knowing her full name made it difficult. The chapel in Hoxton? Why not start somewhere close? If he put himself out there, maybe the universe would somehow guide him. He carefully gathered the letters together, returned them to their hiding place and ducked out of the depot into the dusky light of a crisp London evening. He walked briskly up Redchurch Street, turned right on to Shoreditch High Street and followed the road left on to Old Street. Hoxton Street was just to the right, and the square one more left. William knew this area well; the band used to rehearse in the basement of the George and Dragon pub once upon a time. He paused outside the chapel gates; he couldn't remember the last time he'd been in a church and wasn't sure he'd ever stepped inside a Catholic one.

The golden light flooding through the windows made him feel more welcome as he tentatively pushed the great mahogany doors inwards. Rows of teak pews ran in parallel either side of a plush red carpet, great ivory beams curved overhead, the iridescent altar loomed before him under a circular stained-glass window that looked to William like a flower, but he supposed it held some greater symbolism. A few people were scattered among the pews; whispers echoed in the rafters from the vestibule, where two ladies were poring over a book of psalms. He hesitated before entering further, but the iron casement of flickering votive candles called him forward. To think Winter had sat here, maybe even just days before, and lit one for him. Well, not for him exactly, perhaps, but that's what it felt like.

He sat down in the second-to-last row and allowed the silence to settle upon him. The iconography unsettled him, but he understood why she found it meditative to sit here. He closed his eyes and wallowed in the peace. A hand gripped his shoulder and William yelped so loudly that all the faithful turned to stare. Slowly, he turned his head, to see Ned Flanagan beaming at him from the pew behind. 'You've been avoiding me, Billy!' he stage-whispered, louder than if he had just spoken normally.

William was confused.

'Mr Flanagan, did you – did you follow me here?'

Ned snorted.

'Don't be ridiculous. Just a splendid coinkydink. Come. Let's take a walk. We can't talk here.'

William had no choice but to shuffle along the bench and accompany his boss down the aisle and back into the symphonic onslaught of Hoxton Square. As they crunched across the gravel in the foreground of the chapel, William spoke first.

'Mr Flanagan, I know you think I've been distracted recently, but I can assure you I've been getting results. Did you see the article in the *Guardian* about the whale vomit? I've been meaning to . . .'

Ned looked perplexed.

'Whale vomit? That's not . . . never mind. The reason I wanted to speak to you is that your name came up at our board meeting.'

William sat down on a bench in the square.

'That sounds ominous,' he replied.

'Yes, I would have thought so, too,' Ned said. 'But it seems your little project has attracted the right sort of attention.'

William marvelled as Ned explained how Sally's father had heard all about his work from her, and that her enthusiasm had been infectious.

'They are keen to invest in that book of yours, produce it ourselves, it seems,' he said. 'And, of course, we both know I've always been behind you a hundred per cent.'

He held out his hand and William shook it vigorously.

'We'll iron out the particulars but, suffice to say – congratulations, William. You did it!'

As Ned shuffled away, William remained on the bench a moment longer, watching the lights inside the chapel as they were extinguished one by one. Would he soon hold in his hands the *Volume of Lost Letters*? He chuckled to himself at Ned's about-turn after his adamant opposition but, if this was divine intervention, he would take it. He had even managed to call him by his proper name. Miraculous, indeed.

14

The following evening, William watched the street from their bedroom window, waiting for the familiar grumbling sounds of Clare's racing-green Mini slowing down outside. He arranged the books on the sill in alphabetical order, then by author, before finally returning them to their original positions in ascending height. He desperately wanted to tell her about his breakthrough with the Supernatural Division, but knew he had to tread softly, considering the role Sally had played in its development. He had spent the afternoon calmly working on the fourth floor, refining once again the letters he hoped to include, if he was going to expand the project to incorporate stories such as Prummel's. The anxious anticipation of seeking out a letter from Winter which usually affected him when he worked there was on hold; he had intercepted Marjorie's discovery only the day before. When he found another letter as the final dregs of the day were draining, he was shocked. Two on consecutive days? Were they accelerating in frequency, or had yesterday's been lying dormant while he was in Clovelly? Against his better judgement, he sneaked the letter out of the depot and read it as he walked along the Bethnal Green Road.

It was a blow to walk through his front door, a letter from Winter in his hand, and see Clare's coat back on its hook in the hallway. The heady mix of guilt and anxiety tarnished the relief he felt that she was back in London and would soon be standing in front of him in their home. He was aware how complicated his life had become and, predominantly, at his own hand. Whenever he was away from Clare, he found it so easy to believe in the possibility of Winter, but whenever they were together it seemed absurd to think that Winter was anything more than a ridiculous flight of fancy. Was his instinct for romanticism more powerful than the pragmatic logic he used to reason with himself? This must be how people felt when they had an affair. He had always scoffed when folk spoke of being in love with two people at the same time, but now he had a more empathetic perspective; it wasn't two different people they loved, necessarily, but the two different lives they offered, the two different versions of themselves that they could potentially become. Do we all need someone to see the potential in us for us to be able to fulfil it?

He was wearing a faded red tartan shirt with frayed cuffs and threadbare patches over the shoulder blades; it was Clare's favourite. The first night they spent together, a button had popped free from it while Clare was nervously undressing him. The next morning, he found her sitting cross-legged on the bedroom floor in her nightdress, concentrating fiercely as she sewed it back on. A little white wicker sewing basket was opened beside her. Her grandmother had bequeathed it to her, along with the silk dressing gown Stevie had lost, a set of bonehandled cutlery and an unfinished patchwork quilt. Every so often, she told him, she would pour a bag of materials on to the living-room floor in a fit of reverie and spend an afternoon quietly sewing hexagons together while being serenaded by Nina Simone. Ever since Clare had inherited the quilt, the order and logic of the pattern had gone awry; she had no patience for following the formula of yellows together, blues together, reds and pinks together. Her hexagons placed fuchsia stripes beside sunflower-yellow gingham, cornflower-blue floral connected to forest-green spirals, scarlet polka dots married to purple paisley. It was the disorder of multicoloured silks, cottons, corduroy and velvet that absorbed her, incompatibles forced together with unexpected but beautiful results. William remembered the first day he found her standing over the quilt, rearranging the newly sewn pieces into clusters of seven and placing them in rows underneath their ancestors.

'What do you think? I haven't attached them yet. This is the moment where I always lose my nerve, when they are joined for ever on to the whole.'

She held up the quilt by the top corners and was completely hidden behind it.

'Gosh. It's huge. How big do you want it to become?' he asked.

Clare turned to face him, a puzzled look on her face, as if the end result had never occurred to her before. 'It has become a bit of a monster, I suppose,' she said. 'I don't know if I'll ever be finished, if I'm honest. I guess I'd like it to be big enough to cover the whole bed and touch the floor all around it . . .'

She laid the quilt back down flat on the floor. William crouched over it and spread his fingers over the different fabrics.

'How long did your grandmother work on it?' he asked.

Clare knelt beside him, surveying the work.

'She started it when she first went into the nursing home, but she died six months later. Instead of people bringing her bunches of grapes or crossword puzzles, she asked for material – pieces from old clothes or curtains or whatever they had. These patches here are from my first baby blanket, and these were taken from my gran's old nursing uniform. She loved the stories being sewn into the fabric. My mother hated it. She thought it was creepy. "A blanket full of ghosts", she called it.'

William smoothed away creases in the cloth.

'Have you any more stories here?' he asked.

She leaned across the quilt to point as she explained.

'This peach one is the lining of a bridesmaid dress from my parents' wedding. My Aunt Polly brought that in . . . and this sea-green silk was an old cravat of Daddy's he used to wear on Sundays. I cut this red poppy material from the dress I wore on my graduation from secondary school. It was my favourite at the time, but I spilled blackcurrant juice all down the front of it that night and the stain would never lift. This section here came from Flora's christening dress, and these were cut from a nightgown with rainbows all over it that she loved. I've quite a few patches mixed in now. I was the one most interested in helping her. The rest of the family thought it was too sentimental, and I think they felt silly bringing in their old bits and pieces. Come on. Help me fold it.'

They held two corners each on opposite sides and joined them together. William kissed her forehead over the fabric that divided them and said, 'I'm sure that's why your gran wanted you to have it and would love the fact that you're going to finish it.'

'Maybe,' she answered. 'But she'd never understand why I wouldn't want to make it *nice*. Granny was black and white, rich and poor, good and evil, birds of a feather flock together, but me, I want the quilt to be as random and uncontrollable as the street out there is, as full of colour and contradictions and clashes as Brick Lane Market on a Sunday.'

He realized he hadn't seen Clare sewing in a long time; all her hours and minutes were absorbed by work, or sleeping to recover from work. He forced himself to stop twitching the curtains like an overzealous neighbourhood-watch man and walked downstairs to open a bottle of red wine. He hadn't eaten; the butterflies in his stomach weren't interested in food. Instead, he took down two goblets from the cupboard and placed them on the kitchen table, before changing his mind and returning one, not wanting Clare to think he was presuming anything.

A small wooden button dangled from a thread on the cuff of his shirt. He let it knock a delicate note against their pinewood kitchen table, twisting his wrist slowly left and right to make a rhythm. It reminded him of being a child and watching his grandfather taunt a small ginger kitten with a ball of purple wool. William thought it was cruel how the puppeteer allowed the hysterical creature to tangle its tiny paws in the wool before dragging it away with the kitten's little furry bottom bouncing along behind. He wanted to ask him to stop, but he was more worried about being called a cry baby than he was about the comfort of the entangled kitten. He snapped the button free, but it slipped through his butter fingers and rolled into obscurity beneath a cupboard. William ducked his head beneath the table to make a half-hearted scan across the floor. His eye was caught instead by a lump of green propped against the skirting board; it was the final remnant of Clare's last bowl from Sorrento. He crawled under the table and retrieved it, before bumping the back of his head on the table rim as he clambered back up to standing. The fragment of green sat in his open palm, winking at him in the light, a lost eye looking at him in a state of confusion. He squeezed his fist around it and dropped it into his shirt pocket.

He was debating whether he could pour himself a glass of wine, or whether he should wait, when he heard the front door slowly open. In his haste to hide away the bottle of wine, his foot caught on the leg of a stool and he crashed to a fall. Smithereens of glass scattered across the floor as the Rioja formed gloopy puddles on the white tiles. Clare chased the sound of the crash into the kitchen and screamed when she saw William lying there in a red, sticky mess. He staggered to his feet, his trainers sliding in the wine while he steadied himself and said, 'I'm sorry. It's just wine. I slipped. It's fine.'

William ran his hands under the cold tap at the kitchen sink to clean away the sticky wine. He peeled off his cowboy shirt, tossed it into the washing machine and began sweeping up the glass, smearing scarlet stains across the floor as he worked.

'The grout is the most important thing,' she said. 'Make sure you clean between the tiles.' She stepped into the kitchen and rooted around in the cupboard beneath the sink until she found a bottle of bleach. She mixed it with washing-up liquid and hot water in a Tupperware bowl and passed it to William, along with a scouring pad. 'Are you okay to do the rest? I'll walk around to Mr Patel's to get us another bottle. Do you want anything else?' she asked.

William shook his head as Clare gingerly stepped over the smeared tiles and escaped through the front door. As the power of his elbows fought the strength of the stains, he scrubbed as if the ability to wipe away the darkness in their marriage depended on the force of his will. Could he stem the flow of love that was trickling away, a slow but persistent stream, from what was once a deep, unfathomable lake?

It took Clare longer than it should have to walk to the corner shop, choose two bottles of wine from the range of four, dither over whether to buy some peanuts or crisps and make her way back to the flat. When she let herself in, the kitchen had been restored to order and William was waiting in the living room, now wearing a Beatles T-shirt and a striped woollen scarf. It seemed an odd combination, but she let it pass.

'Do we have to listen to Leonard Cohen right now? I think he might push me over the edge.' William walked to the record player, and turned the volume down before he lifted the needle.

'What will I put on instead?'

'Does there have to be anything playing? What could possibly be an appropriate soundtrack?'

William closed the lid on the turntable and stood against the fireplace.

'We always have music playing, that's all. It feels weird to have the flat totally silent.'

'It's not silent – we're talking, aren't we?'

Clare knew exactly what he meant, though; music was always playing in the background of their lives. She just didn't want to associate any songs, any band, with tonight, the night they might decide to finally call it a day. Was that what she wanted to happen? She remembered making a mix-tape to play if they came back to her flat after their first date so many years before, trying to choose artists who didn't remind her of any other boyfriends or evoke any memories, either happy or sad. She remembered the thrill of discovering a tape that William had made in her locker at university. Each and every song felt like a little piece of magic, a tiny planet of hope and discovery. She had been full of questions. Why did he choose that song? Are those lyrics about me? What do these songs make him think of? And to see his handwriting on the sleeve notes, the curves and strokes and shape of the letters. Clare didn't want a 'Night I left William for ever' soundtrack, songs that would haunt her afterwards, creeping up on her in the supermarket, or on the radio while she was driving to work. She sat in their overstuffed caramel-coloured armchair and pulled their crocheted Afghan blanket around her, as she always had. How much would she tell him of what had happened in Wales? Did everything have to come out now?

William interrupted her thoughts.

'I missed you so much, Clare. I hate this, us sitting here like strangers.'

She sighed and wriggled down further into the chair.

'How could you miss me when things have been so difficult between us?' she asked. 'It must have been a relief to get a break from the way things have been.'

He left his roost on the ridge of the mantelpiece and pulled up a footstool to sit close to her.

'I wasn't relieved that you left, but you're right, we couldn't continue in the way we have been. It's time we started being honest with each other, don't you think?'

Clare looked at the blanket on her knees and smoothed away a wrinkle in the fabric before she spoke.

'Okay, then. Let's hear it . . . the ugly truth, if we must.'

He topped up her wine glass, which was noticeably depleted after such a short space of time.

'You have to just give me a chance to speak, though, without shouting me down or getting defensive. Can you do that? Otherwise, it's pointless . . . and I promise I'll do the same for you when it's your turn. You're not in court now, remember?'

'What do you mean, shout you . . . Okay, okay, I'm listening. Tell me.'

She caught herself biting her thumbnail and quickly withdrew her hand.

He exhaled a deep breath before the words came tumbling out.

'My main worry is that you still seem to be punishing me for what happened with the book. I've apologized so many times, but it doesn't change anything. If I thought it was helping at all, I'd suffer it, but it *doesn't* help. You still seem to think I was some kind of fraud, deliberately making a fool of you, but it wasn't like that . . . No, stop, I can see you waiting to jump in, but hear me out. I hated lying to you, but I kept telling myself that all I needed was to find a way into the novel again, and then I could pull it back and you'd never need to know. It's not like I did nothing – I wrote the first twenty thousand words what feels like twenty thousand times, but I just couldn't move it on. I'm so sorry. I wish I could have. It completely broke my heart walking away from it, and disappointing you crushed me, but I can't change the fact that I failed.'

Clare threw her hands up in the air. A little wine sloshed on her legs, where she held the glass between her knees. She wiped it with her sleeve as she studied him.

'That's the bit you never seemed to get, William. I wasn't disappointed because you *failed*. It was the deception. You were lying to me for *years*, and I had no clue. How could I trust myself to ever know the difference again?'

He reached out to her.

'But you *do* know, Clare. You do know. Are you really telling me you didn't notice anything wrong during that time? That you couldn't see it wasn't working, that I wasn't myself?'

'So it was my fault? I should have somehow noticed and saved you from your own self? The neglectful wife who never bothered to notice that you had *changed*.'

William stood up and paced the floorboards as he tried to douse cold water on the heat in the room, which was escalating rapidly.

'Clare, please don't fight me. That's not what I'm saying at all. I'm just trying to make the point that you've watched me telling the truth a million times longer than you've watched me hide it, and I think, if I am telling you the truth now, you'll recognize it. That's all. I wasn't . . . the words, they just withered inside me . . . I was empty.'

Seeing him so upset, Clare's protests caught in her throat. She watched William's hands shaking as he spoke; his hands were the first thing she had noticed about him. Long, piano fingers. Deep creases in his palms. She wondered what a fortune-teller would say about those heavy lines and what they would mean for her. The wine softened her a little and gave her eyes something to focus on while William paced the room again. He paused in front of the mantelpiece and took another deep breath.

'I also just want to say I have never stopped loving you, but it is very hard to cope with how you blame me for everything imperfect in your life. Any disappointment you feel in your own lot, you trace back to me, and I don't think that's fair.'

He saw her bristle but continued speaking before she could interrupt.

'I completely accept that I've let you down and appreciate that you stayed loyal to us, even though you were disappointed in me . . . but if this is to work, Clare, we need to let go of what's happened and the idea of who we should be and just go into this accepting who we are right now.'

'You mean settle? What if I don't want to just give in and let go of who I think we could be? What if I think there could be more for us?'

He stopped pacing and stood in front of her where she sat. 'I don't mean "settle" at all,' he said. 'I mean letting go of the past to start fresh. You want more for yourself, and I do, too . . . I've had some breakthroughs with the writing recently, and great developments at work. I can't promise you roaring success, but what I do know is there is a much better chance of either of those things happening if I think you're behind me and haven't given up on me.'

She tugged on the end of his T-shirt. A small smile made a shy appearance.

'How many times have you rehearsed that little speech in your head?'

'Many. It's all I've been thinking about.'

William sat down on the sofa and focused his attention on her feet. That was mostly what he had been thinking about – except for the minutes stolen by Winter, of course. He quickly chased that thought away.

Clare swirled the dark red liquid around in her glass and watched William's reflection on the windowpane.

She had underestimated how relieved she would be to hear that he still wanted her. He was going to fight for her, for them, for the little world they had built in these four rooms. The question was, how hard? And was it too late? If they were going to try, she had to tell him the truth. After reprimanding him for so long about keeping secrets, she couldn't in good conscience live with the guilt of hiding her own bad behaviour. It was needling away at her constantly.

'Well, now it's my turn, and I'm afraid there's something you need to know that may change how you feel. Considerably.'

She avoided his eye as he watched her from across the room.

'This isn't easy for me to say, William, but I want to be honest with you, too, so please try to stay calm.'

He held his head in his hands and emitted a low groan. 'Those must be the least calming words ever spoken,' he said. 'What else has happened?'

'What else?' She looked confused, but carried on. 'Not much, I promise, but something. The day of the fundraising benefit at the depot.' She paused. 'I was stressed about the trial and dreading going to that stupid party, and everything just built up in me and I sat in my Mini at the courtroom and I just couldn't stop crying.'

He looked at her, aghast.

'Oh, Clare. Why didn't you tell me? Is that why you were so mad at –'

'Wait. I'm not finished. Maxi saw me there and got into the car to talk to me.'

'No, no, no. Not Maxi. Please don't tell me all of this has anything to do with him.'

'He just put his arms around me to comfort me and, well, we sort of, ended up kissing. That's it. Nothing more than that, but I know it was wrong, so I just had to tell you. It was stupid, I know, so stupid, and I'm sorry.'

She saw the colour in his face change to deep red; he was angry, but trying to control it. She felt tears welling and held her breath in anticipation of him blowing.

'And you had the nerve to accuse me of something happening with Sally? After you had already been with him? That's a staggering act of deflection, Clare. Are you *serious*? You let me stand here, beating myself up about what's happened between us, and all the time, you've been nursing that secret?'

She rushed over and crouched before him but was afraid to reach out and touch him in case he brushed her away.

'I swear, nothing else happened. It was just that one stupid kiss.'

The words swarmed between them like angry bees. A haze of you and me, he and she, why, how, where, when . . . Questions. Accusations. Positioning. Remembering. Pausing. Coaxing. Suggesting. Bargaining. Pleading. Threatening. Blaming. Surrendering. Offering. Rejecting. Shouting. Crying. Rage. Silence.

The curtains were drawn and lamps lit. William started the fire and Clare pulled the blanket from her knees up to her shoulders. The wine bottles were drained, the gin bottle followed and, eventually, the pot whistled for coffee. William stretched out on the couch, his feet resting on the arm of Clare's chair. It was the closest he had come to touching her since her confession. She nudged his feet into her lap, and he was too exhausted to resist. The glow from the streetlight outside crept in around the window frame and cast strange shadows over the tableau. Their conversation was disconnected now, as each of them drifted in and out of dozing, remembered a point from earlier that must be refuted, or was struck by something new. All thoughts soaked in liquor.

Clare's voice was drifting now.

'It's strange seeing the living room at this time, when, normally, we'd be sleeping. It reminds me of being a child; I always wondered what our house was like when me and Flora were at school. I couldn't imagine what my mother did all day when we weren't there.'

'I always tried to picture you at work – bustling about being busy and important, who you are when I'm not there. I used to worry about all the men who would try and sweep you off your feet.'

'None of them ever did, though, William. I swear. Not really. You know this was just a blip, a symptom of everything else that was going on. You believe me, don't you?'

Clare went to the bathroom and released her hair from a messy bun that had all but come undone. Her face was flushed and blotchy; she splashed it with cold water in an effort to cool down. She brushed her teeth and sat on the edge of the tub, enjoying the feel of the chilly tiles underneath her bare feet.

William remained downstairs, body and soul weak and tired. The thought of Clare in Maxi's arms nauseated him, but he knew that this was not the hill his marriage would die on. There was hope for them now, he could feel it, but he would need to dig deep and push past her stupid indiscretion, difficult though it was. He knew he was right to be furious at her about what had happened, but he also felt a blessed relief that things hadn't gone any further. He followed Clare into the bathroom and pulled her upright. She leaned against him, her head finding its old familiar spot in the groove beside his left shoulder as she breathed in the smell of him. He stroked the back of her neck, smoothing her hair up from her skin and letting it fall slowly between his fingers.

'Let's get some sleep,' she whispered.

'Okay. The bed is freshly made. I'll sleep on the couch.'

'Will you sleep in the bed with me? I know a lot has happened, but I just can't face being alone, thinking of you downstairs alone, too. Let's just be together.'

He hesitated but didn't want to argue any more. He led her into their bedroom, pulled back the duvet and turned on her bedside lamp. She stepped out of her dress and pulled on an old white cotton nightdress before slipping under the covers. William removed his clothes and awkwardly climbed in beside her; he felt more nervous than he had the first time she had invited him into her bed. He doused the light and lay flat on his back, afraid to touch her, although he longed to. He listened to her breathing, waiting for it to grow heavy and slow, but he could hear how awake she was, could imagine all the thoughts driving around the streets of her mind. It was a city he feared to tread through in the dark. She wriggled and turned to lay her head on his chest. He stroked her back, startled by how much weight she had lost. He could trace the lines of her ribs where, before, she had always been so soft. He held her as tightly as he could, afraid to wipe away the hot tears that ran down his face in case she noticed. Tried not to sniffle.

Clare heard his breath catching, slid on top of him and brushed the tears away with her hands. She leaned over him and kissed a line from the corner of his eye, over his cheek, past his ear and down his neck to where she had rested her head. It was such a comfort to lie on top of him and feel him respond beneath her as she moved over him in the darkness, swallowing the guilt of a story not fully told. She buried her full confession deep down, where it couldn't accidentally slip from her. So far, no one knew, and she hoped it could remain that way. That this was not the last night she would sleep in his arms.

William followed each movement of Clare's with his breath held. He was afraid a sudden move would scare her away. Was this the first thaw? Their first steps towards a new start?

When they eventually fell into a heavy sleep, mixed emotions crowded the air around them. William had been struggling to reconcile the horror of the thought

of Clare in Maxi's arms with the odd absolution it gave
him for the emotional infidelity he knew he was guilty
of. He slipped out from under the covers and let the
moonlight guide him from their bedroom. He tiptoed
down the stairs and sat in the darkness of the living
room, surveying in the ambient light from the street the
detritus of the night they had spent together. He fumbled in the dark to remove Winter's letter from his
satchel. He knew he had to let Winter and her letters go.
He settled on the windowsill in the living room and
strained to read her last letter again in the dim light.
Where was she tonight while her words kept him
company?

My Great Love, hola,

I write to you from under the Andalucían sun; your
Winter is baking in an untimely heat, for I find myself
on holiday. I have swapped the dreary, blank London
skies so this hot light can drench me instead of show-
ers. I came completely underprepared. My lightest
dresses are too heavy here and my underexposed skin
too white. My legs remind me of bottles of milk sitting
on the doorstep, winking in the dawn light. A little
child pointed at me in the street this morning, and I'm
sure it was shock at my pallor. Maybe she thought I
was a ghost.

At night, I lie under a rotating fan attached to the
ceiling, the sheet clammy beneath me, air smothering
above. I try to bargain with the gods for a breeze that
will blow me to sleep, but I'm always disappointed. If

you were here, I can't imagine two hot bodies could like squirming in these clammy sheets together. Maybe you would surrender and sleep downstairs in the hammock on the porch. Maybe we would just sit up and not struggle against it at all. I wish you were here to wade through the close night air with me. I'd suffer the extra heat of your heavy arm around me if you could tolerate my hot cheek against your chest. Instead, I sit on my own, listening to the songs of the sea, worrying that dark shadows moving across the horizon are sinister figures looking for me. I used to think I would be a fighter if someone attacked me. Here, on the rural coast, I am scared of the night without electric lights. Maybe I'm braver in the city. Here, I would surely flee, if my feet were not sinking in the sand.

This holiday wasn't planned, my love. It wasn't a date circled on the calendar for months. No new dresses or swimsuits were bought. Sadly, I came to recover from the passing of my grandfather – as if bereavement is so easily managed that I can allocate a period of time for it to do its worst to me and send me back to the living. I'm not sure that my head and heart have even fully signed up to try. They refuse to connect to the reality of it all and alter the reasons why am I here; make the funeral that of a stranger, change the identity of the old gentleman lying in the coffin. I've never known anyone who died before – not anyone close to me, anyway. I've witnessed grief, but not felt it beyond a vicarious sadness for other people's suffering. For a moment, you are acutely aware of their pain, maybe even feel the sting of tears, but then, you hug them goodbye and leave the house shrouded in black and your life is exactly the same as it was before you visited. Isn't that the bleakest part of all? The lover or sister or friend goes home after the burial to a coat hanging in the hall like a ghost, spectacles perched lop-sided on the bedside table. There is silence where their words should be. A plate, knife and fork left sitting in the drawer. And the rest of the world carries on regardless.

They laid him out in the parlour of his cottage. It was hard to fathom why his sons and daughters had to watch that beloved man be carried into his home in a wooden box. There was nothing poetic about it. His grandsons struggled to bear the weight. The coffin was too long to turn in the little hallway and they talked of pushing it through the living-room window or carrying it in through the back door. My Auntie May despaired that the back garden was too unkempt to take him in that way. My Uncle Jimmy surveyed the window to see how long it would take to remove. And all the while, neighbours gathered in twos and threes, and children cycled laps on bikes and trikes. His old neighbours hobbled closer on walking sticks if they could, or watched from behind net curtains if they couldn't.

My father stood with his hand resting on the side of the coffin. He is too old now himself to bear the weight on his shoulder, but he said he just wanted to be close to him. It almost broke my heart. I had never seen him cry before. An ice-cream van rollicked past, playing its regular, sunny Saturday siren, before spotting the hearse and dashing away. My sisters and I stood side by side in that little front garden. We didn't touch. Black daffodils standing still, no breeze. No one comforted the other, for we all felt the same. We were broken, watching our father breaking. How proud I was of him that he could show his grief. I saw my mother holding him up and felt so relieved for him that he had her there. How much harder it must be to bear these things alone. I don't want that to be me. I want you to meet my lovely father. Soon. I will miss my grandad terribly: my fiercest critic and my greatest advocate. I'm sorry he never saw me achieve something wonderful, but I know he was sure that I would. Maybe that's just as good. He was a man ahead of his time, encouraged my feminist grandma to pursue all her passions, to become a photographer too, shared the burden at home so she could work. He inspired his children to follow their dreams, and his grandchildren in turn. He gave me my first camera, and the very first picture I took was of my grandparents sitting on the wall outside their house. It sits beside my bedside, a daily reminder that I must not lose faith. 'Have heart, my dear,' my grandmother always tells me. 'Only dreamers find dreams come true.' I know how blessed I am to have had this family to love me; I know their love will be a buffer around me, no matter what this wretched world sends me.

I'm going to wait until I am back in London before I post this. For the rest of my time here, I will let the sun heat my pale skin. I hope my seventy-year-old self will forgive me the wrinkles, and I hope you will learn to love them. You should be here with me. Our time will come, won't it, my love?

Until you find me,

Winter

William lay on the couch and pulled Clare's Afghan blanket over him. The image of Winter as a black daffodil, mourning for her grandfather, her red hair harsh against the funeral clothes, caught him by the heart. He remembered the day of Clare's father's funeral; how distraught her mother and Flora had been, how frozen Clare was. It saddened him to think of Winter alone with her grief. It frightened him to imagine that for himself. Or for Clare.

He couldn't help but compare Winter's attitude about family to Clare's in a manner unfavourable to his wife. She never wanted to hear about his childhood and seemed almost to resent him for the happy family he was born into. He had never been able to explain to her how his middle-class suburban upbringing could be a burden on him, the passive-aggressive expectation that he would build on his parents' success with his own. The Woolfs had never wanted a writer for a son, although they weren't confrontational enough to stand in his way. Deep down, he knew that's what had triggered his writer's block: the knowledge that, if the work was a failure, he would have fulfilled their worst fears for him. The irony of him achieving that by doing nothing at all was not lost on him.

He had never been able to explain that pressure to

Clare; she couldn't tolerate any complaints on his part about his childhood when she had endured proper suffering. He knew it couldn't compare. In truth, he realized that his parents had always been a little too soft on him; they always solved any problem he presented as best they could. If he hadn't studied for an exam, they paid for private lessons, and they had financially supported all his whims without ever expecting him to get a job to support himself. Perhaps that was why he had found it so easy to let Clare take care of him. She had spoiled him, too, and he had revelled in it for too long. Allowing him to enjoy a lifestyle he couldn't afford, indulging him in expensive rare vinyl records and first editions of novels. It was time for him to take responsibility for his actions, late as he was to the realization.

He remembered a terrible row he once had with Clare when his mother went to hospital for an emergency appendectomy. Despite the relatively low-risk procedure, William's father was beside himself with nerves and had burst into tears when he saw William and Clare arriving at the hospital. He would never forget how small Clare looked when she turned and ran from the waiting room. Later that night, they were sitting in the attic at a friend's house party, drinking whiskey, when she tried to explain why it was so hard for her to witness that sort of unconditional love. She said it exposed to her so much that was lacking in her own understanding of what relationships could be, what she could expect from people.

Lying on the couch, agitated sleep washed over William with restless dreams of the sea lapping against the shore, black sails flapping on a boat on the horizon. He was shivering where he sat on the sand but could not move.

Upstairs, Clare had slept soundly, but she woke up to a sinking feeling. She reached out for William, but he was gone. Instead, guilt now filled the bed and smothered her where she lay. Images of her last day and night in Wales flashed in her mind: Maxi's car crunching up the drive-way, their empty glasses in the bar, his knock on the door. She fought them away and resisted the impulse to go to William for comfort; she didn't trust herself to be silent. Instead, she lay diagonally across the bed as the light gathered momentum through the venetian blinds. The darkness she had felt before dawn slipped away in parallel increments until she felt calmer, stronger. Ready to start a new day. Relieved her secret was still safely tucked away, where it could do no more harm.

15.

William bent over his desk, sneaked a segment of chocolate orange from the pedestal drawer, and placed the whole piece in his mouth before straightening in his seat. It wasn't greed that made him so secretive, or a reluctance to share the loot with his colleagues, but rather a desire to be left alone and avoid the jovial banter that shared confectionery always involved. With only the slightest excuse, Marjorie would circle him, like a bird of prey, desperate to indulge in the contraband. He cringed at the thought of the chocolate-orange mush swirling around in her mouth while she regaled him with snippets from the scandalous underbelly of community bingo. He couldn't endure it. Not today. Instead, he closed his mouth firmly around the half-moon slice of sin and swallowed surreptitiously as it melted and folded upon itself. Chocolate orange was Clare's favourite treat. Maybe that's why he chose it. A little taste of happier times, when he was lucky to scavenge the tiniest bite from her: 'I'll buy you one of your own, if you want, but I'm not sharing mine. Take my soul, but you'll never take my chocolate orange.'

She was always quite particular about having her own things, apart from everything they shared or bought together; her own bedside table with a little silver key to lock the drawer, a separate wardrobe for her clothes, shelves in the living room for her books alone, a chest in the attic for her keepsakes and childhood treasures. Once, in an argument about where they were going to spend New Year's Eve, he had accused her of being so independent because it meant she could pack more conveniently if ever she wanted to flee. Her response – silence – was frightening; he hadn't really thought it could be true until that moment. Maybe, in her heart of hearts, she had always carried a seed of doubt that they would stay together. Men had started wars over women they loved; women had moved mountains. Were those people suppressing little niggling doubts throughout? He doubted it.

In the weeks following Clare's homecoming, however, William was relieved to see how much things had improved at home. They were not suddenly reconciled but the atmosphere at home was at least conciliatory. He thought the shock of Clare being in the danger zone of an affair had forced them both to re-evaluate their priorities. When he thought of Maxi, William's jaw clenched, but really, in the scheme of things, it could have been worse. It would be too much to say that it had all been for the best, but he welcomed the sea change her indiscretion had heralded. Clare tried not to work so late in the evenings and they took it in turns to cook more at home: fresh salads and slow-roasted casseroles, Asian stir-fries and spicy curries. Less time was spent watching television and more was devoted to listening to each other. Clare cancelled a ceramics class she had been due to start and suggested they revive their old weekly cinema night instead. One evening, as they drained the dregs from a bottle of Riesling, she turned to him and said, 'It's a relief, isn't it? I feel like I was trying to carry a tray of plates that was too heavy for me up a flight of stairs. Letting them fall was a shock, but something of a relief, too.' William rinsed out the empty wine bottle and threw it in the recycling, flinched at the crash of glass on glass.

An ill wind had cleared the air, but there was still a ghost lingering in the corners of his mind. A question taunted him: if Clare had really left him for Maxi, if their marriage had truly been over, would he have tried to find Winter in earnest? And, if the idea was still tugging at his heart, was he right to be trying so hard to ignore it? He had made a conscious effort to banish Winter from his life but, sometimes, when he least expected it, her words whispered in his ear: *Our time will come, won't it, my love? . . . I'm saving my stories for you.* He was determined, however, to let her go. He and Clare had, just, pulled their marriage back from the brink. He couldn't be the one to run away now. How could he let Clare down like that, when she had always stood by him?

William spritzed furniture polish on to his desk and buffed the mahogany finish with a yellow duster. What a risk he had taken by allowing himself to be so seduced by Winter. All her letters were now sealed inside a brown padded envelope, buried beneath a telephone directory, an atlas and a heavy dictionary in his bottom desk drawer. He knew that he should send them to the shredder but couldn't quite bring himself to just yet. Would it be terrible to include one of Winter's letters in his *Volume of Lost*

Letters? He closed the door on that idea; he would be doing it only in the hope that she might present herself; he couldn't allow anything to jeopardize the progress he and Clare had made. The letters were a distraction, re-igniting the old belief in *the one* of his stubborn heart. He needed to let this foolish idea go: the letters weren't meant for him and he wasn't meant for Winter. Besides, it was weeks now since one had appeared, so perhaps she was done with him, too. The letters had stopped appearing after he had resigned himself to ignoring their call. That had to be a sign, hadn't it?

He picked up a collection of different-sized envelopes that dribbled across the paisley-patterned carpet by his feet and shuffled them into a neater, but still unyielding, pile. Each letter should receive his undivided attention; each deserved every possible chance of finding its way. A squidgy manila envelope, creased and battered, wilfully refused to fall into line and toppled the tower. William's superstitious mind had learned to trust his instincts and accept the letters as they fell. He stretched to reach for it; pulled it closer with his thumb and forefinger.

The address on the envelope had been written in blue colouring pencil, curling letters now bleeding across the page above the Isle of Man postmark. To Gordon? Gerard? Gregory, maybe? What was the surname? Davenport? That might help. The house number and street were smudged, but it seemed to be somewhere in Holland Park. William squeezed the parcel and gave it a little shake; lots of little pieces shuffled within. Was it a jigsaw? A puzzle? Something broken? He gently cracked the seal, and the contents scattered across the table, into his lap and on to the floor: hundreds of individual words cut from newspapers, magazines and goodness knew where else, each one glued to a piece of coloured card. He scooped the words up and gathered them into a little mound in the centre of the table.

Words jumped out at him in a kaleidoscope of so many different colours, typefaces and sizes: eleven, eucalyptus, lemon tree harvest, own goal, dirty washing, panda bear, summer drought, swarm of bees, Doc Marten boots, top hat, jealousy, silk, xylophone, blackbird, duke, nuclear attack, Mars, cellophane wrapping, letter box, penguin compound, snow, polka, paving stones, pumpkin pie, daffodils, anticipation, handwritten, chandelier, lost boys, library, cottage industry, racist attack, Juliet's balcony, protest march, entrepreneur, witchcraft, umbrellas, scarlet, star-struck, soup kitchen, forgiveness, fern, Laurel and Hardy, salt of the earth, Electric Ballroom, warts, shrinking violet, whistle-blower, calligraphy, cymbals, resonate, lamplight, rocking chair, myxomatosis, peaches, float.

William's fingers rifled through the randomness, separating, singling out and congregating the words together again. Why did some words disturb him? Crawl inside his mind and set up camp there? They flashed like neon against a jet-black night: blackbird, witchcraft, scarlet, lamplight, daffodils. He eased the remaining contents from the envelope, along with a sheet of squared paper from a mathematics copybook; it smelled of primary school. Doodles of flowers, butterflies and stars bordered the purple ink, and glitter clung to his fingers as he separated out the pages.

Hi Godfrey,

Thanks for your letter. It came on Tuesday and I managed to meet the postman on the corner, so no fear of my mam or stupid Tracy opening it first this time. Do you know it's actually against the law to open someone else's letters? I told my mam when I found that out, but she just said it was a bigger crime to give her cheek, so I'm not sure she's that bothered. I'll just try and get to the post first from now on, but maybe we can use some code words, just in case? Instead of saying you love me, maybe just say you love mashed potato or something, and I'll know what you mean. Maybe not potatoes, though, but something else that makes you think of me.

You're probably wondering what the bag of words is all about. Well, believe it or not, it's your birthday present. I'm sorry I couldn't get you a real present, but I'm not getting any shifts at the café now it's only open part-time for the winter, and I didn't want to ask Da; he'd only ask me too many questions. The thing is, I'm hoping you'll like this, even though I made it myself. It's to help you with your songs – I know you said that writing the words is the hardest part, and I heard David Bowie talking on the radio about how he writes his songs. He said he just cuts out loads of words and mixes them all together before picking different ones out like in a raffle to put together to make up sentences. It's called a VERBALIZER!! Isn't that the best idea ever?? So I made you one. And I know you said if I asked you to write a song about me you never would, but at least this way maybe I can inspire you, even if the song isn't about me. I hope you like it. It took ages to stick all the bits of cereal box on the back, but I wanted it to last you more than the one song if you liked it.

I have to run to get this in the last post. Good luck with the gig in the social. I wish I could come and see the Mad Frogs' debut gig. That's a much better name than the Slow Turtles, by the way.

Lots of mashed potato,

Tina . . . x

William wondered if Godfrey ever did know how much trouble Tina had gone to. Did he think she had simply not replied to his last letter? He pulled down the telephone directory from the shelf above his desk and flicked quickly through the pages until he reached the Davenports; there were just two in Holland Park. He gave a silent prayer of thanks that Tina's Godfrey wasn't a Smith or a Jones and dialled the first number. It rang and rang until a row of beeps disconnected him. His second call, to the next address, was answered on the first ring and a little girl sang down the phone with well-rehearsed importance, 'Hello, this is the Davenport residence. Who is speaking?'

'Hello, this is William Woolf calling from the Royal Mail. Could I speak to one of your parents, please?'

'We don't know any postmen.'

William struggled to suppress the impatience in his voice. He crossed through items on his to-do list, the receiver cradled under his ear, while he spoke.

'I'm not a postman. Could you call one of your parents for me?'

'They're not here. Daddy's golfing and Mummy is playing tennis.'

'Lovely. Well, who else is there?'

'I'm not supposed to talk to strangers and tell them things.'

'Quite right. So, can you call a grown-up for me?'

William heard muffled whispers as the receiver was intercepted.

'Arabella, who are you tormenting? You were told not to answer the telephone.'

'I think it might be Stranger Danger, Granny.'

'Oh, seriously. What nonsense!'

'Hello, Mrs Davenport speaking. Can I help you?'

William straightened up to answer. 'Yes, hello. My name is William Woolf and I work in a Royal Mail department that deals with undelivered mail. I was wondering if there is a Godfrey Davenport at this address?'

'Godfrey? He's my son, but he doesn't live here; this is his sister Camilla's house. Where did you get this number?'

'The telephone directory. The address on the parcel just told me the name and area so I thought I'd try my luck. Could you give me a forwarding address to redirect it to?'

There was a silence. William suspected she was considering his request.

'Do you know what this *parcel* contains?' she asked, her curiosity barely concealed.

'I'm afraid I'm not at liberty to say, but I do believe it is a personal item that he would want delivered.'

'How intriguing. Well, you can send it to me. Godfrey and his family will be visiting from the Isle of Man at the weekend.'

The Isle of Man! Was he living there with Tina, after all? William carefully collected the jumble of words into a clear plastic envelope and sealed the letter from Tina inside. Would Tina be standing beside Godfrey when he opened it? Or was he summoning a ghost from the past to haunt him? William dropped the parcel into the mailbag for next-day delivery with a short cover note which in no way justified the length of time between posting and receiving, and wished it well. He hoped Godfrey had married the right girl.

Later that evening, Clare laid her new peacock-blue cashmere coat across the bed, fastened the big pearl buttons and stepped back to admire it. She bit her lip, considering for a moment the eye-watering sum she had paid for it, but dismissed her buyer's remorse. It was a long time since she had indulged in something lovely for herself, and this was a special occasion, after all. Her oldest schoolfriend, Enid, was getting married in Dublin the following day, and she was looking forward to escaping London with William. It was almost five years since she had last seen Enid, and she had been relieved to find the wedding invitation on their doormat in the midst of their Christmas post. She was struck by how hurt she would have been not to be invited, despite the distance that had crept between them, which was far wider than geography necessitated. Clare carefully folded the layers of pale-pink tissue that had swaddled her coat and tucked them away in her dressing-table drawer. She caught her reflection in the mirror and smiled at the subtle blonde highlights her hairdresser had scattered through her hair that afternoon. 'Takes years off you,' he'd proclaimed, and she found herself inclined to agree. Baby steps.

Two cases lay open on the floor, Clare's filled with her clothing and belongings, William's still empty, despite the early-morning flight they would catch the next day.

'William, can you come and pack?' Clare called down the stairs, as she unwrapped the new pale-blue tie she had bought him to complement her outfit. She ran the silk through her fingers while she waited to hear some acknowledgment that he'd heard her; a mumble reverberated from the living room and she was content. She rustled through his sock drawer for the least exotic socks he owned, something sensible to peek out from the trouser hem of the navy-blue suit she'd collected from the dry cleaner's earlier. She lined up random trinkets that did not belong there on top of the chest: scissors (lethal, she thought), a used handkerchief, a pamphlet for Madame Tussauds (of all places), a box of plasters that belonged in the bathroom cabinet. She touched something faintly sticky and pulled it out into the light: a Polaroid picture of a pair of boots!

'What are you doing with all my stuff?' William brushed the paraphernalia of his untidiness back into the drawer with one sweep of his arm. 'Can a man have no privacy?'

'What's this picture?' she asked, not once tearing her eyes from it.

William only now noticed Winter's picture in the hands of his wife. He carefully rearranged the socks in an equally chaotic state of disorder as he cleared his throat.

'Oh, that?' he said, pretending to scrutinize it along with her. 'It's nothing. Just something I found in the depot. It ended up trapped in a book I was reading somehow, and I forgot to bring it back.' He saw Clare look at him quizzically.

'Are you sure that's all it is?' she asked. 'It seemed to have been hidden away back there.'

William turned away and shoved the drawer closed. 'Not hidden, just lost!' He plucked the photo from her fingers and tossed it in the waste-paper basket beside his bureau. 'Just some more of the random madness discovered in the daily mission.'

William pretended not to notice as Clare picked it back out of the bin to stare at it again, and focused on removing his suit from the plastic covers.

'Should I wear the jacket on the flight, do you think?' he asked. 'Save it getting creased in the case?'

Clare was still frozen in concentration over the image. 'I just feel like I've seen these boots somewhere before,' she said. 'But I can't place it. Don't worry, it will come back to me.' She smiled as she placed it down on top of the chest. 'Let's finish packing so we can have an early night.'

Later, William lay flat on his back, staring into the darkness. Why had he hidden that picture at home? So foolish! Why had he even kept it at all? He jolted as Clare grabbed his arm and gave him a little shake.

'William,' she whispered. 'Are you awake? I've got it!'

He rolled over on his side to face her, saw her silhouette sitting upright. She flicked on her bedside lamp; the sudden brightness dazzled him. 'I saw a girl wearing those boots a few days ago. I just remembered!'

William's heart pounded. He didn't trust himself to maintain a neutral expression and turned to drink from a tumbler of water on his bedside cabinet.

'Who?' he croaked. 'What do you mean? Where?'

Clare snuggled back down under the duvet. 'When I was waiting in the car for you outside the Indian restaurant the other night. She walked past and, honestly, it was like a scene from a film. That's why it stayed with me. She was wearing the boots, and this big white fur coat, and she had miles of red hair.' Her last thought trailed off into a question. 'It looked like maybe a costume of some sort?' She clicked off the light again. 'That's a relief. I *knew* I recognized them. Do you think they really could be the ones in the picture? Can't be too many glittery white cowboy boots walking around!'

'No,' William sighed. 'I would think not. Small world.'

He listened to Clare's breathing grow steady while he struggled to control his own. A white fur coat? It must be her. He felt the walls closing in around him. Would he never be free of this? He lay perfectly still under the duvet, eyes closed tight. Why was the universe so determined to throw this woman in his path? Had he fallen foul of some cruel trickery? For months, he had been scanning the streets for a sighting, and then, when Winter had finally appeared, he had been looking in another direction. What would he have done if he'd spotted her while Clare sat watching? He couldn't have just allowed her to walk past, could he? His restless legs started twitching under the covers. Worried that he would wake Clare, he tiptoed to the living room and lay on the couch watching *Fawlty Towers* with the sound turned off. It made for a confusing silent movie.

When Clare found him the next morning, he was contorted into an awkward shape under her blanket, cold toes stretched over the end of the sofa.

'I couldn't sleep, and I didn't want to disturb you.' he explained.

'Don't worry,' she answered, pulling the blanket away. 'But it's time to get up now. We are off on an adventure.'

16.

It was raining in Ireland, as it always seemed to be, but as they walked down Wexford Street, huddled together under an orange-canopied umbrella, William was thankful that the skies had opened. On the flight over, he had fought hard to squash the lingering anxiety he felt at Clare's unexpected encounter with Winter. Deeply engrossed in his novel, *The Haunted Bookshop*, he deflected Clare's chatting while the words swam before his eyes. Was Dublin really the best place for them to be visiting? The city was so firmly associated now in his thoughts with his secret lady of the letters. The invitation Winter had extended to explore her old haunts lingered in his mind, but he tried not to dwell on it. He linked arms with Clare and splashed through dirty puddles with enthusiasm. He was determined not to scan the streets for a redhead in a white rabbit-fur coat, but the habit was so instinctive to him now that it was almost impossible for him to resist. He stopped abruptly outside a narrow little pub with square glass windows running the full width of the exterior. A red-and-white-striped awning hung over the door, making the building look more like a barber's shop than a pub, but its name was painted in cursive scarlet script along a white banner: The Long Hall. Wasn't this the place Winter had spoken about in her letters?

Clare nudged him with her shoulder and asked, 'What is it? Are we lost? I think Temple Bar is just ahead.'

'It's nothing. Just this pub. I remember someone telling me about it once. I was just surprised to see it; you know the way you can never usually find places that people recommend.'

She stood on her toes to peer through a clearing in the condensation on the window.

'It's so tiny . . . but it looks like a nice old-man pub. Maybe we could come back later for a nightcap if the reception doesn't run too late.'

He gripped Clare's elbow and guided her to the pedestrian crossing. 'No, it's not important. We'd better hurry.'

He knew it was ridiculous, but the thought of taking Clare in there seemed somehow disloyal to Winter. Was he losing his mind? Surely the betrayal lay in thinking about another woman in the first place while he was away with his wife. And it wasn't as if Winter expected anything from him – she didn't even know he existed! As they waited for a break in the traffic so they could cross the street, he couldn't resist turning back to take one last look at the Long Hall. He felt sure someone was watching him. His skin prickled but, when he looked back over his shoulder, there was no one there.

The wedding ceremony of Enid and Seamus was held in the Smock Alley Theatre on Exchange Street. Their immediate families sat on long wooden benches in front of the black panelled stage, white ribbons running along each edge. Old milk bottles, painted in different shades of red and purple glowing from candles inside, made impromptu chandeliers that dangled from the wooden rafters over the stage. The remaining guests were crowded into three tiered balconies with cast-iron railings that surrounded the performance space. Garlands of calla lilies and cornflowers stretched along the railings. Night-light candles in china teacups were set into recesses of the stone walls throughout the venue. The acoustics of the room transformed the buzzing chatter of the guests into a melodious hum. Clare gripped William's hand as they found a spot on the second tier.

Instead of Mr Buckley walking his daughter down the aisle, they wove along each balcony, swamped by gushing excitement and thunderous applause as they moved. Enid's father walked one step behind her, guiding her elbow with one hand, dabbing his eyes and shining bald head with a ridiculously large white silk handkerchief with the other. The skirt of Enid's dress was so wide that, on the corners, she had to turn sideways to proceed, laughing all the time at the absurdity of it. Her blue-black hair had come undone from the elaborate style the hairdresser had conjured that morning; it collapsed about her shoulders under the crown of white roses that circled her head. It looked perfect. When Enid saw Clare, she hugged her old friend, kissed her forehead, before she was swept along by the current of well-wishers. In her wake, William put his arms around his wife, and she rested her head on his shoulder. He hated to think of not being there with her today; to imagine her standing alone in her silver taffeta dress, feet side by side in her white velvet Mary-Janes and new coat.

As Enid reached the stage, Seamus stepped forward, handsome in a seaweed-brown tweed suit that suited his dark colouring. He was an island man, with wild, black curls, and piercing blue eyes glistening out from under one bushy eyebrow. His right arm was in a sling from a surfing accident the week before, his cast covered in scribbled good-luck messages. The shaman who would lead them through the ceremony hushed the whooping from the audience. Silence descended as he guided them through each ritual before the couple pledged their vows: the lighting of their individual candles at the beginning and the united flame at the end; the binding of their hands together. As they exchanged rings, Enid's mother stood and sang 'She Moved through the Fair', her hands straight down by her side like a soldier. The white chrysanthemum posy on the lapel of her fuschia blouse glowed in the theatre spotlight.

> I dreamed it last night
> That my true love came in
> So softly she entered
> Her feet made no din
> She came close beside me
> And this she did say:
> 'It will not be long, love,
> Till our wedding day.'

William handed Clare his handkerchief and she dabbed her eyes carefully. He smudged away a gloop of mascara from her temple with his thumb and she gripped it for a second like a newborn. Seamus dipped Enid for a

Hollywood kiss and the wedding party jumped up to cheer in chorus, stamping their feet on the floorboards beneath them. 'Go on, Seamus, lad,' a heckler called from the back and his entourage whooped. As the newly married couple climbed down from the stage to lead their guests through to the reception hall, William and Clare stood in one shadowy corner of the balcony and melted into a long kiss.

Long wooden banquet tables stretched the length of the converted church where dinner was served; sunlight streamed through the stained-glass windows, dispersing prisms of coloured light on the white stone walls. A low river of green moss, pine cones and branches of fir trees ran down the centre of each table, interspersed with tea lights in green glass dishes and clutches of daisies. Each guest's name was handwritten in white ink on a pistachio-coloured envelope that rested in the centre of their moss-green linen table mat.

The hall reminded William a little of the place where he and Clare had been married. Though less beautifully preserved, the town hall in Islington was of a similar vintage. At their reception, the Turkish rugs were threadbare and the brass chandeliers missing the odd bulb, but they had been drawn to the character of the rooms and felt the hall was just the right size for their wedding. Fifty maroon velvet chairs had been placed in two semicircles which faced each other, creating a natural pathway between them. There was no seating plan, but everyone organically found his or her place in the circle. Before the ceremony, Clare had struggled with the idea of walking down the aisle without her father to escort her. When William suggested that they arrive together, she threw her arms around him, covered his face with kisses and said, 'I knew that there was a reason I was marrying you.'

Clare dressed and beautified herself in Flora's flat before the two sisters took a taxi together to the hall, where they found William and Stevie awaiting their arrival. Stevie wore a silver suit with drainpipe trousers that were slightly too short; one hot-pink sock and one black-and-white chequered peeped out above his white Chelsea boots. William wore a plum velvet blazer with deep red lining and black trousers with braces over a starched white shirt. He still wore the blazer now sometimes, on special occasions; he felt it brought him luck. When Clare stepped out of the taxi, William was confused for a moment; she looked so different from what he had expected. No white dress or veil or bouquet of flowers; instead, a sophisticated black chiffon dress that hugged her waist and kicked out to the knee, and a white velvet bolero over her shoulders. Her hair was swept up into a glossy bun, a single red rose behind her ear. She wore little white gloves, a short string of pearls, red glitter shoes and carried a white rose tied in a scarlet silk bow. Clare resembled no bride he had ever seen and looked all the more magnificent for it. They stood in silence for a moment, absorbing what was happening.

'Are you disappointed, William? Would you have preferred a blushing bride in white?' she asked, her voice barely audible over the traffic that rushed past.

William held her by the arms, afraid to pull her too close in case he ruffled her outfit, and leaned towards her until their noses touched.

'Disappointed? You are the most fantastic, most beautiful, most brilliant bride there ever was, and I'm going to march you into that hall right now before you realize how ridiculous it is that you are marrying a silly fool like me and change your mind.'

Stevie and Flora went ahead to put on the music; Flora tucked Stevie's shirt in and made him tie up his wild (then lilac) hair on the way. William and Clare waited outside for the opening notes of Michael Dees singing 'What are You Doing for the Rest of Your Life?' before Stevie opened the door and everyone stood to watch William, adorned in plum, and Clare, elegant in black, walk down the aisle together. When they reached the registrar, everyone drew their chairs together to complete the circle. There was no religious element to the ceremony, no prayers to a God they didn't believe in, no words written for them to repeat by people who had never known them. Instead, they wrote their own vows, simple and honest, but with enough love in them to draw a little tear from even Stevie's cynical eye.

Before the end of the ceremony, the registrar called on the guests to step forward if they had particular good wishes or any wisdom from their own marriage to share with the newly married couple; a few brave souls did. Clare's uncle surprised them both by digging deep into his gruffness to speak. He revealed that her father had told him that he knew Clare would grow up to be an amazing woman and that he hoped she wouldn't let the failings of her parents turn her against the idea of spending her life with the right man, should he come along. Uncle Jimmy said her father would be delighted to see that his wish had come true.

After the ceremony, Clare and William snaked around the semicircles of chairs to accept congratulatory hugs, then they all walked to the Crooked Billet. The function room had been reserved for them, and a buffet of potato and chickpea curry, moussaka and bowls of salad and rice prepared. Fairy lights were strung in garlands around the room and tea lights sat on the windowsills in recycled jam-jars, transforming the dingy space into something a little bit more magical. Stevie's band played, until the landlord threatened to cut the power, and they danced until the final note rang out. William's favourite photo of the day caught him singing with the band while Clare danced beside him. They looked so happy. Just as Enid and Seamus did today. Could they tether the island of their love to the mainland once again before it was lost for ever at sea?

Giving the final speech, Mr Buckley drew to a close on the subject of his daughter, his elaborate handkerchief close to hand. 'My last wish for Enid and my new son-in-law today is this: when you have a choice between winning a row or saving the day, save the day. Remember: cynics may win battles, but romantics win the war. To Enid and Seamus.' The guests all stood, and echoes of 'To Enid and Seamus' rippled about the room as glasses clinked.

Clare lost her balance as she stretched across the table with her champagne flute. She knocked over one of the green tea-light holders and extinguished the flame.

'I think the fizz has made me a little soggy,' she whispered to William.

She poured herself a full glass of water and nudged her empty flute further away to prevent her topping it up again too quickly.

While the bride and groom slipped away for photographs, a space was cleared for dancing. Seamus's family band of traditional Irish musicians needed little encouragement to launch into a rousing sequence of set dances. From nowhere, a semicircle had formed at the front of the room: an accordion, bodhrán, tin whistle and fiddle poised and ready to play.

'Ladies and gentlemen, "The Siege of Ennis".'

Enid's family and friends from England watched in amazement as Seamus's contingent rushed forward and began to form orderly rows in sets of four; they weren't to remain bystanders for long, however. Seamus's mother circled the room, canvassing and cajoling, until everyone was on their feet. William and Clare partnered up with Seamus's Uncle Niall and Aunt Audrey.

'Don't look so frightened,' Audrey laughed, as she swapped places with William. 'You stick with me, and Niall will look after your good wife, there.'

And, with that, they were off, Seamus's father calling commands in Irish from behind his accordion: *Amach! Isteach! Brostaigí! Brostaigí!* William had no idea what he was saying but allowed himself to be swept along by the beat. His and Clare's feet found the rhythm and followed the pattern as they moved in lines up and down the room, swinging around in circles, crossing partners and ducking under arms to meet the next row of four. He caught Clare's eye as a giant of a man spun her so fast in his arms that her feet left the ground; she was doubled up in laughter when she staggered back into position. This music didn't tolerate melancholia; it was just the tonic they needed.

For the last dance of the evening, the DJ played 'Careless Whisper' by George Michael; Clare and William sat together and watched Enid and Seamus slow-dancing in the centre of the floor while their friends linked arms in a circle around them. 'I'm not sure that DJ Cliff Seacrest has really listened to the lyrics,' William joked. 'Maybe that wasn't the best choice of song to end the evening.'

He stopped laughing when he saw Clare's eyes flood.

'William, there's something you should know.' She moved her chair closer to him and picked up his hand in both of hers. She started again: 'I haven't . . .' But she never finished her sentence, because Audrey and Niall interrupted her.

'Come on!' Audrey called. 'They're doing the going-away.'

She pulled Clare to her feet and on to the dance floor, where, two by two, all the guests formed an archway for Enid and Seamus to run through before they left for their honeymoon. As the DJ cranked up the volume for Cliff Richard to serenade them with 'Congratulations', the bride and groom were stopped every few feet by couples dropping their arms to trap them and smother them in final well-wishes. William and Clare locked hands and bobbed along to the music while waiting for the newly-weds to reach them.

'What were you going to say, Clare?' William shouted at her over the din. 'Are you okay?'

He was relieved when she nodded, smiling now once again.

'It was nothing. I was just going to say I haven't felt this happy in such a long time.'

Enid and Seamus drove away in his green Peugeot 205, tin cans and old soccer boots clattering from the exhaust and white balloons filling the back seat. The wedding guests stood waving until they had vanished from sight up the quays. Clare and William strolled alongside the river.

'I don't feel ready to go back to the hotel yet, do you?' Clare asked as she hesitated outside the welcoming glow of the Boulevard Café on Exchequer Street.

William pushed the door open and they found a table in the window, where they watched revellers cavorting through Friday night. Every so often, a flash of red hair would dance past and catch his eye, despite himself, but he tried his best not to react. They ordered two hot whiskies for a nightcap and shared a basket of hot, fresh bruschetta. Sitting as they once had many years before, shy but hopeful, William was optimistic, albeit a little wary of saying too much. The day had been perfect; he didn't want to spoil it now by talking once again about worries that had been too big to squeeze through their front door.

Clare leaned across the table and brushed a curl behind his ear.

'Oh, William, maybe we should just pack it all in and move to the south of France or something. We could open a *boulangerie*, or a *chocolaterie*, and descend slowly into middle age, plump and happy, while we live the good life. No Tube. No clients. No letters!!'

His stomach flipped a little at the thought of a fresh start with this woman; he savoured for a moment how beautiful she looked in her silver dress. What was he doing still scanning the streets for Winter when his incredible wife was right here in front of him?

'We should do it. Let's just go. Anywhere. What's keeping us in London, really? We could just go and start again.'

Clare pulled her hand back into her lap and sighed. 'William, you know it's not as simple as that. We can't just run away and hope all our problems get left behind. They would just come with us and set up camp in Provence, or wherever we were, and we'd feel even worse.'

He reached for her hand once more. 'I know it seems mad, but maybe a fresh start is all we need?'

She took a deep breath and squeezed his knee under the table.

'I hope so, William. I really do.'

'And maybe we could even think again about starting –'

'No!' she snapped. 'Don't even go there. We can't try

to make a baby into some kind of bandage to paper over the cracks in our relationship. We've only just –'

He held his hands up in a gesture of surrender.

'Okay, let's drop it for the moment, but I really want you to think about it. Not just for my sake. If you're really sure you don't ever want to have a child, then that's fine. I know we can have a great life together, regardless, but please be sure you aren't just saying no out of fear, or stubbornness, or lack of faith in me, because we would work it out. I know we would. People in much worse situations than ours manage every day.'

She busied herself pouring them glasses of water from a carafe.

'Okay. I hear you,' she replied. 'But can we please talk about something else? Let's pretend we're just two people on a date. Tell me things about you that I've forgotten I know. Let's not try to fix everything in one evening. Let's just be glad we're here.'

The waiter came and cleared the empty bruschetta basket. When he left, William nudged his glasses further up the bridge of his nose and asked, 'Have you ever read *Ulysses*? I tried to start a book club of the classics in college, but there wasn't much interest.'

Clare laughed.

'I'll never forget your face when I walked in. You looked like you'd been caught red-handed, stealing biscuits or something.'

He shook his head at the memory.

'I was so mortified. The rejection of no one coming

was hard enough to endure on my own, but to have a witness, and such a gorgeous one, well, that hurt!'

All of a sudden, the lights dimmed and the waiting staff meandered their way through the restaurant with a cake and sparklers, singing 'Happy Birthday'.

Clare leaned into William and whispered, 'How embarrassing. I would die if that was for me,' but the performance came closer until she was laughing in shock as they screeched, 'Happy birthdaaay, deear Cllllllaaaaareeee, Happy birthday to you.' She stammered a protest but the head waiter made her stand up on a chair to blow out the candles. The restaurant cheered while she tried to modestly hold her skirt down as she climbed back into her seat.

'You absolute rotter! I can't believe you did that to me! It's not my birthday for five months!'

Clare was beaming, despite her embarrassment. Was this all they had needed all along? A little fun? A little time away from the pressures of playing out the self-inflicted roles of their marriage?

As they strolled back to their hotel, they were happy, arms entwined, feet in step, and after they turned out the light later that night, Clare fell asleep on her spot on William's shoulder and, for what felt like the first time in a very long time, she felt like she belonged there.

17.

The telephone ringing on the night stand seemed part of Clare's dream at first. Who could be calling at this time? She shoved William to wake him, and nestled further into her pillow. He groaned at her, but groggily picked up the receiver. The night receptionist told him how sorry they were to disturb them but there was an urgent call from London. William shook Clare awake. They had left the hotel number on their answering machine in case the hospice called about Clare's mother. It had to be them. 'Clare, wake up! I think it's about your mum.'

She sat up in bed, confused by the hour and the worry in his voice.

'What is it? What's going on?'

'I think it's the hospice. The receptionist is putting them through.'

Clare turned on the overhead light and pulled a blanket around her. William watched her as he held the receiver to his ear, impatient to know what was happening but afraid of what was coming. Why would something bad have to happen now? A man's voice slurred down the phone. He was shouting over the din of a noisy pub.

'Clare, is that you? It's me. Clare?'

'No, it most certainly is not. This is William. Her

husband. Who is this? What is this about? Why are you calling at this time of night?'

'Oh, it's you, is it? The cuckold! Well, you should know, *William*, that she doesn't want you any more. Not really. Why don't you just let her go? She's too good for you. I could give her the life she deserves. You're wasting her –'

William threw the receiver down on to the bedspread. 'It's for you,' he said, and walked into the bathroom, where he sat on the edge of the bathtub in the dark.

'What's going on?' Clare called after William as she scrambled across the blankets to reach the receiver.

Through the bathroom door, William heard Clare whispering under her breath before slamming down the telephone. He waited for her to rush to him, but the moment stretched on. That was when he knew she had been lying to him. He walked back into the bedroom and plucked his shirt off the floor. Struggling to button it with his fumbling fingers, he realized he had put it on inside out. Clare stumbled towards him, her feet tangled in the discarded sheets, and tried to stop him pulling on his trousers next.

'William, stop. Let me explain. It's not what you think.'

He staggered away from her, the red of his face deepening.

'How long have you been sleeping with him?'

'William, it's not like that . . .'

He raised his voice.

'If you don't tell me the truth right now, I will walk out of here, and I swear you will never see me again.'

He watched the tears start to stream down her face, but the sight of them repelled him now. How could he have been such a fool? His instinct had told him there was more to what happened with Maxi, but he just hadn't wanted to believe it.

'It was just the one time, I swear. He came down to collect me from Wales —'

'*From Wales?* He was with you that whole time? For —'

'*No!* He just offered me a lift home, and then we ended up having too much to drink and stayed an extra . . . It wasn't planned, William, I promise. I'm so sorry. Please . . . it just happened —'

'Is that the best you can do? Just stop it. You made a choice. I never thought you could become such a walking cliché. The fancy lawyer with the big car and the house in the country he bought with his trust fund. You just couldn't resist it, could you? You've been trying to crawl up that social ladder your whole life, and when he handed it to you on a plate you just couldn't say no. So much for us.'

The colour drained from her face; she sobbed, making big, gulping noises. William stormed around the room, picking things up and throwing them back down.

'You're like a total stranger to me. And the *lies* you've told. You must think I'm such a fool . . . A right cuckold, as your *boyfriend* himself said. You bare-faced lied to me and lived with it day after day.'

Clare sat down on the edge of the bed with her head in her hands.

'Maxi shouldn't have said that,' she whispered.

'*Don't say his name!*' William slammed his fist into the

pillow, which was still warm from where he had been sleeping moments before. She stood up, tried to put her arms around him, but he pushed her away with such force that she splayed across the bed. He stopped himself from reaching out to her.

'I wanted to tell you!' she cried. 'I did! But I didn't know if we could survive it, and I thought it was better just to try and put it behind us, because it was just that one time.'

He stood over her, his voice cold now.

'Why would I believe anything you say? You could just be confessing this much for now, until I find out the next grizzly detail. And anyway, Clare, *once is enough!* You've never had a one-night stand or slept with anyone you didn't care about.'

She knelt on the bed and tried to pull him towards her.

'William, please. Tonight still happened – the things we said we meant. Please don't give up on us now!'

'I'm not the one who gave up on us, Clare. If you knew how hard I've tried not to get pulled out of our marriage . . .'

He stopped himself before he said too much.

'What is that supposed to mean? William?'

'Nothing, it doesn't mean anything. I'm going home and, lest there be any doubt in your mind, *you* are not. Hopefully, *Maxi* will let you stay with him. I'm sure he'll be only too delighted.'

'No, William. Please don't go!'

Her shoulders heaved as she watched him, gulping in deep breaths of air.

William struggled into his socks and shoes, distractedly checked his blazer for his passport, clutched his satchel by its handle and walked out, leaving the rest of his belongings behind. Clare followed him into the hallway and shouted after him. The hotel porter delivering champagne next door looked away, embarrassed at seeing her in her nightdress, her distress.

William didn't turn around but called over his shoulder, 'Don't you dare follow me!'

Despite his fury, it was gut-wrenching to listen to her crying as he walked away. He kept staring straight ahead so she would not see the tears that were rolling down his face, too.

18

After William left, Clare curled up in a ball on the floor of the hotel bedroom. She couldn't crawl back into the bed where they had lain together. Her mind flitted from rage at Maxi to anger at herself. Now that she was faced with the bleak consequences of what she had done, the thought of Maxi repulsed her. How could she have been so cavalier about her marriage? Had she felt so secure in William's devotion to her that she thought it would be possible to play out her experiment without any retribution? The last thing she had wanted to do was hurt William – what had possessed her? What upset her most was the realization that, inebriated as she was when she invited Maxi to her room, she could even then feel regret prickling along her spine, but she had forced her own hand. She was compelled to follow through and see what another life, another Clare, might feel like. Fraudulent. Now, she knew.

The claustrophobic hotel room overwhelmed her; she couldn't wait there until morning, driving herself more and more insane with thoughts of where William might be, cursing her mistakes. How could she have done this to him? Deep down, she knew that if their marriage dissolved now, it wouldn't be only because of what she had done, but she couldn't tolerate the idea of this being how things ended between them. She couldn't – wouldn't – bear the burden of that on her shoulders alone. Not when they had been so close to finding each other again. It was a shock to realize how much she wanted to save their marriage when faced with the reality of losing William for ever. For months, she had lived with one foot already out of their front door, and now she wanted to barricade herself inside. She tried to quieten the conflicting voices in her head. Was it just fear of the unknown that trapped her? Or did she really want to make her marriage work? Everything had become so confused.

Clare departed for the airport to wait for the first early-morning flight back to London. Maybe William was doing the same thing and she would see him there. Packing their suitcases, her heart was in ribbons as she folded his trousers and shirt, balled his stripy socks and laid them in his suitcase. She pulled on his discarded T-shirt and breathed in the still-living scent of him before slipping into the night, pulling both their cases, enveloped in her big blue jumper with the crooked white stars.

In the taxi on the way to the airport, the driver tried to coax her story from her. Where was she off to? What had brought her to Dublin? She tried to shut down his questioning with murmurs about 'some bad news from London' and 'being called home unexpectedly', and stared out of the window to avoid his eyes in the rear-view mirror. The streets were filled with people spilling out of pubs on Wexford Street into the pouring rain.

The drops cascading down her window blurred the lights and smeared the colours across the pane. She had stopped crying. For now. Watching the tears of the city sky streaking down the glass, it felt as if the heavens were crying for them, but she didn't feel she deserved their sympathy.

In the deepest, quietest part of herself, she knew that William was right. A part of her must have wanted this to happen, willed for something irretrievable and powerful to force them to stop the procrastination, desperate for redemption, rejuvenation, salvation. Her mind scattered thoughts like ashes in the breeze. How could she ever expect him to respect her again? To trust her again? How would she ever be able to respect herself? She rustled in her handbag for a compact, smoothed some concealer on the dark circles under her eyes and traced a ribbon of red across her lips. Little threads to keep herself sewn together for what lay ahead.

At the airport, she scanned the departures area for William, walking through Duty-free in a robotic state. What would she say if she found him? Would he cause a scene? Blank her? Was there any chance he would take her in his arms? Instinct told her no. It was going to be a long walk back from here to the couple kissing in the shadows of a wedding that day. If they could ever find their way. She hoped that her legs had the strength to carry her.

19.

William waited at the airport on a hard grey plastic chair, a brown paper bag containing an uneaten toasted cheese sandwich by his feet, a cardboard cup with the cold dregs of instant coffee balanced between his legs. The interval to board his flight felt interminable; he was too mentally electrified by the night's events to sleep and yet he felt physically demobilized by them. No flights were arriving or departing at this time; his only companions were other displaced travellers lost in transit. When he saw Clare on the escalator, struggling to negotiate it with their two suitcases, his heart leaped to call her name but his head silenced him. He crouched down lower in his seat, hiding behind the pillar that shielded him from her vision as he watched her scanning the departures lounge – for sight of him, he presumed. Seeing her like this, he felt as if he were witnessing his own heart walk around the airport in another body. The further away she walked, the smaller and emptier he felt. He did not trust himself to see her now; he was weakened by the weight of his damaged love, crushed by her crime.

Before a plan had fully formed, William was on his feet and darting for the exit, his ticket discarded with the remnants of his unwanted breakfast. As he burst through the revolving doors to escape the airport, the sun was just beginning to rise; light diluted the dark sky, turning it a moody blue. He was the only person waiting for the bus to the city centre; he was happy to climb aboard as the sole passenger and take a quiet, leisurely route into town while he collected his thoughts. He sat on the upper deck in the front seat and watched the city roll out before him through the wide pane of glass as the morning brightened. When he was little, he liked to sit in this seat with his dad and pretend he was driving the bus through the streets of Cambridge. It was a shadowy day when his father told him he wasn't sure his knees could take the stairs. They had to sit on the ground floor, across from a grumpy old lady wearing a pink plastic visor and steadying a tartan shopping bag on wheels. He didn't want his dad to be one of those old people who chatted about the weather and the graffiti in the town square. And he didn't want another little boy taking his place in the best seat in the house.

It struck him for the second time in as many days that the drive into Dublin offered a grim first impression of the city. He wondered if tourists were shocked by the towers of council flats, the suburban housing estates and the miles of concrete all around. Where were the lush green pastures of the Emerald Isle they had been promised? No doubt the picture-postcard island would reveal itself in due course; he would love to explore it properly one day. Maybe take a train into the west? How he wished that was what he was doing now, instead of unravelling his whole life into a pile of tangled wool.

He wanted to explore Winter's Ireland; if he was honest, he wanted her to show it to him.

He jumped off the bus at O'Connell Street and walked across the bridge over the River Liffey. The light on the water made it glisten in silver and he recognized why Dublin was considered so magical; you could feel the fairy tale spinning from the old stone of Trinity College, dancing up Grafton Street and scampering down the side alleys. It was painful to absorb the beauty of it all while he was feeling so broken. Especially given how happy he had been to walk these streets with Clare the day before. He walked with his head down, listening to Morrissey sing harmonious songs about disharmonious minds on his Walkman; it soothed him like a lullaby. Why do we take such perverse pleasure from sad songs? Do they make us feel less alone?

He didn't stay in the same Dublin hotel as he had with Clare. There was no need this time for room service, jacuzzis or opulent surroundings; instead, he found a cheap room in a backpackers' hostel on the quays. As he waited for the receptionist to register his details, a wave of nausea washed over him.

'Sir, are you okay? You look very pale. Can I get you anything?' The touch of the girl's hand on his arm made him jump.

'What? Oh, yes, no, I'm fine. Just a bit dizzy. Maybe some water. Thank you.'

He fished the ice cubes from the plastic tumbler she handed him and allowed one to melt on his tongue, flinching when the cold exposed a sensitive tooth. Grinding the ice with his back teeth, cold rivulets of water escaped down his throat, a delicate relief. When he saw the reality of his accommodation, he regretted his pragmatism; the room smelled of onions and a plastic sheet lay under the thin grey one on his bed. What past indiscretions had prompted that act of protection from the management? He looked out of the window at a yard full of rubbish bins and bits of old machinery. An ebony coat stand stood forlornly in the midst of it all. How could such prime real estate in the city centre have become so neglected? He pulled the margarine-coloured curtains closed and lay gingerly on the crinkling mattress; he would just rest his eyes for a moment.

When he awoke in the hostel later that morning, the glorious sunshine bursting through the thin curtain fabric disoriented him. Where had yesterday's downpour gone? He washed as best he could in the cracked porcelain sink in the corner of the room, draped his blazer over his arm and walked to the grocery shop next door to buy some essentials. Despite his foul mood, he welcomed the unexpected warmth on his face as he breathed in the air; it smelled so much cleaner than London's. An instant remedy. He purchased a double espresso from a coffee trike called Java the Hut, sat on a marble stone bench beneath a lime tree and watched the light skip across the glittering surface of the Liffey as the city symphony tuned up for another day. A brown plaque rested on the bark of a nearby tree. It read, '60,000 street and roadside trees inhabit Dublin city centre, with an average of 5,000 new trees planted every year.' He wondered who had been given the task of counting them; pictured a man walking the streets with a spiral-bound jotter, losing track and starting again at the beginning.

The shock of the previous night was waning a little, the reality of why he was still in Dublin dawning. Clare's confession sat like a ball of iron in his stomach, but he forced the image it conjured from his mind. He hadn't allowed himself to try to find Winter before but, now, well, things were different. In his bones, he knew that some prescient instinct told him that coming to her city would be revelatory. Wasn't that why he had felt compelled to tuck her Polaroid picture beneath the cover of the moleskin-covered notebook he always carried? From his breast pocket, he removed this now and stared at it; how the shimmering morning light infused it with energy!

Compared to London, Dublin was a village. He even knew the name of Winter's favourite pub; surely if he asked some questions at some of her old haunts, it would help narrow down the search? He wondered how long it was since she had moved; it sounded quite recent in her letters. And if her name really was Winter, the chances seemed high that someone would remember her. Perhaps it was madness to chase a ghost through this city, but what was the alternative? Go home to pace the flat all weekend, worrying himself into a knot, arguing with Clare? William's thoughts bounced back and forth in agonizing indecision, until a stubborn peace settled upon him. He could not endure another day of dithering and withering under Ned's relentless scrutiny. It gave him a momentary relief to think he could refine his approach; Dublin seemed a much less overwhelming haystack to find a needle in. Everything was becoming more real, and that was a good thing. He couldn't play this out in his mind much longer; he needed some answers. And Clare no longer stood in his way. Winter's letters had struck a nerve; he couldn't allow life to just happen to him any more. Wasn't that what Clare had been trying to tell him for years? Maybe the impetus to get him here was involuntary, but now that he had finally taken some action, he had to follow through.

First things first: he needed to buy himself some time. He marched down the boardwalk, eyes peeled for a telephone box, until one presented itself, just before the Ha'penny Bridge. He folded himself inside it; the smell of the rotting fish and chips on the floor took his breath away. As he lined up neat piles of ten-, twenty- and fifty-pence pieces on the metal shelf covered in sticker advertisements, he propped the door open a crack with his foot to let some air circulate. He dialled his own telephone number, wobbled to hear Clare's voice on the machine; he remembered how many times she had recorded the message before settling on this one. 'That's not what my voice sounds like, is it?' she'd despaired. She deleted it and started again, while he threw cushions at her to make her laugh each time. As he listened, he heard his own faint laugh in the background. To his ears, his voice sounded weak and watery as he spoke but, this time, there was no opportunity to re-do it.

'Clare, I don't quite know if you deserve this message but, in case you call the police or some such, I wanted to let you know I'm staying in Dublin for a few days. Please don't be there when I do come home. I'll find you when I'm ready.'

He hung up the receiver and strengthened his resolve for call number two.

'Dead Letters Depot, Miss Clarke speaking.'

William recognized her telephone voice and a strange nostalgia touched him.

'Marjorie, it's William. I need your help, but why are you in on a Saturday? I was just going to leave a message for you.' He paused, dreading the outpouring of scorn and derision to follow but, in its place, her voice softened into a conspiratorial whisper.

'Oh, sometimes I like to come in to water the plants, do a few bits. The weekends are long. What can I do? Shoot!'

He pictured her sitting alone there, paused to consider it, but garbled on, 'I don't have much time to explain, but I'm stuck in Dublin and won't be back for a few days. Can you cover for me if I'm not in on Monday? Maybe you can say –'

'Don't worry. I'll think of something. Leave it to me. Everyone will be in a tizz because twenty-five life-sized mannequins arrived yesterday evening and they've taken over the place!'

The beeps warned him that time was running out, and he fed his last two coins into the slot.

'Thank you, Marjorie. I mean it. I know I haven't been my best recently.'

'Don't you worry, ducky. Just get home safe to us, okay? And William?'

'Yes?'

'Anything you need, I'll be here.'

The line disconnected. William emerged back on to the street with the dawning realization of how much Marjorie must care about him. Why had he always been so hard on her? Relieved to have completed his tasks, he continued across the Ha'penny Bridge to begin his mission in earnest. Now that he was on his way, the enormity of his actions enveloped him, and the lack of a concrete plan. He walked in long strides, avoiding cracks in the pavement. Supposing he did find someone who knew Winter – how could he explain why he was looking for her? What if they told her a strange Englishman was hanging around town asking questions about her, someone she had never even met but who knew so much about her? She would probably call the police, he would definitely lose his job, and any chance of ever resolving things with Clare would be completely gone. If that was even what he wanted any more. He compelled himself to remember that this was the woman who had cheated on him. Anything else would be a lie. He thought about her earlier confession: the slip of the kiss. In his gut, he had known that there was more to it than she had told him. If he had been prepared then to accept the implicit knowledge of betrayal and reach out a conciliatory hand all the same, what had really changed now that it had been made explicit? Should he have sat down wearily on the side of their hotel bed and tried to reach an understanding? Could he have just redrawn the line under the whole affair in a heavier, more permanent ink and allowed their weekend of rediscovery to continue? Would she love him more or less for his forgiveness? He closed the door on this line of thought. Nothing could ever be the same now, because the truth could never be unknown. He could never unlearn that she had lied to him and that she had chosen to continue to do so when the opportunity to tell the truth had finally presented itself. It was her ability to live inside that fraud that really sickened him. And that was before he even let himself think of what she had physically done. He could never have stayed in that hotel room and lived with himself.

He turned right along the river until a stone arch enticed him into Temple Bar, where the cobbled streets had become thronged with shoppers and tourists enjoying the unexpected sunshine. He paused outside the Rock Garden and read the billings for that night to see if anyone he had heard of was playing, but he didn't recognize any of the names. Who knows, if he and Stevie had stuck at it, maybe the Bleeding Hearts might have played here themselves. He strolled down Crown Alley, where all the rock-and-roll kids hung around in awkward little groups in self-conscious poses. A lady sporting a vintage tuxedo, her hair gelled into a bleached-blonde quiff, was dragging a clothes rail heavy with retro band T-shirts and denim jackets down two steps to rest in front of the purple-and-white-striped walls of her store. William helped her position it, and she winked at him.

'Thanks, chicken,' she said.

He followed her back inside as he wriggled Winter's Polaroid picture from his pocket.

'Excuse me!' he called after her. 'You don't happen to know where I might find a pair of boots like these?' He ignored how foolish he felt as she absorbed the image then quickly looked him up and down.

'My wife,' he offered. 'She bought a pair somewhere around here a few years ago but lost them. I wanted to try and replace them for her. Her favourite pair, you see.'

She pulled out a pair of round gold-rimmed spectacles from under the counter and studied the picture more closely.

'Hhhmmmm, I can't say I've ever seen boots like them before,' she said, with a drawl. 'You're not in Nashville, ya know. I wouldn't fancy your chances.'

A teenage boy, resplendent in yellow denim flares, black polyester shirt and orange platform boots staggered through from the back room, the top of his Afro just visible above the huge cardboard box he was hugging.

'Alex! Just the man!' she exclaimed. 'Here, take a look at these. Ring any bells?'

He dropped the box with a slap on the concrete floor and leaned over to peer at the picture.

'What am I looking for?' he asked. 'Who's this guy?'

He nodded towards William, who jumped in to answer.

'I'm trying to find a shop that sells them, or used to, anyway. Any suggestions?'

The young man drummed his fingers on the counter-top, chewing on the question for a moment. A look of hard concentration on his face gave William hope, but it quickly vanished.

'Nope, sorry,' he said with a shrug. 'I'm going to get a breakfast roll, okay?' he asked the tuxedoed lady, as he headed for the door.

In every shop along the alley where William enquired, he received the same incredulous looks, hopeless shrugs, offers of alternatives. He was sitting on the steps of Central Bank, contemplating his next move, when the yellow-flared teenager from that morning strutted past, paused and turned on his heel to call back to him.

'Yo! Boots guy!' he hollered. 'I just thought of somewhere! There is *one* place you could try . . . on Dame Lane. They do more costumes, but I *think* they used to do cowgirl stuff.' He held up his hands in question. 'Worth a shot?'

'Yes, yes, definitely,' William answered. 'Thanks so much!' but the boy had already resumed his parade down the city catwalk, leaving William to watch him walk away.

Dame Lane – hadn't Winter mentioned that street in one of her letters? With revived purpose, William paused at the pedestrian crossing, looked at his street map to find the way to Dame Lane and discovered it was a little alleyway running parallel to where he stood. He picked up the pace as he travelled along its curling pavement, looking through the windows of a taxidermist's, at the closed blinds of a beauty parlour and the lonely white walls of a gallery empty of art. He was relieved to find the lane so short and the shops so few as to eliminate any chance of him mistaking the place.

A bubblegum-pink clapperboard hung on the black railings of a stairway leading down to a basement unit. Curly white lettering spelled out the name Gúna of Una, above drawings of ladies' hats with legs sticking out beneath them that appeared to be doing the can-can. He climbed down the stairs, pausing to look into the window, past the jailhouse bars to the lair within. The interior looked as if it had been dropped into Dublin from a Hollywood movie set. Mirrors framed by strings of white lights stretched along one of the whitewashed stone walls. Black-and-white portraits of fifties starlets adorned the rear, looking down on a turquoise chaise longue scattered with voluminous velvet cushions in myriad shades of blue. Red and black feather boas dangled from the ends of white wooden clothes rails, kissing the plush peach carpet underneath. Instead of changing rooms, a hot-pink velvet curtain was draped across one corner on an ornate silver rail. A woman's head and shoulders were visible over the top as she wriggled into something metallic-looking; her feet peeped from the bottom, where her trousers gathered around her ankles.

When William pushed through the glossy black door, little bells tinkled and the aroma of vanilla essence was overpowering. It was obvious this shop was not a domain designed for the comfort of men. Enthroned in a purple velvet armchair behind a black marble counter, a woman looked out at him from under a ruby-encrusted pill-box hat that sat neatly on rolls of shiny ebony hair. Her face was powdered chalk-white with eyebrows drawn on in black, sweeping false eyelashes, two circles of blush on each cheek and a perfect pout of sticky redness. She appeared to be wearing a short wedding dress. When she spoke, her voice was a raspy whisper, as if it had become tired from too much singing in smoky jazz clubs.

'Well, now, are you lost or on a mission?'

She beckoned him towards her with a frosted-pink talon, and William stumbled down the last step into the shop, steadying himself against a glittering ladder of stilettos that wobbled perilously.

'Um, I'm not quite sure what you mean.'

'I *mean*, have you stumbled in here by accident? Or have you sought out a secret wonderland where a man of certain persuasions can find another identity?'

'Oh, gosh, no, well, I did come looking for you, but not for my own benefit, per se. You see, I have a friend who I think likes to shop here, or liked to, anyway.'

'Marvellous. She has excellent taste, and you would like to buy her a present! Come with me.'

She stood up and rested a hand on her hip as she sashayed into the middle of the room. She pointed at a red-and-white polka-dot footstool before ducking behind the pink velvet curtain herself.

'Wait here, I shan't be a moment,' she cooed over the top.

William hesitated before lowering himself on to the little seat, which brought his knees in line with his chin.

His eyes wandered around the twinkling room, lingering over the cacophony of fabrics and colours. He tried to imagine Winter here, trying on exotic dresses and assessing her appearance in front of the mirrors, but couldn't really picture her, just the shimmering daydream his mind's eye conjured up. He certainly couldn't imagine Clare here; there wasn't a pair of black trousers or a two-piece suit in sight. He reprimanded himself for the unfair comparison: Clare hadn't always been that way. Slowly, over the years, the flowery dresses and stripy jumpers had been muscled out by the uniform of work which eventually became the norm. He had to admit, though, it was exciting to think of the sort of woman who would shop here; it raised his expectations further of how glamorous Winter might be. He just couldn't shake the image of scarlet hair tumbling down the back of her white rabbit-fur coat.

He tried to ignore the muted conversation of the ladies behind the dressing screen, but they weren't being very discreet.

'I'm just not sure it's very flattering. I don't know if I want to draw that much attention to my backside.'

'Sweetie, it's not the dress's fault. That's just your shape. Embrace it. Shake it. Love it.'

He heard a firm slap, followed by a little squeal of laughter, before the owner of the bottom appeared in front of him.

'What do *you* think? Do you like it?'

He surveyed the woman wriggling in front of him and tried to work out which 'it' in particular he was supposed to be remarking on. Her baby-blue hair was teased into a beehive rising a foot above her pixie-like face. Little blue silk butterflies were scattered throughout, as if they had become trapped there and set up home. A pink fish dangled from a hook in each ear and dozens of strings of multicoloured glass beads encircled her throat. The dress itself appeared to be made of tinfoil on the top half, with chains of metal hoops resting on silver paper at the bottom.

'Well? Do you like it? If you saw me in a bar, would you want to talk to me? Do you think I look ravishing? I won't settle for anything less than ravishing. You hesitated. It's awful. I knew it. Una, get me out of this contraption.'

Una started adjusting the dress on her shoulders.

'Nonsense, he's just shy. Look at him, he's spellbound. Aren't you?'

'Oh, yes, quite. I don't think I've ever seen anything quite like it before.'

'But, do you *like* it?'

'I'm really not a very good judge of these things. I don't really know anything about fashion or . . .'

His words were left suspended as she flounced back behind the screen. She wrestled out of the dress and tossed it over the top of the curtain.

'I knew it. Una, it just won't work. Let's try again next week.'

Una scooped up the fallen outfit and smoothed out the panels as she nonchalantly reclaimed her seat behind the desk. William shuffled over in front of her again.

'You just lost me a big piece of business, mister. I hope you're planning on splurging, big time.'

'I'm terribly sorry, I'm just not really the right person for this sort of thing. And the truth is, I'm not actually here to shop.'

She picked up a hand mirror, turned away from him and fiddled with the net at the front of her hat.

'Well, we're not a spectator sport. So, if you'll excuse me . . .'

The pixie lady bustled past him. The jingle of the bells was violent as she slammed the door behind her.

'Please, I just wanted to ask you about my friend.'

'Sale first. Conversation later.'

'But that's exploitation. Surely, you can't charge me for asking a few questions. I just want to see if you can help me –'

'I think I'll take an early lunch, so, if you'll excuse me.'

Una reached under her desk for a gold-plated handbag with tassels around the edge and removed from it a single avocado.

'Okay, okay, I have . . . let me see' – he rustled in his blazer pockets – 'twelve pounds and seventeen pence. What can I buy for that?'

She sighed, spun back to the counter and opened a deep drawer underneath.

'Some fishnet tights. What size would you like, sir?'

William ran his fingers through his hair with frustration.

'This is ridiculous; I don't care what size. They'll be going in the bin as soon as I leave.'

'Oh, darling, there's no need to be so hostile. We just want to make sure all our customers have a wonderful experience here.'

She smiled at him as she wrapped them, first in pink tissue paper, and then white, before tying the package with black silk ribbon. William was convinced she moved as slowly as possible to aggravate him and waited impatiently for her to finish before shoving the beautiful parcel into the front pocket of his satchel. She pushed her chair back and crossed her legs, revealing some elegant stockings of her own.

'So, tell me about this *friend* of yours.'

'Well, it's a little complicated. I'm not entirely sure of her name but I believe she may be called Winter.'

'You *believe*? I thought you said she was a friend. A lot of ladies love this shop; I don't recall ever meeting anyone called Winter.'

'She's more of an acquaintance, of sorts, and, you see, I'm trying to find her, but I only have a few clues, like, for example, I happen to know that she loves this shop. And I think she might have bought these boots here.'

He held the Polaroid out to her; she glanced at it without taking it from him.

'Yes, I remember those boots; they were for a child, actually. Sat here for ages before someone with small enough feet came in and wanted to buy them.'

'Gosh, do you remember who you sold them to? Do you keep records of your sales?'

'Oh, darling, I wasn't even here that day. Maybe the

old owner, Gloria, might know her, but she lives in Canada now. I bought the shop when she left.'

William stood in silence.

'I'm sorry I couldn't be of more help, but at least you've got some lovely stockings,' she offered.

He turned to leave, but he had one more question, 'Why is the shop called Guns of Una? It seems a strange name.'

She laughed and shook a handkerchief at him. 'Not "guns", you silly man,' she cooed. 'Gúna – *gooooona* – it's the Irish for dress. Gúna of Una, and that's me – I'm Una.'

Humiliation complete, William climbed the steps back out on to the streets of Dublin with the tinkle of bells and laughter in his wake. It was so frustrating to have such a strong lead go cold, but the palaver had not been entirely in vain. He left with a stronger sense of Winter than before; the sketch in his mind was filled in with a little more colour. The more he knew, the more enticing Winter became.

20.

Clare arrived back in London after an interminable spell at the airport waiting for the first flight to take her home. When she eventually arrived back at their flat, she was disappointed to find the hallway dark and silent when she pushed the door open. William must have waited to catch their original flight home, after all, she thought. It was crushing to see the evidence of their departure littered around the flat; was this the last remains of their final happy time together? Two unwashed teacups upside down in the sink; the shoe polish left open on the mat from William's last-minute shining; the curlers she had removed scattered across her dressing table. She swiped them on to the floor in an angry blow. How had she allowed this to happen? Just when she had started to believe in their future again, everything had imploded. She couldn't face unpacking their luggage, seeing their clothes from the wedding crinkled and used before going to bed alone. Instead, she went back downstairs to wait for him.

Clare's hands shook as she spooned coffee granules from the canister on the windowsill and dropped them in a waiting mug. The boiling water splashed over the sides as she tried in vain to steady her hand. The more she willed herself to act normally, the more her body failed her. She placed the mug on the table, took the milk from the fridge. As she poured, a sour stench struck her. She cursed in frustration and threw the carton into the sink, watched the thick, curdled mess clog the drain for a moment before breaking apart under the force of the water from the tap she ran. She sat at the kitchen table. I'll just rest my eyes for a second, she thought, before a heavy sleep seized her, her head lying on her forearms on the table. In her dream, the telephone rang, in the distance at first, then louder, as her consciousness rose. As her eyes blinked awake, she heard William's voice, shot up straight and called his name. She ran into the hallway, the living room, listened for movement upstairs. 'William?' she called, into a vacuum. Had she dreamed it? As she walked back towards the kitchen, rolling the stiffness from her shoulders, the flashing red beacon of the answering machine caught her eye. She pressed play and William's voice filled the hallway once more.

He sounded a million miles away: sad, lost and lonely. She rewound the tape and played it through again. And again. And again. When she could bear it no longer, she lay on the living-room sofa, listening to Morrissey on the record player. It made William feel closer. Eventually, she felt ready to formulate something of a plan. From the basket of white paper that lay beside his typewriter, she pulled a sheet and wrote him a note.

William, my love,
    You don't know how much I wanted to be here when you came home; how hard it is for me to resist trying to

make you forgive me with pure strength of will. But I know that you deserve some time alone to process what's happened, much as it terrifies me to think of what conclusions you may reach.

What I did was indefensible but, I hope that, in time, you will see that, although it was awful, it may have been understandable; something so ugly and profound it would force me to confront how I feel, about us, but also about what my life has become. I was desperate, and behaved desperately.

For what it's worth, I want you to know that there is nothing between me and that man and, even if we don't survive this, there will never be anything between us again. I promise you. I think we both need some time to take stock of what's happened, but I want you to know I think we can move past this, if we both really want to.

Please don't close a door that we can't ever return through. Maybe things can never be the same again, but couldn't that be a good thing?

I am going to stay with Flora – please come and find me when you're ready.

All my love,

Your Clare

She folded the letter and left it on William's pillow, tidied away the curlers she had swept to the floor and filled a backpack with some things she might need. Before she left the house, she paused at the front door and thought for a moment before running back upstairs to their bedroom. From under their bed, she dragged out her old portfolio and knelt before it. The dust it unsettled made her cough as she brushed it clean with a discarded nightdress that lay at the foot of the bed. Without really understanding why, she tucked it under her arm to take with her. As she propped it against the back seat of her Mini, she felt better for having it there. A little piece of her from before she lost her way.

21

While Clare was writing William her note, William was pounding back up Dame Lane as an onslaught of spitting rain attacked his hunched shoulders. Droplets on his glasses blurred his vision, but he was too frustrated to unclench a fist from either pocket to wipe them. Instead, he kept his head down, too stubborn to pull his hood up, and continued marching blindly, until he almost walked into a lamp post. Resting his forehead against the damp blackness of the iron, he emitted a low whine. A hand on his left shoulder blade made him start, and the force of his reaction startled the owner of the hand in turn. A young woman with a nest of messy fair hair escaping from a pea-green beret looked at him with conflicting expressions of curiosity, suspicion and concern. They began apologizing at the same time. Her accent carried the sing-song cadence of somewhere beyond the city, each sentence ending in a high note, leaving him confused as to which sentences were questions and which were statements.

'I'm sorry – I thought maybe you'd had an accident, or hurt yourself? I can't help myself. I'm a nurse, you see, and whenever I think someone might be in trouble, I have to ask, or else I'd be thinking about it all evening and worrying I'd read about them on the news. Everyone would say how the world had become such a terrible place that no one would stop and ask a fella if he was okay, too busy minding their own business . . . it would put me off my supper . . . Anyways, I'm just blathering on now, and I can see you're okay, and we're both getting soaked to the skin. You are okay . . . aren't you?'

William waited a beat beyond what was comfortable before he began to speak. He had just about followed what she was saying but, now that it was his turn to speak, her jumble of words seemed to have rendered him incapable of making any sense himself.

'Yes, I just needed a minute. Sorry, it must have looked a bit odd.'

'Well, it's a funny spot to stop with the heavens opening above us. As long as you're okay?' She tightened the belt on her navy-blue raincoat and tucked a few soaked tendrils of hair back under her beret as she skipped backwards into the flow of pedestrians.

'You should get yourself home, have a bath. Steam the damp out of you.'

Her face broke into a lopsided grin that changed her appearance completely. Her expression became illuminated like a starlet in a silent movie with no words to tell the world what was on her mind. He waved to her as she turned away, little rivulets of water trickling down the sleeve of his coat, before darting through the traffic that had stopped at the lights. He ducked under the archway of a market arcade and shook himself like a shaggy dog. A chuckle escaped him as he remembered his glee at the sunshine state he'd awoken to that morning. Was this his punishment for tempting fate? He let his eyes wander to the source of the clatter behind him. Market traders packing away their wares from stalls that ran in two lines down the centre of the archway. Little shops on either side were growing dark as shutters were drawn, signs switched off, lights quenched and doors locked. He strolled through the detritus of the Saturday sales: war memorabilia, trophies won at long-forgotten sports days, football matches or tennis tournaments, rails of vintage dresses, floppy hats and moth-eaten fur coats, tiers of twinkling fairy lights, costume jewellery, and candles being snuffed one by one.

Should he bring something home to Marjorie? To thank her for looking out for him? Perhaps also to make up for stealing back his Winter letter and allowing her to think she lost it. He idled at a stall with racks of vinyl records and battered hardback books naked without their dust jackets and chose a slim volume for her: *The Love Letters of War.* Her valentine-soaked heart would revel in it. Some of the traders smiled at him hopefully as he continued on and trailed past their displays, a last-minute sale before home time would finish the morning off nicely, but he didn't linger at any one spot for long. He could tell some people were tired and just wanted to pack up as quickly as possible, resigned to the fact that it would all have to be unpacked again the next day. An impatient teenager stuffed colourful woollen tights and patterned knee socks into black plastic bags with no care for the meticulous manner in which they had been hung and displayed that morning. A lady dressed in baker's whites carefully flattened cream cardboard boxes. A young man, worse for wear in a dirty shell tracksuit and unlaced trainers, watched her out of the corner of his eye as he leaned against a closed shop front. William hesitated and pretended to browse through an album of old stamps as he surveyed the scene. What would he do if the watcher grabbed the woman's cashbox of takings? At least he might be able to startle him before it went that far, if he timed it correctly. In what looked like a painful manoeuvre, she dragged a stuffed plastic crate from under the rose-patterned tablecloth. The young man made a start towards her and William rushed forward, too, just in time to hear him gargle at her, 'Let me do that for you, Mrs Gallagher, you don't want to be puttin' your back out again.' She smiled at him and turned to look at William, who was now standing far too close for comfort and, for the second time that day, an Irishwoman gave him a worried look and asked him if he was all right.

'Indeed, I just wanted to catch you before you closed up.' He smiled weakly and mumbled an ineffectual, 'Smells delicious . . . mmmm.'

As the chap lifted the crate, he threw William a suspicious glance.

'Shall I take them to the car for you, Mrs Gallagher?'

'That would be lovely, dear. I've left a bag inside for the young fella, so help yourself. Take the keys and you can pop them in the boot.'

William hovered at the edge of the stall, feigning interest in a display of eccentric umbrellas in a shop window.

'Now, what were you after yourself? I've only got

one spelt loaf left, but there's a dozen or so scones still up for grabs, and a couple of cream buns. The market's closing early today so I brought less than usual with me. Fancy them doing works on a Saturday, the busiest day of the week. Thoughtless –'

'I'll take a cream bun, please.'

'Right, was that it?'

'And the spelt loaf,' William gulped. 'And the scones.'

'Lovely. Fifteen pounds all in, so.'

William added the unwanted baking to the superfluous stockings in his satchel. He walked purposefully away towards the beckoning lights of the busier end of the market, wondering what he could possibly do with it all. He cursed himself for his own inability to just say no. It was nearly time for lunch. A steaming bowl of soup was just what he needed to recalibrate and make a plan for the rest of the day. He strolled up George's Street, nodding at the closed shutters of the Long Hall pub, to which he knew he would return, and turned up side streets that led back towards Grafton Street and St Stephen's Green. He thought of Clare remarking that Dublin was a lot like Manhattan, really; the way the city sat around the lush green park at its heart. It was ludicrous; Manhattan could carry Dublin around in its smallest pocket, but still, he understood what she meant.

He found himself a temporary home in the library bar of the Central Hotel, where the atmosphere reminded him of Christmas Eve. An open fire was roaring in the hearth. Chesterfield sofas and plush armchairs were scattered around on thick, rich carpets in sets of twos and threes; all the lighting came from lamps and tea-light candles in crystal holders. What a dangerous place to encounter on a damp day such as this; he might never leave again. A softly spoken waitress with wing-tipped tortoiseshell spectacles and two long auburn plaits trailing down her back brought him a bowl of country vegetable soup and warm crunchy rolls slathered in butter. He tried not to think of the brown-paper bag of bread hidden under his seat as he relished the comfort food, having already decided to leave the bag behind him when he left.

After the soup had warmed his bones, an Irish coffee with its whiskey kick seemed the only option. He sank back into a rust-red leather armchair and stretched his toes to within inches of the flames flickering in the hearth. Stress ebbed from the tension in the back of his neck down his spine and out through his aching legs before wafting with the smoke up the chimney. He decided that missing his flight had been worth it, for this moment's grace alone. He closed his eyes and felt he was hovering a few feet above the room as he tuned in to the sounds around him: clinking glasses behind the bar, the pages of a newspaper being snapped taut after each turning, a vacuum cleaner murmuring in the hallway, animated chatter from two ladies surrounded by shopping bags, their high heels temporarily abandoned, sipping gin and tonics. Clare would love it here. The thought sunk him in gloom. He wanted to be angry at her, to hate her, even, but every time those dark feelings bubbled inside him they burst before they grew real legs. Deep down, he knew that what she had done was just a terrible symptom of how wretched they had become, but that didn't mean he could make peace with it. And definitely not yet.

He pushed the memory of last night from his mind and turned his thoughts to Winter instead. Had she ever lounged here on a lazy Saturday afternoon? Sometimes, it's harder to surrender to indulgences of that nature where you live; there's always some small task to be accomplished. Library bars, even one as seductively comfortable as this, could never be his weekly ritual in real life. Obligations would get in the way and turn the whole business into a spate of guilty mental list-making as he catalogued all the other ways he could be – should be – spending his time. This sort of pleasure had to be reserved for holidays, or the occasional spontaneous moment. What a sad truth to confront. Perhaps if he and Clare had enjoyed more of this and fixated less on accomplishing things on their to-do lists, they would be here together now with Clare's feet tucked in beneath him. Perhaps. He wriggled into a more upright position, rummaged in his satchel for his notebook and flicked through the history impressed upon its pages that stretched back to the time before this calamitous period in his life. He pined for the innocence of his scribblings:

Potential birthday presents for Clare:

A first edition (if can afford) . . . but of what?
Weekend abroad (is this just present for me, though?)

Telescope for star-gazing (can you see enough stars through the smog in London?)
Fountain pen (too work-related?)
Cooking classes (too open to misinterpretation?)
Espresso maker? (too domestic?)
Lingerie? (again, present for me?)

Directions to Karen and James's: Overground to H'bury and Is; change at Dalston Junction; turn right until giant street mural and next left to No. 11 over the dry cleaner's.

Shopping:

Paella rice (medium grain; regular if none)
Pimms (and lemons/limes/cucumber)
Cardamom pods
Non-alcoholic wine for Mrs C
Pesto (green & sun-dried tomatoes)
Honey – squeezy
Green olives (some stuffed with cheese for C.)
Chocolate digestives
Sweet potatoes

To do pre-Christmas:

1. Bleed the radiators
2. Order wine hamper
3. Bag of clothes to charity shop
4. Replace lights on bicycle
5. Arrange night with Stevie and the band

6. Xylophone!!!
7. Secret Santa

He hadn't done any of those things and couldn't remember at all what the xylophone reference meant. Perhaps Clare's frustrations at his alleged inability to get anything done weren't entirely misplaced. At least he had seen Stevie, although not under the circumstances he would have liked. He scribbled from memory a list of people and places Winter had mentioned in her letters; how he wished he could lay all her letters out before him and scour them for clues. He remembered her old career promoting records in radio stations and tried to consider how useful that nugget of information was. How many radio stations could there be in Ireland? If he spoke to one of the DJs, they would know all the radio pluggers, wouldn't they? It was hard to gauge what sort of relationship she might have had with them without him having any insight into how the industry worked, but it was definitely a lead worth exploring. He caught the eye of the waitress and gave her the universal gesture to request the same again. As she placed the hot glass tankard before him on a tomato-red napkin, he asked, 'Odd question, but do you listen to the radio much?'

'At home, I do. It doesn't really work to have music playing in here, though, if that's what you're thinking?'

'No, no. I was just wondering about the local radio stations, what I should tune in to while I'm in town.'

'Well, I listen to some of the pirates myself, but the main one is 2fm. That has all the big DJs on it and is a bit more mainstream. Apart from Dave Fanning. He's deadly and plays great tunes after eight o'clock. Rock and alternative stuff, mostly. Would you be into that sort of thing?'

'Sounds great. Like the Irish John Peel? Where is the station itself? In Dublin, I'm guessing?'

'Yeah, in RTÉ, out in Donnybrook. It's not far from here but, if you're into it, the Roadcaster is outside St Stephen's Green shopping centre today. You can go see the legend Larry Gogan in action.'

His antennae twitched at the mention of Donnybrook; wasn't that where Winter had lived, over a cake shop? He could have kissed the waitress for mentioning it, as he wasn't sure he would have remembered it otherwise.

'The Roadcaster?' he asked, hopeful for more intelligence that could help him.

'Yep, it travels all over the country with Larry playing the hits and his Golden Oldies. You should take a stroll up and check it out. You can play a request for Maggie and the gang in the Central Hotel, and my ma might hear it.'

William gulped down the hot Irish coffee as quickly as the scalding liquid would allow before heading back out into the warren of Dublin. The rain had stopped and the wet cobblestone paths glistened under the pale watery sunlight that tried to break through. As he drew closer to the gates of St Stephen's Green, he saw a little crowd gathered around a big black-and-yellow bus that was pumping out 'Teenage Kicks' by the Undertones. He edged his way to the front, where one of the happiest-looking men he had ever seen was chuckling behind a clipboard and wearing giant yellow headphones. A beaming young woman wearing a black jumpsuit with a thick cerise-pink belt was holding the microphone for him while he shuffled through his papers. The music ended abruptly and the spectators all shared a titter as the DJ jumped and giggled himself at nearly being caught out. A voice of chocolate, so warm and friendly, boomed out from the speakers. This must be the legend Larry himself, thought William. Larry turned to a blushing middle-aged woman who was bursting with pride at the attention. She kept fluffing her ginger perm as she watched him, shifting her weight back and forth from one foot to the other.

'So now we're going to have our last Just a Minute quiz of the day. Who do we have here?'

'Oh, Larry, I'm Ursula, and that's my friend Carole hiding over there, but she's too shy to go on the radio.'

'What's that, Carole? Carole, come over here and help poor Ursula answer a few questions out of that.'

Carole turned scarlet and waved madly, as if the nation of Ireland could see her gesturing over the radio waves.

'It's no use, Larry. She'll murder me after.'

'Don't mind her, Ursula. We'll give it a go ourselves. Are you ready?'

'Don't ask me any hard ones, Larry.'

'We'll let the clock start, then, Eddie, and away we go.'

A clock started counting down and Larry jumped into action:

'How many in a baker's dozen?'

'Thirteen.'

'How many times did Johnny Logan win the Eurovision?'

'Twice. Oh, I love him, I do.'

'Name the capital of Germany.'

'G.'

'Finish this famous proverb: as happy as . . .'

'Oh, as you, Larry.'

The crowd started laughing, but Larry managed to keep going with the questions.

'What do you put on before you go to bed?'

'Perfume.'

'Can you divide 144 by 12?'

'Yes.'

'A stitch in time saves . . . ?'

'Nine.'

'What do vegetarians not eat?'

'Vegetables.'

'What do caterpillars turn into?'

'Dust.'

The alarm sounded, and the crowd gave a big cheer while Larry's assistant counted her score.

'Ah, they didn't suit you, Ursula, but how many did she get, Anne?'

'Only four this time, I'm afraid.'

'Aw, don't worry a bit, Ursula. You got a few sticky ones there, but you did great. What do we have for her, Anne?'

'A great prize – two tickets to see Twink in her new show at the Gaiety and a Cadbury's chocolate hamper.'

'Great stuff. Let's hear it for Ursula, and it's back to the studio for the Boomtown Rats. Hit it, Eddie.'

Carole and Ursula posed for a photograph with Larry before he escaped, but William managed to catch the attention of Anne before she jumped on board the bus behind him.

'Excuse me, do you have a second?'

'Hello there. We're not doing any more quizzes today, if that's what you're after, but I can give you a form to fill out if you'd like to have a request played?'

'That's okay. I was just wondering if you might know a friend of mine who works for one of the record companies.'

'Maybe, but it depends on what they do.'

'She's a plugger, as far as I know.'

'Oh, well, Larry would probably know her, then. He listens religiously to every new track that comes out. What's her name?'

'Winter, although that could be a nickname.'

'Ooh, that's unusual. Doesn't ring any bells but, if you wait until the end of the show, you could ask Larry himself, if you'd like to.'

William started backing slowly away as he realized that he couldn't really ask this DJ if he happened to know Winter and, if so, where she used to work, without looking pretty peculiar. Was this blind alley just indicative of the end results he would face from all his clues? The futility of his search seemed ever clearer, and he started to panic about what exactly he was hoping to achieve. Was he hoping that whatever magical force had brought the letters into his life would also help him find the woman who wrote them?

He told Anne he might pop back later and ran to catch the number 10 bus that would take him to Donnybrook village. He asked the driver to let him know when they reached his destination, then watched Dublin city roll by. Larry's quiz reminded him of the challenge he had taken at last year's depot Christmas party; he was called up on stage to name something he had found in the depot for every letter in the alphabet. The audience shouted out the letters and, flustered though he was, he managed to call out a discovery in response to each one. He ran through the list in his head until the driver gave him the nod as he pulled up outside a huge chapel. A, apple tree; B, butterflies; C, chandelier; G, gnomes; J, jalapeño peppers; K, kaleidoscope; M, marzipan; P, picnic basket; V, ventriloquist's dummy. William jumped off the bus, his mind a momentary blank for what he had had for Y, before it hit him as he waited at the pedestrian crossing. Y, yo-yo! Of course!

He walked along the high street, with its artisan shops and ornate streetlights, hoping he hadn't missed the bakery as he strolled past. All these shops looked as if flats could exist above them. Did Winter walk along here every day? Buy her groceries in that market? Pore over paperbacks in that bookshop? Find bunches of flowers for friends in that florist? Anyone here could have known her, could still know her now. Everyone spread a web of connections across the world they inhabited: acquaintances, friends, chance encounters. Surely some sticky fragments of Winter's time here must exist along this street.

A cake shop sat on a curved corner, its stained-glass door opening on to the connecting street. This must be the one. In the window, a display of wedding cakes blocked most of the interior from view, but he saw that the bakery stretched further along the street; a row of little tables for two with blue-and-white-check table-cloths lined a long window. Each table had a red bud vase in the centre that held a sprig of winter jasmine. His favourite flower. In fact, the only flower that held any emotional significance for him at all. When he was a little boy, every November, his mother would take him out into the fields at the back of his grandmother's house in Devon to gather armfuls of it. They seemed to herald that Christmas was coming. His granny filled the house with them; in vases of all shapes and sizes but in empty milk bottles and tall drinking glasses, too. Whenever he could, he took a bunch to her grave in Highbury.

He was disappointed to discover that the flowers were plastic, but then, it was the wrong season. Goodness, where would he be spending Christmas this year? Would he and Clare be apart? Where on earth would he go if they were? Stevie's house? Thoughts of Christmas Eve without Clare made a cold mist gather on his skin. If he couldn't imagine Christmas without her, what was he doing sitting in a cake shop in Dublin, trying to track down a ghost? Even as every iota of common sense told him to leave and go straight to the airport, however, he was incapable of surrender. An important, essential part of himself had committed to this quest and, whatever his better judgement told him, he could not give up now. He forced himself to focus; he had lost sight of why he had come here.

William approached the counter, ordered a chocolate eclair and a peppermint tea, immediately questioning their compatibility, before starting to quiz the silver-haired gentleman in a starched white shirt and royal-blue tie who was so elegantly preparing his tray. William wondered if the clientele came as much for his attentions as for the little pastries that, he later discovered, were made by the man's wife.

'I'm visiting from London and remembered my friend, Winter, saying she lived above a cake shop around here. I don't suppose it was this one, by any chance?'

The gentleman's voice was slow and soft, only just more audible than a whisper. William felt they were already participating in a shared confidence.

'I don't suppose so.'

'Oh? Any particular reason?'

'A very particular one. I've lived upstairs with my wife for twenty-five years and, although we've had all the seasons living with us through that time, to the best of my knowledge, they have never taken on any human form.'

William concentrated on stirring his tea, watched the colour darken within the thick, glass-walled mug.

'I see. Twenty-five years. It's a long time. You must be very happy here.'

'Oh, we've had our ups and downs. And we did try to

leave once. My wife, Sylvie, became poorly, and we made an effort to retire in the west, but it wasn't for us. Syl spent all day making cakes without any neighbours for miles to give them away to. I thought I'd never be able to suffer the sight of them again. So, we came back to work, and my daughter kindly let us take the reins again.'

'Did she mind the shop for you while you were away?'

'Yes, she took over the whole business and lived upstairs but, really, I think she was relieved not to have to keep going. She had loftier ideas than inheriting the family business and always hankered to move abroad, to a bigger city where something exciting could happen.'

William's teaspoon clattered on to the silver tray while he registered this news.

'So, all for the best, then? Did she make the move? America? Or closer to home?'

'No, she wanted to go to America, but her mother's heart was broken at the thought of her being so far away, so she settled for London. Syl still feels guilty about that. Maybe if she had just gone to America, things would have turned out differently.'

William kept his voice steady as his heart banged and thrashed inside his ribcage. He rested his clammy hands against the tiled countertop to steady himself.

'Did she not like it, then? What's she up to now?'

His confidant took off a pair of wire-rimmed spectacles and patted his brow with a white handkerchief before polishing the lenses.

'I'm afraid she's not up to anything. Things took an

unfortunate turn over there and she got herself into some trouble. We've never really been sure exactly what happened; dodgy boyfriend at the heart of it, though, of course. Anyway, she passed away and was found in a horrible little flat in Shepherd's Bush, and by then it was too late to ever know the whole story.'

He started coughing, and William struggled to find something to say, before stammering out, 'I'm very sorry for your loss, sir.'

The gentleman folded and refolded the napkins on the counter while William gathered up his tray.

'I don't really talk about it that much, have to put a brave face on it. I'm sorry if I made you uncomfortable. It hits you at the strangest of times.'

'Not at all, it's the comfort of strangers.'

'Quite. Let me know if you need anything else.'

The man turned and pushed through the glass doors to the bakery, where William saw him circle his arms around a small, homely lady, her white hair in a net and flour on her bare arm, the sleeves of a yellow cotton blouse rolled up to her elbows. She leaned into him, and they rocked together for a moment, until she stepped away to pull a tray of loaves from the oven.

William sat back at his table for two and forced the eclair into his dry mouth. He couldn't taste anything and swallowed it in two forced bites that caught in his throat. This man's daughter couldn't be Winter. The timing was all wrong. Winter lived in East London, not West. And the letters were still arriving. Unless she wasn't posting them, or had sent them a long time ago.

What if she had found her great love in the guise of some awful man who had taken her to live in Shepherd's Bush and destroyed everything? Would he ever be able to find out? He finished his tea and carried his tray back to the counter. The man smiled as he took it from him.

'You can see her on the wall as you leave, our Moll. I give her a wave every day when I lock the shop door. That photo was taken the day she left for London. In my heart, I think of it as the day she died.'

On his way out, William paused in front of a lavender-coloured wooden photo frame that held a black-and-white photo of the man's daughter. It was hard to tell what colour her hair was – maybe light brown, maybe red – but her skin was powder white, with dark lines smudged around her eyes. Standing to the side of the frame, with a giant rucksack on her back that shaped her like a snail, she wore an army jacket over a black frilly skirt and above tartan tights and army boots. The camera froze the moment in time: she had an enormous grin across her face and a pillow tucked under her arm. William gave her a self-conscious little wave before jingling the bell over the door as he exited into another downpour.

He wrestled his satchel into a better position on his shoulders and began walking towards the city centre. He didn't care if he was soaked to the skin, if he got lost, or even if he never found his way back to the hostel. With no regard for avoiding puddles or pedestrians, he ploughed onwards, past pubs welcoming damp Dubliners in for warming pints, and parents running with strollers, groceries hanging from the handlebars. Hordes of supporters were pushing through the gates of the rugby grounds, and William enjoyed being tousled along by the groups of lads, the excuse it gave him to push a little and be a bit rougher than he needed to. He stood on a bridge and wondered if the river below was a tributary that flowed into the Liffey. He assumed it must be. The raindrops exploded on the surface as the water raced along, and William wondered how deep it was, if anyone ever swam there in summer. He watched a red scarf being dragged by the current, until it became tangled in some reeds. A swan pecked at it and swam away in disappointment.

He marched onwards, resigned to the squelching discomfort of his soaked socks squeaking inside his shoes, and crossed the intersection to Wexford Street. He recognized it as the road that would take him back to the hostel. Stopping outside the window of Whelan's, he watched a group of musicians setting up in the corner for a session. The fire was glowing and the people already dotted around the bar looked happy to have escaped another rainy day in Dublin. It was tempting to join them, but he dragged himself away from the honey pot and strode on. There was only one destination left on his itinerary, before he subjected himself to a night of scratchy sheets and the constant fear of an intruder. He couldn't shake the feeling that Winter and the bakers' daughter may be one and the same. The thought made him feel a sense of despair that his limited acquaintance with Winter should not produce. His spirits were low, but he wasn't quite ready to give up on his ghost yet. He had always thought the Long Hall held the best chance he had of finding information that would lead him to Winter. For better or worse, he was pinning his last hopes there.

22.

The Long Hall had emerged from Victorian Ireland with all the paraphernalia of the era still intact. The deep oak panelling, velvet upholstery, chandeliers and brass fixtures proudly held their place as modern times swept past the heavy red wooden door. The ruby walls and tapestry carpets whispered secrets as clocks from times gone by tick-tocked down the hours to last orders. When William arrived, a gentle hush hung in the air and there were just a few customers propped against the bar, waiting for pints of Guinness to settle. William mooched towards the last stool and hung his drenched coat on the brass hook underneath the bar. As he walked past the gallery of photographs hanging on the wall, he scanned the captions for Winter's name and the faces for anything he might recognize, but to no avail. The *Irish Times* was open on the polished bar, with a half-completed crossword facing upwards, a pen resting on top, as if it had been patiently waiting for him. He leaned over to read the unsolved clues as the barman wandered over.

'Help yourself. I've done all the ones I know. What can I get you?'

William felt compelled to order Guinness, although he wondered how it would mix with the Irish coffee, peppermint tea, vegetable soup and eclair he had already consumed that day. He spread the newspaper out before him and scanned the headlines without really absorbing any of the content. He didn't recognize many of the faces that were famous here. He struggled with the heavy black drink; it was too much for him, and he sipped from just below the creamy head. The barman saw him grimace and folded his arms across the bar in front of him.

'Will I put a drop of blackcurrant in that for ya? It sweetens it up a little and helps you get it down.'

William slid the glass back across the counter and the barman added a splash of dark purple cordial from a decanter under the bar.

'You here on business or pleasure?'

'Well, sort of a mixture of both. I just came to do some research for' – he sighed – 'for something I'm working on.'

'A book, is it? We get plenty of writers in here. Tucked away in corners scribbling in their notebooks, cursing reviews in the paper.'

'Not exactly, but I can see what attracts them. It's a great little pub. How long has it been here?'

'Since before the turn of the century,' he said, polishing wine glasses with a tea towel adorned with a map of Ireland. 'Wouldn't say it's changed much, either. It'll be heaving in a few hours but, I have to say, it's one of the few pubs in Dublin where, even when it's bursting at the seams, you can still have a conversation. People appreciate that, I think, not to be screaming at each other over blasting music or being blinded by lights. It's always fairly civilized in here, compared to some of the places I've worked.'

William glanced around the room, his eyes lingering once again on the framed photographs.

'A friend of mine recommended it to me,' he said. 'She used to come here a lot before she moved to London.'

'Aye, we get a lot of regulars all right. Same faces every week.'

'Do you ever remember meeting a girl called Winter?'

'Winter?' He slapped the tea towel over his shoulder. 'What sort of a name is that? I've met a Summer, and a Spring, too, but never anyone called Winter. That's a bit depressing, isn't it? There was a girl in my class in school called Nollaig, mind you, which is "Christmas" in Irish, but that's different. Winter? Her folks might as well have called her Rain or Cloudy.' He chuckled at the thought.

'So, it doesn't ring any bells?' William asked, without much hope.

'No, but I've only been here since I moved up to start college in September. You'd want to ask the boss man. He's been here since he was my age, and that wasn't today nor yesterday. He'll be in at some point later on. You'll know him when you see him. Six foot seven and bald head shiny as a new penny.'

William moved from the bar to one of a nest of round tables at the rear and waited for the landlord to make an appearance. He examined the glass in front of him and doubted a pint had ever lasted so long in this establishment before, but he was content to let the warmth of the bar dry out his clothes and to give his bones a chance to settle.

At the stroke of six, as if the school bell had been struck, the neighbouring businesses released workers into the streets, and it seemed many of them proceeded directly to the sanctuary of the Long Hall. Pints lined up on the grille behind the bar at various stages of completion, and the barmen performed a beautiful choreography as they danced past each other, switching between tasks with the efficiency and grace of men who loved their job and took pride in doing it well. Coats were abandoned on hooks and stands to dry off, ties were loosened or stuffed into pockets. One woman shook down her hair from a tight bun into waves of golden blonde that shimmered in the light from the chandelier. William wondered if she was standing there deliberately because it cast her in such favourable light. He envied the patrons the ease with which they immersed themselves in the atmosphere of a Saturday evening on the town; pined for the nights he, too, had spent with little to care about other than not missing the last Tube home. Who knew, though, what sadness lay in the hearts of these people? What strife awaited them at home, what darkness weighed down their shoulders. From where he sat, however, all he saw was merriment and the easy company of comrades celebrating their survival of another week. He tried to seem relaxed himself and not to start at every swing of the door, like a man waiting on his blind date to appear. Whiskey after whiskey was his short-term solution.

William looked around him and wondered how he'd

ended up sitting on his own in a pub in Dublin city with no idea where his wife was or what she was doing.

'Do you mind if we jump in here? Are these free?'

Two young women stood over him, laden with two umbrellas, a Dunnes Stores plastic bag of groceries and what looked like several coats, hats and scarves.

'No, that's fine. I'm by myself,' he answered. William stood up as they squashed all their belongings into the tiny space under the table.

'Thanks a million,' one of the new arrivals answered. 'This is actually our table, you see; we sit here every week. Normally, we try to get here early to snatch it up, or else we just hover menacingly until whoever is sitting here gets the hint.' She laughed. 'So, what's your name? I'm Winter and this is Ailbhe.'

William spat a mouthful of Jameson on to the table, narrowly missing the sleeve of one of the pair.

'I'm sorry, what did you say your name was?'

'Indra. Although it doesn't normally get quite that reaction. What did you think I said?'

'Sorry, I just misheard you. It's been a long day.'

Ailbhe, who was swathed in multiple layers of wool, rolled down the polo-neck of her black-and-white houndstooth dress and pulled her polished black bob out to perch atop. She seemed not to be wearing any make-up, but her complexion was pure peach. Her eyes were a very dark blue, and she looked at William in a knowing way that unnerved him. When she eventually spoke, her voice had a husky Northern Irish lilt that William thought she could surely make a career from.

'So, what brings an Englishman to a Dublin pub on his lonesome on a Saturday night?'

'Well, I've been in town all day, and I thought it might be nice to stop off for a drink before I head back to the hotel. I wasn't expecting it to be quite so busy, though.'

Indra looked the exact opposite to her companion. She had platinum-blonde hair cropped close to her head, a slinky black dress barely covering her toned, tanned body and a lot of make-up: dark green around her brown eyes, something pink and sticky on her lips.

William chose his words carefully; he could hear a slight slur creeping in.

'How do you two know each other? Been friends for long?'

Indra laughed. 'You could say that. She's my big sister.'

'Really?' William looked back and forth from one to the other. 'You look so different!'

'Meaning she's gorgeous and I'm not,' Ailbhe sighed, rolling her eyes.

'No, not at all, that's not what I meant.'

'So you *don't* think I'm gorgeous?' Indra shot back.

William scratched at his beard.

'That's not what I meant. You don't even have the same accent.'

'Well, we didn't grow up in the same part of the country. You see, our father –' Indra began, but Ailbhe cut her off.

'Indie, there's no need to go into all that, okay? He doesn't want to hear our life story. And I definitely don't want to tell it. Again.'

William stood up. 'I'm sorry, it's really none of my business,' he said. 'Can I buy you both a drink? Then I won't feel so bad about you keeping me company.'

Indra clapped her hands.

'That's a marvellous idea. What's your name?'

He told her, and she held out her hand to shake his; on each finger twinkled a different silver ring.

'Fabulous, William. I can tell we are going to be great friends altogether.'

William yelped as a sharp kick found his shinbone. Ailbhe reddened a little.

'Sorry, my foot slipped.'

'That was quite the delivery for a slippery foot.'

'It was meant for Indy. I'm sorry, it's just we have some things to discuss, and we weren't really looking for company.'

'You do realize that you came to join me, and not the other way around?'

'Well, we thought you might be leaving soon and didn't expect you to join us, really. Sorry, I didn't mean to be rude. No offence.'

'Ailbhe, stop it! Please don't mind her. She's a stroppy cow when she wants to be. We'd love to have a drink with you. One vodka and white, and one white-wine spritzer, please. With lemonade, not soda.'

'Tell you what, I'll get you the drinks and then find somewhere to wedge myself at the bar out of your way. Best of both worlds, eh?'

He edged away from the table and started squeezing his way to the service area, ignoring Indra's protests and

Ailbhe's sulky silence. In the mirror of the bar, he saw Ailbhe watching him from under her fringe while Indra berated her, gesticulating madly with her hands. What an odd girl. He didn't particularly want to spend the evening being prodded and poked by these two. It definitely wouldn't help him accomplish his mission. He caught the eye of his new best friend, the barman, and ordered their drinks, with another shot of whiskey for himself. He squeezed on to a bar stool in the corner that had become a coat depository and beckoned to Indra to come and collect their drinks so he wouldn't lose his spot. She teetered over in pink wedge sandals.

'Why don't you come back over and join us, eh? Ailbhe doesn't mind, not really. She was just worried she wouldn't get a chance to give me a lecture about college if we had company.'

'No, that's okay, I'm not really in the mood for conversation much myself. You two have a good night.'

As he pushed his stool back away from the bar so he could pass her the drinks, Indra put her hand on his forearm.

'You've very sad eyes, do you know that? They are ruining your whole look. I bet that you're quite handsome when you're happy. Maybe we can cheer you up.'

He jerked away, spilling some of the white-wine spritzer in his haste. 'I don't think so,' he answered, as he tried to steady himself. 'But thank you. Maybe see you later.'

Indra shrugged her shoulders and went back to Ailbhe, who was staring intently at the floor. There was a time, long before Clare, when William would have found it irresistible to try to solve the puzzle of girls like that, but not these days. He swirled the whiskey around in his tumbler and tried to zone out of the conversations swirling around him. His ear couldn't resist tuning into the odd phrase here or there, though. Little exchanges caught his attention, as if he were spinning through different frequencies on the radio dial:

'He clearly fancies you. Just admit it.'

'But darling, he's my fitness instructor. He has to be friendly to me, that's his job, to be friendly. I'm sure he's the same with everyone.'

'He's never put his arm around me – not once – and I'm pretty sure I've never seen him do it to anyone else, either, for that matter . . .'

'I just feel like she's deliberately excluding me. I mean, it was my idea to include the snow globe, and then she didn't even invite me when they went to pick it out. Now, she'll get all the credit again, but I suppose that's what she wants, really, isn't it . . .'

'He keeps spouting Latin at everyone, and it could be entirely made up, for all anyone else knows, but it's not like you can challenge him on it. The only Latin I know was our school motto, *Fortiter et suaviter* or something, but I'm not sure how you pronounce it, even if there was an opportunity for me to roll out "Strength and gentleness" in conversation . . .'

'I heard the funniest joke ever today: what do you call a cat with no tail?'

'A Manx cat.'

William was growing more and more inebriated. He hadn't eaten any dinner to line his stomach and fortify him for the quick succession of drinks he was consuming. With no sign yet of the landlord, he questioned what he was still hoping for. That a group of people would just start talking about Winter within earshot and he could casually join the conversation? He lost his balance when he tried to stand up from his stool, and the room swirled as he stumbled on the way to the bathroom. The fluorescent light in the small, wood-panelled room dazzled him at first, but he pressed his forehead against the cold tiles around the mirror and found a little relief. He gripped the sink, closed his eyes and breathed deeply, despite the heady mix of disinfectant, men's cologne and something damp and moist that permeated from the walls. He sat on the steel-blue pipes that bordered the perimeter of the room, holding his throbbing head in his hands. Every so often, someone stepped over him to go to the cubicle, but he managed to mumble that he was fine convincingly enough not to raise alarm. The din from the lounge sounded far away, and he wasn't quite sure how long he had been resting there when a tall, imposing figure who looked alarmingly like a professional wrestler nudged him with a steel-toe-capped boot.

'Everything all right in here? You're the last one.'

William scrambled to stand up. The room had stopped spinning, but his head was pounding.

'Gosh, I'm sorry. I must have dozed off. One too many, I think. I'm a bit of a lightweight these days.'

The man shrugged and picked up the bin, which was overflowing with paper towels, and let the door close behind him, leaving William to pull himself together. He splashed cold water on to his face and rinsed the fuzzy feeling from his mouth. That must be the landlord, but William knew he hadn't made the best first impression. It suddenly struck him that he had no coat, no bag. What if someone had stolen his satchel with his passport and wallet inside it? He would be stranded in Dublin. He rushed out of the bathroom, back to where he had been sitting, but all the stools were upside down on the bar and a cleaning lady was hoovering the carpet.

'Don't worry. I have your things behind the bar for you.' His barman friend from earlier walked past him with a tray of empty glasses. 'I thought you'd left without them. What happened to you?'

'I'm ashamed to say I fell asleep on the floor of the bathroom. Your boss woke me up.'

The barman laughed, shaking his head. 'I'm surprised he didn't throw you out,' he said, 'You're not in Temple Bar, you know.'

'It's very out of character, I can assure you. Is he still around? I was hoping for a word.'

'He's in the cellar, but he'll be back in a minute . . . Good luck. He's not the most pleasant at the best of times. Most of the time, I just try to keep out of –'

A clearing of the throat interrupted them.

'Who, may I ask, is not the most pleasant, Mr Fitzpatrick?'

The landlord stood before them, his arms crossed in

front of his black leather waistcoat and skin-tight white T-shirt.

'Oh, no one, boss. We're just talking about some eejit from the telly. This chap here was looking for a word. I'll be in the cellars if you need me.'

The landlord didn't look at William as he spritzed the bar top with furniture polish and wiped it down with a wet cloth.

'So, Sleeping Beauty, what can I do for you? We're officially closed, you know.'

William followed him as he worked. 'I was just wondering if you might know a friend of mine, a girl called Winter?' he asked. 'She used to drink here all the time. Long red hair? She told me to say hello.'

He gave a little snort. 'I find that hard to believe. I don't really socialize with my customers. And I never met nobody called Winter.'

William tapped him on the shoulder. 'Maybe it was a nickname. You sure you never heard it before?'

The landlord turned to William and looked him straight in the eye.

'Positive. Now, if you're done, the door's that way.'

William struggled back into his coat, grappled to open the solid oak door. He made two unsuccessful attempts before stepping out into his third rain torrent of the day. It was strangely refreshing after his hot and sticky collapse on the floor of the bathroom. He ran to a bus shelter to try to get his bearings and come to terms with this latest blow. He stood before a map of the city centre, tracing his finger along the path he believed would take him back to the unwelcoming stench of his hostel. Out of the dark night, a soft voice spoke to him.

'Are you lost, William?'

Ailbhe sat on the bus stop bench, reading a book by the light of a torch no bigger than a pen.

'Ailbhe! Hello, well, no, not really. I was just confirming my route. Where's your sister?'

'Oh, she got a better offer. I was just letting the shower pass before I walk home. Usual story with Indie, I'm afraid. I'm sure you would rather find her sitting here.'

He sat down beside her on the bench.

'Not even a little bit – honestly. I find your sister quite scary, and she told me I looked sad, which is actually the sort of thing that, if you weren't depressed beforehand, would certainly bring on a bout.'

Ailbhe smirked at him.

'Oh, don't worry. She says that to all the boys, even the jolly ones.' She paused. 'In fact, especially the jolly ones. She has this theory that, deep down, all men are sad about something and are looking for a girl to make them feel better, so she pretends to sense it inside them and uses it to reel them in. It's very effective, actually, if horribly manipulative. When we were living in London, it seemed to work even better for her with the English boys. All those repressed feelings.'

'Crikey. Such cynicism in one so young!' said William. 'And here I was, worried that I looked a complete pitiable wreck when I thought I was putting on such a convincing brave face.'

'Oh, no, don't get me wrong: you look completely

broken by life. It's just she would have said that to you, regardless.'

Ailbhe turned her attention back to the book she was reading, as if to end the conversation.

'Is that it? We're done here?'

'Why? Is there more?'

'Well, you perform such a casual assessment of my person and then just opt out of the conversation. That doesn't seem very fair.'

'I didn't mean to offend you. Anyway, you started it, looking for sympathy because Indie called you out. Looks like the rain is easing off now. I might make a run for it.'

William was suddenly a little panicked by the thought of confronting the failure of his Dublin expedition by himself, even if the alternative was this spiky lady.

'Wait, how about a bag of chips to warm us up? Loads of salt and vinegar? You can eat them walking home.'

'You're not walking me home. You could be a serial killer, for all I know, though I do admit I'm not feeling hugely threatened.'

He experienced the odd sensation of being slightly offended that she didn't think he had the makings of a serial killer in him but decided against insisting that he would be able to murder her if he wanted to.

'That's fine. I'm not suggesting anything untoward, just some chips. I really feel partial to a bag but have no idea where to find some and thought you might accompany me in the right direction.'

'You're standing across the street from a chip shop, William.'

She lost her icy aloofness for a moment, unable to resist a little laugh at his expense.

'Marvellous. Let's go. You can tell me about your time in London.'

They dashed across the street through the slow-moving traffic and joined the noisy queue of post-pub famished masses craving curry chips, onion rings and garlic dip.

'You never told us what you are in town for.'

'Well, I was looking for something – for someone, sort of. But it didn't really work out.'

'A girlfriend?'

'No, I had a chance encounter with someone, of sorts, and I remembered they mentioned the Long Hall so, when I happened to be in town, I thought I would pop in and see if the universe might cut me a break. Silly, really. She doesn't even live in Dublin any more.'

'Unfinished business.'

'Exactly.'

'What's her name? It's a small town – maybe I know her. Maybe I'm your moment of serendipity in Dublin.'

'You won't. I'm starting to wonder if she even exists. Maybe I imagined her, or my wife invented her as . . . Oh my God, could that be it?' William put his hands on her shoulders and gushed, 'What if Clare wrote the letters? What if, all this time, it was her? Trying to tell me things about her? Oh God, what if she knows I'm here? This could be a total disaster.'

'I'm sorry – you're married? What letters? You look like you've seen a ghost.'

William paced up and down alongside the steamed-up glass window of the chip shop and put his thoughts back in order. A man in leather trousers and a white vest threw a chip at him.

'Jaysus, stop fidgetin' man, you're twistin' me melon!'

William ignored him and rejoined Ailbhe in the queue, whispering now.

'No, no, that's crazy. It couldn't be. The details were too specific, and she could never get into my office, and Marjorie had one, and anyway, what would be the point? To test me? No, stop it, no. That's not it, I'm just freaking myself out.'

'Have to say, you're kind of freaking me out, too, at the moment.'

William stood in silence as she ordered two bags of chips, with salt and vinegar on both but extra salt on hers.

'Together or separate?' barked the man behind the counter.

'Separate. Definitely separate,' Ailbhe shot back.

'Do you not want some chips with your salt? You'll end up with really high blood pressure if you keep that up, you know,' said William.

'That's great advice, Dad, and you probably shouldn't have nervous breakdowns in strange cities, either, but hey, at least your cholesterol is okay.'

She handed him his chips and they bumped into each other as they both tried to leave at the same time. William stood back and held the door open for her.

'So, tell me about her – your *unfinished business . . .*'

'Well, her name is Winter . . . and she lived here for quite a while, before –'

'Ooh, how exotic, like the burlesque dancer?'

William stopped in the street and turned to face her.

'What do you mean? What burlesque dancer?'

'Winter! She's fabulous, like a white-witch character. She has this stage persona that's all about magic and casting spells over men so they do her bidding. She really works the Celtic thing – she looks like a model from a *Visit Ireland* catalogue. All red hair and pale skin and these piercing green eyes. I saw her at the Clapton Working Men's Club last summer, and it was frightening how good she was. Nothing tacky or sensationalist, just a proper vintage burlesque routine.'

William dropped his bag of chips and they scattered about his feet.

Ailbhe jumped out of the way and shouted, 'Dear God, what is it this time? What have I said now?'

He once again put one hand on each of her shoulders and locked eyes with her.

'Are you telling me that there is an Irishwoman performing burlesque under the stage name Winter, in Clapton?'

'Well, yes. Why? Do you think that's your girl? If it is, you have no chance, I'm afraid. She is stunning – I mean, terrifyingly beautiful. Way out of your league.'

Her voice was fading away as the reality of the situation sank in. All this time, Winter may really have been sitting – or dancing – on his doorstep. He kissed Ailbhe on the forehead and did a little skip as he set off for his hostel. So many thoughts collided in his head: how Winter had written of a new persona, of how far the feathers would take her, Clare seeing her in a costume. He couldn't quite believe it, but it looked like this god-forsaken trip had yielded some results after all. A burlesque dancer, though? Was it remotely conceivable that a woman like that would be interested in someone like him? He felt so pedestrian. The thing was, though, she *was* searching for someone like him. Her letters told him so. And was her burlesque costume any different, really, from the one Clare wore to court or the one he wore to the depot? Was it strange she hadn't mentioned her performances in her letters? No, he decided. She wanted her great love to understand her interior world; she didn't want him to be seduced by the sequins. He was sure that must happen to her all the time. She was looking for someone different.

When he got back to the hostel, he peeled off all his clothes and sobered up a little under the ice-cold spray of the rickety shower. He climbed into the abrasive sheets, which no longer bothered him, and stared blankly into the darkness while the city cing on outside his window. When dawn broke, he was still lying in the same position, not quite asleep, not quite awake. He now knew where he could probably find Winter, so that's what he would do – wasn't it?

23

Clare lay on an inflatable mattress dressed in grey pin-striped bedlinen in Flora's living room/kitchen/dining room. To call it open plan would be generous; there was very little open about that space. Fitting the mattress on the floor had involved pushing Flora's two-person pine-wood dining table against the wall and stacking the chairs on top. When Clare reached out to the right, she could touch the teak sideboard that stood against the magnolia wall. To the left, the thin brown carpet gave way to the lime-green linoleum that differentiated the kitchen from the rest of the room. Her hand crossed the border as she traced the diamond pattern on the floor with her finger. Looking around the room in the morning half-light, it struck Clare how much of a stranger her sister was to her now. All these vinyl records; when had Flora started listening to soul music, fallen in love with the blues? Who were all those letters from, bundled together on the windowsill? Somehow, she had managed to splash colour and personality across every available surface that the tired little flat offered. Most of it had been collected on her travels, she'd explained. The row of terracotta pots with the family of succulents she brought home from Crete; the curtains made from woven blankets were from India; the Murano glass bowls had been carefully transported in tissue paper from Venice. A stuffed pheasant perched on the sideboard, its beady eyes watching Clare where she lay.

Over the kitchen table, dozens of photographs and postcards told a thousand tales of her adventures overseas. What did these smiling faces mean to Flora? Were they strangers passing through, or had some of them come to mean more to her? Any one person in particular? For so long, Clare had judged her little sister's roaming to be irresponsible, flighty, feckless. When was she going to settle down? Commit to something? Even when Flora told her she had trained as a doula, Clare wouldn't take her seriously. She realized now that, while she had been berating her sister for the choices she had made, Flora was out in the world, squeezing every spectacular second from life, experiencing so much more than her sensible older sister. At what point had Clare decided that only the lifestyle she chose had any value? Why was it so important to her that others reflected and reinforced her behaviour with their own? As she waited for the city, and her sister, to wake up into a new day, she was pleased to realize that she wasn't jealous, she harboured no resentment. All she felt was a renewed optimism that the world was still out there. And that it wasn't too late to get to know her sister on an equal footing, as adults.

She heard Flora gently creak the door open and pause.

'Don't worry, I'm awake. Come in!'

'Sorry, sis, if I woke you. The night ran much later than I expected. That little baby was in no hurry to meet us, but he got there in the end.'

Clare sat up in her charcoal silk pyjamas and propped herself against the radiator with some pillows.

'I don't know how you do it, Flo. You must be exhausted.'

Flora stretched out on the tattered beige corduroy sofa, her two feet propped on the armrest, twisting her wrists back and forth.

'Oh, it's worth it. They called him Lennon Presley, after John and Elvis.' She smiled. 'That baby has a lot to live up to. When I left them, his dad was cradling him in his arms and singing "Heartbreak Hotel".'

'That's sweet.' Clare yawned and rubbed her sister's arm.

Flora's voice dropped a tone. 'So you don't still think I should train *properly* and become a midwife?' she asked, raising her chin to look out at her sister from under her fringe.

Clare flinched, pulled the duvet up around her knees.

'I'm sorry, Flora. You know I've only ever wanted what was best for you –'

Flora swung her legs around so she sat facing her sister.

'It's okay,' she said. 'Annoying as it can be, I'd rather have someone nagging me than no one caring at all. It was almost like having a proper mum.'

Clare stretched her back like a cat and let the silence sit between them. She stood up, bounced along the mattress to make her way to the kitchen, and put the kettle on. While she waited for it to boil, she rummaged through Flora's fridge, sniffing different containers and tossing some in the rubbish bin. After a moment, Flora spoke again.

'I was thinking about you tonight – you and William.'

Clare closed the fridge door but remained staring at it, nudging a fridge magnet from Reykjavik along the edge with her index finger.

Flora leaned on the back of the sofa, watching her sister. 'I think you'd be great parents, that you'd be a great mum. I wish the whole baby thing –'

'*The baby thing!*' Clare pulled open the one tiny cupboard over the sink, snatched two mismatched mugs and shoved them on the counter-top. 'Please don't, Flora. I always said we couldn't even consider it until we had our lives set up properly – a proper home, his career sorted. And he never got it together so, case closed, as far as I'm concerned.'

Flora stood up, pulled the sheet off the mattress and released the valve to deflate it. The trapped air escaped with a high-pitched whine while Clare slapped two tea-bags into the flip-top bin. Flora folded the mattress into a clumsy square in her arms, speaking again to Clare, but without looking at her.

'Are you sure you're not just using all that as an excuse? You were never keen, even before William.'

'And what if I am?' Clare snapped, as she started gathering her clothes together from where they were draped over the back of a kitchen chair. 'It's still all true, and do you blame me? We didn't exactly have a great role model for mothering, growing up, now, did we? I would rather not have any children than risk turning out like her!' She turned towards the hallway.

Flora pushed past her sister to block the living-room door and stretched her arms across the frame.

'*No!*' she shouted. 'I'm not having it. You're nothing like Mum! You've no reason to think you'd make the same mistakes she did. You looked after me when she couldn't. And she was sick.'

Clare tried to squeeze past her, but Flora wouldn't budge. Clare tried to calm down, shocked how quickly this conversation had turned; her heart raced as if a mouse had suddenly scampered across the floor. She forced her voice to become neutral.

'Stop it! She wasn't sick. She was a drunk, and still is. You and Dad always make excuses for her, but I protected you from so much of it. I have no idea how to be a good mother, because I never had one. The older I get, the more I see her in me, and the harder it is to stay in control.'

She dropped her clothes in a heap on the floor and sat down beside them, holding her head in her hands. She was too tired for this. Any time she felt even a semblance of normality, she was thrown off course again. Flora slid down the wall beside her and put her arm around her.

'I'm sorry for pushing,' she whispered, 'but can I just ask you something? If you could be sure that you wouldn't end up like her, if your relationship was strong, would you want a baby, then? Because it's a hundred per cent fine if you just don't think it's right for you, but if there is even a small part of you that wants it, you need to be very careful about your next move, because it's one of the few choices you make in life that can't be reversed if you leave it too late.'

Clare rested her head on her sister's shoulder. 'That's what William said too.' She sighed. Flora remained silent.

'Okay,' she said eventually. 'If I could wave a magic wand and fix everything, then, yes, maybe I would consider it, but I couldn't do it by myself.'

Flora squeezed her hand. 'You wouldn't be alone,' she said. 'William would be there, I'm sure of it. And me, too.'

She stood up, offered her hand to Flora to pull her up also, and said, 'You have to understand, Flo, that us staying together isn't the only possible happy ending for us. There are no plan Bs now . . . only plan As. Does that make sense?'

'It does,' she answered. 'But I can still root for you, though, right? I think William'll come through.'

'Maybe he will,' Clare said, 'but I've hurt him a lot. You don't know the whole story, Flo.' Flora's head whipped around to look at her sister but Clare ignored her arched eyebrows and continued towards the bathroom. She called back over her shoulder, 'Do you fancy taking a drive? I've been working on something and want to show you the results.'

One shower and two slices of peanut butter on toast each later, Clare drove her sister through Camberwell, Shoreditch and De Beauvoir Town until her Mini rattled to a stop in front of what looked like a derelict building in Dalston. Flora pressed her hands on the glass of the passenger window while she peered out.

'Come on! All will be revealed,' Clare said, as she jumped out of the car and hauled the rusty corrugated gate open.

She punched a code into a security box to release the cast-iron front door and led Flora inside. A long concrete corridor stretched ahead, with burnished black doors to the right and left, and a steel staircase curled upwards at the rear. Flora followed her sister as she ran up the steps two at a time. At the top, she produced from her bag a silver key attached to a ring of turquoise fluff as big as a tennis ball. With it, she opened a white panelled wooden door and swung it wide to allow Flora to enter first into the wide, rectangular room. One wall consisted purely of windows; light flooded the room and clouds of dust danced across the old floorboards under their feet. Bits of threadbare grey carpet still stuck to the perimeter of the room; the previous tenant must have had the vision to tear most of it away to find out what the original floor was. A paint-splattered butcher's block ran down the centre, and a Belfast sink, chipped and cracked, stood in the corner.

'It still has running water,' Clare announced, turning on the taps to demonstrate.

'Wow! What is all this?' Flora was wide-eyed as she walked across the room to look out across East London through the cracked windowpanes.

'It's my new studio!' she said, turning slowly on her heel to survey the room. 'I paid six months upfront and, tomorrow, I'm going to blow a small fortune on a new easel and every oil paint they have for sale in Ferguson's. I don't think I've felt so excited in a long time.'

Flora squealed and ran back across the room to throw her arms around her sister. They spun in a circle, holding hands like they had as children, before collapsing on the dusty floor, laughing.

'Tell me everything! Does this mean it went well with your boss yesterday?' Flora asked.

Clare wiped the palms of her hands on her jeans.

'Oh, it was just what I expected,' she answered. 'I'm just glad it's over. He said I can take the year and they will hold my job open, but that "leaving at this point in my career will have a serious impact on my ability to make partner".'

A wrinkle of worry creased Flora's brow.

'Are you not bothered about that?' she asked. 'You've worked there for so long. And that ladder was so hard for you to get on in the first place. You're the first woman they've even considered for partner, you said it yourself. That's a big deal!'

It was Clare's turn now to put her arm around her sister.

'Not as much as it should. I just know that, if I don't take a break now, I probably never will. And, at this point, the fear of working for ever at a job I don't love far outweighs the fear of falling a few steps down the ladder if I have to go back. I mean, have you seen my porcelain sink?' She winked at her little sister. 'C'mon. I'll treat you to lunch at Soup Opera.'

★

As they drove back to Flora's, Clare felt as if the spring sunshine was glowing from within her and spreading out across the city. She knew in her bones that this was the right thing for her to do, but worries about William tailed her like a thundercloud. They stood at a cross-roads. A large part of her wanted them to reinvent their lives together; the other worried that they might need space from each other to be able to do that. Either way, she knew she had to forge her own path so that, whether they stayed together or not, in a year from now she could be happy, or at least happier. She knew that she couldn't keep blaming him or their marriage for hold-ing her back. It was on her now, and she wouldn't let herself down, but she hoped she could find a way to save their marriage. And she already had one idea about how she could do it.

Flora was singing along with the Bangles' 'Eternal Flame' on the radio when Clare pulled the Mini over. 'Do you mind if we take a detour past the flat?' she asked. 'I need to pick up a few things.'

'Sure thing,' Flora said, and she smiled at her sister. 'My big sister, the artist. Who'd have thunk it, eh?'

Clare tapped out the beat of the song on the steering wheel. She liked the sound of that.

24

Discovering Clare's letter, instead of her physical presence, in their home was mostly a relief to William, but he couldn't shake a tinge of disappointment that she had done as he had asked and left him alone. He couldn't, however, deny what a comfort it was to hear that she was staying with Flora and not with that man. It was too soon, he thought, to consider when he might see her again or what he would say when he did. For now, he had to follow through on solving the mystery of Winter, for both their sakes.

William had heard about the Clapton Working Men's Club but had never been himself. Stevie, who had led many a conga line there in his time, had told him it was a giant dress-up box for students, eccentrics, performers, voyeurs and the fabulous to dance, play, perform and mingle with many unlike-minded people. On the top floor, it still existed as a club for working East End men to socialize, play cards and pool, and listen to records on the original gramophone that had been preciously maintained since the club had opened in the sixties. These members had their own entrance, a private stairway to their rooms, which minimized but didn't eliminate entirely the opportunity to converse with lindy hoppers, drag artists and adherents to the current craze Shoreditch inhabitants had for dressing up as Hollywood stars and staying in character all evening. It was exactly the sort of club that Stevie had moved to London for, and his only disappointment came with the realization that, with this crowd, he would never be the most interesting or flamboyant person in the room. He made a valiant effort for a while, experimenting with dressing up in a three-tiered-cake costume, as a fearleader – which William later realized was a dead cheerleader – and trialled numerous creative ideas involving body paint, glitter and carefully positioned feathers. Eventually, however, he grew fatigued and decided it was far more intriguing just to go as himself; it was one of the few places where Stevie, dressed normally, didn't cause a stir. He had invited William along a few times to 'broaden his horizons' and 'set him free', but William had always resisted. He considered asking Stevie to accompany him now. He might even be able to pass it off as a symptom of his general malaise in response to recent events, a need to embrace the world that existed outside the marital home. He was sure Stevie would support him fully, however he wasn't quite ready to admit to anyone, even Stevie, about what he had been up to in Dublin. He decided to investigate quietly by himself to begin with and call for reinforcements later if required.

The number 48 bus dropped William at Clapton Pond, and he patrolled the avenues, looking for the right address. When he finally arrived at the venue, he almost walked past the entrance, it blended so perfectly with the residential houses along the street. A brass plaque adorned a white iron gate at the end of the driveway with the letters C.W.M.C. and an engraving of the happy/sad Greek-theatre masks connected by a snooker cue. He creaked the gate open and continued up a path that wound around the side to the rear. The whole building was much larger than the front exterior implied; the back garden revealed a world of wonder at play. Festoon lighting draped from the roof of the house through the branches of the trees. Oversized swings and hammocks rocked gently in the breeze as they waited impatiently for someone to fill them. A giant chess set sat on the lawn; the queens stood with their backs to each other, wearing lipstick, plastic sunglasses and baseball caps – the bishops, too. A dozen tutus of varying sizes were drying on a washing line; they looked rather disturbing as they danced in the wind, like discombobulated ballerinas. Tables and chairs painted in proud rainbow stripes were scattered around the garden, behind bushes and in nooks and crannies, to accommodate private mischief. The door of a shed painted scarlet was swinging open, and William could see that the interior was red, too: the walls and floors, sofas and chairs. He didn't dare to cross the threshold, but wondered what lay further inside, what activities were enjoyed there after dark. William felt a bolt of envy towards those who came here freely and weren't ashamed to act on their desires; something he struggled to do more and more as time passed.

The back wall of the house was covered in graffiti: giant flowers and kaleidoscopes of colour, peace slogans and dancing zebras. Perhaps there were all sorts of subliminal messages at play that William was innocently absorbing. The windows were covered in starry cloth that prevented him peeking at the interior, but in the centre of the back door sat a frame made of white lights and miniature crystal balls containing the programme of events. It offered the Sailors and Sweethearts Swing Ball, the Camping in the Countryside Sleepover, Hollywood Bingo, Fun and Funky Friday, The Cocky Horror Picture Show, Rock and Roll in the Hay . . . and there, in a cursive silver font, Winter Wonderland: Burlesque Revue. There was a photo of a lady in silhouette lying atop what looked like a giant block of ice with cascades of fiery red hair flowing over the edge. It had to be her.

The heavy black wooden door opened a crack and a head emerged, wearing what looked like the gusset of a pair of tights on top of it and very white powdered make-up. The man's lips were painted red, but so far only one eye had been decorated with elaborate make-up and false lashes; altogether, it gave him the appearance of a very disturbed china doll.

'You're not a journalist, are you? I don't even have all my face on.'

His voice was very deep, with a strong northern accent.

'No, no. I was just checking the listings. The burlesque show sounds interesting. I might come along.'

The character behind the door swung it open to reveal a black fluffy bathrobe with white fishnet stockings peeking out beneath.

'Oh, you definitely should. Those girls are just fabulous,

and they'll move on to other, bigger things soon, I can tell you. I've been the manager here for ten years now and they all move on in the end, but these girls in particular are far too good for this dump. You just can't get the talent, usually, to turn out a decent show. Do you perform yourself?'

For a fleeting second, William considered that this could be the in he needed, but caught himself before he opened up another Pandora's box of ridiculous behaviour on his part.

'No, no. I'll definitely come along to see one of the shows, though.'

'All right, then. Close the gate on your way out. We're keeping a low profile today. Bit of trouble last night.'

'Oh, what sort of trouble?'

He paused for a moment as he surveyed William further, and then the whole story came gushing out as his shoulders collapsed forward.

'Dolly Get-Your-Part On was whizzing around on rollerskates while under the influence and accidentally fell through the curtain while the Von Tramps were performing, and that horrible old queen Dixie Trix pushed her off the stage, and Dolly's wig came off, and the wheels were spinning underneath her while she tried to stand up, and she got madder and madder and pulled at Dixie's skirt for balance, and the two of them ended up rolling around the floor, with hair and lashes flying and pantyhose ripping, and then all the Von Tramps piled in and it became a bit of a free-for-all.'

He took a breath before he continued. 'Some fool in the audience called the police, which was completely unnecessary, as we always resolve these little matters ourselves, but when they arrived we were still serving – after hours – so now I'm in so much trouble you just wouldn't believe it.'

He sat down on the doorstep and held his head in his hands. William awkwardly patted his shoulder and mumbled something reassuring about first offences and extenuating circumstances. The manager patted his hand, nodding his head like a toy bobbing dog.

'Maybe a little sleep would help?' he suggested, as he peeled his hand away. 'I hope you get everything sorted.'

Turning the corner to follow the pathway out, he looked over his shoulder and saw the old dear wiping his eyes with one of the tutus as he collected them from the line. Winter's show was scheduled for the following Thursday, so William knew exactly where he could find her then. He could ask Stevie to come to the show with him, but the prospect of watching her perform made him terribly uncomfortable. Winter hadn't told him about it herself, and to go and see her on stage felt as if he were stealing something from her, something she hadn't chosen to share with him. Maybe he could see her afterwards? Or leave her a note. Or a letter? Yes! A letter was definitely the right way to contact her after all this time. His new friend could pass it on, perhaps.

Back on the 48 bus, William forced himself to consider why the club had affected him so much, why he felt so jealous of a life that could so easily be his. Had Clare been right all along? Had he just convinced himself that he was happy at the depot because he didn't think he deserved another chance to live a more creative life? Maybe he saw Winter as his portal to a second chance. He knew, though, that only he could set himself free. For too long now, he had been a passive observer in his own life. Could Clare ever support him if he tried again to succeed as a writer while she was still trapped in the snares of her job? Did they each need to start again as individuals to have the freedom to let go of their past selves? Maybe Winter had come for him so that could happen. Or maybe her letters would help him find his way home. Whatever the outcome, he knew he was close to the truth.

25

Two blue Basildon Bond envelopes sat on William's desk, one addressed to Winter, one to Clare. They waited like a pair of starched pillows anticipating a pair of tired heads. He traced his forefinger over one name and whispered it aloud into the deserted office space. *Clare*. How easily his pen had scrawled her name, how practised those letters in that order were by his hand, how effortlessly his pen nib scratched their shape. His fountain pen formed the word 'Winter' more clumsily; he had smudged the crossing of the 't'.

He felt compelled to read both letters again, hoped the words found at midnight were not so soaked in Jameson as to prove incoherent. Beyond the windows, a wet blackness was spilling across the skyline, an inkpot toppled on sheets of pale-grey paper. The office was too dark to award him a reflection; he looked beyond the glass out to a city hushed and shrouded in mystery. The city lights were blurred in silver rain as black cats raised black kittens in alleys more puddle than path.

In this enveloping gloom, it was hard to imagine sunlight could ever sweep this town, illuminate corners, coax it to shimmer. It was even more difficult to think of those two women with only their absence in common. Where was Clare tonight? Was she sitting hunched over a computer at work, pale face, tired from the longest of days, glowing in the electric-green light? Had she kicked off her stilettos and slipped her stockinged feet into the wine wool stockings she hid in her bottom drawer for nights when she worked late alone? Or would she have pulled her hair from its daytime knot, swapped a suit jacket for a leather one, carefully applied scarlet lipstick and absconded to a cellar bar to drink expensive white wine with the men from her office, or with one in particular? The thought made him want to race into the wet night and trawl the streets looking for her. Would she want to be found? He wasn't sure any more. It was less than a week since she had left him in Dublin, but what a difference those days had made.

Where was Winter tonight? Whenever his mind turned to her, splashes of vibrant, energizing colours shot through him: crimson, sunburst, shades of the sea. He imagined a scarlet head bent in laughter over clinking cocktail glasses, saw her huddled under an old-fashioned black umbrella held by another, a long, green scarf dancing behind her in the breeze. He could not summon her face. Sometimes, when he hovered in half-sleep, a flash of apple-green eyes forced him awake. Where did he draw them from? Could you fall in love with scarlet hair, green eyes and words on a page intended for someone who might not be you? Could that be enough? Words rising in a smoke plume that curled down your throat, a searching light exposing cobwebs and evaporating shadows. He extended his forefinger and drew circles in the condensation on the glass, his nail hidden by a blackened bruise. A set of Russian dolls, porcelain dolls, paraded across the windowsill. Marjorie's work, he presumed. He smeared his left hand across the pattern he had made, dried his palm on his corduroy trousers and turned back to the desk. The two letters glowed in the lamplight. He picked up his missive to Winter first.

Dear Winter,

Is that your real name? Since I've started reading your letters, the word has stopped meaning a season to me. Instead, it has become an answer to a question I did not know I had been asking. In my line of work, I endeavour every day to find resolution for undelivered letters, to help them find their homes. This is how your letters found me. In truth, it feels like something much more than a professional inevitability; that letters such as yours would always end up on my desk. It's quite the opposite, in fact. The unlikelihood of each one reaching me is staggering, even with my determined searching every day. For I have come to believe that they were intended for me – only me – and that some divine or magical force guided them to my anxious hands. This, of course, may not have been your intention. You may have hoped for so much more than me. You may have expected nothing at all.

I hope it doesn't alarm you to hear that I have been searching for you. For a number of weeks, I have pieced together the clues you laced through your letters, little lighthouses that have helped me find you. But, now that I have, I cannot imagine walking up to you in the street, mouthing this confession and surviving the shock it would give you.

Instead, I thought I would write these lines, explain where I have come from, introduce myself a little. Perhaps then we could arrange a time to talk, if it doesn't all feel too peculiar for you. I know this is highly unorthodox: I have had months of getting to know you; you have just these few lines. Maybe it will be too strange for you; I can understand if that is so, and will not trouble you again. I shall return your letters, and you can save them for someone else you feel should have been standing at the shore when they washed up in a bottle.

I hope you will choose to meet with me, though. Your letters have joyridden through the streets of my mind, and I long to meet the driver who disturbed my peace. I come with no expectations; I am not in a position to have any, other than a closing of a story that will otherwise haunt me. If you would like to sit with me a while, you can leave me a note at the Dead Letters Depot on Redchurch Street, letting me know where and when, and I will come to you.

John Donne once wrote, 'More than kisses, letters mingle souls.' I believe he spoke the truth.

Yours,
William Woolf

It was difficult for William to judge whether or not his letter hit the right tone. Would it frighten Winter to think that, in order to find her, a stranger had used private details she had innocently shared? His instinct told him no, that she would want him to reach out, that, on some level, Winter had hoped that the letters would lead someone to her. He squashed the lingering doubt that he may have projected more meaning upon this woman than was sensible and carefully folded it over on its original crease. He guided it back into the envelope before reaching for the letter to Clare.

My dear Clare, my wife, my friend, my heart,

I have lost you, and there is a great hole in my life where you should be.

Since I came home alone, I have allowed myself to fantasize that true love is not this difficult, hurtful, destroying; that if we were meant to be together, then none of this would have happened. I have dreamed of starting again with someone else who understands me, where the loving comes easy and I have an unblemished heart to offer. The road back for us seemed too hard; surely it would be easier to go on alone.

But I couldn't make it ring true. Even these terrible months of anguish are better than no you at all, for at least it means our story continues, and continue it must.

I could leave you for ever but you will never leave my heart. We can part, if we choose it, both leave this marriage, broken and bruised, try to build ourselves anew somewhere else. Or we can build our marriage anew together.

We had so many years of happiness before things went wrong. Surely it is naïve to think that nothing testing would ever come our way, that we wouldn't fail at some point. What you did? It makes me feel like you have become a stranger to me. I want to decide instead that it was the deed that was strange and not you – that I am still your husband. For I am.

We can come back from this, my darling Clare.

Please don't give up on us. Let us put the world to rights.

We should be together again.

All my love,

Your William

He lined up Clare's letter beside Winter's. Did he believe what he had written? Or was he fighting for her because he felt he should? Was his heart more deceitful, or his head? Could he really be so sure that Winter was just an escape pod? A fantasist reaction to a horrible reality? Was it just immaturity that made him believe in Winter? Or was it immature to think his love with Clare was valid only if it endured?

He flicked the desk lamp off and moved through the sleeping office with just the spill from the corridor light to guide him. As he passed Ned's desk, he paused to run his fingers over the final draft of the *Volume of Lost Letters* that awaited him there. One hundred and eleven pages. Forty-one letters, and the stories that accompanied them. To think, in a matter of months, the Supernatural Division would be immortalized for ever in hardback books. The name gave him pause: was it quite right? He ignored the niggling doubt. Just two hundred copies, initially, to be distributed to libraries across the country, but it was a start. He longed to show Clare, but had waited to show her the finished product, had planned to wrap it and present it to her as a fait accompli. He hoped he would still get the chance.

He couldn't resist taking a detour past the fourth floor, teasing himself with the sight of three new sacks awaiting his attention. He was tired, too tired to think of tackling one now. He knew that, if he started, he would feel compelled to empty them all. He turned out the light and left the room in darkness. On the landing, he paused as prescient instinct tingled; the idea that a letter from Winter could be lying there waiting for him was more than he could bear. His antennae were erect, his gut urging him onwards.

The contents of the first bag spilled across the floor. William raked through impatiently, allowing the envelopes to sieve through his fingers like flour. Nothing. He hastily shuffled them together and poured them back into the mouth of the mail sack. How his attitude towards these little mysteries had changed. No delicate hands now, or slow, respectful movements. All tenderness lay in reserve for just one type of letter. And there it was, buried deep down in the second batch. Brazen and shocking in its sudden appearance, as if he had summoned it out of sheer will. Goosebumps marched a slow beat down his spine. How had he known there would be one? Hadn't he wished and willed for one before, with no results? William felt a quiver run through him as he picked it up.

He slid his back down the pale-mint wall and leaned uncomfortably against the rickety cast-iron radiator. He could feel the cold metal hugging him through his clothes but did not wriggle away from it. He just wanted to read what she had written.

My Great Love,

Should I be posting this to you or handing it to you? Now that I've found you. Now that I must believe you have found me. These last few months have been a miracle. My mother said I was just the type to be swept away in a whirlwind romance. How that galled me. As if my fondness for you was born of nothing more than a romantic predisposition or lack of independent thought. When I think of all the secrets we have shared, the unravelling of old lives, the threading together of a new one, it feels like there is no good reason to wait. The only cloud that lingers around me is these letters. Why haven't I told you about them? Isn't it silly to think if you were he – the love – you would have found them somehow? Of course it is. Of course it is.

So why do I feel confused, writing this letter? I feel as if I am writing to a wish of a man and hoping the real man grants it. Is this one last chance for the universe to allow me to marry the wish and the reality both? Before I marry you, or him? Oh, how I hope it is you. I am in a muddle. On the last Saturday of April, I will don a white dress and my father will walk me down the little aisle of the chapel in Hoxton Square. I hope the right man will be waiting for me there. I have waited so very long for you.

Winter

The information slapped William like waves on a sailboat. Winter was getting married. Tomorrow. To someone else. And he knew where to find her. Was she hoping he would? Or was she just a nervous bride, full of anxiety as her wedding day drew closer? Imagine the shock she would get if he did try to intercept her at the chapel.

The Dead Letters Depot shrank around his shoulders. The walls and ceiling and floor inched closer until he was afraid to open his eyes, lest the room had become a cell with no windows, no doors. William scraped his back up the wall and stood. He returned, at a funereal pace, to the front door of his flat. The light was glowing from the hallway, even though he was sure it was off when he left that morning. He pushed the door open, and knew Clare had been and gone. The scent of cinnamon lingered in the air, but the rooms were too quiet for her to still be there. The flat sounded different when Clare was home, even when she was completely silent. He walked into the kitchen and saw a crisp white envelope sitting on the table; his name, written in Clare's handwriting, on the front. He turned it nervously over and back in his hands, unsure what to hope for inside.

Still standing, wearing his coat, scarf and gloves, his woolly fingers clumsily prised it open. He had to shake the contents free, and a folded sheet of dove-grey paper floated to the floor. William tore off his gloves and knelt down to rescue it from beneath the table. He stayed sitting there as he read it.

William,

I am more sorry than you can ever know. Please don't let all that we shared be reduced to that one awful happening. I don't know if we have moved too far away from each other to find our way back. Maybe we have grown into versions of ourselves that can't connect in the way we once did, but the memory of those two people gives me hope. Do you remember how it used to be? Do you believe our love can endure and heal the rift that has separated us? Before you decide, I've left you something in the living room that I made for us. Open your heart, William, and let me back in.

All my love,
Clare

William swallowed hard as he moved to the living room and cautiously swung the door open. A white sheet was draped over the window; his old super-8 projector resting on a pile of poetry books, e e cummings on top. He flicked the switch to let the film play, and the picture crackled into life. He knelt behind the projector as Clare's face glowed on the screen. It was their wedding day: scenes from the ceremony, the reception, the dancing, all edited together. It cut to William on a boat on their honeymoon in Sorrento; they were searching for the local resident dolphin and he was gesturing madly at Clare to where it swam behind her. She swung around too late to catch him and the camera wobbled as she lost her balance. To the Isle of Man, where Clare blew him a kiss from the back of a motorbike as she spun past along the cliff road. Next, William waved a bottle of cheap champagne at her as he climbed the rocky road to Edinburgh Castle, weighed down by a backpack and too many layers of clothes. The film cut to Clare and William dancing on a bandstand in Kent; he remembered Flora had filmed them when they went to a Carpenter family wedding. Memory after memory flashed before him. The final scene was Clare making snow angels outside his college bedsit on the night of their first date. The picture crackled and the screen turned to white.

William slumped on to his side on the carpet. A draught from the chimney danced a lock of hair across his forehead, but he did not brush it away. The sky was lightening before he finally creaked up to sitting. He spread four letters on the floor in front of him: two written to him, two written by him. Was what had gone before with Clare enough to see them through? Would he ever forgive himself if he let Winter go? He felt torn in two, with only blind instinct to guide him.

26.

William abandoned the idea of sleep and climbed out of bed still wearing his clothes from the night before. He pulled the curtains wide and stood in the flood of weak dawn light. He stripped the bed of all its linen and bundled it into the washing basket with the other clothes that had been discarded haphazardly throughout the room. He stretched fresh sheets across the bed and made it perfectly, collected the half-empty water glasses and coffee cups from the bedside locker and swept the floorboards with more enthusiasm than he had ever shown them before. Even under the rug. The bathroom was next; he scrubbed the tiles, polished the taps, tossed the hard, gnarled soap that rested on a ceramic dish shaped like a fish. He mopped the floor until it gleamed, slipping on the wet surface in his haste to move on. His cleaning frenzy carried through the living room, the kitchen and hallway; it shocked him to see how filthy the flat had become while he had been distracted by his calamitous affairs of the heart. He folded the sheet that had been hanging over the window in the living room and placed it on top of the projector; tidied both away in the upstairs cupboard. The film Clare had made rested on top. He reached out to touch it again before he returned downstairs to vacuum, dust and polish. He angled the sweeping brush upwards to disturb each of the cobwebs that had gathered in the ceiling corners of the kitchen. There would no longer be any evidence of heartache in this flat. It was time for a new beginning.

The final cleansing was of his own body; he stood beneath the shower spray and washed any last remnants of indecision away. He felt focused. Clear and confident. After today, there would be no unfinished business. William left the bathroom spotless, as if it had not been used, and returned to the bedroom to dress. He paused in front of his wardrobe while considering what would be appropriate to wear that day, idly flicked through the shirts that hung there, rifled through the pullovers and T-shirts on the shelf, before it came to him. He wrestled free a hanger that housed in plastic the plum velvet blazer from his wedding day and laid it on the bed. Nothing else would do. He dressed in black trousers, a white shirt, then eased himself into the blazer. It felt a little tight across his shoulders, but the buttons still closed. He looked at himself in the mirror as he smoothed the velvet on his lapels – how much had changed since the first time he wore it. How much he had changed.

27

William's socks grew damp inside his leather brogues as he stood in the park; the grass was doused in morning dew and long enough to creep inside the hem of his suit legs. Small mounds of freshly cut blades were scattered behind him, their fragrance drenching the air, but the perimeter remained wild and unmown. With both hands, he gripped the black iron railings that encircled the park, his knuckles white with the cold, blue veins transparent. Across the street, people peacocked in their wedding attire, adjusting their posture in new shoes, fingers fidgeting at hats with feathers. Spring flowers spilled from weather-beaten crates, ceramic pots, hanging baskets; ropes of daisies entwined the church gates; an archway of yellow roses bordered the door. Columbia Road Flower Market decamped to Hoxton Square, William thought, with a small smile of acknowledgement. A swing-band trio – double bass, saxophone and guitar – in turquoise linen suits performed acoustically in the churchyard. They followed guests in serenade as they passed by, encouraging them to sing along. It was a spirited ensemble, and their enthusiasm was contagious; William caught laughter on the breeze and watched folk clutch each other for photographs and scan the new arrivals for familiar faces. He recognized the manager from the Clapton

Working Men's Club walking up the path in a pristine double-breasted burgundy suit and pulled back into the shadow, lest he himself be seen.

William clenched and released his toes inside his shoes. A Volkswagen campervan spluttered to a stop in a cloud of black smoke, the horn beeping wildly as white balloons tied to blue ribbons strained to take flight from where they were tied to the door handles and rear-view mirrors. A cluster of guests in the porch cheered and applauded before the van struggled away, leaving a tall, slim man with a mop of golden curls posing shyly for photographs in its wake. This must be the groom. He wore a midnight-blue suit. As he turned to greet the arrival of a black taxi, William saw his silver silk tie fluttering in the breeze and felt as if it were tightening around his throat. Had Winter chosen that suit for him? It must be so.

The groom opened the passenger door of the taxi; the lady who emerged took William's breath away in a cloud of confusion. Were the gods playing a cruel joke on him? A fragile woman engulfed in a sea of moss-green chiffon, a long, red braid snaking down her spine, placed her hands on the groom's shoulders and leaned forward to whisper something to him. William watched him blush and pull her close into an embrace. His memory searched for her name before he called it to mind in a moment of clarity. Could that truly be Alice-Ann? His photographer friend from Clovelly? What a sonic boom to the soul! Haphazard realization buzzed inside him: was she the grandmother Winter had spoken of who had pursued her passions and inspired her so? Could he have solved this mystery all those weeks ago if he had trusted his instinct to tell Alice-Ann his story? He started coughing as a teenage boy, awkward in an old man's tuxedo, stood at the doorway and beckoned everyone inside.

'The bride is coming!' he heard him call to the stragglers.

William craned his neck to watch for a car turning into the square, knowing that at any moment it would appear. He counted slowly backwards from one hundred, looking from his feet to the corner of the street and back again. As the fifties petered out, a white Beetle spluttered into sight and slowly chugged to a halt outside the chapel. His discomfort mounted. Had he invaded someone else's dream uninvited? Gatecrashed reality while hunting a ghost? The satellite he had orbited from afar was drawing ever closer; the earth tilted beneath his feet and left him spinning. He could see wispy clouds of white and a flash of scarlet blur through the window as the wedding car slowed to a stand. He saw the bride look to the left; one hand paused as it reached to smooth a stray red curl behind her ear. William touched his beard, held his breath.

Their eyes met.

The usher opened the car door and a white lace glove reached out to him. He steadied the bride as she climbed out and smoothed the skirt of her gown. It was an old-fashioned dress, knee length, full skirt of lace, long sleeves, a silk bow at the nape of her neck. The scarlet hair he had long imagined erupted from a boxy hat with a white lace veil. On her feet, sparkling white cowboy boots. An elderly man, resplendent in top hat and tails, climbed from the car and walked slowly but with great presence towards her to take her arm. William watched the man he was sure must be Winter's father hand her a bouquet of yellow daffodils; she reached her hand to touch his face and he kissed her on the cheek. As Winter took his arm, she turned her gaze towards William.

Their eyes met.

William jolted at the flicker of recognition that passed between them. Alice-Ann approached Winter and a photographer ran from the chapel yard to capture the bridal party in the moment of arrival. Winter's face froze into a perfect smile as she looked directly into the lens, before linking her grandmother to the right, her father to the left, and crunching up the gravel pathway to the chapel door. William moved along the railing, feeling for the gate without ever looking away from her. The Beetle backfired as it spluttered away. Winter jumped and whipped her head back towards the noise.

Their eyes met.

William walked to the kerb and paused as a stream of traffic whizzed past him. He stepped backwards towards the railing once again. At the church door, Alice-Ann's fingers fluttered over the bride's dress as Winter adjusted her veil. She paused, turned, before lowering it. The traffic cleared and, with it, the congestion blocking the avenues of William's mind dissipated.

Their eyes met.

He was lost and found.

One Year and One Day Later

Clare lay on a battered dusty-pink velvet love seat in her studio. Kate Bush played on the record player behind her; it looked as if the cherry blossoms on the tree outside her window were swishing in time with the music. The radiator cranked and groaned as it tried to warm the cold, exposed brick walls that surrounded her. She pulled the patchwork quilt she had finally finished the weekend before around her shoulders and smiled in contentment. She loved how the fabrics felt as she ruffled them with her fingers; she was surrounded by memories.

Clare looked up at the sounds of footsteps on the stairs and glanced at her easel; a sheet covered the painting. Good. She wasn't ready to show him yet. Her swollen belly strained against the paint-splattered fabric of her smock as she turned. She squirmed back into a more comfortable position and rested the book she was reading on top of the bump with the cover facing her. She was tickled by how well it balanced there: *The Lost Letters of William Woolf.* Resting her head on the cushion behind her, she closed her eyes and listened to the footsteps drawing closer. As the door to her studio creaked open, she turned.

Their eyes met.

Acknowledgements

First and foremost, I would like to thank my literary agent, Peter Straus, for taking a leap of faith on both this novel and the writer within me. I am eternally grateful to him and the entire team at Rogers, Coleridge and White for their endless support and dedication.

Thank you also to:

- My superhuman UK editor, Jessica Leeke, at Penguin, who guided me so mindfully through my first editing experience.
- The indefatigable Jillian Taylor, and her amazing comrades at Penguin for the boundless energy they devoted to bringing this manuscript to life.
- My agent in America, Kim Witherspoon, of Inkwell Management, for introducing this book to a whole new world across the pond.
- Margo Lipschultz, Melanie Fried and my magnificent publishing team at Graydon House in America for their insights, support and enthusiasm.
- Michèle Roberts, an inspirational writer and my mentor, who gave me permission to think of myself as a writer for the first time and encouraged me to just keep going.

- The fellow writers in my writing workshop for their encouragement and feedback; Natalie, Francis, Deb, David, David and in particular, Marc Lee, for his reading of early drafts and ongoing belief in the work.
- My parents, Frank and Margaret Cullen. All they ever want for their children is their happiness; unconditional love such as this is a tremendous gift.
- My late grandmother Julia for passing down bravery in the blood, and to my siblings, Patricia, Ger, Frank, Mary and Lynda and the extended Cullen clan.
- Hans, Gaby and the Wieland family of Cliffoney, Co. Sligo, where the mountains meet the sea, and many of these words were written.
- Karen Connell, who has believed in all my mad schemes since we first met at school, not least of all, that I would one day write this book. I would be lost without her.
- To all of my incredible friends who have taken such joy in watching this book come into being. I love and appreciate you very much – you all inspire me in a million different ways.
- To you, dear reader, for crossing the threshold to the Dead Letters Depot.

My final words of thanks go to Demian Wieland. The book is dedicated to him; he watched over me tirelessly as I watched over these words. Thank you, Demian. This one's for you.

Reading Group Questions

1. The language of Winter's letters is quite distinct and poetic. What kind of image did they conjure up of Winter? Did she turn out to be what you expected? Why was William drawn to her and what do you think this says about William and the ideas he holds about love?

2. From the beginning we get to see Clare's point of view and her reasoning behind her actions. How did this help inform your thoughts on their marriage and the different actions they took? Did you feel any empathy for William or Clare? How did this change as the novel progressed? Did you end up feeling more empathy for one character than the other?

3. William tells Clare in the heat of an argument 'I just enjoy the company of a beautiful young woman at work. So what?' (p.83). Do you think Clare's reaction was justified? And when we later discover that she cheated with Maxi, how did it change your opinion of this incident?

4. Conflict between adult responsibilities and following your heart is an important strand in the novel. Discuss the different ways that Clare and William deal with this.

5. Clare's childhood is a constant shadow over her current life, in the choices she makes and the person she wants to be. How does this affect her relationship with William? Should William have been more understanding of her overall? Or was he justified in his feelings?

6. Flora suggests to Clare to 'let go of feeling disappointed and start imagining what a new future together could look like, you might feel better about everything and he might get his confidence back' (p.160). Do you think this advice applies to Clare? What would be the practical ways for her to take it on? Would changing her viewpoint ultimately change William?

7. Clare and William's relationship is affected by all the things they don't say to each other and the ideals they hold of how their relationship should be. What do you think these ideals are? How are the expectations they have of each other informed by this?

8. Letters, and the act of writing them, are a major part of the novel. How are they used as tools of change throughout the arc of the story?

9. There is a degree of ambiguity surrounding the ending, particularly between the final words of 'their eyes met. He was lost and found' and the little snippet we see a year down the line. What was your interpretation of this? What ideas do you think author Helen Cullen wanted to offer up about love and relationships? How does this feed into your own opinion of these themes? And, ultimately, did it affect how you thought the story should have ended?

10. The author hints at the era the novel is set in with the use of payphones and mentions of events around the world, conveying a sense of nostalgia and charm. Do you think it had that effect? How would the story have been different if it had been set in the present day?

The Lost Letters of William Woolf Playlist

1. Chet Baker – Old Devil Moon
2. David Bowie – Wild Is The Wind
3. Nina Simone – My Baby Just Cares for Me
4. The Cure - Pictures Of You
5. Kate Bush – Hounds Of Love
6. Beethoven – Moonlight Sonata
7. Culture Club – Karma Chameleon
8. Sonny & Cher – I Got You Babe
9. Madonna – Like a Prayer
10. The Platters – The Great Pretender
11. Leonard Cohen – Suzanne
12. George Michael – Careless Whisper
13. Michael Dees – What Are You Doing for the Rest of Your Life?
14. The Undertones – Teenage Kicks
15. The Bangles – Eternal Flame
16. The Smiths – There is a Light That Never Goes Out

A Q and A with Helen Cullen

On the Book

What inspired you to write this story?

It all began with that line of poetry from John Donne: *'More than kisses, letters mingle souls.'* When I first sat down to tentatively write the first word, of the first page, of the first chapter of what would become this book, those words leaped from my memory and the premise for the narrative was established. I wanted the book to meditate on the lost art and power of letter writing, and knew that letters would remain at the heart of whatever I wrote. I was also very conscious of wanting to explore the juxtaposition that often exists between the way romantic love is portrayed in the media and the arts, and the pragmatic reality of sustaining a relationship over a long period of time. I was interested in the idea of second chances, and if they always necessitate something, or someone, new or if they could be found in the life you already inhabit. All of these ideas, and more, formed the emotional infrastructure of the novel, and these questions became the scaffolding on which the narrative was built.

The letters and the backstories to them are so personal and important to the recipient. How did you find the ideas for them?

Placing this story in the Dead Letters Depot was the greatest gift I could unwittingly have given myself as a writer; it allowed me to pull on the threads of so many short stories in the form of the letters that arrived there. It is a world where magic and reality could collide and co-exist on a daily basis, a place borne purely of the imagination where the gritty examination of relationships could be interrogated whilst also allowing for the potential magical elements of life to play: the serendipitous, the fated, the charmed. As I walked through the streets of London or along the lanes at home in Ireland, I found inspiration for the letters in the depot everywhere: the David Bowie exhibition at the V&A, an abandoned silk glove at the foot of Benbulbin mountain in County Sligo, a biscuit tin of wedding photographs, a cabinet of medals at the Imperial War museum, a walk-through Columbia Road Flower Market, listening to 'Bloodflowers' by The Cure on vinyl. In myriad different ways, inspiration was drawn from the flotsam and jetsam of life that we bob along with every day, the overheard conversations and silent observations. None of these letters were based on actual people, but they still felt very real to me.

Music features heavily in the book. Why was it important to you that the book had its own sound-track?

Curating the songs to accompany the narrative allowed me to indulge in the perfect intersection of my two great loves: music and literature. One of the most revelatory moments in my relationship with each character came with the realization of who their favourite artists were and what music they chose to listen to at pivotal moments in their lives. Knowing that William Woolf was listening to The Smiths as he strolled through Dublin city made the whole scene crackle with life for me; I could place myself in the very heart of him. Understanding that Clare's musical heroine was Kate Bush gave me insight into the longings she nursed in private, the artistic instincts that she was working hard to oppress. Discovering that Winter's favourite band was The Cure reinforced in me her melancholic disposition, and how art could articulate sadness for her in a way that was restorative, uplifting and, ultimately, joyful. There is little in my novel that is biographical or inspired by events from my own life. The one thing that is borne of my own bones, however, is the importance of music in the character's lives. My great gift to these fictional folks that I developed such empathy for was the music that has been the soundtrack to my own life so far.

Why do you think letter-writing is such a powerful way to communicate?

I believe that when we sit down to write a letter it changes how we express ourselves: we become more thoughtful, more considered. In this digital world that we live in, we can communicate with more immediacy and efficiency than ever before, yet so many of us are also more isolated than ever before. Technology can give us all a false sense of connection that really doesn't permeate to the heart of who we are or eradicate loneliness. If those other mediums were all to vanish overnight, and we became dependant on letters once again, I think we would all get to know each other in new and profound ways. Yes, we would communicate less, but what we said would matter more. It is only when you create the opportunity of writing a letter that all the things you have to say reveal themselves, safe in the knowledge that the recipient won't, and can't, reply immediately but will also have time to think and reflect about what they want to say in return. I worry that there are generations of people now who will never know the thrill of seeing a letter on their doormat, with their name written in the handwriting of someone who loves them. I believe we are really pining for these physical connections in our lives now and hope that we will have a letter-writing revival.

And finally, what's one thing you'd love people to take away from *The Lost Letters of William Woolf*?

The instinct that they will probably never regret writing *that* letter and the impulse to begin it.

On Writing

As a debut writer, how did you find the writing journey?

It has been a roller coaster! From the ups and downs of writing the first draft through to the unmitigated joy of finding William's story on bookshop shelves, it has been a learning curve that I know still has plenty of bend to go. Like so many people, my dream was always to one day write a book, and I sometimes still cannot believe that it has come true. I am so grateful to everyone who has helped make it a reality and to the readers and literary community who have shown me such kindness and support.

What's one thing you wish you had known before you started writing *The Lost Letters of William Woolf*?

That creativity happens when you create the opportunity for it. I've learned I don't need the perfect mood, environment, or practicalities to be the catalyst for inspiration – I just need to sit down, anywhere, and get to work irrespective of how I am feeling thirty seconds before. The words are usually always waiting patiently for me to just get on with it.

Who or what inspires you to write?

One of the great lessons I have taken from writing this book is that inspiration is present all the time, all around us, in the life we are living right now, even in the moments when it feels its dullest. I am always amazed and thrilled when I feel the little tingle that comes with recognizing a sign or moment that feels created by the universe just for you.

And finally, any tips for budding writers?

I think it is helpful to try to keep moving forward one word at a time without rewriting too much until you have a first draft. You can finesse and correct anything in the edit, but working out the story you want to tell until the very end will give you the perspective you need regarding what actually needs to be edited, and hopefully the confidence to do it.

Quick-Fire Round

What was your favourite childhood book?

There is no doubt in my mind that I am a writer now because of the foundations laid with my childhood reading.

I loved Enid Blyton and my mother introduced me to all of the classics she in turn had loved as a little girl: *Little Women*, Laura Ingalls Wilder's Little House series, the Anne of Green Gables books, the Chronicles of Narnia, *The Secret Garden*, *Heidi*, *Black Beauty*, *Alice's Adventures in Wonderland*. I remain eternally grateful to my younger self for absorbing all that those incredible stories have to offer.

Favourite music?

The soundtrack to my life is an eclectic one, but there are some artists who are permanent residents in my heart: David Bowie, The Cure, The Smiths, Suede, Kate Bush, Feist, Tori Amos, Jeff Buckley, Radiohead to name but a few. I still think the planet is mourning David Bowie; I know I am.

Favourite artist?

I feel so fortunate to have wonderful work by Jennifer Rosemary Hooper hanging in my home. Both her art and her friendship are blessings in my life.

A quote to live by?

As with so many of life's big questions, I can find the answer to this in a line of poetry from Seamus Heaney: 'Walk on air against your better judgement.'

The new book from

HELEN CULLEN

Coming 2020

Read on for a sneak preview . . .

Inis Óg, 2005

It was Christmas Eve.

Murtagh wore tan sheepskin slippers, broken down at the heel.

He shuffled backwards and forwards along the well-worn floorboards in the shadowy hallway of the Moone family home.

Smoothing his crown of tousled golden curls back from his forehead, he gently touched where his temples throbbed. Still damp from the rain, he hugged his Aran cardigan tighter and the wooden robin brooch on his lapel turned upside down.

The ticking of his wristwatch was amplified in the silence, its pearlescent moon face catching the street-light through the window and winking back.

The door to the living room remained firmly closed. Christmas waited inside.

The branches of the lopsided fir tree he had dragged home across the Gallaghers' field seven days before were weighed down by decades of tinfoil garlands that the children had clumsily stitched together with red wool. None would ever be thrown away, however tattered they became. Every year, as the Moones assembled to transform their island cottage into something akin to Santa's grotto, each child claimed their own creations with jealous possession. With ceremonial grace, their mother carefully unrolled their handiwork from the fraying white tissue paper that protected the decorations for the other forty-eight weeks of the year. One by one they were placed on the tree.

Over these festivities, as with all others, Murtagh's wife reigned supreme.

His Queen Maeve.

None of the children challenged the traditions; their mother had sewn them so meticulously into the fabric of their being.

Stitches that could not be outgrown.

How he loved her for this gift she bestowed upon the family: permission to remain childlike in their enthusiasms, never to become embarrassed by what they had once loved. 'You never have to lose anything or anyone,' she often said, 'if you just change the way you look at them.'

And yet he had lost her.

Even while he held her close.

Even with his eyes wide open.

Murtagh had woken that morning, once again, to an empty bed; the sheets were smooth and unruffled on Maeve's side. He had expected to find her sitting at the kitchen table wrapped in her hound's-tooth shawl, pale and thin in the darkness before dawn, a tangle of blue-black hair swept across her high forehead like a crow's wet wing, her long, matted curls secured in a knot at the nape of her neck with one of her red pencils. He had anticipated how she would start when he appeared in the doorway. How he would ignore, as he always did, the few moments it would take for her dove-grey eyes to turn their focus outward. For the ghosts to leave her in his presence. The kettle would hiss and spit on the stove as he stood behind her wicker chair and rubbed warmth back into her arms, his voice jolly as he gently scolded her for lack of sleep and feigned nonchalance as to its cause.

But Maeve wasn't sitting at the kitchen table.

Nor was she meditating on the stone step of the back door drinking milk straight from the glass bottle it was delivered in.

She wasn't dozing on the living-room sofa, the television on but silent, an empty crystal tumbler tucked inside the pocket of her peacock-blue silk dressing gown, the one on which she had painstakingly embroidered a murmuration of starlings in the finest silver thread.

Instead, there was an empty space on the bannister where her plum woollen coat should have been hanging.

Murtagh opened the front door and flinched at the swarm of spitting raindrops that assaulted him. The blistering wind mocked the threadbare cotton of his pinstripe pyjamas. He bent his head into the onslaught and pushed forward, dragging the heavy scarlet door behind him. The brass knocker clanged against the wood with the force of his effort; he flinched, hoping it had not woken the children. Shivering, he picked a route in his slippers around the muddy puddles spreading across the cobblestoned pathway. Leaning over the wrought-iron gate that separated their own familial island from the winding lane of the island proper, he scanned the dark horizon for a glimpse of Maeve in the faraway glow of a streetlamp.

In the distance, the sea and sky had melted into one anthracite mist, each indiscernible from the other. Sheep huddled together for comfort in Peadar Óg's field, the waterlogged green that bordered the Moones' land to the right; the plaintive baying of the animals sounded mournful. Murtagh nodded at them with empathy.

There was no sight of Maeve.

As he turned back towards the house, he noticed Nollaig watching him from her bedroom window. The eldest daughter, she always seemed to witness the very moments her parents had believed – hoped – were cloaked in invisibility, and then remained haunted by what she had seen. Over the years, Murtagh had monitored how understanding began filling her up from the tips of her toddler toes, and knew it would soon flood her eyes, always so questioning, permanently.

Born on Christmas Eve, twenty years before, she was the only one of their children who came into the world via Galway maternity hospital and not into the impatient arms of Máire O'Dulaigh, the midwife of the island. She resented it: how it made her feel less of a true islander. What was more, the specialness of her own day for individual attention, her birth day, was irrevocably lost in the shared excitement of Christmas. In retrospect, it had been a mistake, perhaps, naming her Nollaig, the Gaelic for Christmas, and further compounding the association. No nickname had ever stuck, however. She wasn't the sort of child who inspired others to claim her for their own with the intimacy of a given name.

'Born ancient,' her little sister, Sive, always said of her with bored disdain.

And Murtagh sympathized. Nollaig carried the weight of being the eldest with pained perseverance, responsibilities heavy like stones in her pockets that she had purposefully chosen for herself; no one needed her to supervise them. Her mother certainly harboured a silent resentment of it, felt piqued at the implication that she needed the support. It seemed only natural, if unfair, that Maeve and Sive gravitated more towards each other; the baby of the family shared her mother's wit and wildness and often expressed the irritation her mother tried to hide at Nollaig's sense of duty.

Murtagh waved at his daughter as he blew back up the pathway. Later, he would feel the acute pain of finally understanding the prescience his daughter seemed to have absorbed from the womb.

'How long is she gone?'

Nollaig was standing before the hallway mirror, her face contorted as she vigorously tried to brush her frizzy mouse-brown hair into shape. She scraped it together into a tight ponytail that thrust from the back of her head as if it were a fox tail.

'Ach, you should leave your gorgeous curls be, Noll,' her father cajoled, 'instead of fighting them.'

She smiled at him but slammed the mother-of-pearl hairbrush down on the oak sideboard.

'I don't have curls, I have Brillo pads,' she sighed. 'Did she say where she was going?'

Murtagh squeezed his daughter's arm as he continued into the kitchen. 'I'm sure your *mother* is just out for a walk. Happy birthday, love. Lá breithla shona duit.'

He placed a small copper saucepan of water on the range to boil and waved the invitation of an egg at his daughter. She nodded begrudgingly and curled into the green-and-gold striped armchair that sat in front of the stove.

'With your white nightdress, you could almost pass for the Irish flag,' he joked, and was gratified when she emitted a spontaneous snort of glee in response.

He watched the clock hand count three minutes in silence. Expected any moment to hear his soaked wife splash through the door. He was poised, ready to run towards her with a towel and hushed reprimands for her careless wandering, but the boiling, cooling, cupping, cracking and spooning of each egg passed uninterrupted. Nollaig yawned, stretching her arms and legs before her in a stiff salute.

'Why don't you go back to bed for an hour?' her father asked. 'We'll all have a proper breakfast together later.'

She eyed him with suspicion but acquiesced. 'If she's not back soon,' she said, sidling away, 'come and wake me. Promise? We'll go out and find her. Remind her it's Christmas Eve, for God's sake.'

Murtagh nodded, ushered his daughter out of the kitchen and watched her climb the stairs.

As soon as he heard Nollaig's room grow still, he pulled on waterproof fishing trousers over his pyjama bottoms, thick yellow socks and wellington boots. He struggled into a heavy jumper of itchy grey wool, impatiently yanking the sleeves of his nightshirt down from where they were caught at the elbows, and pulled on the olive-green duffel coat that remained his favourite, though long past its prime. It was eight in the morning now; the sun would not rise until closer to nine. As he reached into the cupboard under the stairs for a torch, he was relieved to find only one waiting on the shelf.

At least she's taken a light.

The beam from his flashlight showed him little but the safest path for his own feet, but he was glad of it as he waded through the inky blackness.

Come meet me, Maeve.

Show yourself.

Come meet me, Maeve.

Show yourself.

As he marched a beat down the long, narrow lane towards the pier, trailing his left hand along the stony walls covered in moss, he repeated his mantra.

Not another soul stirred.

What would call them from the warmth of their own homes to be drenched in this storm? When the weather enveloped the island in an angry embrace such as this, the isolation became almost unbearable. The elements made prisoners of the islanders, who could be convinced they had

387

been swept out to sea, lost and untethered, never to reach the mainland again.

As Murtagh leaned against the weather-bleached clapboard sign that shouted the ferry times in bright-orange paint, the sky became diluted with the first strata of light.

The rain eased.

The darkness slunk away in a mood, but only by as little as it had to for dawn to be officially broken.

Perhaps Maeve was already at home, she in turn now worried for him.

In the watery winter sunlight that was more skimmed milk than golden honey, he trudged through the sand to retrace his steps, willing with each breath for his home to have sprung to life with the dawn while he'd been gone.

The sound of the twins arguing in the kitchen heartened him as he wiped his boots on the back-door mat. Eighteen now, they occasionally loomed before him as fully grown men. At other times, they were still the small boys who hadn't liked sharing the same supermarket trolley seat, letting their objections be known.

'How hard is to toast bread, Mossy?' Dillon said, scraping the charred surface of a cremated slice of soda bread into the sink. 'Every. Single. Time.' He enunciated each syllable with a violent scratch of the butter knife.

Mossy, nonplussed, stood drinking orange juice straight from the carton, ignoring the rivulets that dribbled down his chin. His face lit up as his father peered around the door.

'Da! Where were ye? What's the story with breakfast?' He shoved the carton back in the fridge, the lid discarded on the counter top.

'Yeah!' Dillon chimed in. 'Where's the feast Mam promised? We're half starved waiting!'

Murtagh swivelled his head around the kitchen. 'She's not back then? Your mother?'

The twins caught each other's eyes, Mossy's cornflower blues meeting Dillon's charcoal greys, before their gaze fell back on their father as he wrestled off his boots.

'Was she not with you?' Mossy asked, dragging his floppy blond fringe across his forehead and plastering it behind his ear.

Son Day, his mother called him. Tomás Moone, the pale, blond, waifish bookworm who inherited not only his paternal grandfather's name but his colouring and temperament, too. Son Night, his brother Dillon, with his ebony-black curls, high cheekbones and grey eyes, was unmistakably his mother's son. Named in honour of two of her heroes, Bob Dylan and Dylan Thomas, the artistic mantle lay heavily on his shoulders. He had the dream to be an artist, but not the driven determination. Dillon was never really interested in struggling, only in enjoying what came easily. Mossy was the one who worked hard, persevered conscientiously with any task until it was complete. Sometimes Murtagh wondered how each would have developed if their names had been swapped at birth, or if, with the christening, their fates had been sealed.

Nollaig reappeared at the kitchen door, dressed now in the white velvet pinafore and red polo neck she had planned to save for Christmas Day. 'Has Mam not resurfaced?' she asked, her face flushing.

Murtagh looked at the questioning expressions on the faces of his three children and shook his head. 'I better wake Sive,' said Nollaig, and pounded back upstairs.

Sive had turned sixteen that summer and relished her new, more mature-sounding number. Obsessed with the Manic Street Preachers, Placebo and Suede, she wore fandom like a uniform, her jet-black bob curled under her chalk-white-painted face like the Lego hair of the figures she'd played with as a child. Eyeliner rimmed her eyes in rivers of kohl black, the same dove-grey eyes she saw mirrored in her mother. Blood-red lipstick emphasized how little she smiled. Her clothes, usually striped, always sooty-black, battleship-grey or midnight-blue, she wore in layer upon layer, with garlands of silver stars draped around her throat. A full-length fake-leopard-print fur salvaged from a charity shop on Eyre Street in Galway city was her most prized possession. It was this she wore over her Emily the Strange nightdress now, as she reluctantly followed Nollaig into the kitchen. She pulled the coat tighter around herself when she detected the melancholy cloud that lingered in the air, the private smoke signals the twins passed from one to the other. Her father was busily burning sausages in the pan. She was surprised to hear him curse when the sizzling oil spat at him.

'So, what's the plan? Is Christmas cancelled, then?' Sive asked, checking the temperature of the coffee pot with the palm of her hand.

Murtagh poured her a mugful and scoffed. 'Don't be daft! We're just going to have a little fortification, and then perhaps we can all take a stroll and go and meet your mother. She's lost track of time, that's all.'

Sive reached for the mug and they both held it for a moment. 'So, a search party. That's what you're saying. Great!' She slumped in a chair at the kitchen table and elbowed Mossy to give her more room.

Her father turned back to the pan, his voice strained. 'That's not funny, Si. And it's nothing of the sort. I think we'd all just like to start the day together. And you know your mam – she'll be having a great time walking the roads and will be delighted to see one of us coming to meet her.' He put the ham that Maeve had prepared the night before in the oven and set the timer for noon.

Not long afterwards, as the rain started to pour again, the twins forged ahead towards the rusty shipwreck on the east of the island.

Nollaig and Sive elected to walk past the chapel, on to Tigh Ned's pub, and agreed to then carry on to the castle ruins if they hadn't found her first.

Murtagh set out for the lighthouse, convinced if Maeve was gone this long that must be the road she had taken. Although, the thought struck him, he did not know how long it had been since she left the house.

Why hadn't he insisted she come to bed with him? She was too restless, she'd said. Too full of the moon for sleeping.

They would reconvene back at the house after they reached their destinations instead of continuing on; the chances were their mother would be waiting at home when they came back, wondering where they had all gallivanted off to.

Nollaig and Sive returned empty-hearted first. Nollaig scraped the ashes from the grate in the living room while Sive set the kindling for a fire. They stood in front of it in silence, waiting for the others, warming their hands near the flames without feeling the heat at all.

The twins burst in next, Dillon's soaked fluorescent trainers squelching as he walked. When they saw the sisters were alone, they backed out of the living room without a word; Mossy climbed back under his duvet, fully clothed, his brown brogues dangling over the foot of the bed, and pretended to read a book of poetry by Keats. Dillon drained the tank of hot water in the shower, his discarded clothes a soggy pile outside the bathroom door.

When Murtagh's arrival wasn't accompanied by the fluttering sing-song of their mother's voice, Sive's eyes flooded. Nollaig snapped, told her to pull herself together and hurried out to the kitchen to speak to her father alone. The aroma of roasting ham percolated throughout the silent house, as if in spite. When the electric beeps heralded its readiness, Nollaig turned off the oven without even looking inside. She hoped her mother would be home soon to reprimand her for not taking greater care. Dinner was sacrificed to a God she wasn't sure she believed in as her father prepared to face the elements once again. Nollaig called her brothers and sister together and they divided up the island paths between them for a second search. Nobody spoke as they marched out of their cottage in single file, back into the storm.

Minutes of acute expectation bled into anxious hours of increasing alarm. By mid-afternoon Murtagh and his four children were wet, exhausted and turning on each other. In vain, their father encouraged them to eat bowls of lukewarm vegetable soup that he ladled out slowly. He choked his own down, spilling some on his cardigan, dropping his spoon on the floor tiles with a clatter. Nollaig caught his eye and he nodded.

'We need more help,' he said, as he eased himself up from his chair. 'I won't be long.'

Murtagh walked to Tigh Ned, where the islanders were gathering for hot whiskies and shepherd's pies before the evening mass. The lime-coloured plastic Christmas tree on the windowsill wore the wine-and-white Galway jersey, circled by pint glasses holding beeswax candles donated by the parish priest, Father Donal. The *RTÉ Guide* bumper Christmas edition stood on display by its side with a small laminated sign perched against it: *Not to be removed from the premises*. The air was heavy and moist as a result of the condensation rising from damp clothes and human bodies huddled together.

Murtagh spoke to Father Donal, whose white denim jacket sat stark against his black shirt and slacks, a sprig of holly pinned to his breast pocket. With head tosses and clicking fingers, Donal summoned a semicircle of islanders before draining his tumbler in one, crunching an ice cube with his back teeth as he delivered instructions.

The Moone children would come to the pub, eat some dinner there, no objections entertained. Murtagh himself was to wait at home for Maeve.

'In case,' Father Donal said, before correcting himself, 'I mean, for *when* Maeve comes back by herself.'

In groups of twos and threes, they dispersed, half-consumed pints of Guinness left resting on the grille in the hope of a speedy return.

And so Murtagh found himself pacing the floorboards of the hallway, fingering rosary beads in the pocket of his cardigan more out of superstition than faith. What little light had broken through that day had once again dissolved into darkness.

From the little window in the hallway, he watched the streetlamps flicker into life in quick succession as the cuckoo clock chirped four with inconsiderate glee. He shouted at it to stop its keening and then found himself apologizing to the little yellow bird. A knock pounded the front door.

Murtagh hid in the study for a moment, covering his ears.

He didn't want the news a knock like that would bring.

What he wanted was a hand to reach for that door that belonged to someone who could unlock it, walk herself in and wrap her arms around him.

He blessed himself with the ruby-red beads and opened the front door a crack. Father Donal stood on the doorstep, his denim jacket soaked through, his hands wringing a tweed peak cap. Over the priest's shoulder,

Murtagh saw Seamus McCann and Áine O'Connor waiting outside the gate, huddled under a huge canopied umbrella advertising Tayto crisps, their eyes focused on the laneway beneath their feet.

'Why don't they come in, Donal?' Murtagh opened the door wide and beckoned them with his arm, but the priest reached for it and held it in his own.

'Tell me, Murtagh. Your currach, is it still in the boatyard? When did you last have her out?'

Murtagh took a step back, the priest a step forward, still holding his arm.

'Only yesterday. Where else would it be? No one would be out in this weather. No one. What are you asking me that for?' He stood up straighter.

Father Donal squeezed Murtagh's arm tighter, his icy blue fingers exposed in black fingerless gloves. 'There's a currach caught in the rocks by the westward cliff. A few fellas are climbing down now to release it. Could you come with me, Murtagh? Just so we know it's not yours. To eliminate it.'

Murtagh shook away the priest's hand and pushed past him without stopping for his coat.

Father Donal hesitated before pulling the door closed behind them.

Murtagh threw his shoulders back as he repeated his walk from that morning to the pier. His name deigned him protector of the sea, and now he pleaded with the melanoid Atlantic for protection.

Father Donal, Seamus and Áine rushed behind him in silence, but no one tried to match his step.

At the boathouse, he found the door unlatched, and the discovery stuck the soles of his shoes to the sandy path beneath him. Áine stepped forward, gently swung the door wide and pulled the string to light the bulb that dangled from the ceiling. With a glance, she quickly knew what Murtagh's eyes would not believe, however hard they scanned and searched.

The boat was gone.

From the distance, Murtagh heard voices calling from the shore. Ignoring protestations from the priest to wait until he had learned more, he staggered down the sand dunes to where a cluster of men stood in a half-moon around a currach, their hunched shoulders turned away from him. As he approached, Peadar Óg, owner of the whining sheep, moved towards him. His clothes were drenched, his face red raw and freezing, eyes wet and wild.

'I'm sorry, Murtagh,' he croaked. 'It's Maeve. We have her. She was tethered to the currach by a rope. Her pockets . . .'

His voice broke.

'Her pockets were full of stones.'

He stood aside, and Murtagh dropped on his knees in the wet sand beside the boat. In the silver light, blue veins traced delicate pathways across Maeve's face, like tiny cracks in a porcelain vase. He traced a line over each one with his little finger while the islanders turned their faces away.

Father Donal began a decade of the rosary and, in quiet voices, each one joined in, even the ones who weren't believers.

In fact, theirs were the loudest voices of all, as with each 'Amen', the darkness crept closer.